Plate 1. Bromhey Farm, COOLING, Kent: R. F. Muggeridge's 1932 excavation. Vessels laid out on the kiln include grave-goods from adjacent burials as well as black-burnished ware (BB2) kiln products.

Royal Commission on Historical Monuments

Supplementary Series: 5

THE POTTERY KILNS OF ROMAN BRITAIN

Vivien G. Swan

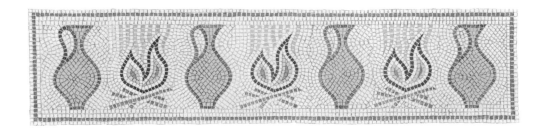

LONDON·HER MAJESTY'S STATIONERY OFFICE

'A good knowledge of local kilns will add greatly to our knowledge of earthworks; . . . No more useful study could be undertaken by anyone anxious to contribute to the ground work upon which the investigation of British Camps and Earthworks will have to be based.'

General Pitt-Rivers, *Excavations in Bokerley and Wansdyke,*
Dorset and Wilts. 1888–91 III (1892)

© Crown copyright 1984
First published 1984

ISBN 0 11 701203 3

CONTENTS

LIST OF ILLUSTRATIONS

MAPS

The following Commission staff have contributed substantially to the production of this volume: Jean Bryant (editing), Tony Berry (graphics), Philip Sinton (cartography), Sally Glazier (typing), Patricia Drummond (background research), Peter Williams (locational photography), and Bob Skingle and Tony Perry (photographic processing and printing).

ACKNOWLEDGEMENTS

I would firstly like to acknowledge the very substantial contribution of my R.C.H.M. colleagues in the production of this book, particularly A. M. Berry, P. M. Sinton, Mrs J. Bryant, Mrs S. Glazier, Mrs P. Drummond, T. E. Buchanan, A. D. Perry, R. A. Skingle, P. M. Williams. I am especially grateful to Mr Collin Bowen (formerly Principal Investigator in the R.C.H.M.'s Salisbury office) for suggesting that my initial private research on pottery kilns should proceed under Commission auspices, and to Dr Graham Webster, Mr John Gillam and Mr Richard Coleman-Smith for their encouragement and helpful comments on an early draft of the text. Thanks are due as well to Dr P. J. Fowler and those individual Commissioners, particularly Professor S. S. Frere and Professor A. L. F. Rivet, who suggested many improvements which I have incorporated in the volume. I would also like to express my gratitude to Drs Michael and Marianne Gechter for their hospitality and academic help during my visit to the Rheinisches Landesmuseum in Bonn, to Professor Harald von Petrokovits for the generous loan of his card index of kilns within the Roman Empire, and to Dr Ninina Cuomo di Caprio of the Laboratorio di Termoluminiscenza Applicata all' Archeologia, Milan for much valuable discussion on Roman kilns during her research-visits to Britain over the past twelve years.

Thanks are also due to the Directors, Curators and Officers of numerous Institutions for their ready assistance: notably Buckinghamshire County Museum, Aylesbury, Bedfordshire County Council Planning Office Archaeological Section, the Rheinisches Landesmuseum, Bonn, the British Gas Corporation, the British Museum, Cambridge County Council Planning Office Archaeological Section, University Museum of Archaeology and Anthropology, Cambridge, Canterbury Archaeological Trust, Canterbury City Museum, Chelmsford Excavation Unit, Chester Archaeological Excavation Unit, Clwyd Record Office, Colchester Archaeological Trust, the Colchester and Essex Museum, Derby Museum, Devizes Museum, Doncaster Museum, Essex County Council Archaeological Unit, Exeter Museums Archaeological Field Unit, Farnham Museum, Gloucester City Excavation Unit, Gloucester City Museum, Grantham Museum, Guildford Museum, Hampshire County Museums Service, Hertford County Museum, Ipswich Museum, Kingston upon Hull Transport and Archaeology Museum, Leicestershire Museums Archaeological Field Unit, Lincoln Archaeological Trust, Lincoln City and County Museum, Maidstone Museum, Malton Museum, Manchester University Museum, Mildenhall Museum, Milton Keynes Development Corporation Archaeology Unit, Mucking Post-Excavation Unit, Nene Valley Research Committee Archaeological Unit, Newport Museum, Gwent, Norfolk County Museums Archaeological Unit, Northampton Development Corporation Archaeological Unit, Northampton Museum, Northamptonshire County Council Archaeological Unit, The Castle Museum, Norwich, the Ordnance Survey, the Ashmolean Museum, Oxford, Peterborough City Museum, Portsmouth City Museum, Rochester Museum, Suffolk County Council Archaeological Unit, the Verulamium Museum, Wessex Archaeological Unit, Wiltshire County Council Archaeological Unit, the Yorkshire Museum, York; also the Libraries of the Society of Antiquaries of London, the London University Institute of Archaeology, the Institute of Geological Sciences, London, the Society for the Promotion of Roman Studies, London, the University of Leeds, the Department of Archaeology of the University of Newcastle upon Tyne, and the Yorkshire Archaeological Society, Leeds.

I am also indebted to the many individuals who so willingly communicated to me the results of their excavations and research, including A. S. Anderson, F. K. Annable, P. S. Baker, C. Balkwill, C. Barnett, B. Barr, P. Bennett, J. Beswick, G. Bevan, P. Bidwell, T. Blagg, B. P. Blake, N. M. Booth, P. Booth, D. Boyce, M. Brely, J. Bromwich, A. E. Brown, D. Browne, G. F. Bryant, P. C. Buckland, D. G. Buckley, P. Carrington, P. Catherall, A. J. Clark, J. Collins, D. Compton, the late D. B. Connah, K. Crouch, P. Crummy, N. Cuomo di Caprio, G. B. Dannell, M. Darling, R. Davies, A. P. Detsicas, D. Devereux, M. J. Dolby, J. Dool, A. G. Down, C. M. Dring, G. T. Dring, P. J. Drury, B. R. K. Dunnett, S. M. Elsdon, F. H. Erith, P. Fairweather, M. Farley, R. A. H. Farrar, K. R. Fennell, P. J. Foster, P. Gailliou, C. Going, C. Gouge, B.

Green, H. J. M. Green, J. A. Greenaway, A. Gregory, D. H. Hall, W. S. Hanson, S. R. Harker, B. R. Hartley, K. F. Hartley, M. W. C. Hassall, R. H. Hayes, C. M. Hills, E. W. Holden, J. Holmes, A. W. J. Houghton, M. Howe, R. G. Hughes, K. Hunter, A. Hurst, H. R. Hurst, R. F. Hutchings, D. A. Jackson, I. Jackson, C. M. Johns, G. D. B. Jones, M. U. Jones, D. B. Kelly, P. Kenrick, D. Kenyon, L. J. F. Keppie, D. C. King, E. King, A. K. Knowles, G. C. Knowles, H. Lane, A. Lawson, G. M. Leather, R. H. Leech, J. Mostyn Lewis, A. Light, J. E. A. Liversidge, N. Loughlin, B. Lovegrove, M. A. B. Lyne, A. G. McCormick, D. F. Mackreth, A. D. McWhirr, C. M. Mahaney, P. Marney, J. Marjoram, G. Marsh, J. May, J. Mellor, A. Miles, R. Moore, D. Mynard, E. J. Owles, C. R. Paine, M. Petchey, B. Philips, J. Plouviez, R. Pollard, J. Pullinger, R. Rattray, G. G. S. Richardson, R. J. Rickett, V. Rigby, K. A. and W. J. Rodwell, A. Rogerson, A. Rook, J. Samuels, C. Saunders, M. Shaw, H. L. Sheldon, M. G. Simpson, J. P. Smallwood, P. Smith, G. Soffe, M. Stone, R. P. Symonds, A. Taylor, C. C. Taylor, M. Todd, H. Toller, D. J. Tomalin, R. Trett, C. Tubbs, R. Turland, R. and C. Turner, P. Tyers, S. Upex, G. Usher, B. Vyner, F. Waters, P. L. Waters, G. Webster, P. V. Webster, W. A. Webster, S. Weller, L. P. Wenham, S. E. West, J. B. Whitwell, J. P. Wild, J. H. Williams, M. J. Winter, the late K. F. Wood, P. J. Woods, P. Woodward, C. J. Young.

Thanks are due to the various copyright owners, both individuals and institutions, for permission to publish the following illustrations: Plates: 1, 5, R. Bucknell; 9, 10, 15, L. Davies; 11a, 11b, 11c, 11d, 39, R. H. Hayes; 12, 33, the late D. B. Connah; 16, the Norfolk Archaeological Unit of the Norfolk Museums Service (photographer, R. J. Rickett); 17, the British Gas Corporation (photographer, P. Catherall); 18a, 18b, 20, 22, 24a, 24b, G. T. Dring; 19, 21, 23, R. Turland; 27, J. May; 32, K. F. Hartley; 35, 36, 37, 38, Doncaster Museums (photographer, J. R. Lidster); 40, Newport Museum and Art Gallery, Gwent (photographer, Cefni Barnett); 41, Mildenhall and District Museum (photographer, the late Lady G. Briscoe); 42a, 42b, A. Scott Anderson (photographer, Bryn Walters); 43a, 43b, A. K. Knowles; 44, Lincolnshire Museums (City and County Museum, Lincoln); 46, J. B. Whitwell; 25, 26, Figure XXII, Norfolk Museums Service (Norwich Castle Museum); Fig. V, A. R. Mountford; Fig. XXIII, Society of Antiquaries of London. Plates 3 (photographer, R. Parsons), 13, 14a, 14b, 17, 30a, 30b, 31a and 31b (photographer, P. M. Williams) are from photographs in possession of the National Monuments Record (Crown Copyright).

No approach to the study of kilns would be feasible without some understanding of their products. In this I owe much to the work of earlier students of Romano-British pottery, and to current members of the Study Group for Romano-British Pottery. I am especially indebted to John Gillam and Katherine Hartley for their stimulating discussions and their readiness to share their unrivalled knowledge with me, much of it unpublished. I hope that this volume will compensate in some measure for the precious time which they and the many others have so generously given to this study.

V.G.S.

FOREWORD

Pottery manufacture in Roman Britain was a major industry; its products were traded in quantity, sometimes over great distances. The kilns and kiln sites of this industry possess an intrinsic interest, and also illuminate aspects of the social, economic and technological history of Roman Britain. The development or decline of a pottery, and the structural characteristics of its kilns, may reflect the arrival or departure of the Roman army and its *negotiatores*, the interplay of Iron-Age and Roman traditions, the progress of Romanization, the immigration of alien craftsmen, the exploitation of local resources and the consequent development of a local landscape, or fluctuations in the prosperity of a region. Studies of the products of kiln sites can also advance our knowledge of trade and of the chronology of Romano-British pottery.

This publication brings together a body of information relating to all known Romano-British pottery kilns and kiln sites in England, Scotland and Wales. Tile kilns are omitted since they are being studied by others (McWhirr and Viner 1978; McWhirr 1979). The survey falls into two sections: the first is a discussion of the siting, historical development and technology of kilns and associated features; the second, in microfiche, is a gazetteer of kiln sites with their structures and products. The material is arranged according to the traditional counties (pre 1974) with concordances listed in Appendix A. The gazetteer is correct up to October 1982. It can be made available, if required, as a print-out from the National Monuments Record (Archaeological Section), Fortress House, London W1X 1AB.

Work on a select gazetteer of kilns began as a private venture by the author, resulting from a small invited week-end meeting held in 1971 to plan the 1972 CBA Conference on 'Current Research in Romano-British Coarse Pottery' (Detsicas 1973). At the same meeting, the Study Group for Romano-British Pottery was founded. All participants agreed on the need for a complete list of Romano-British kilns and kiln sites (with the location of their material as an aid for pottery researchers), to stimulate field-workers to search in areas deficient in kilns and to encourage the publication of the many important kiln groups still to be published. These aims remain but, when the Commission accepted responsibility for the continued investigation and publication of a, by then, growing body of information, other hitherto neglected aspects, in particular the morphology of kilns, began to receive attention. It was also considered desirable to examine aspects of kilns and kiln sites in broader terms than hitherto.

The large number of entries in the gazetteer (*c.* 1383), and the nature of the remains of kiln structures on and in the ground, have precluded that personal inspection by the author of all sites which is normal Commission practice. Nevertheless, of excavated but unpublished kilns, all available records and almost all assemblages deposited in museums have been examined and, where archival material and finds are not in public repositories, the excavators or other appropriate individuals have been approached for detailed information. Most kiln sites known from unpublished surface evidence have received similar treatment. It will be abundantly clear from the gazetteer how much is owed to the many excavators who have completed the author's formidable questionnaire, or have given time to comment orally on their kiln structures and show their pottery assemblages to the author. Many excavators supplying details of their discoveries wished, however, to emphasize the interim nature of their conclusions. These were, inevitably, often derived from material only partly processed and may ultimately be modified or superseded. For some of the more important kiln sites, critical reconsideration has been given to the published chronology and in a number of instances amended dating is suggested here, in the light of recent advances in pottery studies.

One bonus of the research for this volume has been to draw attention to the existence of a number of substantial but little-known archives of unpublished records of excavations of kilns and other types of site. The Archaeological Section of the National Monuments Record has been able to proceed with the microfilming of several of these in order to make them nationally available. In one or two cases, copies of unpublished plans, records and verbal information were obtained from individuals who have since died.

This gazetteer is a continuing archive which will be maintained as part of the National Monuments Record. The Commission would welcome emendations and additions to it and may well consider publishing a supplement in due course, should there be a need. It is especially hoped that this volume will act as a stimulus to further fieldwork and research, to the preparation and deposition of better archives and to the publication of more kilns and kiln sites both in Britain and on the Continent.

ADEANE
Chairman
October 1982

CHAPTER 1

The history of Romano-British pottery-kiln studies

The first person to record Romano-British pottery kilns was apparently John Conyers, 'an Apothecary formerly living in Fleet-Street, who made it his chief business to make curious observations, and to collect such Antiquities as were daily found in and about London'. Some kilns were found in 1672 when the foundations for the NW corner of St Paul's Cathedral were being dug and they were drawn and discussed in his diary (now in the British Museum). Although he observed their siting, his main interest seems to have lain in the pottery found in the vicinity (Marsh 1978, 195–7). His attitude was typical of that in the following two centuries: a preoccupation with kiln products as distinct from the means by which they were manufactured. The most notable exception was the work of Edmund Tyrell Artis in the 1820s to 40s in the Lower Nene Valley, Hunts. and Northants. Artis was not a mere collector of antiquities. He produced careful drawings of a number of the kilns which he excavated (Pl. 29), including cross-sections. Some of these were annotated with measurements. He also gave some serious thought to kiln-firing techniques, such as loading and the need for a 'smother kiln' to produce grey as opposed to orange wares. Indeed he seems likely to have been the first person to conduct pottery-firing experiments (Smith 1846).

By the end of the 19th and beginning of the 20th centuries, scholars began to be aware of the need to excavate and study pottery-production centres. In 1892, general Pitt-Rivers in his preface to *Excavations in Bokerley and Wansdyke* wrote: 'A good knowledge of local kilns will add greatly to our knowledge of earthworks; but investigations into the sites of ancient potteries can hardly be said as yet to have become so serious a study as the subject demands. As a rule, when kilns have been discovered and described, no attempt has been made to classify the different kinds of pottery found in them. I admit that the identification and classification of fragments of pottery is difficult, but not so much so as to discourage the attempt. No more useful study could be undertaken by anyone anxious to contribute to the ground work upon which the investigation of British Camps and Earthworks will have to be based'. Pitt-Rivers clearly saw kiln excavations as a means of studying and locating the source of the pottery found on settlements. His words did not go unheeded. By 1930 three substantial studies of pottery industries had been published, each embodying elements of the new standards of classification and publication adumbrated by Pitt-Rivers himself.

The report on the Roman pottery kilns excavated at Horningsea, Cambs. (Walker 1912) included as an appendix the first gazetteer of pottery kilns in Roman Britain. It was short, confined to published kilns, and without critical commentary, but its author mainly intended it as a way of comparing the kiln structures which he himself had excavated at Horningsea. It was, moreover, accompanied by the first published discussion of methods of loading and roofing kilns, with illustrations of relevant kiln-furniture from the Horningsea potteries.

In 1927 a kiln study of a very different character was published. *Excavations in New Forest Roman Pottery Sites* by Heywood Sumner is now better remembered for the author's delightful 'art nouveau' illustrations (Fig. I) than for some of the conclusions relating to the kiln structures which have been shown to be erroneous. Nevertheless it was the first study of the history of a large industry by classifying the style of its pottery in the context of its topographical background. The book also included an elementary distributional study, the results of simple experiments in firing samples of local clays and the first reconstruction drawing of a kiln in the process of being fired.

Fig. I. Rough Piece, Linwood, ELLINGHAM, Hants.: Heywood Sumner's 1925 kiln excavation: *after* Sumner (1927, *opp.* 93).

The most advanced kiln study of all at this early period was that appended by W. F. Grimes to his report on Acton's excavations of the remarkable legionary kilns at Holt, Denbigh. (1930). It included an annotated list of all known Romano-British kilns and, even more important, a classification, for the first time, of the types of structure comprising tile and pottery kilns: A. up-draught; B. horizontal-draught; and C. clamp, with subheadings (I–VI) for the various types of permanent internal structures used

to support a raised oven-floor. The work was a landmark, a model of its kind. Fifty years later, Grimes's classification still forms the basis of most discussions on pottery kilns, nor has his kiln gazetteer been updated.

In 1957 Grimes's scheme was developed, with the addition of a few supplementary details, by Philip Corder in a classic paper. Its main contribution was to draw attention to the very wide variety of temporary raised floors, as distinct from the permanent raised ones, and to describe a range of baked clay kiln-furniture, other than fire-bars, to which, Corder hoped, excavators would pay more attention in the future. Unlike Grimes, however, he dismissed the possibility of Roman pottery ever having been fired, like tiles, in clamps.

The next landmark in the study of Romano-British kilns was an article by Peter Woods on Late Belgic and Early Romano-British kilns in the Nene Valley (1974). This defined for the first time a range of very rudimentary surface or near surface-built kilns, constructed mostly without permanent walling and utilizing portable supporting kiln-furniture. Such kilns are typologically not far removed from 'clamps' or 'bonfires'. There seems little doubt that the next few decades will see increasing recognition and elucidation of the sites of true Romano-British pottery clamps or bonfires. The first possible example, already published (Farrar 1975, 49–50, fig. 4) was connected with the Dorset black-burnished ware industry (BB1).

Although in the past decade there has been a considerable number of publications relating to Romano-British kilns and kiln sites (e.g. Hartley 1973a), in only one (Young 1977, 29 ff.) was the comparative study of kiln structures taken beyond local boundaries. Nowhere have Romano-British kiln types been set in the wider context of the other Roman provinces. This situation contrasts sharply with the present state of Romano-British pottery studies, where the increasing trend has been to define regional wares, to trace migrations of potters and, where applicable, to relate wares to their Continental background. For several other areas of the Roman Empire, such as Italy and France, kiln gazetteers already exist (Cuomo 1972; Duhamel 1973). In Britain medieval kilns have also been listed (Musty 1974). There is undoubtedly room for a comprehensive treatment of Romano-British kilns.

The one related discipline in which substantial advances have been made in the past two decades or so is the study of the technology of clamp and kiln-firings (Coleman-Smith 1972; O'Brien 1980 and undat.; Reynolds 1979 and undat.; Anon. 1972; 1973; Bryant 1970; 1971; 1973; 1977a, b; 1978; 1980; Fanthorpe 1977; Gunn 1971; Lyne and Jefferies, unpubl.; Mayes 1961; 1962; Reynolds 1976; Watson 1958; Wood, unpubl.). Experimental firings have, however, encompassed only a limited variety of kiln types. It is hoped that the following discussion of the full range of archaeological evidence for Romano-British kilns and the appended gazetteer will now form a basis both for further experimental work and for varied archaeological research on the subject.

CHAPTER 2

The siting and distribution of kilns

The basic requirements for pottery production are the availability of suitable clay, tempering material, water and fuel. To make mass production worthwhile, the existence of potential local markets and easy communications for bulk transport are of equal importance.

Physical factors

Britain is well served by river valleys: in these by far the greatest number of Romano-British kilns are sited because they provided most of the basic necessities outlined above (Maps 1–7). Valley alluvium frequently contains not only deposits of secondary clays (*see below*), but also quantities of sand. The latter was undoubtedly the most frequent non-plastic constituent in the fabrics of Romano-British pottery, whether present naturally in the clay or, as was frequently the case, deliberately added as temper. Sand often contains a large proportion of silica which enables it to withstand high temperatures, and to counteract excessive shrinkage, warping and splitting when added to a clay. Its traditional importance to the Romano-British potter is clearly indicated by the dumps of sand, sometimes non-local, recorded on a number of kiln sites.

River valleys were naturally attractive to the rest of the community as well as to potters. They were consequently often the most densely and continuously settled areas of Iron-Age and Roman Britain. Topographical and geological reasons apart, then, it follows that a relatively high frequency of kilns should be expected in them because the communities living along the valleys provided the necessary local market.

Clays

Even beyond the river valleys, few areas of Britain are very far from sources of secondary clays. These tend to be more plastic than primary clays (*see* p. 6) and require only simple techniques of preparation. Most would have been adequate for the manufacture of the everyday kitchen-wares of Roman Britain. As a result of mixing with impurities by natural geological processes, secondary clays almost always contain iron compounds. For this reason they generally fire to a browny-orange to red colour in an oxidizing atmosphere (*see* Glossary), and grey to black in a reducing atmosphere (*see* Glossary), although other complexities are known to have affected vessel colourations (Shepard 1954, 16–17). In Roman Britain, reduced kitchen-wares tended to predominate throughout the regional industries, with a few notable exceptions, such as Severn Valley wares for which an intrusive, possibly military origin is suspected, and some of the late calcite-gritted wares produced at Harrold, Beds., and Lakenheath, Suffolk.

The ready availability of secondary clays meant that, particularly in the Lowland Zone, most pottery (perhaps at least 70 per cent) could be produced on a local basis by potters who were often attached to a settlement or group of settlements. Such workshops are rarely likely to have traded their wares more than 16–24 km. The ubiquity of small deposits of clay in many areas

4

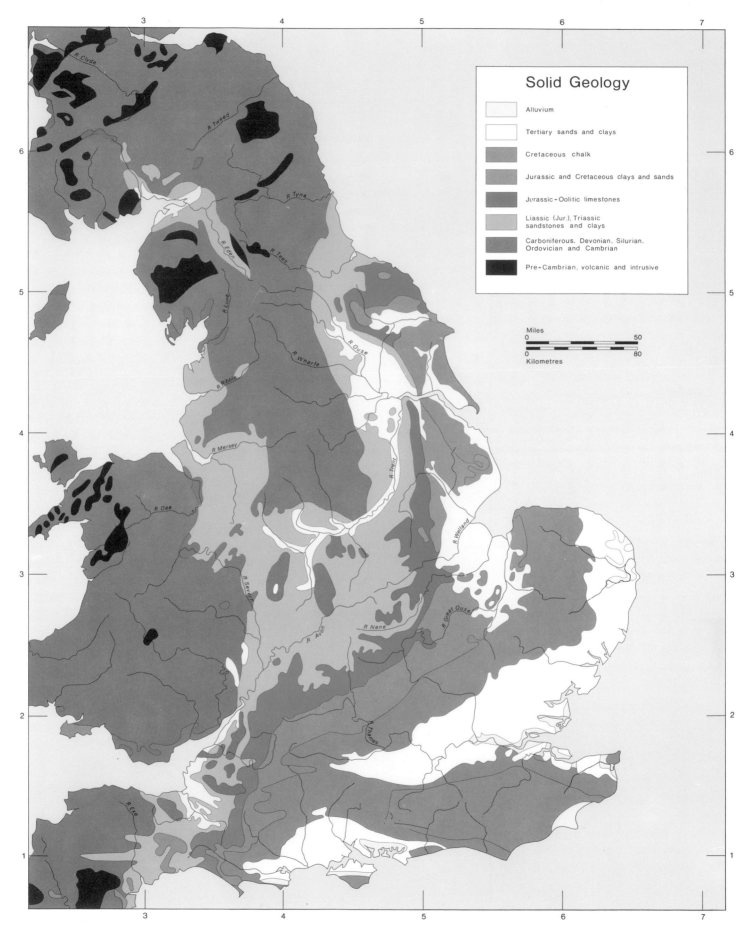

Solid Geology

Alluvium

Tertiary sands and clays

Cretaceous chalk

Jurassic and Cretaceous clays and sands

Jurassic - Oolitic limestones

Liassic (Jur.), Triassic sandstones and clays

Carboniferous, Devonian, Silurian, Ordovician and Cambrian

Pre-Cambrian, volcanic and intrusive

Miles
0   50
0   80
Kilometres

R Clyde
R Tweed
R Tyne
R Tees
R Eden
R Lune
R Wharfe
R Ouse
R Ribble
R Mersey
R Dee
R Trent
R Welland
R Severn
R Great Ouse
R Nene
R Avon
R Thames
R Exe

Map 1

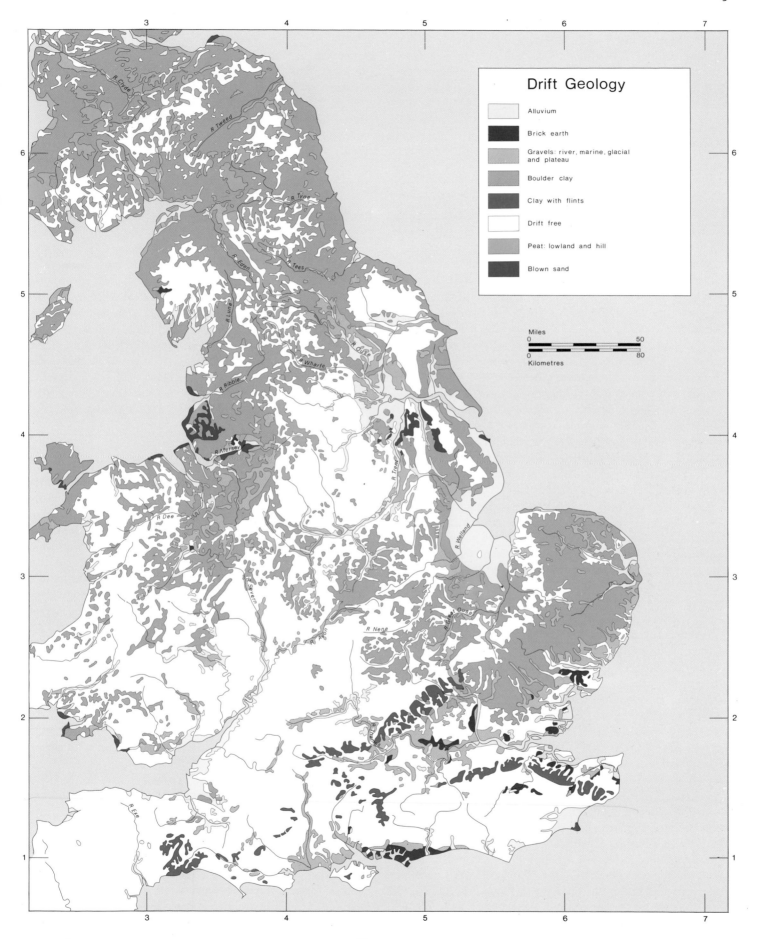

Drift Geology

- Alluvium
- Brick earth
- Gravels: river, marine, glacial and plateau
- Boulder clay
- Clay with flints
- Drift free
- Peat: lowland and hill
- Blown sand

Miles
0 _____ 50
0 _____ 80
Kilometres

R Clyde
R Tweed
R Tyne
R Eden
R Tees
R Lune
R Ouse
R Wharfe
R Ribble
R Mersey
R Trent
R Dee
R Welland
R Severn
R Nene
R Great Ouse
R Exe
R Thames

Map 2

would also have given peripatetic potters a livelihood. Instances of this have been recorded in Crete and the Aegean area until relatively recently (Nicklin 1979, 443; Hampe and Winter 1962, Taf. 1). In Britain, the possibility of itinerant potters has, indeed, been suggested in connection with the kilns at Highgate Wood, London (Brown and Sheldon 1974, 224–5) and also at Mucking, Essex (Jones and Rodwell 1973, 15). General similarities between the kilns and products at Mucking, those at Orsett Cock, only 4 km to the NW, and at Buckenham's Field, Billericay, 16 km to the N, may imply that these sites lay on the itineraries of generations of the same group or firm of potters (Map 17). The kilns of potters possibly operating on this basis seem to have been built and rebuilt at periodic intervals in the same general areas. They were often peripheral to occupation sites, sometimes just within their outer boundaries, or even in small reserved industrial compounds attached to settlements. Their apparent density could give an excavator a totally false impression of the intensity of activity, and a careful assessment of the chronology of each kiln in such a group is vital. Potters working in this way would have required only small deposits of clay. In contrast, the survival or evolution of a static industry was closely conditioned by the size of its clay source. The few non-specialist, purely regional potteries whose production reached abnormally high levels, were all sited near very substantial clay deposits, as at the Wattisfield, Suffolk, complex and the Alice Holt/Farnham industry in Hants. and Surrey (Lyne and Jefferies 1979, 3, fig. 1).

Only the specialist industries of Roman Britain required the rarer, primary clays, such as the Jurassic clays. These comparatively direct derivatives of feldspar have relatively few impurities, tending to be more or less iron-free. They were needed to produce the traditional pale colour of mortaria and flagons, often preferred for decorated table-wares too. In general, however, they required more elaborate processing than secondary clays. Specialist manufacturers were not, in normal circumstances, prepared to transport clay to their kilns over long distances, so were naturally more limited in their choice of a centre for production. There is growing evidence that a number of such potters moved workshops, sometimes substantial distances, in order to exploit large seams of exceptionally good white-firing clay.

The migration of mortarium-manufacturers from Radlett and the Brockley Hill area just S of Verulamium, Herts., to the Hartshill/Mancetter, Warwicks., area early in the 2nd century (p. 98) appears to be such an example. The greater potential markets for their products further N, however, would certainly have been another major motive. The potters involved in this move were possibly beginning to experience or to foresee difficulties in the availability of the superior white-firing clays in their home territory. From c. AD 90 onwards (inf. J. P. Gillam) a number of their fellow Brockley Hill manufacturers were reduced to making some mortaria in an iron-bearing orange-firing fabric and coating them with a white slip to produce a pale surface appearance. This almost certainly indicates the exhaustion or near-exhaustion of their white clay resources (Castle 1976a, 224). A similar technique was used within the Oxfordshire industry at Baldon, a site away from the white clay supply of the region (Young 1977, 117).

The crucial significance of a good source of white or cream-firing clay to a Romano-British workshop cannot be overestimated. The sudden discovery of a substantial new deposit could rapidly transform an industry of relatively local status into a specialist producer of major provincial importance. The Norton, Yorks. E.R., potters were just such a case (p. 111). They moved $7\frac{1}{2}$ km SW to Crambeck, Yorks. N.R., shortly before the middle of the 4th century, presumably following the discovery there of a good seam of cream-firing clay. This enabled them, for the first time, to manufacture fine specialist vessels in quantity, as well as their existing ranges of local grey kitchen-wares. The move ultimately had far-reaching consequences for the whole balance of the pottery trade in Northern Britain in the second half of the 4th century (Gillam 1973, 61–2).

While it was normal practice for potters to move their workshops as near as possible to the actual sites of such special clay sources, several exceptions existed within some of the more long-term industries, for example in the Lower Nene Valley (Hartley 1960, 8) and in the Oxford region (Young 1977, 16). In the latter area, the mineral constituents for the trituration grits of the mortaria, as well as the pale-firing clay, were transported to the kiln sites over distances of up to 10 km (ibid., 16). No doubt selective scientific work would identify other instances where special ingredients for slips and colour-coats were imported from elsewhere.

Water

Few recorded Romano-British kilns appear to be sited farther than about 400 m from a spring or other water-source. At many sites there must also have been wells, tanks or other provisions for water-storage in or near the actual workshop area. These have been found on some of the extensively excavated kiln sites, as at Stibbington, near Peterborough (Wacher 1978, fig. 40) and Mancetter, Warwicks. The many potteries which lie close to a river or large stream would have had the added advantage of ready access to water-transport for distributing their products, or for importing raw materials (Webster 1977, 326, fig. 25.1). This is particularly clear from the mid 2nd century onwards in the Lower Nene Valley. Here the marked spread of major factories along the valley (Map 14), never far from the Nene, must surely be an indication of the importance to them of that river.

Fuel

No kiln could be operated satisfactorily without an adequate supply of fuel. Pottery, in general, can be fired with a wide range of fuels, including dung, peat, straw, reeds, chaff (Cockle 1981, 94), coal and wood. The first four tend to be more suitable for clamp or bonfire-firings. Dried dung in particular has the advantages of burning quite rapidly and evenly and, by holding its shape as an ember, of protecting the pottery from cooling too rapidly. The presence of burnt grain in the stokehole of a kiln at Stowmarket, Suffolk, nevertheless, has led the excavator, J. Plouviez (pers. comm.), to suggest that straw may have been used initially to produce a good blaze and, as a result, a strong draught through the kiln before more substantial fuel was added. The use of straw for this specific purpose in 16th-century Italian kilns was described by Cipriano Piccolpasso (Rackham and Van de Put 1934, 40, pl. 46).

Coal can only be used for firing in conjunction with a grate. There is no conclusive evidence for the use of either in Romano-British potteries, although coal may have been used in a pottery-drier at Norton (Hayes and Whitley 1950, 17). Bryant's experiments (1977a, 11–12) have shown that charcoal is impractical for firing kilns of Romano-British type.

Wood is an eminently suitable fuel provided that it is thoroughly dry. If it is even slightly damp, the heat required to evaporate the water will tend to cancel any gain in temperature. Small quantities of carbonized wood, found in association with Romano-British kilns, have been identified from a number of sites in widely-separated locations. They comprise numerous species, sometimes several different ones from a single deposit, but with no clear preference for any individual type of tree. Bryant's experiments (1973, 154) have shown that apparently any type of wood used in kilns of Romano-British type will easily fire earthenware to over 800 °C, that is usually to a non-porous state. As Rhodes (1969, 61) has pointed out, however, soft woods yield more heat because it is released at a faster rate, an important factor in raising the temperature of a kiln.

As at Mucking (Jones and Rodwell 1973, 17), many Romano-British potters presumably employed whatever wood was grown locally. The diameter of the specimens of wood recorded from the Nene Valley and many other kiln sites is invariably small, implying the use of faggots, small branches, twigs and brush-wood rather than timber proper (Hartley 1960, 8). As Rackham (1976, 50–51) has pointed out, in the Roman period no suitable tools existed for chopping into usable sizes any great trees surviving from what he calls the 'wildwood'. This is his name for the long-established 'primaeval' natural forest, although it had probably largely vanished from most of the lighter land, such as river-gravels and chalk-land, by the time of the Conquest. The agriculture of the Roman period, however, probably left un-cleared some areas of 'primary' woodland and wood-pasture, remnants of prehistoric forest now managed as a resource without total tree-felling. An isolated local kiln, operated on a short periodic basis as by peripatetic potters, might in some instances have been adequately supplied with fuel from a few small areas of the local 'wildwood'. On the other hand, areas of woodland, properly managed to grow small and medium-sized trees, would have been essential both for the fuel needs of any larger industrial establishment and for the construction of its associated buildings, such as workshops and stores. Some kind of permanent coppice system must surely have stood behind the large-scale, long-established potteries, such as those in the Nene Valley, at Hartshill/Mancetter, at Colchester, in the New Forest, the Oxfordshire region and the Alice Holt/Farnham area (Rackham 1976, 51). Such a system seems far more likely than the cyclic reoccupation of pottery sites on the regeneration of underwood fuel supplies suggested by Fulford for the New Forest potteries (1975, 8). The possibility, however, that some

industries may have moved because of fuel shortages should not be totally discounted (cf. p. 19).

Coppices require some sort of enclosure to keep out the various animals which would otherwise eat the young tree shoots. Rackham (1976, 115) has discussed boundary-earthworks of coppices for the medieval and later periods, but there seems no reason why similar Romano-British enclosures should not have existed within reasonable access of most moderate-sized, or larger, kiln complexes. Some of the irregular, undated enclosures recorded by Sumner and others in the New Forest (1917; Pasmore 1967, 14 ff.) could well relate to the timber supply of the adjacent Romano-British kilns. Another possible Romano-British coppice might explain the enclosure illustrated by Lyne and Jefferies (1979, 16, fig. 4) just SW of the Alice Holt kilns. Its purpose has not been established but morphologically it is unlike any known settlement or stock-enclosure; evidence of Romano-British occupation lies just outside it. In Straits Enclosure, Alice Holt, some of the enigmatic earthworks pre-dating the formal enclosure of the woodland in Edward III's reign could perhaps relate to a Romano-British coppicing system for the nearby kilns.

Kilns near military sites might well be expected to have shared the same timber sources as the army itself. Potters might, additionally, have utilized 'off-cuts' from the construction of timber fort buildings and any small wood surplus to other military activities. In the kilns of several potteries with potential relationships to military establishments (p. 83 ff.), as at Manchester, impressions of the carefully squared-off timbers used to support the raised oven-floor before firing have been recorded. This may represent the use of surplus wood, initially pre-shaped for other, possibly military purposes. Where observed, the underfloor impressions in kilns elsewhere mostly suggest the use of withies or small unshaped branches.

There may be a direct relationship between elements in the design of kiln structures, and the size, type and relative abundance or scarcity of the fuel with which they were fired. Some of the Alice Holt/Farnham twin-flued kilns have letter-box-shaped apertures only 0.16 m high at the junction of the flue and furnace-chamber (Fig. XVIII). This surely reflects the use of fuel of relatively small diameter. Bryant, experimenting in the firing of a copy of a Romano-British kiln with a long flue (1977a), found that in normal operation it apparently had no obvious techno-logical advantage over shorter types. This design, however, was possibly a response to the particular type of fuel available at the time. In clamp-firing, it has been observed that one large well-insulated bonfire uses a limited supply of fuel more economically than do several smaller ones, and that a dearth of suitable firing materials may be one factor in the practice of firing many pots in one bonfire. The same assumptions could be applied to kilns proper.

In the Hartshill/Mancetter potteries, the development, to-wards the end of the 2nd century, of very large kilns (Fig. XIII), some shared by major potters, has usually been associated with the streamlining of the industry and the need to fire more pots because of increased demand (Hartley 1973a, 144). It is possible, however, that after a century of pottery manufacture in the same area, there was a greater need for fuel-conservation, a factor reflected in the size of the kilns. By no means all of the kilns of the long-term major specialist industries of Roman Britain show such a marked proportional increase in size at any stage in their history. Some major producers used very small kilns, for example the Crambeck potters (Corder 1928; Corder and Birley 1937). Fuel availability and kiln structure may well have been more closely linked than hitherto realized.

Markets: political, social and economic factors

The need to establish pottery workshops near or within easy access of potential markets scarcely needs reiteration. The overall siting and distribution of kilns in Roman Britain was conditioned by several major consumer considerations: (1) the native pre-Conquest background; (2) the dispositions of the Roman army, particularly in the 1st and early 2nd centuries, and its changing supply procedures, both affected by centralized policy decisions; (3) the relative speed of Romanization of the inhabitants concomitant with the development of towns, at first related to the deployment of the army units.

(1) The distribution maps (4–7) clearly show a dearth of Roman kilns in the 'Highland Zone' of Britain, that is in most of Wales, much of Northern England and Scotland. This was not due to an absence of suitable clay and other raw materials, although clay supplies were undoubtedly better S and E of the Jurassic ridge; a few kilns were after all set up for short periods to supply forts in the Highland Zone (Maps 4, 5). From the natives, however, there was relatively little demand for pottery and therefore no incentive for potters to set up kilns for them. With a few exceptions, these areas were thus essentially aceramic throughout the late Iron-Age and Romano-British periods.

In certain areas of Britain at the time of the Roman Conquest, particularly central Southern England, S of the Thames, and the South-west, relatively coarse handmade, and presumably clamp-fired, wares had been produced for 4000 years and were in regular use, mainly for cooking and storage. The trend in these areas was for existing industries to expand enormously, initially stimulated by the immediate needs of the Conquest-period army. Such native-inspired potteries were non-specialist and served the local population, but sometimes traded further afield. Except in the *vici* and developing towns in these regions, the demand for specialist vessels, such as mortaria and fine table-wares, was negligible at first and did not become a significant factor in the siting of industries until the 3rd and 4th centuries. These trends are reflected in the relative lack of specialist kilns in these areas in the 1st and 2nd centuries (Maps 4, 5, 18) and the general sparsity of kiln structures overall. Many of the native pre-Conquest industries apparently continued to fire pottery by their traditional clamp methods, for example the Dorset producers of black-burnished ware. The few specialist industries existing in such areas at this period were usually short-term, linked to local forts, and ceased when the troops moved on. Exceptionally one might survive because its access to communications enabled it to continue supplying the army economically from a distance.

In contrast, wheel-thrown pottery, sometimes including high-quality table-wares, was already being manufactured in some places before the Conquest. These essentially comprised most of the Thames Valley and Estuary, Essex, Hertfordshire, the Trent Valley, and those valleys and hinterlands converging on the Wash. Some, particularly those in the South-east, were also importing table-wares before the Invasion. In these areas, existing pottery manufacture expanded most rapidly at the Conquest (Map 4), since many of the potters were already capable of making almost the whole range of fabrics and forms required for Roman military supply. From such regions, too, a number of potters migrated to adjacent areas in the wake of the Roman army. These factors are reflected in the great density of 1st-century kilns in these areas, particularly in the Upper Nene Valley (Maps 4, 14, 17), and in the sprinkling of kilns in immediately adjacent, formerly aceramic, regions (Maps 4, 13). It was in these so-called 'Belgic' areas of Britain that the earliest specialist industries tended to flourish (Maps 4, 15, 14). The local population was already familiar with the concept of 'table-wares' and in certain areas, as at Braughing, Herts. (Partridge 1981), had been importing wide ranges of these since the beginning of the 1st century. They were thus receptive to the other classes of Roman vessels newly introduced at the Conquest. From the start, therefore, specialist industries established in those areas were not entirely dependent on their trade to military consumers. In some instances, they were able to function without it or survive when it ceased.

(2) The Roman army used vast quantities of pottery of all kinds. Its policy at the Conquest was to obtain pottery locally as far as possible, to import small quantities of specialist wares where necessary, and to make its own pottery only as a last resort when no local or easily accessible supplies were available (Darling 1977, 68–9). Military establishments thus attracted civilian potters from far and near to work in their immediate vicinity. Some craftsmen may even have come from the Continent, for example to Longthorpe, W of Peterborough (Wild 1974, 160). The progress and impact of the 1st-century army can be seen in the number of early kilns near towns, since the latter usually developed on the sites of earlier forts (Map 4). It is also represented by the burgeoning of existing industries such as those in the Upper Nene Valley (Map 14), by the presence of kilns in areas which were essentially aceramic before the Conquest, and by the number of early specialist kilns near major roads, such as Watling Street, and near rivers or the sea. This last element marks the need to transport such items as mortaria and flagons to the troops as they moved northwards. Since water-transport was the cheapest, fastest, and most convenient method in the Roman world, the relationship of sea or rivers to military suppliers, in particular, was critical, for example to the mortarium manufacturers of North Kent late in the 1st century (Hartley, K. F. 1977), and those of Hartshill/Mancetter from the 2nd to 4th century (Wacher 1973, 327). The bulk and weight of the mortaria and flagons, so essential to military messes, may have stimulated the specialist production of such items to develop and expand in Britain earlier and more rapidly than that of fine table-wares such

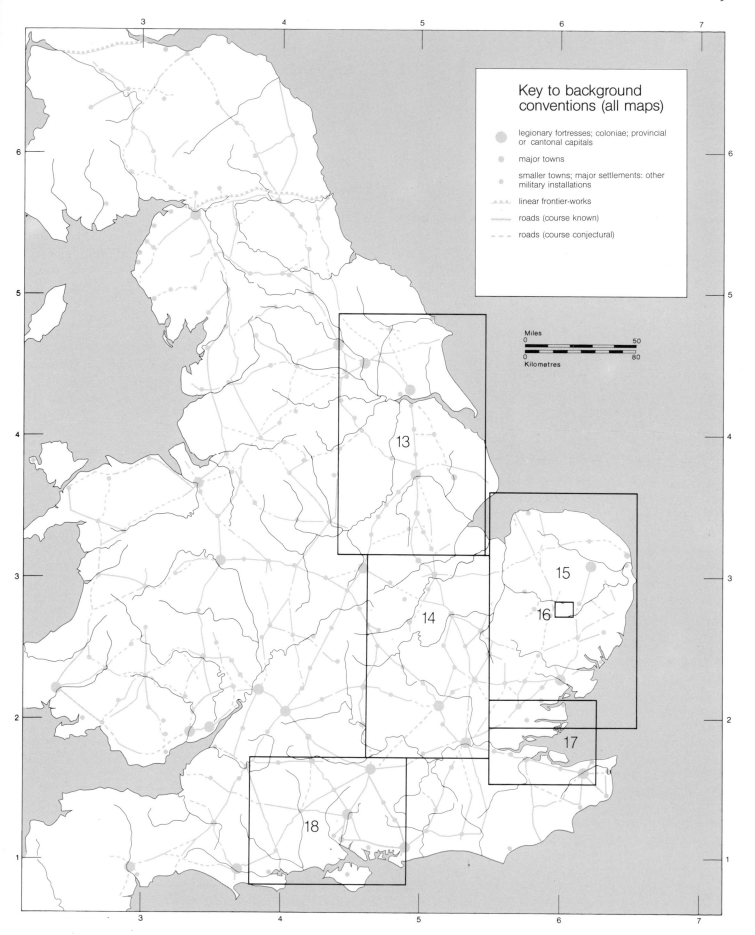

Key to background
conventions (all maps)

legionary fortresses; coloniae; provincial
or cantonal capitals

major towns

smaller towns; major settlements: other
military installations

linear frontier-works

roads (course known)

roads (course conjectural)

Miles
0   50
Kilometres
0   80

Map 3

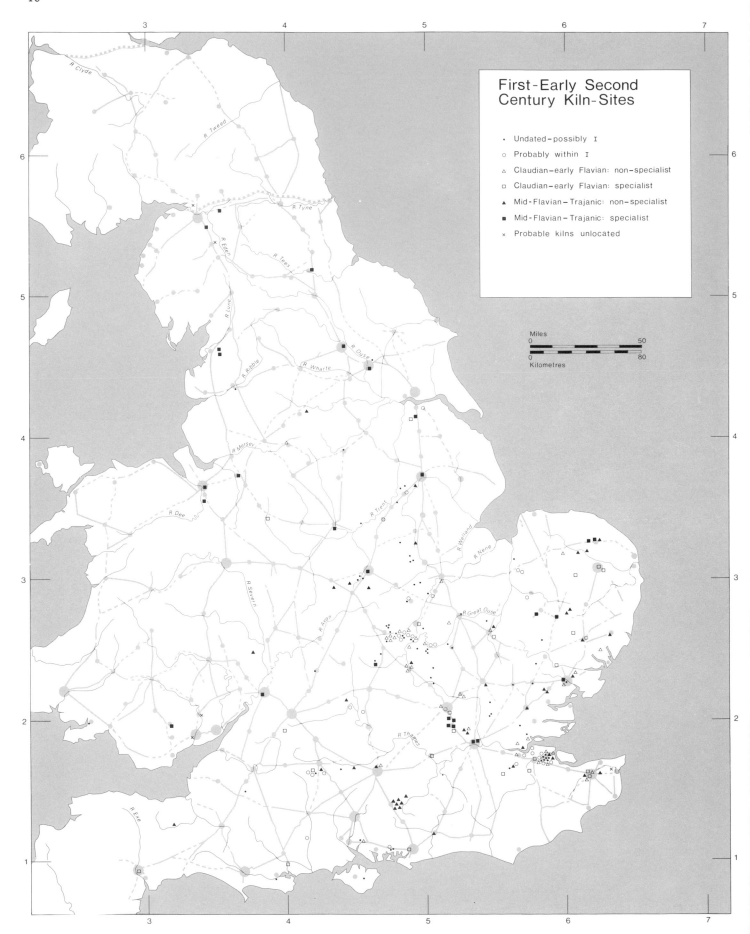

First-Early Second Century Kiln-Sites

- **·** Undated—possibly I
- **○** Probably within I
- **△** Claudian—early Flavian: non-specialist
- **□** Claudian—early Flavian: specialist
- **▲** Mid-Flavian—Trajanic: non-specialist
- **■** Mid-Flavian—Trajanic: specialist
- **×** Probable kilns unlocated

Miles
0 — 50
0 — 80
Kilometres

Map 4

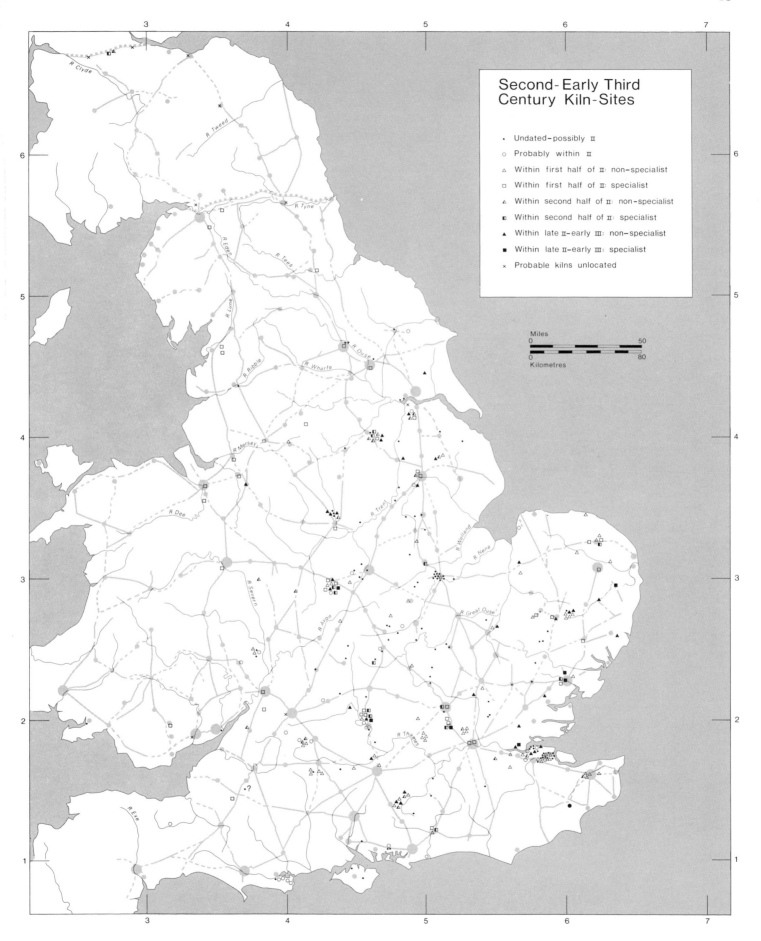

Second-Early Third
Century Kiln-Sites

- • Undated–possibly II
- ○ Probably within II
- △ Within first half of II: non-specialist
- ▢ Within first half of II: specialist
- ▲ Within second half of II: non-specialist
- ◪ Within second half of II: specialist
- ▲ Within late II–early III: non-specialist
- ■ Within late II–early III: specialist
- ✕ Probable kilns unlocated

Miles
0   50
0   80
Kilometres

R Clyde
R Tweed
R Tyne
R Eden
R Tees
R Lune
R Ribble
R Wharfe
R Ouse
R Mersey
R Dee
R Trent
R Severn
R Welland
R Nene
R Avon
R Great Ouse
R Thames
R Exe

Map 5

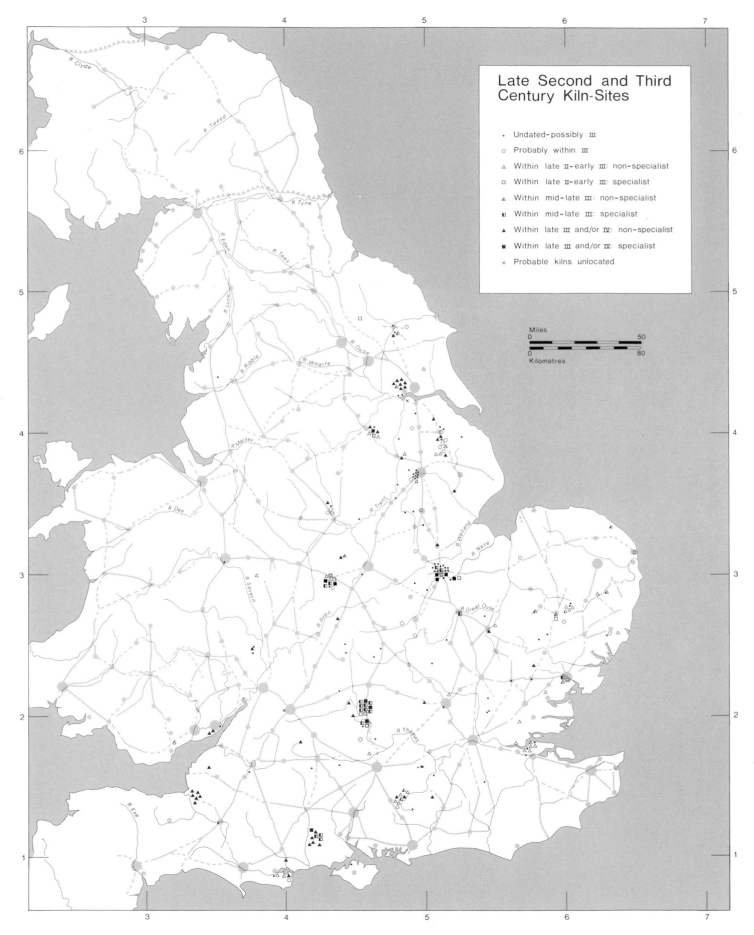

Late Second and Third Century Kiln-Sites

- **·** Undated-possibly III
- **○** Probably within III
- **△** Within late II-early III: non-specialist
- **□** Within late II-early III: specialist
- **▲** Within mid-late III: non-specialist
- **◪** Within mid-late III: specialist
- **▲** Within late III and/or IV: non-specialist
- **■** Within late III and/or IV: specialist
- **×** Probable kilns unlocated

Miles
0   50
0   80
Kilometres

R Clyde

R Tweed

R Tyne

R Eden

R Tees

R Ure

R Ribble

R Wharfe

R Ouse

R Mersey

R Dee

R Trent

R Welland

R Nene

R Severn

R Avon

R Great Ouse

R Thames

R Exe

Map 6

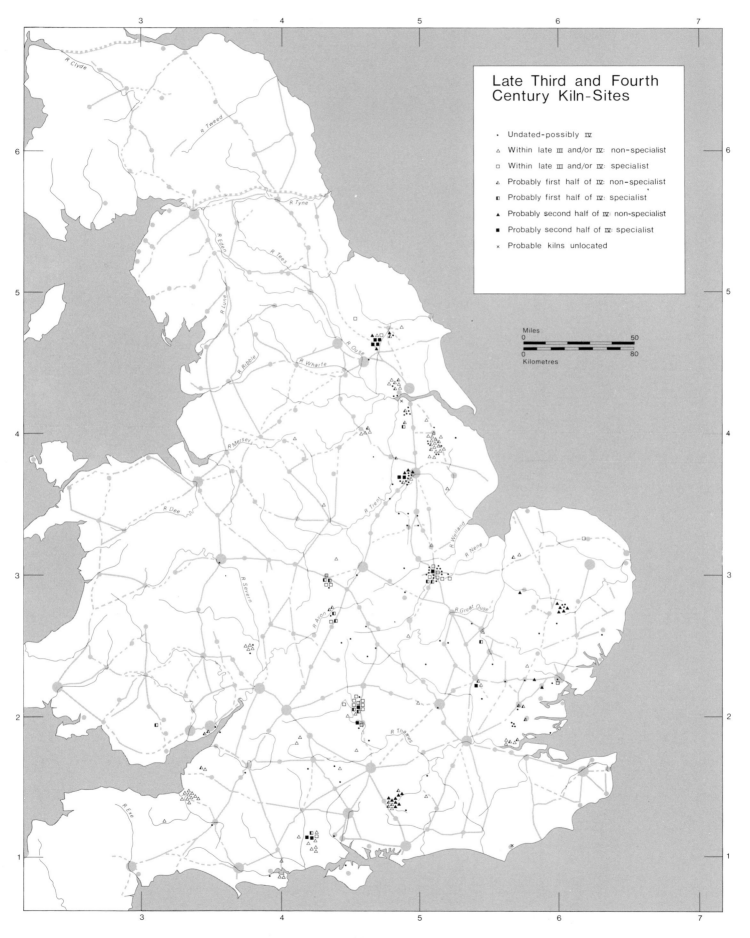

Late Third and Fourth Century Kiln-Sites

- • Undated—possibly ⅣV
- △ Within late Ⅲ and/or Ⅳ: non-specialist
- □ Within late Ⅲ and/or Ⅳ: specialist
- ▲ Probably first half of Ⅳ: non-specialist
- ▣ Probably first half of Ⅳ: specialist
- ▲ Probably second half of Ⅳ: non-specialist
- ■ Probably second half of Ⅳ: specialist
- × Probable kilns unlocated

Miles
0   50
Kilometres
0   80

Map 7

13

14

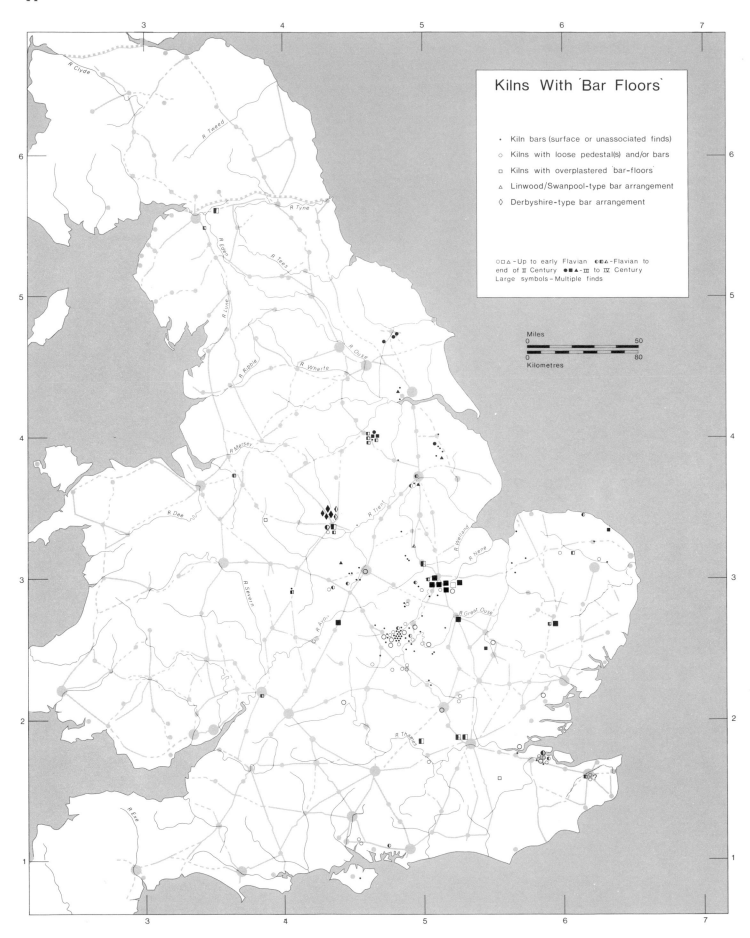

Map 8

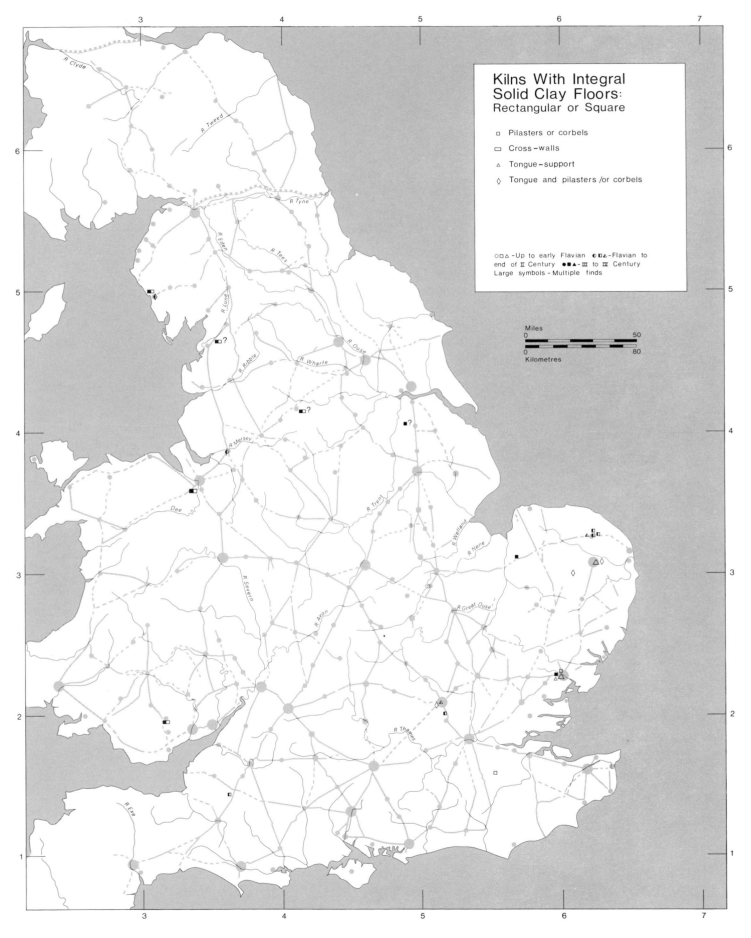

Kilns With Integral Solid Clay Floors:
Rectangular or Square

□ Pilasters or corbels

▭ Cross-walls

△ Tongue-support

◇ Tongue and pilasters /or corbels

○□△ -Up to early Flavian ◐◨◮-Flavian to
end of Ⅱ Century ●■▲-Ⅲ to Ⅳ Century
Large symbols - Multiple finds

Miles
0   50

0   80
Kilometres

Map 9

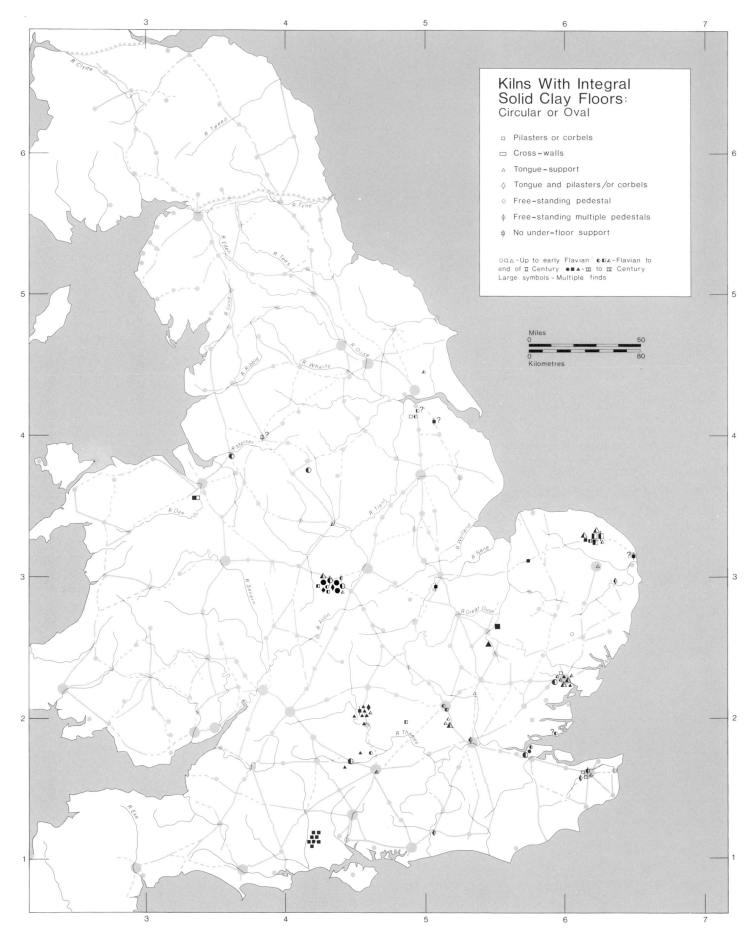

Kilns With Integral Solid Clay Floors:
Circular or Oval

   ▫ Pilasters or corbels

   ▭ Cross-walls

   △ Tongue-support

   ◇ Tongue and pilasters /or corbels

   ○ Free-standing pedestal

   φ Free-standing multiple pedestals

   φ No under-floor support

○▫△ -Up to early Flavian · ◐▫△ -Flavian to end of II Century ●■▲ - III to IV Century Large symbols - Multiple finds

Miles
0   50

0   80
Kilometres

Map 10

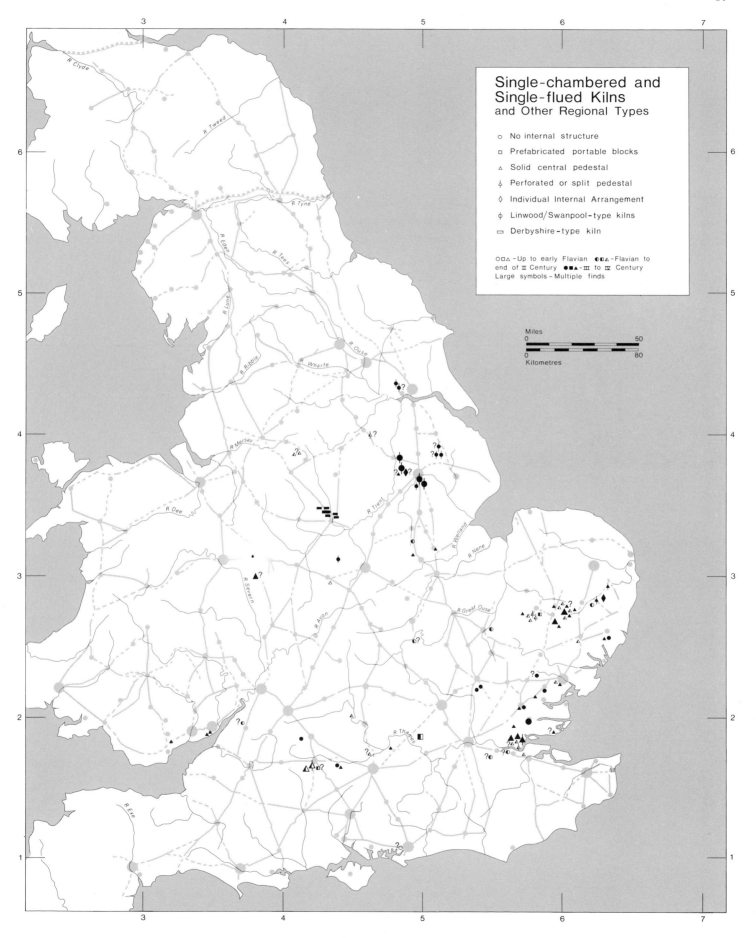

Single-chambered and Single-flued Kilns
and Other Regional Types

○   No internal structure

□   Prefabricated portable blocks

△   Solid central pedestal

⚲   Perforated or split pedestal

◇   Individual Internal Arrangement

φ   Linwood/Swanpool-type kilns

▭   Derbyshire-type kiln

○□△–Up to early Flavian   ◐◱◪–Flavian to
end of II Century   ●■▲–III to IV Century
Large symbols – Multiple finds

Miles
0   50
0   80
Kilometres

Map 11

18

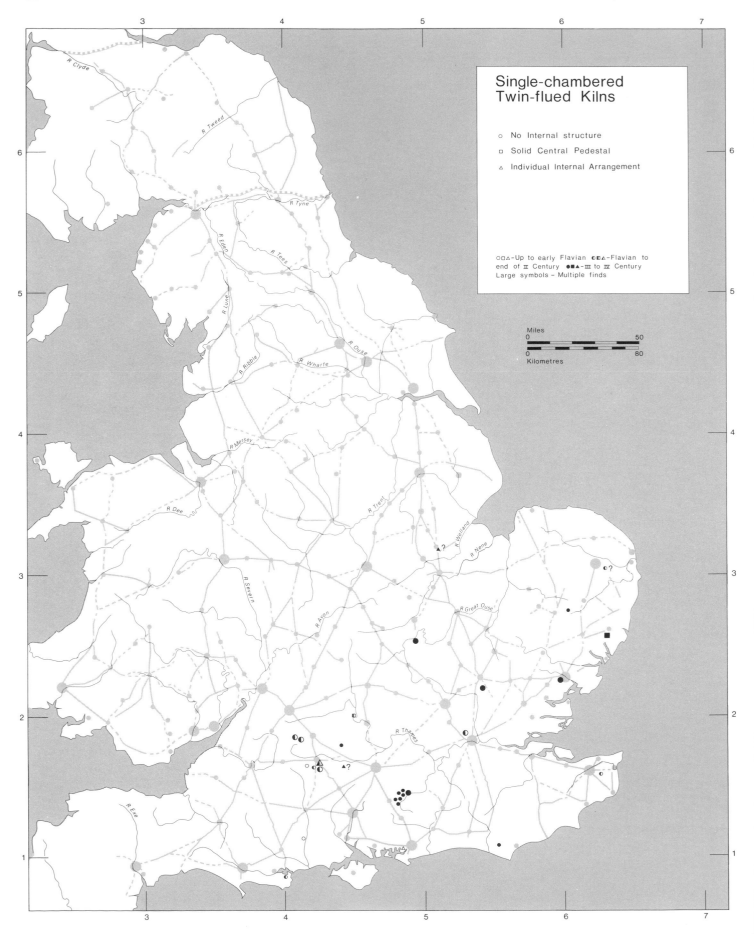

Single-chambered Twin-flued Kilns

o　No Internal structure

□　Solid Central Pedestal

△　Individual Internal Arrangement

o□△–Up to early Flavian o□△–Flavian to
end of Ⅱ Century ●■▲–Ⅲ to Ⅳ Century
Large symbols – Multiple finds

Miles
0　　　　　　　　50
0　　　　　　　　80
Kilometres

Map 12

as colour-coated beakers, cups and bowls. The latter being smaller and lighter continued to reach the province from the Continent in quantity for much longer.

The pottery evidence suggests that in the Trajanic period Roman official policy towards military supply changed radically (Gillam 1973, 53–4). A number of legionary and auxiliary depots was established for the manufacture of tiles and pottery, and these can be clearly distinguished on the Stanegate and elsewhere in the North (Maps 4, 5). One effect of this was possibly to accelerate the decline of some of the earlier specialist industries such as the Kent mortarium manufacturers (Hartley, K. F. 1977). Under Hadrian in c. AD 120, another drastic turn-about in military supply-policy is implied by the ceramic evidence. These depots were closed and the army of the North was left dependent on supplies from civilian sources further S (Gillam 1973, 54 ff.), a policy seemingly adhered to thereafter. This must have contributed to the rapid expansion of the Dorset black-burnished ware industry and the Hartshill/Mancetter potteries, among others. It also encouraged other specialist producers to set up in the North-east, the Midlands and North, for example the Wilderspool, Carlisle/SW Scotland, Corbridge and Lincoln potters. Some even moved into Scotland in the Antonine period (Hartley 1976a; Swan 1982, *forthcoming*). From c. 120 onwards, the regular shipping of black-burnished ware to the northern frontier along western sea-ways (Gillam and Greene 1981, 9 ff.) may well have stimulated the establishment or expansion of industries within easy access of such routes or along them, for example the Wilderspool, Cheshire, Muncaster, Cumberland, and Severn Valley potteries (Webster 1976). Their distributions (Map 5) indicate a steady expansion in the number of potteries throughout the 2nd century, including more specialist factories than at any other time in Roman Britain. Many of these supplied relatively small quantities of their wares to the garrisons in Wales and the North. Most of them were relatively small and by the mid 3rd century many had either ceased production or become of purely local significance (Map 6). This was part of a general trend for specialist production to be concentrated in the hands of fewer but larger manufacturers, a trend reaching its climax late in the 4th century. At the same time the continuing tendency for the northern garrisons to draw supplies from closer sources culminated in the floruit of Crambeck and the Yorkshire, East Riding kilns. They virtually monopolized northern markets in the second half of the 4th century (Maps 7, 13; Gillam 1973, 61–2).

(3) Romanized communities tended to use pottery for a much wider variety of purposes than was normal before the Roman Conquest, even in the so-called 'Belgic' areas of Britain. The adoption from the classical world of the mortarium for the preparation of food is an example. In the Midlands and South, in the 1st century and early in the 2nd, the rapid growth of towns on the sites of earlier Roman forts provided nucleii of Romanized people. They required not only native kitchen-wares, but also the ranges of special vessels whose traditional use had already been established on the sites by the earlier garrisons. Even in places such as Verulamium and Colchester, where garrisons were very short-lived, the compulsions of the Romanized way of life must have resulted in sharp increases in the demand for vessels of Roman type. In the 1st and 2nd centuries, then, the siting of many kilns related primarily to urban consumers (Maps 4, 5).

From the 3rd century onwards, the *Pax Romana*, the resultant general increase in prosperity, and the Romanization of the countryside led to the additional burgeoning of industries in more rural locations (Maps 6, 7). Most of them were producing primarily kitchen-wares, but a few were also making specialist products, as in the New Forest (Swan 1973) and at Pakenham, Suffolk (Smedley and Owles 1961b; Maps 18, 15). Fulford (1975, 7) linked this trend to a shortage of timber supplies near towns (cf. p. 7). It was, however, the first time that many rural potteries could survive without being primarily dependent on urban or military consumers. The siting of several industries away from major rivers and roads tends to confirm this idea. In the New Forest potteries, manufacture may have helped to compensate for the low agricultural productivity of this tract of land, a factor possibly also influencing the siting of kilns elsewhere (p. 108).

Young has suggested (1977, 13) that the establishment and expansion of some industries was possibly restricted by pre-existing agricultural activity, such as villa estates. In the Roman world, however, pottery manufacture, like tile-making, was apparently often regarded as a normal part of agriculture (Helen 1975, 13, 97 ff.). The establishment of potteries in Britain might therefore sometimes have gone hand in hand with the development of villa estates. Clay, fuel, water, and other basic supplies could have been leased in return for rent or for pottery containers to hold farm produce, as in Egypt (Cockle 1981) and elsewhere within the Roman Empire. The possibility of a correlation between the distribution and siting of villas and kilns is worth detailed consideration. A possible link between the villas and kilns in the Claxby/Walesby area of the Lincolnshire Wolds was noted almost twenty years ago (*Lincolnshire Hist. Archaeol.* I, i (1966), 46–7).

The 4th century, particularly the second half, witnessed a definite decline in the total number of kiln sites (Map 7). At the same time, however, the fewer centres tended to become larger, and also important to wider areas (Map 7). In some quarters this has been considered indicative of a general decline in the last half-century of Roman rule. On the other hand, as Nicklin (1979, 455) has pointed out, the same phenomenon in modern Nigeria has accompanied a phase of accelerated economic development. Clearly the factors affecting kiln distributions in Roman Britain are complicated, and all are not yet fully understood.

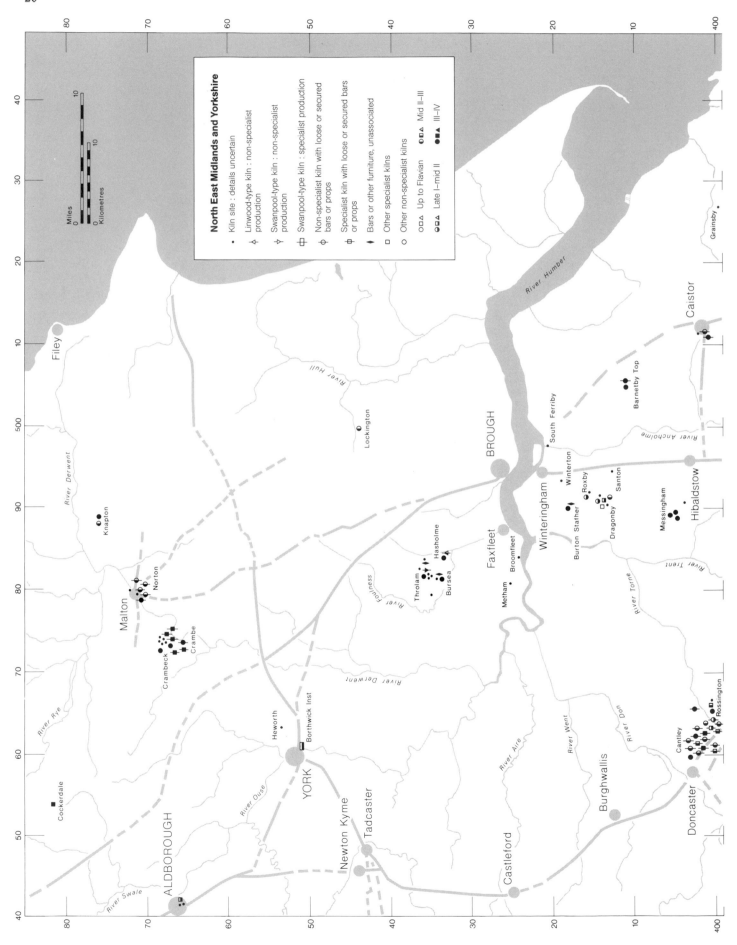

North East Midlands and Yorkshire

Kiln site : details uncertain
Linwood-type kiln : non-specialist production
Swanpool-type kiln : non-specialist production
Swanpool-type kiln : specialist production
Non-specialist kiln with loose or secured bars or props
Specialist kiln with loose or secured bars or props
Bars or other furniture, unassociated
Other specialist kilns
Other non-specialist kilns
Up to Flavian
Late I–mid II
Mid II–III
III–IV

Miles
Kilometres

River Humber
River Hull
River Derwent
River Rye
River Swale
River Ouse
River Foulness
River Derwent
River Aire
River Went
River Don
River Torne
River Trent
River Ancholme

Filey
Knapton
Malton
Norton
Crambe
Crambeck
Cockerdale
Heworth
Borthwick Inst
YORK
ALDBOROUGH
Newton Kyme
Tadcaster
Castleford
Burghwallis
Doncaster
Cantley
Rossington
Lockington
Throlam
Hasholme
Bursea
Metham
Broomfleet
Faxfleet
BROUGH
South Ferriby
Winteringham
Winterton
Roxby
Santon
Burton Stather
Dragonby
Messingham
Hibaldstow
Barnetby Top
Caistor
Grainsby

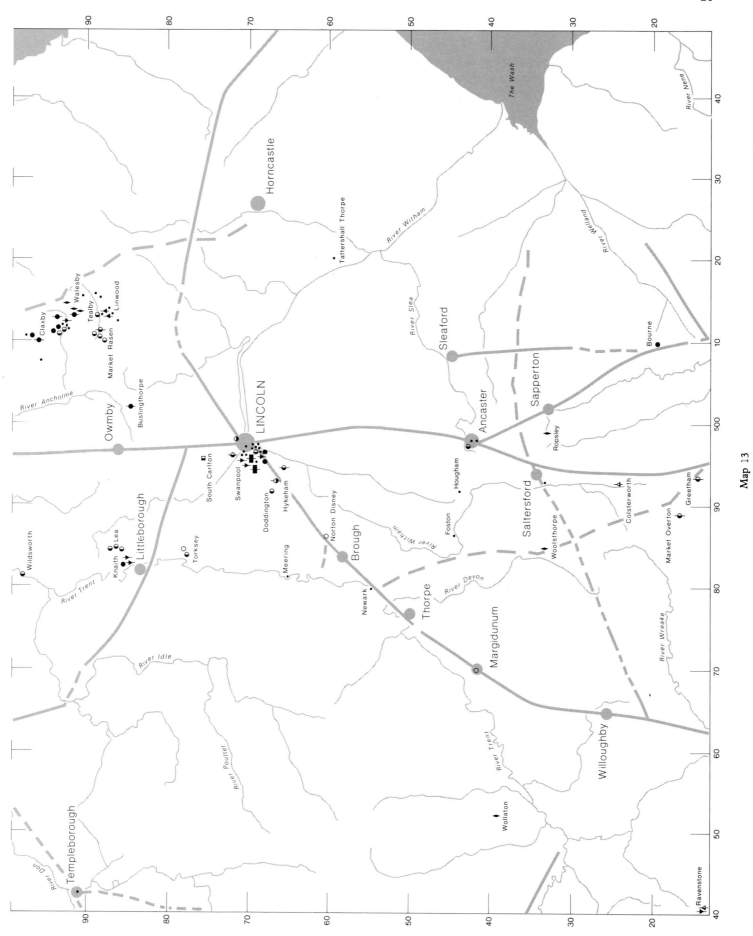

Map 13

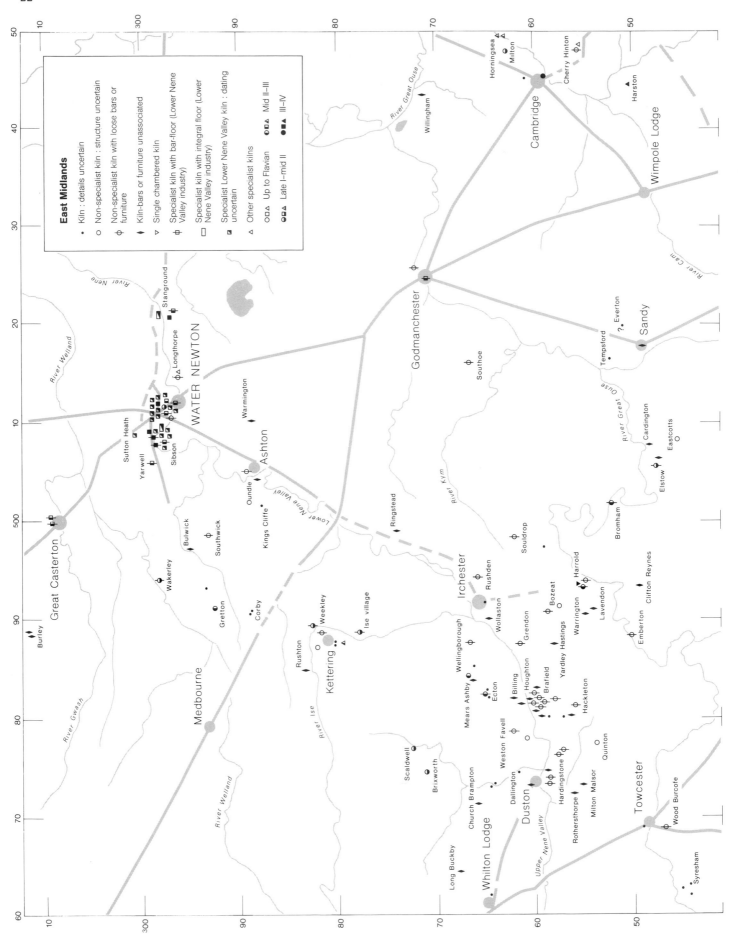

East Midlands

- • Kiln : details uncertain
- ○ Non-specialist kiln : structure uncertain
- ⊕ Non-specialist kiln with loose bars or furniture
- ◆ Kiln-bars or furniture unassociated
- ▽ Single chambered kiln
- ⊞ Specialist kiln with bar-floor (Lower Nene Valley industry)
- ▢ Specialist kiln with integral floor (Lower Nene Valley industry)
- ▪ Specialist Lower Nene Valley kiln : dating uncertain
- △ Other specialist kilns

  ○◻△ Up to Flavian
  ◑◻△ Late I–mid II
  ⊕◻▪ Mid II–III
  ●▪▲ III–IV

Great Casterton

Burley

River Gwash

River Welland

Medbourne

Whilton Lodge

Long Buckby

Rushton

Kettering

Scaldwell

Brixworth

Church Brampton

Dallington

Duston

Hardingstone

Rothersthorpe

Milton Malsor

Towcester

Wood Burcote

Syresham

River Ise

Weekley

Ise village

Mears Ashby

Wellingborough

Ecton

Weston Favell

Billing

Houghton

Brafield

Yardley Hastings

Hackleton

Quinton

Upper Nene Valley

Wakerley

Gretton

Corby

Bulwick

Southwick

Kings Cliffe

Oundle

Lower Nene Valley

Ringstead

Irchester

Rushden

Wollaston

Grendon

Bozeat

Warrington

Lavendon

Emberton

Clifton Reynes

Souldrop

Harrold

Bromham

River Nene

River Welland

Stanground

Longthorpe

WATER NEWTON

Sutton Heath

Yarwell

Sibson

Warmington

Ashton

Godmanchester

Southoe

River Kym

River Great Ouse

Willingham

Horningsea

Milton

Cambridge

Cherry Hinton

Harston

Wimpole Lodge

River Cam

Sandy

Everton

Tempsford

River Great Ouse

Cardington

Eastcotts

Elstow

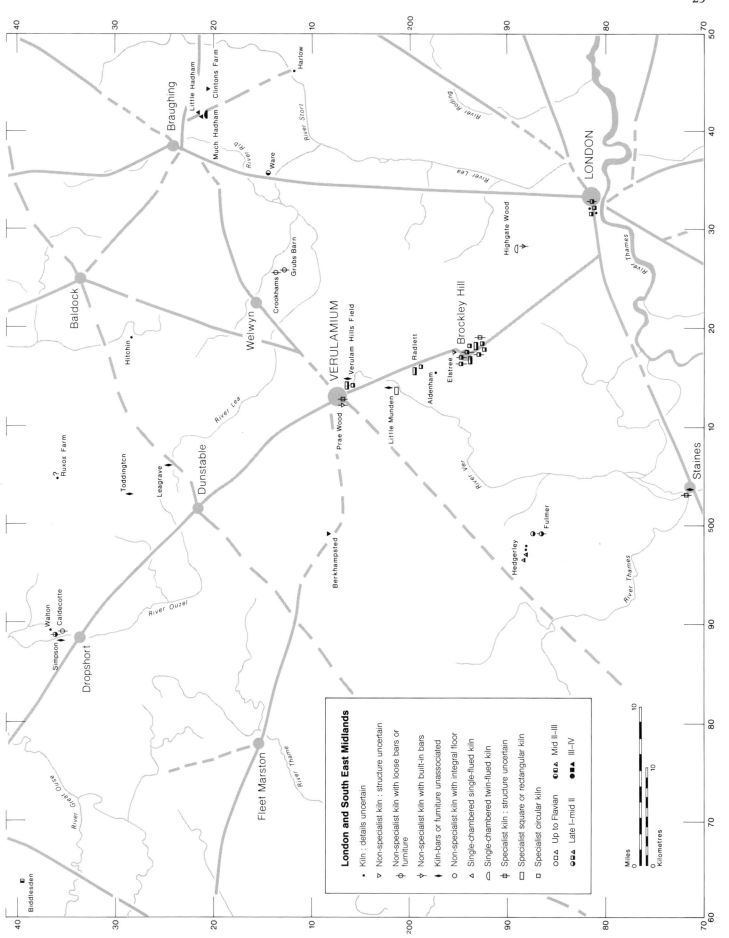

London and South East Midlands

- •   Kiln : details uncertain
- ▽   Non-specialist kiln : structure uncertain
- ⌀   Non-specialist kiln with loose bars or furniture
- ⍓   Non-specialist kiln with built-in bars
- ◆   Kiln-bars or furniture unassociated
- ○   Non-specialist kiln with integral floor
- △   Single-chambered single-flued kiln
- ⌓   Single-chambered twin-flued kiln
- ⊕   Specialist kiln : structure uncertain
- ▢   Specialist square or rectangular kiln
- ▫   Specialist circular kiln

○▢△   Up to Flavian   ◐▢△   Mid II–III
◑▢△   Late I–mid II   ●▪▲   III–IV

Miles

Kilometres

Map 14

Biddlesden

River Great Ouse

Fleet Marston

River Thame

Dropshort

Walton
Caldecotte
Simpson

River Ouzel

Berkhampsted

Dunstable

Leagrave

Toddington

Ruxox Farm ?

Hitchin

Baldock

Braughing

Little Hadham
Much Hadham
Clintons Farm

Harlow

River Stort

River Rib

Ware

River Roding

River Lea

Welwyn

Crookhams
Grubs Barn

VERULAMIUM
Verulam Hills Field

Prae Wood

Little Munden

Radlett

Aldenham

Elstree

Brockley Hill

Highgate Wood

LONDON

River Thames

River Ver

Fulmer

Hedgerley

Staines

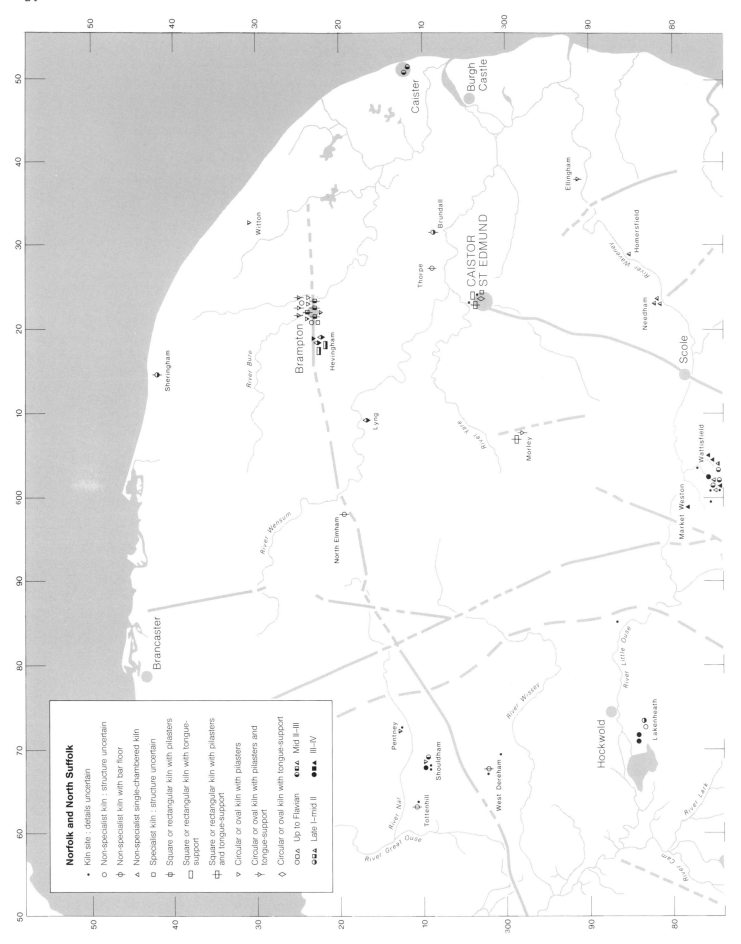

Norfolk and North Suffolk

- Kiln site : details uncertain
- ○ Non-specialist kiln : structure uncertain
- ⌀ Non-specialist kiln with bar floor
- △ Non-specialist single-chambered kiln
- □ Specialist kiln : structure uncertain
- ⊞ Square or rectangular kiln with pilasters
- ▭ Square or rectangular kiln with tongue-support
- ⊞ Square or rectangular kiln with pilasters and tongue-support
- ▽ Circular or oval kiln with pilasters
- ⴼ Circular or oval kiln with pilasters and tongue-support
- ◇ Circular or oval kiln with tongue-support

○⌀△ Up to Flavian ○▭△ Mid II–III
◐⌀△ Late I–mid II ●■▲ III–IV

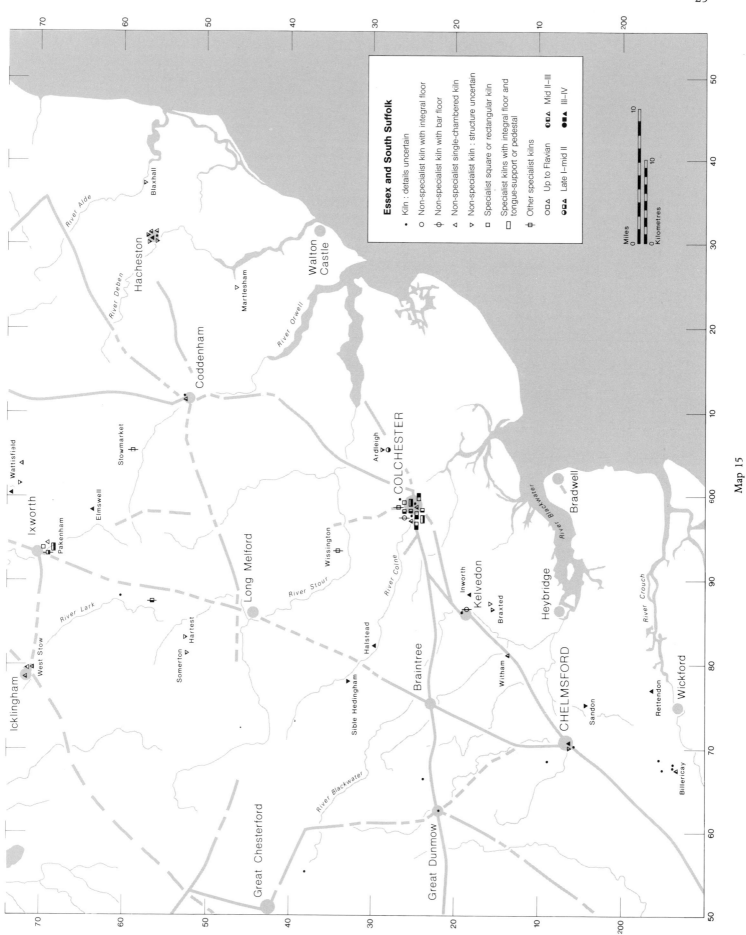

Essex and South Suffolk

- • Kiln : details uncertain
- ○ Non-specialist kiln with integral floor
- ⏀ Non-specialist kiln with bar floor
- △ Non-specialist single-chambered kiln
- ▽ Non-specialist kiln : structure uncertain
- ☐ Specialist square or rectangular kiln
- ▭ Specialist kilns with integral floor and tongue-support or pedestal
- ⏀ Other specialist kilns

○⏀△ Up to Flavian	⊙⏀▲ Mid II–III
⊙⏀▲ Late I–mid II	●■▲ III–IV

Map 15

26

Map 16

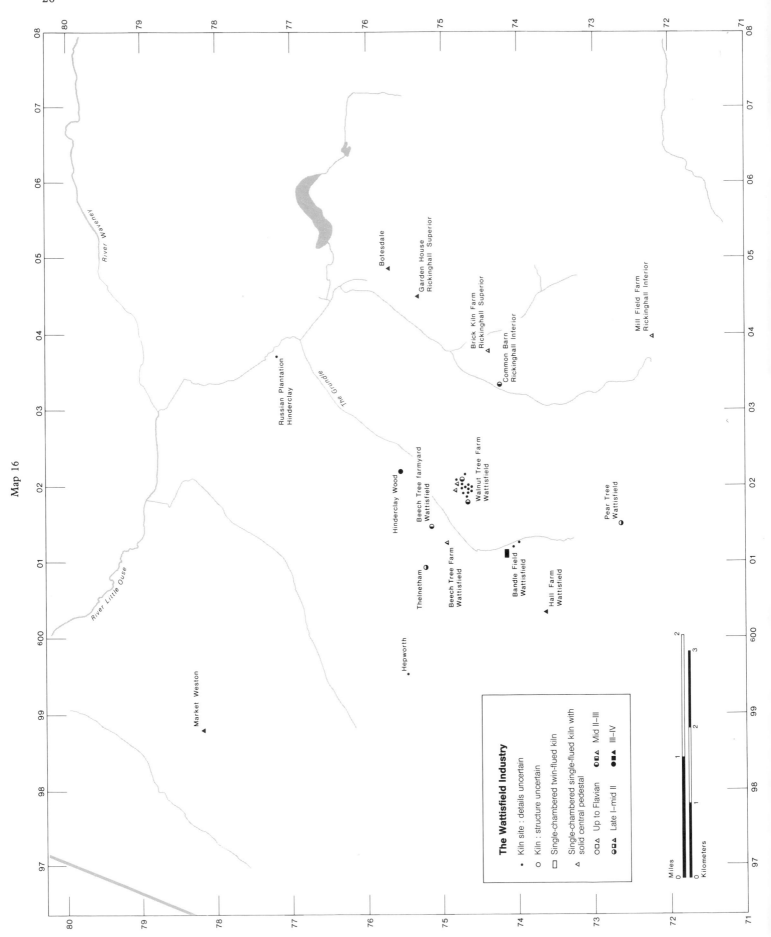

The **Wattisfield** Industry

• Kiln site : details uncertain

○ Kiln : structure uncertain

▭ Single-chambered twin-flued kiln

△ Single-chambered single-flued kiln with
    solid central pedestal

○□△ Up to Flavian   ○△ Mid II–III

○□△ Late I–mid II   ●■▲ III–IV

Miles
0   1   2

Kilometers
0   1   2   3

River Waveney

River Little Ouse

The Grundle

Botesdale

Garden House
Rickinghall Superior

Brick Kiln Farm
Rickinghall Superior

Common Barn
Rickinghall Inferior

Mill Field Farm
Rickinghall Inferior

Russian Plantation
Hinderclay

Hinderclay Wood

Beech Tree farmyard
Wattisfield

Walnut Tree Farm
Wattisfield

Thelnetham

Beech Tree Farm
Wattisfield

Bandle Field
Wattisfield

Hall Farm
Wattisfield

Pear Tree
Wattisfield

Hepworth

Market Weston

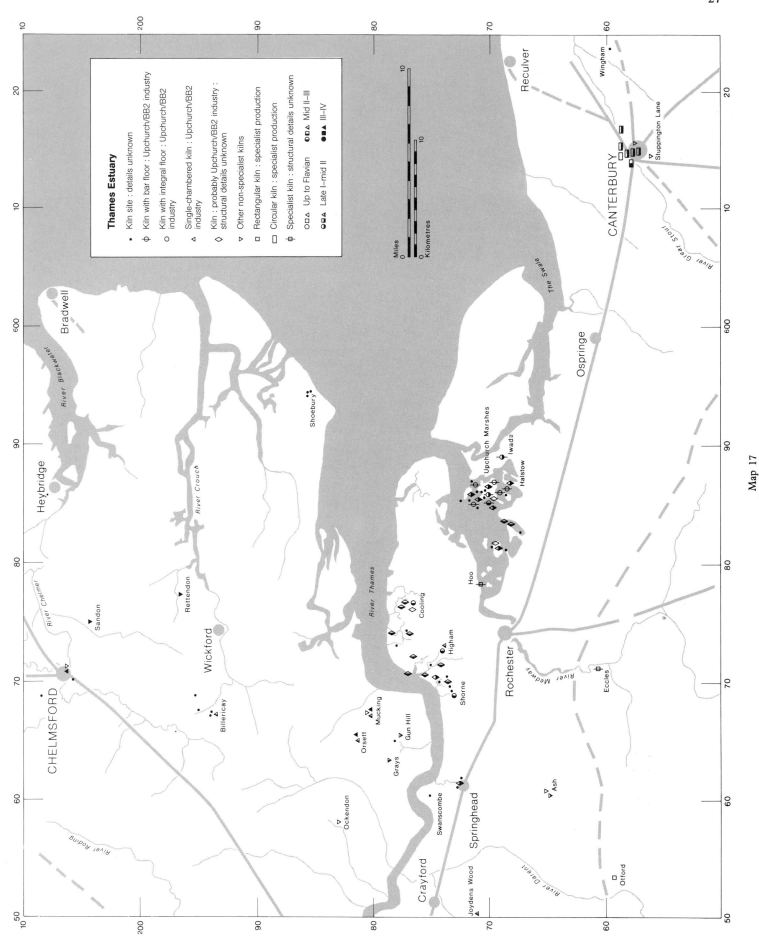

Map 17

28

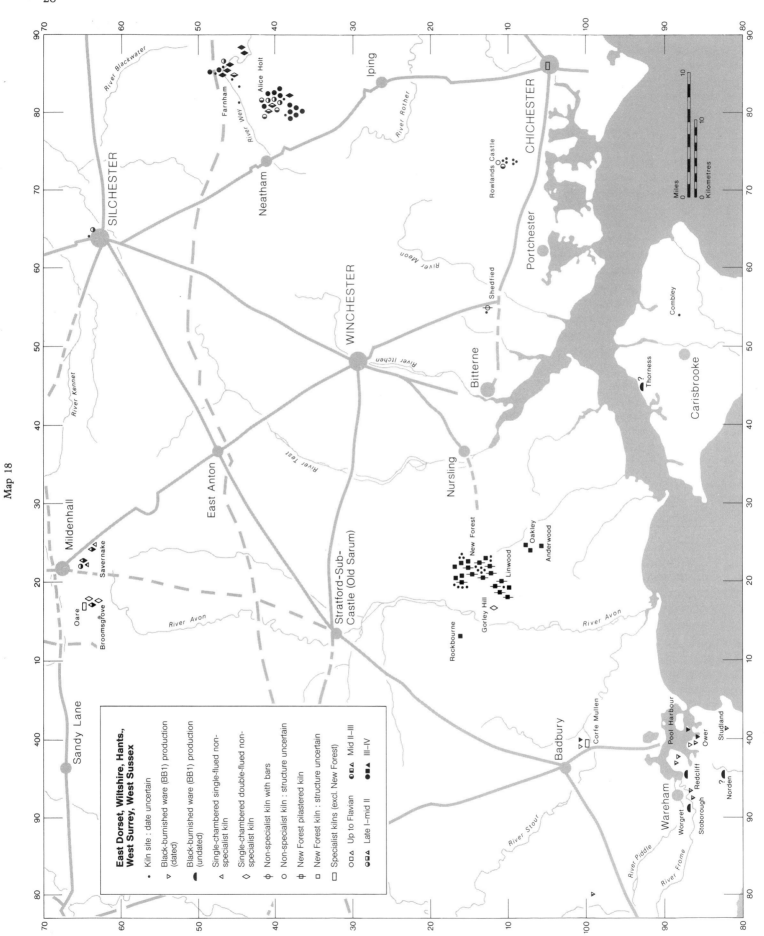

Map 18

East Dorset, Wiltshire, Hants.,
West Surrey, West Sussex

• Kiln site : date uncertain

▽ Black-burnished ware (BB1) production
  (dated)

◖ Black-burnished ware (BB1) production
  (undated)

◁ Single-chambered single-flued non-
  specialist kiln

◇ Single-chambered double-flued non-
  specialist kiln

⬥ Non-specialist kiln with bars

○ Non-specialist kiln : structure uncertain

⬦ New Forest pilastered kiln

▢ New Forest kiln : structure uncertain

▭ Specialist kilns (excl. New Forest)

○◨△ Up to Flavian   ●◨▲ Mid II–III

◐◨▲ Late I–mid II   ●■▲ III–IV

CHAPTER 3

Techniques of kiln building and operation

Kiln components

The essential parts of a Romano-British up-draught kiln (Fig. II) comprised: (a) the *stokehole, stoke-pit* or, in surface-built kilns, *stoking-area*; (b) the *flue*; (c) the *furnace-chamber, combustion-chamber* or, in single-chambered kilns, *oven-pit*; (d) *support*; (e) *raised oven-floor* or, in single-chambered kilns, *kiln-floor*; (f) *oven*; (g) *superstructure*; (h) *exhaust-vent*; (i) *capping* or *topping*.

(a) The *stokehole* or *stoke-pit* (Fig. II.ii) was usually a hollow dug into the ground from which fuel was fed into the fire burning in the adjacent flue and combustion-chamber. Excess ash could be raked out of them into the stokehole, where sometimes the fire was probably also started. In surface-built kilns, stoking was often carried out at ground level, and the term *stoking-area* is then used (Fig. II.iii).

(b) The *flue* or *fire-tunnel*, referred to in some kiln reports as the *furnace* or *praefurnium*, linked the stokehole to the furnace-chamber. It varied in length. In single-chambered kilns (Fig. II.ii) this was where the fire burnt, and through it the draught would draw flames into the furnace or combustion-chamber. In kilns with a raised oven-floor where the flue was short, the fire was probably kindled there and burning embers would be pushed from it into the furnace-chamber (Fig. II.iv, v). In some excavation reports, and in a number of potters' manuals, the use of the word 'flue' is not confined to this area. It is often applied to the gaps or channels between the oven-floor supports in the combustion-chamber, or to apertures in the kiln-superstructure for the emission of gases. The latter will here be termed '*exhaust-vent*' (*see below*; Fig. II.ii).

(c) The *furnace-chamber* or *combustion-chamber*. Except in single-chambered kilns, this was where at least part of the fire burnt and from which hot gases percolated upwards (up-draught) through the raised oven-floor to the superimposed oven (Fig. II.iii). In single-chambered kilns, where there was no such raised floor or chamber, the fire tended to be confined to the flue and so vessels could be stacked in the adjacent sunken chamber, then termed the *oven-pit* (Fig. II.ii).

(d) *Support.* A protruding, recessed or raised structure, temporary or inbuilt, positioned in the combustion-chamber to support the superimposed raised oven-floor. It could take the form of pilasters or piers (Fig. III.v), ledge(s) (Fig. III.vii), cross-walls (Fig. III.iv), or corbels (Fig. III.vi) protruding from the interior of the kiln-wall, holes in the kiln-wall (Fig. III.viii), one or more free-standing pedestal(s) (Fig. III.ii), an inverted pottery vessel (Fig. III.i) or a 'tongue' protruding from the back of the combustion-chamber (Fig. III.iii). The term 'pedestal' has been applied loosely to both tongues and free-standing supports. For clarity it should be prefaced either by 'free-standing' or 'tongue' to distinguish between the two.

(e) The *raised oven-floor*, or false floor, spanned the combustion-chamber and upon it vessels were stacked for firing. It was built of portable components such as bars (Fig. II.iii), positioned at intervals, or of solid clay perforated with vent-holes (Fig. II.iv).

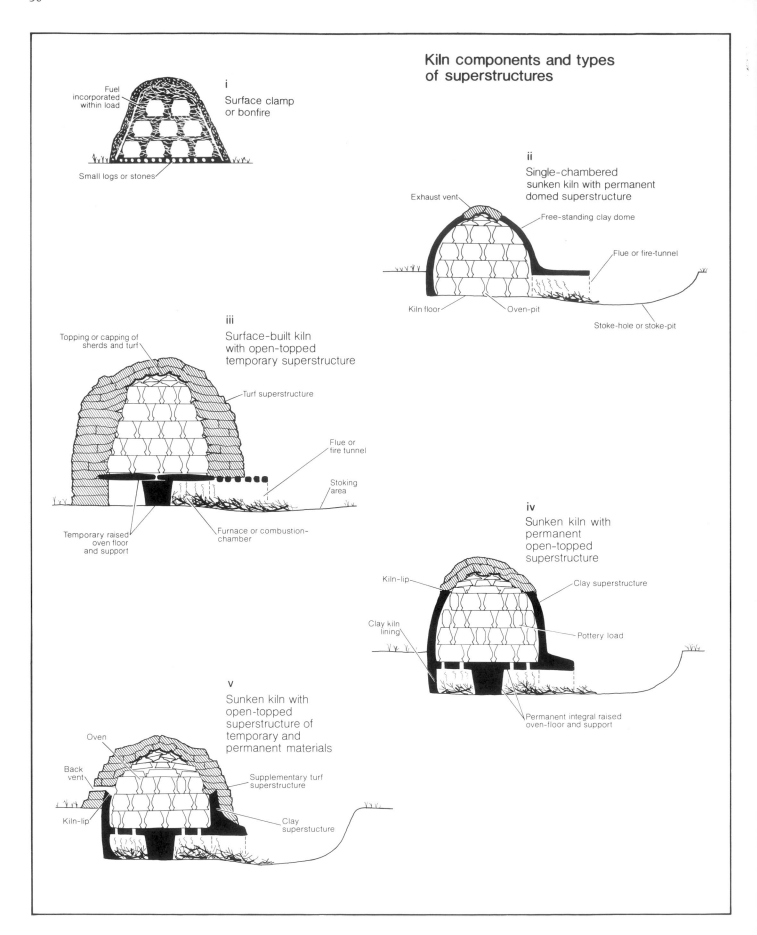

Fig. II.

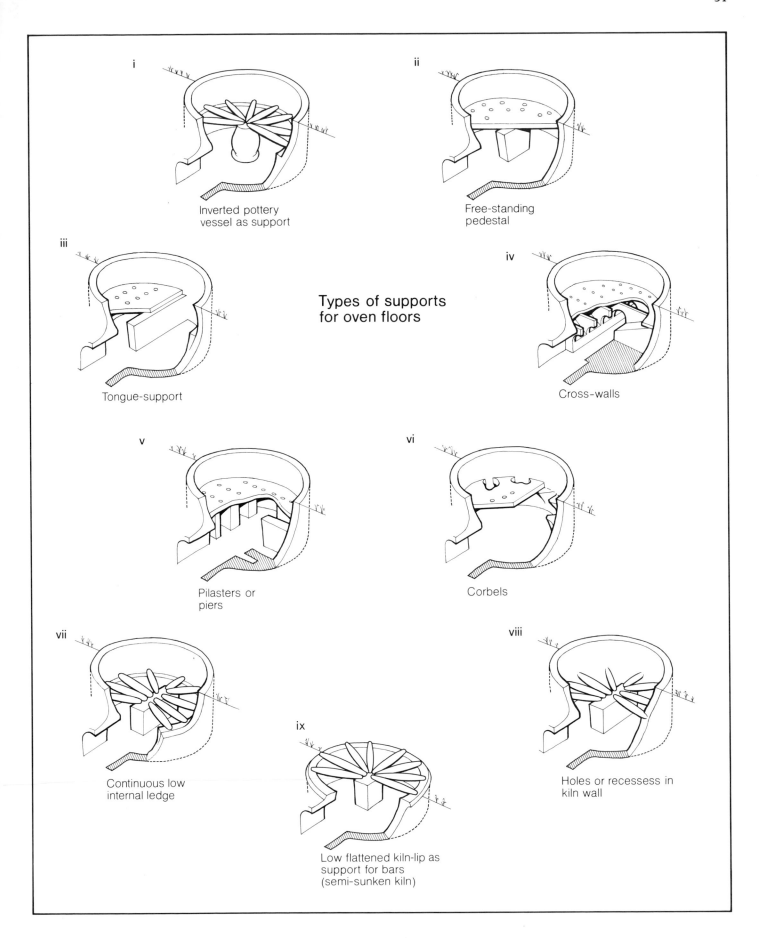

i   Inverted pottery vessel as support

ii   Free-standing pedestal

iii   Tongue-support

iv   Cross-walls

Types of supports for oven floors

v   Pilasters or piers

vi   Corbels

vii   Continuous low internal ledge

viii   Holes or recessess in kiln wall

ix   Low flattened kiln-lip as support for bars (semi-sunken kiln)

Fig. III.

Both allowed the through-passage of hot air from the combustion-chamber below. In single-chambered kilns, the bottom of the oven-pit is frequently known as the *kiln-floor* (Fig. II.ii). This term has often been used too loosely, and should not be applied to a *raised oven-floor*.

(f) *Oven.* An independent raised chamber in which the vessels were stacked for firing and into which hot gases and flames rose from the combustion-chamber immediately below (Fig. II.iii–v).

(g) *Superstructure.* This usually applies to the free-standing, temporary or permanent walling of the kiln above ground, but occasionally to the kiln structure above oven-floor level whether below ground or otherwise. For details of various types, *see* p. 34 ff. (Fig. II.iii-v).

(h) *Exhaust-vent(s).* One or more hole(s), often at the top or back of the oven-superstructure, through which hot gases could escape into the atmosphere (Fig. II.ii, v). At certain stages in the kiln-firing they were either left open or blocked, as necessary, to increase or decrease draught upwards.

(i) *Capping* or *Topping* (Fig. II.iii; *see also* p. 34) comprised material used as a temporary covering for the open end of a kiln-superstructure. Its prime purpose was to prevent excessive heat loss, but in a reducing firing it could be totally sealed to prevent oxygen entering the oven.

It is not proposed to discuss in detail the problems involved in the construction and operation of kilns, but merely to indicate some of the archaeological evidence for these processes. Good accounts of experimental kiln building and firing have been published (for list *see* p. 2). It is important, however, to appreciate the limitations of the evidence available from excavations. Of most kilns, little or nothing survives above ground. Any understanding of the structure as a whole is often exactly proportional to the depth to which the kiln-chamber was sunk into the natural subsoil, thereby preserving it. As a result, we know much about the structures of the deeply-sunken Derbyshire-ware kilns (Fig. XXI).

Some Romano-British kilns were constructed of stone plastered over with clay internally, but the vast majority had a solid-clay lining. Clay is, of course, an excellent refractory material and kiln-chambers cut into a clay subsoil were often left without any independent lining, for example at St Stephen's, Canterbury (Jenkins 1956, Area I). Most surface-built kilns lacked a substantial permanent lining and must have been walled primarily with turf for which little evidence now survives. (Fig. II.iii). As a rule, the clay used for the lining of a kiln was similar to that of its products but more coarsely-tempered. Frequently sand was included and, sometimes, sherds, pieces of fired clay, lumps of stone, broken kiln-furniture and vegetation. The main function of such material was to bind the clay together, to reinforce it at vital points of wear and, above all, to stop excessive shrinkage and cracking of the kiln structure. The Swanpool kiln experiments suggested that this problem was most serious at the early pre-firing drying stage in surface-built kilns with permanent clay walling (Fig. XX; Wood, unpubl.). It was successfully solved then by placing sand or turves against the outside of the kiln-walls and flue. Possibly the same purpose was served by the soil banked up externally against the lower part of some of the surface-built clay-lined kilns at Highgate Wood (Kilns 2, 3, 5; Brown and Sheldon 1969; 1970), and also by the ash dumps deliberately allowed to accumulate around some of the Alice Holt and Throlam, Yorks. E.R., kilns (Lyne and Jefferies 1979, 17; Corder 1932). Clearly, the relationship between an upstanding kiln-wall and its immediate area deserves careful examination.

The most usual technique of kiln building involved plastering with clay the sides of a hole of requisite size and shape. The finger-marks and other impressions visible on the interiors of many kilns suggest that this was mostly done by hand (Pl. 2). At Cantley, Yorks. W.R., however, the use of a tool, possibly a trowel, was evident in Kiln 25 (Cregeen 1965, 45), and the walls of Kiln 7 appeared to have been built up in coils (Annable 1960). In contrast the wall of a kiln at Pitts Wood in the New Forest (unpubl.) was built of raw clay blocks, a technique made difficult to detect by the subsequent smoothing-over of surface joins. The use of prefabricated sun-dried or pre-fired clay blocks (Figs. X, XI; Pls. 26, 27), or tiles is not common and is generally confined to specialist kilns, particularly those in early workshops probably working in military tradition, as at Morley St Peter, Norfolk (p. 84), and in the major industries with close Continental connections, such as Colchester and the Lower Nene Valley (pp. 94, 96). Such blocks may have been more stable at high temperatures, and their use must certainly have facilitated localized kiln repairs.

Some kilns embody the impressions of burnt-out withies used as reinforcing material, occasionally in the lining as at Mucking (Jones and Rodwell 1973, 17), but more particularly on the underside of the raised oven-floor and its supports, or in the region of the flue-arch. It seems probable that such details as the impressions of under-floor supports or the use of prefabricated bars within a floor seemingly of solid clay have not been noted in many older excavations. Careful observation is also needed at the junction between the kiln-wall and the raised oven-floor. Many reports fail to indicate whether there are scars or other evidence of flooring having been removed at this point, a vital factor in deciding whether a kiln was single or double-chambered.

The flue, together with the raised oven-floor, was the weakest part of any kiln structure, partly because of its proximity to the fire. This was very noticeable in the various experimental kiln-firings. In most kilns, flues seem to have needed frequent replacement or repair. The flue-roof of each Mucking kiln appeared to have been rebuilt for each firing (ibid., 17). Potters often went to great pains to reinforce them with local stone as at Norton (Pl. 39), coursed tiles as at Colchester (Fig. X), or prefabricated clay components such as bars or arched pieces as in the Nene Valley (Fig. XI). In Kilns 6, 8 and 20 at Cantley (Annable 1960; Gilmour 1955, pl. II), the flue was cut through a massive frontal block of clay, constructed separately from the kiln-chamber. At several other sites, flues were tunnelled through the natural subsoil.

Plate 2.

Lower Sloden Enclosure, FORD-INGBRIDGE, Hants.: Kiln 1, detail of interior of furnace-chamber: *Centre*, finger impressions between two pilasters where clay lining had been plastered on by hand. *Bottom right*, impression of burnt-out withy. *Far left*, sherd incorporated in repair to flue-arch.

When built, the kiln structure itself would have needed preliminary firing at least once to give it stability. In some kilns, various stages seem to have been consolidated separately. The furnace of Highgate Wood Kiln 2 was apparently fired before the addition of the pedestal (Brown and Sheldon 1969, 41). Floors of prefabricated overplastered bars were almost certainly fired independently. Some kilns were completely remodelled, relined, refloored, or had their axes re-aligned during their life-span. The evidence of the Swanpool kiln experiment (Wood, unpubl.) suggested that, provided no initial constructional faults existed, the damage to a kiln from its first full firing was normally relatively minor and easily patched up. This implies a relatively long life for most of the more substantial kiln structures, with scores rather than dozens of firings.

Overall design

The design of some kiln structures was influenced primarily by the traditions and ancestry of the potting background to which they belonged. Many structures, indeed, must have been conditioned by the special technological needs of the types of vessels which they produced and the firing properties of the potting clay used. Very high or relatively low kiln-temperatures, long or short firings, oxidation or reduction were all critical factors. More experimental kiln-firings need to be conducted with these points in mind, although gradual heating and cooling were clearly the general rule.

It seems likely that for specialist wares a relatively sophisticated kiln with a raised oven-floor was essential to keep the

vessels away from the ash and flames. The high temperature to which Derbyshire wares were fired depended on an exceptionally high, chimney-like firing-chamber to produce a strong draught (Fig. XXI). The capacious combustion-chambers of the New Forest kilns, free of large protruding supports and with relatively high oven-floors and high, very short flues (Fig. XV), may have been designed to achieve the high temperatures characteristic of most of their lustrous wares or for burning bulky bundles of wood. In some kilns, the form of a flue is noticeably linked with the design of its kiln-chamber. Kilns with cross-walls or long pilasters almost always have long flues, presumably because there was little or no room for fuel to be raked into the furnace-chamber beneath the oven-floor, as in Brampton Kilns D2, E, G, G1 (Fig. XIX). Similarly, a large, long flue was characteristic of Swanpool-type kilns, probably because of the lack of space for fuel within the kiln-chamber itself (p. 123; Fig. XX; Pl. 46). In some smaller kilns, as at Norton (Pl. 39; Hayes and Whitley 1950) and at West Stow, Suffolk (Pl. 3; Prigg 1881, Kiln 1), fuel raked too far into the furnace-chamber might have displaced the portable furniture or vessels stacked at the bottom of the kiln. To prevent this a long or relatively wide, sometimes bulbous, flue was adopted, perhaps explaining the character of the original arrangements in Kiln C at Brampton, Norfolk (Knowles 1967). This had such a flue, but evidence for the layout within the kiln-chamber was lacking, possibly because the portable furniture had been removed.

That wide flues were also a response to the type of fuel used in them has yet to be satisfactorily demonstrated. Experiments with a wood-fired kiln with permanent floor-supports (Bryant 1977a,

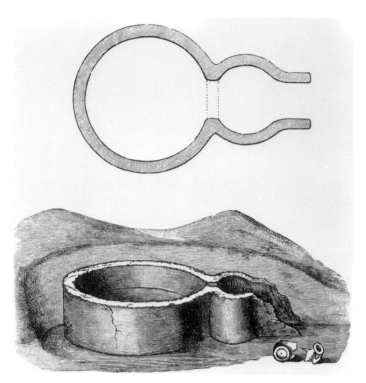

Plate 3. WEST STOW, Suffolk: kiln (internal diam. approx. 1.08 cm) with bulbous flue, excavated in 1879: *after* Prigg (1881, *opp*. 152).

Roman Britain but that several were in use simultaneously in various locations and even, sometimes, within a single factory, as at Hartshill/Mancetter (Hartley 1973a).

In the interpretation of a kiln-superstructure the intended firing atmosphere is crucial. Bryant (1973, 149) has noted that to oxidize pots is relatively simple, whatever the character of the superstructure, since permeability is not a prime consideration. The top of the pottery stack itself needs only a light temporary capping of loose material, such as potsherds or tile, resting on it to insulate vessels in the upper tiers of the kiln-load (Fig. II.iii). Sealing is unnecessary.

On the other hand, reduced wares, which formed the bulk of native-derived production, call for slightly more complicated firing techniques. For these, the whole kiln-superstructure must be completely impermeable, at least during the latter stages of firing and cooling, to prevent the seepage of oxygen into the oven. To achieve this, the flue or flues are blocked immediately after stoking and the insulating capping of the kiln-load sealed simultaneously with impervious material, such as clay, turves, sand, or dust (Rhodes 1969, 10, fig. 9). This covering, again resting ultimately on the pottery stack, is necessarily temporary since it must be removed after firing in order to unload the pottery. In the following discussion, this element, part of which was possibly added during the course of firing, is termed the 'covering' or 'capping', while the basic or above-ground element in the kiln-superstructure present at the outset of a firing is termed the 'dome', 'top', or 'superstructure' as appropriate (Fig. II.ii–v).

The standard reconstruction of a kiln-superstructure accepted for many years was that proposed by Corder (1957, 14, fig. 3). It comprised a 'free-standing, temporary dome, formed of turves, straw and clay, built up on a framework of branches around the pots' as they were stacked before firing. Such a structure, it was considered, would have had either a 'vent left at its apex' or 'some other means by which hot gases could permeate the walls'. The dome would have been completely demolished when cooling was completed and renewed for each subsequent firing. Experiments (Mayes 1961; 1962; Bryant 1973, 155) have shown, however, that the burning-out of the substantial framework of branches, and the shrinkage of the clay during the firing of such a dome, would have made it difficult to maintain the completely air-tight conditions essential for holding a reducing atmosphere at the cooling stage. These problems would have been particularly acute in large kilns. As Bryant pointed out (1977b, 109), moreover, 'it is hard to see any potter taking more time and effort to build a temporary structure than is evidenced (from experiments) for the vast majority of permanent domes'. As he suggested, the use of the term 'temporary' dome', indicating a free-standing structure built over a loaded kiln, is better discontinued.

On the basis of the archaeological evidence available, Romano-British kiln-superstructures seem to have been of three types:

(1) Permanent free-standing domes (Fig. II.ii).
(2) Open-topped superstructures:
    (a) of permanent materials, and occasionally tall enough to be described as chimneys (Fig. II.iv);
    (b) wholly or partly of temporary materials (Fig. II.iii, v).

11 ff.) suggested that the advantages of a long flue, with an ashpit at its junction with the stokehole, were of marginal technological significance and offset by some disadvantages. Its use with other types of fuel, however, may yet indicate a technology different to that involved in firing a short-flued kiln with wood. In some of the Alice Holt kilns the flue narrows quite markedly towards the interior, resulting in a letter-box-shaped opening at its junction with the kiln-chamber (Fig. XVIII). Experiments in firing such single-chambered twin-flued kilns have shown that this flue design creates enormous suction, thereby substantially increasing the draught and drawing the flames into the chamber (inf. M. Lyne). The high temperatures resulting from this feature are evidenced in many Alice Holt/Farnham products.

Kiln-superstructure

The methods and materials by which kilns were covered have long been the subject of much controversy and speculation, mainly because this part of a kiln rarely survives intact and is almost impossible to reconstruct from fragments. On many kiln sites little attempt has been made to consider in detail the evidence for them.

Over the past decade or so, the techniques of kiln-covering have been better understood, largely because of the firing experiments conducted by Bryant (1970; 1971; 1973; 1977a, b; 1978; 1980). A re-examination of archaeological records, in the light of these experiments, shows that they contain more details of kiln-roofing than was hitherto realized. It now seems certain that no single type of kiln-superstructure predominated in

Permanent free-standing domes

For these an igloo-type roof was constructed as an integral part of the kiln-oven, with a small vent at the top just large enough for loading (Fig. II.ii). Although such a dome must have involved the potter in an initial outlay of much time and effort, its great virtue was that it could be used for many successive firings. Furthermore, experiments in the production of reduced wares have shown that permanent domes have a substantial advantage in holding a reducing atmosphere within a cooling kiln (Bryant 1973, 151). The vent-gap covered by the makeshift temporary capping would have been small and thus easier to seal than the larger aperture of an open-topped kiln. Experiments, however, proved that permanent domes complicated and prolonged the loading process. It is difficult to arrange a stack of pottery through a small aperture in a stable manner and in such a way as to ensure a good flow of hot gases around the vessels.

Kilns with permanent domes are known to have existed in the Mediterranean area and the Near East for at least five millennia (Hodges 1970, 58, figs. 51 and 3; Singer *et al.* 1954, 392 ff.). From the Classical Mediterranean World their use probably spread to other parts of the Roman Empire, including Britain, in the wake of Conquest. A model of a kiln found in the potters' quarter at Nijmegen (Loeschcke 1922, 3, Abb. 3) shows a domed oven with a 'cowl' protruding on one side of the top vent, possibly to prevent a sudden wind gusting down the dome. The domed kiln structures painted on Greek vases (Richter 1923, 76–8, figs. 72–94; Noble 1965, 73, fig. 231 ff.), and the structure and firing techniques of many primitive domed kilns in the Mediterranean area still being operated in the same basic traditions, both suggest the frequent use of a blockable door in the side or back wall of the oven. This facilitates loading and sometimes acts as a spyhole during firing (Hampe and Winter 1962, 44,

Abb. 26–7, 83, Abb. 50–51; 1965, 53, Abb. 43, 77, Abb. 69–70, 154, Abb. 134, Taf. 25.1–4, Taf. 54.5). Except for those involved in Attic pottery, most of these kilns seem to be intended essentially to produce oxidized vessels, thus presenting no problems of protracted air-tight sealing in the region of the door. Certainly there is no evidence for such doors in Romano-British kilns, perhaps because of the difficulties they pose in maintaining a reducing atmosphere. On the contrary, the few recorded examples of domed kilns in Britain were of much squatter proportions, as at Cooling, Kent and Shepton Mallet, Somerset (Pls. 4, 5), than most of those recently recorded in rural potteries in the Mediterranean area (Hampe and Winter 1962; 1965). They must have been loaded through a hole in the top of the dome. A number of references to the discovery of apparently well-preserved Romano-British kilns mention 'domes' or describe them as 'like beehives', but do not give details. It may be reasonably presumed that these too refer to kilns with permanent domes. All known domed kilns apparently had a relatively small capacity and were built of clay as a continuation of the below-ground lining of the oven-chamber.

Evidence from a number of sites suggests that withies were sometimes incorporated in the clay superstructure to help in holding its shape before firing and to reduce shrinkage, as at Hardingstone, Northants. (Woods 1969, 4). At St Stephen's, Canterbury, impressions on the 'dome' debris were thought to indicate that the withies had been grouped into bundles (Jenkins 1956, 51–2). Highgate Wood Kiln 2 had a series of holes in the kiln-wall. Kiln 3 had stakeholes in the top of the kiln-wall, along its circumference, perhaps part of a light wooden frame supporting the superstructure before firing (Brown and Sheldon 1969, 40–41). Judging from primitive potteries in the Mediterranean area, numerous waster vessels placed inside one another to form a

Plate 4.

Bromhey Farm, COOLING, Kent: part of the permanent, shallowly-domed clay superstructure of kiln; finished edge of loading vent is visible at *top* (*see also* Pl. 1, frontispiece).

Plate 5. The Brewery, SHEPTON MALLET, Somerset: kiln (internal diam. approx. 1.42 m) found in 1864; the 'dome' survived for 'two feet' above oven-floor at back of kiln: *after* Scarth (1866, *opp.* 1).

curve may also have provided a light yet rigid element for vaulting the kiln-dome (Hampe and Winter 1965, 71, Abb. 64, 192, Abb. 142, Taf. 16.2, Taf. 27.3). There is good evidence that stacks of pots were incorporated in this way in the vertical walls of some of the kilns at *Novaesium* (Neuss), Germany (Filtzinger 1972, 52, Abb. 3, Taf. 97.1; unpubl. records in Rheinisches Landesmuseum, Bonn, *per* Dr M. Gechter). The method would also have provided excellent insulation comparable with that afforded by the jacketing of tubes in the walls of some samian kilns (Hull 1963, 20 ff.).

Open-topped kilns of permanent materials

Here the kiln-wall continued vertically, or nearly vertically, above ground like a cylinder and was not substantially corbelled inwards to form a dome (Fig. II.iv). The oven would have been loaded with pottery up to the top of the lip, namely the top of the kiln-wall above ground level (Fig. II.iv), or perhaps even to almost 1 m above it. The whole stack then had to bear the weight of a temporary capping, initially to prevent heat loss. Most superstructures of this type were built of clay but a few, as at Harrold, were probably of stone bonded with clay (inf. A. Brown). In experiments, those of clay were easy to build and fire, and more convenient to load efficiently than domes. Extra care was, however, needed in the ultimate sealing of the load capping in order to maintain a satisfactory reducing atmosphere at the cooling stage.

This type of kiln, also apparently of considerable antiquity (Hodges 1970, 58, fig. 52), is still frequently found in some of the more primitive Mediterranean potteries working in the same traditions. These, like some of their domed contemporaries in the area, often have blockable loading doorways (Hampe and Winter 1965, 109, Abb. 104, 49, Abb. 40, 71, Abb. 64). There is no evidence for such doorways in Britain, partly because oven-chambers here are often sunk below ground. It is possible, however, that in some Derbyshire kilns (Fig. XXI) the front, above flue level, was removable and replaceable (cf. Hampe and Winter 1962, Taf. 40.3–6).

A large, clay probable model from Holt apparently represents a circular open-topped kiln with a thickened rim indented with thumb impressions (Fig. IV; Grimes 1930, 184, fig. 60, no. 9). These impressions may be purely decorative but could represent the point at which small flue-vents occurred at the junction of the kiln-lip and the topping of the load, since the Holt kilns were producing oxidized pottery.

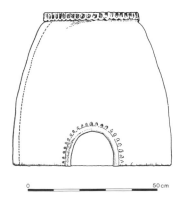

Fig. IV.

HOLT, Denbigh.: the so-called 'oven', probably model of a circular open-topped kiln; *after* Grimes (1930, Fig. 60).

During the past few years evidence has increased for Romano-British kilns of this type, mostly sunken, a circumstance aiding their preservation. Some of them show a flattening or slight widening at the lip, presumably to stabilize the turves or other material used for the temporary capping. At Cantley, the lip of Kiln 20 was flanged, perhaps to help key-in the covering material at the point at which it would be sealed with clay (Gilmour 1955, pls. I–IV). Sometimes the flattened top of the lip slopes downwards towards the interior of the kiln (cf. Hampe and Winter 1962, 24, Abb. 20–21). This would have been particularly convenient in the more squat kilns, where the stack rose in a mound above the lip of the kiln-wall and the capping had to be corbelled over rather than laid horizontally across it (Bryant 1977b, 108, fig. 38). Some open-topped kilns in Britain, as at Mucking (Jones and Rodwell 1973, 15–17, pl. I) and at Wilderspool, Cheshire (Pl. 34), have walls which are not vertical but cambered slightly inwards, and thus resemble very truncated cones. Such superstructures, nevertheless, do not 'arch over' sufficiently to be classed as true domes. There is indeed a wide variety. Included in this open-topped class are the chimneys of the Derbyshire-ware kilns, set almost completely below ground and sometimes rising at least 2.1 m above the bottom of the furnace-chamber and 1.8 m above the level of the raised floor (Fig. XXI). Since loads were unlikely to have been stacked more than ½–1 m above the level of the lip of such kilns, it is possible to calculate their approximate size. There are stark contrasts, for example, between the capacity of the tall Derbyshire-ware kilns, and some of those at Mucking, Essex (Jones and Rodwell 1973, pl. I) and Mancetter (Hartley 1973a, fig. 2, H).

Free-standing open-topped kilns wholly or partly of temporary materials

A number of kilns, which had no permanent lining of clay or stone, including the La Tène-derived types (p. 55 ff.), must have had open-topped superstructures with vertical walls built of turves (Fig. II.iii). Some clay-lined kilns, in which both the oven-floor and the lip of the kiln-wall were at, or near, ground level, must have had similar superstructures (Fig. II.v). Examples are known at Hartshill (Pl. 32; Hartley 1973a, fig. 1, Kiln B), at Oakleigh Farm, Higham (Pl. 17; Catherall 1983, *forthcoming*), and at Slayhills Salting Kiln 1 and Barksore Farm, Lower Halstow, in the Upchurch Marshes of North Kent (inf. I. Jackson). In some, the lip was splayed outwards over the ground surface, presumably to provide a broad base on which to stack the turves, as in Kiln 5 at Horningsea (Walker 1912, fig. 10).

Some of the Alice Holt (Fig. XVIII) and Crambeck (Corder 1928, figs. 3, 24) kilns had one or more layers of flat stones at ground level, presumably for the same reason. Where the ground surface was inclined to be wet, such a course would also have ensured a dry foundation for a turf superstructure. In some kilns the lip of the wall rose above ground level, but its height above the oven-floor would have been insufficient to enclose a pottery stack of viable size. In such cases the clay walling would presumably have been continued upwards with turves into an open-topped superstructure. As turves in general require a broad foundation, such a supplementary stack would probably have been based on both the clay kiln-wall itself and the ground immediately behind (Fig. II.v). Careful observation of the outer circumference of a kiln-wall is called for during excavation in order to determine whether there is a cleaner or paler area representing the protected surface where turves rested, or where clay was applied behind the sods to seal them at ground level (Bryant 1970, 8). At Alice Holt (AH 52, phase 2) the very broad turf superstructure of the Antonine kiln appeared to have been cased or revetted into bays with short protruding stretches of clay walling. On the outer circumference of a later kiln on the same site was a row of stakeholes, presumably the remains of a fence intended to prevent the turf superstructure from spreading (inf. M. Lyne).

Turf superstructures were probably topped in the same way as clay ones (Fig. II.iii–v). One of their great advantages was that the height could be adjusted to suit the size of the kiln-load. A turf stack, moreover, could be raised during firing, if necessary, to help increase the temperature in the kiln. Experiments at Doncaster, Swanpool, and Barton-on-Humber (Fanthorpe 1977; Wood unpubl.; Bryant 1973, 153; 1977a, 14) have shown that the great disadvantage of turf superstructures was their permeability. They apparently suffered greater heat loss than those of clay or stone; they were also difficult to seal adequately for a reducing firing and, therefore, more prone to gas leaks. This may explain why La Tène-derived kilns operating before or shortly after the Conquest, as at Hardingstone, often seem to have produced both oxidized and reduced wares, probably the result of unreliable atmospheric control in their firing (Woods 1969). Not surprisingly, little evidence of any turf superstructure has survived *in situ*. At Alice Holt (AH 52), however, a small segment of turf walling, overlaid by a later kiln, apparently had a thin internal plastering of clay, presumably to prevent gas leaks. The extent of this practice is unknown. In experiments, the gaps between sods have often been infilled with clay during construction and the whole turf stack subsequently coated externally with clay. Sand and dust may also have been used to plug gaps (cf. Rhodes 1969, 10, fig. 9).

An important result of experimental kiln-firings has been to determine, in some measure, what archaeological traces might survive from turf superstructures and kiln-stack coverings, both often made of identical materials (Bryant 1971, 18). The clay in the turves facing the interior of the kiln baked into distinctive fragments, oxidized orange or reduced grey depending on the atmosphere, with clear marks where the roots had been burnt out. Some of the shapeless pieces of 'straw and grass tempered-clay' frequently described in kiln reports as 'dome plates' may, therefore, be the remains of burnt sods, or fired remains of clay plastered over such sods on the interior of the kiln-wall or within the temporary turf covering of a pottery stack. In contrast, clay plastered on to the exterior of a turf superstructure was found to remain moist and plastic, and to be suitable for reuse after a firing. It would not, therefore, necessarily leave any identifiable trace. On the other hand, experiments showed that a clay sealing put on the covering of the load at a late stage in the firing became oxidized. It was not, however, fired enough to be reduced with the load during the cooling period (Bryant 1971, 18). No doubt further experiments will reveal more details of this nature.

In 1957 Corder advocated the collection and study of fired and unfired clay debris found in the excavation of kilns. Even now, however, very little of such material survives primary sorting at excavations, or subsequent 'weeding out' by museum curators economizing on space. Though unfired turves rarely survive in an identifiable form, their remains might well be expected among the material back-filled into a stokehole. Careful sampling here for plant seeds may prove informative. The identification of buttercup seeds within a 'chunk of black crumbly soil' from the stokehole of Slayhills Salting Kiln 3 suggests that this may have been part of a turf sod from the kiln-superstructure (inf. I. Jackson).

Because of the absence of evidence, it is uncertain whether, in a Romano-British kiln, a side or back-vent (Fig. II.v) was ever left in the superstructure during firing and closed up during cooling. Excavators from the late 1920s onwards were influenced by Heywood Sumner's reconstructions (1927, fig. XVI) and tended automatically to assume the existence of such a feature at the back of the kiln immediately *below* oven-floor level. Once his conclusions were shown to be erroneous (Swan 1971), the idea of any sort of back-vent went out of favour. In the Claxby and Swanpool kiln experiments (Bryant 1977a; Wood, unpubl.), a vent in the rear of the kiln, *above* oven-floor level, was found to aid the flow of warm air and eliminate a potential cold spot at the back of the oven. In kilns with tall superstructures any vent must have been positioned relatively high in the wall; otherwise parts of the upper layers of the pottery stack would have been underfired. The effect of a back-vent in kilns with low domes is discussed elsewhere (p. 120).

Loading ('setting')

Experiments have shown that the reasonably careful arrangement of a load is essential to its even firing. Vessels were stacked upside down with a free passage of air around them and, where possible, with open mouths, namely each with its rim in a central position on the base of that below to avoid sealing. They formed a series of domes within the oven, thus helping to retain the heat within the load (Fig. II). With larger vessels at the bottom, uniform ranges of shapes and sizes aided this process, and could have resulted in some measure of standardization of loads. Sand may sometimes have been used to prevent vessels sticking together. Fused stacks of wasters from Colchester (Hull 1963, pl. XVIII), the New Forest (unpubl.) and elsewhere (Pl. 6) suggest that colour-coated wares were often stacked inside one another. Often a sharp change of colour between the lower and upper half of a pot indicates where another superimposed vessel protected it from the atmospheric changes within the oven (Swan 1980, cover). Evidence from Classical Greek vase-painting, and the stacking arrangements used by many rural potters in the Mediterranean area still working on primitive lines, may imply that vessels near the top of a load did not need to be inverted but could be fired on their sides (Richter 1923, 78, fig. 80; Hampe and Winter 1965, 231, Abb. 148–9, 35, Abb. 25, Taf. 25.1, Taf. 26.2–3). Detailed arrangements within kilns were, no doubt, peculiar to individual potters. Most up-draught kilns fire relatively unevenly. Once a potter had familiarized himself with the idiosyncrasies of his kilns, he probably adjusted the arrangement of his wares accordingly, giving products which were more delicate, more expensive or which needed high temperatures, a special 'safe' position. This is evident in Cipriano Piccolpasso's treatise of *c.* 1556–9 on the manufacture of Italian earthenware. It gives very detailed instructions on the preferential setting of different vessels within rectangular kilns not unlike some Romano-British ones (p. 84; Rackham and Van de Put 1934, 40, pl. 34, 67 ff.). In the Swanpool kiln-firing experiments, the flagons in particular posed loading difficulties. The participants suggested that these might have necessitated smaller loads (Wood, unpubl.). A full kiln is essential for an efficient firing. On some sites, therefore, small kilns alongside apparently contemporary larger ones, as at Lower Sloden, Hants. (unpubl.), could perhaps have been for such vessels.

The problems of differential stacking dependent on the varying friability of vessel forms and fabrics are not yet fully understood by archaeologists. How, for instance, were lead-glazed wares stacked and fired in factories where evidence for the use of stilts and saggars (protective enclosing vessels) is lacking, for example in the Derby Racecourse kilns?

As might be expected, in Britain only a few partial kiln-stacks, comprising the lowest tiers, have been found *in situ*, abandoned due to some disaster within the kiln. The best known, found at Water Newton, near Peterborough (Hartley 1960, pl. IB), shows clearly the inversion for firing of a mixed load of vessels. At Markshall, Caistor St Edmund, Norfolk (Layton 1829, 412–3, pl. XXXVI), a partial kiln-load found in 1822 was illustrated and described as having been arranged in a series of compartments, divided by 'peat' and tiles (Pl. 7). This precise layout is possibly more imaginative than real. Alternatively, the tiles and peat may represent the demolished capping and the turves of the kiln-superstructure, which had slipped between the lower layer of vessels in an abandoned kiln-load.

Not all vessels found in a kiln-chamber were necessarily

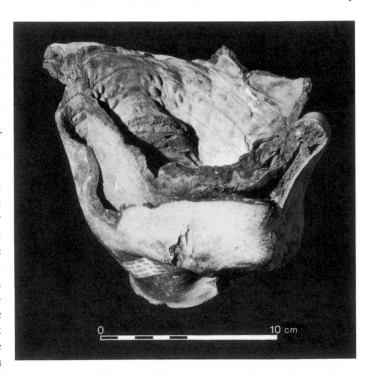

Plate 6. STANGROUND SOUTH, Hunts.: stack of Nene Valley vessels, distorted and fused together due to excessively high firing temperatures in kiln.

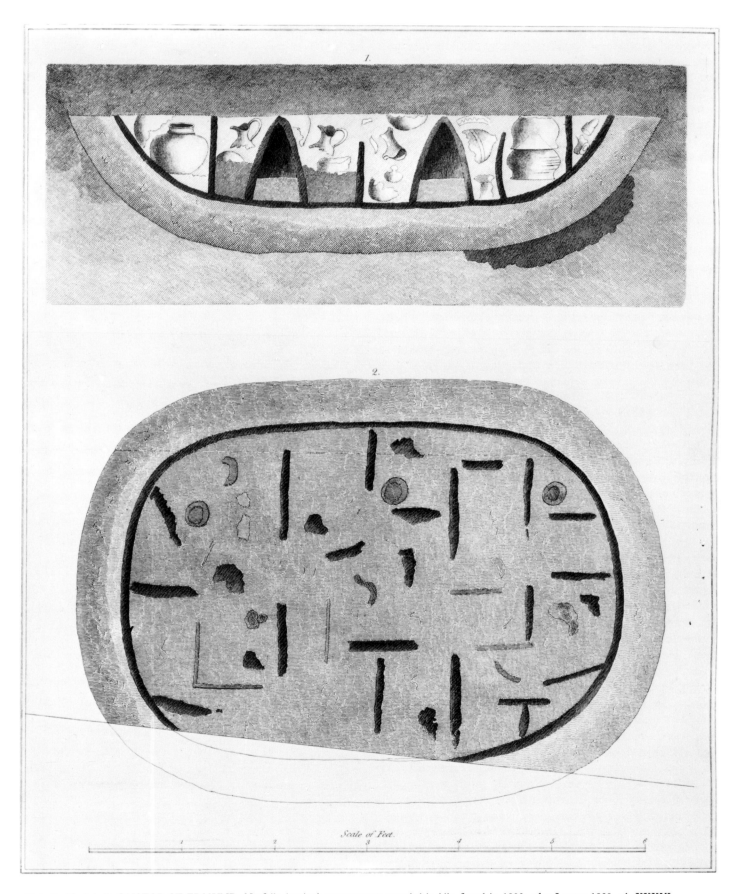

Plate 7. Markshall, CAISTOR ST EDMUND, Norfolk: 'setting' arrangements recorded in kiln found in 1822: *after* Layton 1829, pl. XXXVI.

products of that particular kiln. Unless clearly stacked in the position in which they were fired, they are more likely to have been dumped as waste from another kiln, or back-filled from the levelling of adjacent waster heaps. Published reports, however, frequently contain such a false assumption and reasonably reliable information may be possible only when large areas adjacent to kilns have been stripped.

There is ample evidence from kiln sites for various stacking aids of clay, used to separate vessels horizontally in the kiln, to span awkward gaps, or to level layers. Such spacers, sometimes called 'stackers' or 'setters', included rings or squat cylinders of various sizes such as occurred at Crambeck (Corder 1928, fig. 18), Throlam (unpubl., in the Yorkshire Mus., York) and Little Munden, St Stephen's, Herts. (Saunders and Havercroft 1977, fig. 15.264). These are not unlike modern examples in Mediterranean peasant potteries (Hampe and Winter 1965, 118, Taf. 113). Bobbin-shaped objects, probably setters, occurring at Upchurch, Kent (Hume 1954, fig. 1, nos. 3, 6), Brockley Hill, Middlesex (Suggett 1955, pls. 1, 2, no. 8), and Elstree, Herts., are generally similar to recent examples from Sicily (Hampe and Winter 1965, 100, Abb. 96, Taf. 38.4–6). Sausage-shaped distance pads were interleaved between the mortaria at Holt (Pl. 8; Grimes 1930, fig. 79) as were more irregularly-shaped wodges of clay at Radlett (VCH, *Hertfordshire* iv (1914), pl. XVI). Bun-shaped pads and ring-supports were used at Horningsea (Walker 1912, figs. 40–42). At Water Newton, flat stones were used directly on the uneven oven-floor of Kiln A to level the lowest vessels in the stack (inf. B. R. Hartley). Reused bases of pots or tile fragments, broken fire-bars and other makeshift fired clay objects would have been equally effective. Some of the smaller, so-called 'Belgic bricks' from various sites, such as Orsett Cock, Essex (Rodwell 1974, fig. 9, nos. 2–4), possibly fulfilled such a function. Similar small square clay briquettes in the Overwey, Surrey, kilns (Clark 1949, 40) were interpreted as aids for stacking, a possible explanation also for the 'finger-like' clay objects from the Highgate Wood kilns (unpubl. inf. A. Brown).

Since such objects were used within the kiln-oven, their colour almost certainly reflects the firing atmosphere, a useful observation when the nature or intended finish of a kiln's products is in doubt. Hampe and Winter (1965, 75, Abb. 68, Taf. 38.3–6) noted that clay setters are also used in the Mediterranean area to separate vessels during drying and to keep them off the ground. This could explain why several have been found inside buildings of the Norton potteries (unpubl.).

In many reports, kiln-setters are erroneously referred to as 'saggars'. True saggars were bowl or box-like vessels with domed lids which enclosed pots requiring special firing conditions. They are known only at Holt (Grimes 1930, frontispiece, fig. 78), where they were connected with the production of lead-glazed wares. In this process the vessel was placed in an inverted position on a three-pronged stilt to avoid its rim sticking to the kiln, as lead glazes tended to run (Pl. 9). The whole was then enclosed in the saggar to protect it from the flames and hot gases. Saggars took up a great deal of space, which possibly explains the very large size of the Holt pottery kilns.

Plate 8. HOLT, Denbigh.: sausage-shaped clay distance-pads to aid stacking of mortaria during firing.

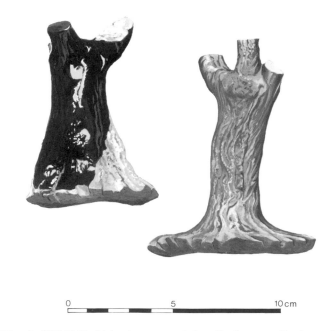

Plate 9. HOLT, Denbigh.: three-pronged clay stilts for suspending inverted lead-glazed vessels during firing to prevent their rims sticking to kiln. Glaze, dripped off a superimposed vessel, is visible on side of left-hand prop.

The most common items of kiln-furniture were flat or slightly concave, approximately circular plates, either plain or with a central hole. These were sometimes tempered or marked with vegetation on one or both sides, as at Horningsea (Walker 1912, 4–52). They have often been termed 'dome plates', since Corder and others thought they were used to reinforce so-called 'temporary domed' kiln-superstructures (1957, 14, 26). As they are not present in all Romano-British industries, it is important to distinguish them from the much rougher, thin, flat, shapeless pieces of fired clay found on kiln sites, also sometimes described as 'dome plates' (cf. p. 37). In 1962 Annable (1962, 148) suggested that because of the care in making the plates or discs, they were unlikely to have been used in domes. Such items, particularly those with a central hole, would have functioned well as setters. The unperforated ones might also have been used for the initial layer of the temporary topping of the pottery stack, as in one of the Barton-on-Humber kiln experiments (Bryant 1971, 3, 8, 17). Large waste sherds, pot bases, and tile fragments would have fulfilled this role equally well (Fig. II.ii–v). They are certainly used in this way in primitive potteries in the Mediterranean area (Hampe and Winter 1965, Taf. 2.1) and may have been so at Brockley Hill. The possibility requires a search for refired, reused ceramic items during the excavation of kilns.

Some kiln-superstructures had a ledge, either continuous or in several short stretches, moulded into the interior of the kiln-wall well above oven-floor level, as in Kilns 2 and 6 at Mucking (Jones and Rodwell 1973, fig. 3, pl. 1A), in kilns at Orsett Cock and Buckenham's Field, Billericay, Essex (inf. H. Toller and D. Buckley), and in Cantley Kilns 31 and 32 (inf. P. Buckland). It was thus unlikely to have had any connection with the raised oven-floor and possibly acted as a stabilizer for the kiln-load. When the pottery-stack had been built up to the ledge, vessels would have been positioned to straddle them both, thereby keying the load into the kiln-superstructure. It is difficult to see what other function such protrusions could have served.

In the Derbyshire kilns, small internal recesses moulded high in the clay superstructure of several kilns (Kay 1962, 28–9, pl. III) have been interpreted as foot-rests for the potter stacking the load. In most cases their shape and position do not seem to have been particularly apposite. Often there appear to have been too few niches for this purpose. In several of the potteries still working in ancient traditions in the Mediterranean area, some very tall kilns are apparently loaded by an unexpected method. A plank or pole is positioned across the kiln, resting on two opposing protrusions or sills moulded into the wall. From it the potter hangs by his legs to stack pots on the lowest tiers of the load (Hampe and Winter 1965, 110, Abb. 105). This could explain the niches in the Derbyshire kiln-walls.

Stokeholes

Stokeholes, in general, are rather featureless and it is difficult to see any coherent pattern of relationships in their shapes and sizes.

These, presumably, mostly reflect the whims of the potter or kiln-builder rather than any technological considerations. Experiment has shown, however, that in kilns with long flues, a pit in the stokehole just in front of the flue, as at Claxby, Lincs., and Branton, near Doncaster, did facilitate the raking-out of ash (Bryant 1977a). Some stokeholes seem to have a 'step' at the back or side, as in Chichester Kiln 2 (Down 1978, fig. 7.8). Although often interpreted as a seat for the stoker of the kiln, it may merely have been used for getting in and out of the stokehole, particularly in wet weather when the ground was slippery.

The positioning of a permanent baffle near the flue-mouth, thus producing a 'fire-box', may ultimately prove to have been an exotic practice. It has been found only in connection with specialist kilns at Colchester (Fig. X) and Pakenham (see p. 111). A very similar baffle in the flue of a simple kiln still used in the Mediterranean area was recorded by Hampe and Winter (1965, 234, Abb. 150). Experimental firings at Swanpool and Barton-on-Humber, Wood (unpubl.) and Bryant (1977b, 14) showed that a temporary movable screen, used as a wind-break baffle in the stokehole region in the early stages of firing, helped to direct the wind into the kiln. It could also prevent an exceptionally strong wind from gusting directly up the flue and making temperature control difficult. A temporary screen, unlike a permanent baffle-block, would not have impeded the raking-out of the flue. Some of the unexplained stakeholes found in the stokeholes at Lockington, Yorks. E.R. (Lloyd 1968, 31), and elsewhere, may indicate the former positions of temporary wind-breaks. Certainly there is no evidence that the orientation of kilns was determined by the direction of the prevailing wind.

The contents of stokeholes require detailed study (see p. 129). Bryant (1971, 18) has shown that the quantity of ash produced by a firing reflects the character of the atmosphere in the kiln. In an oxidizing firing the fuel becomes completely burnt out, leaving little ash. In a reducing firing, however, wood stoked into the flue and furnace-chamber to burn up excess oxygen at the pre-cooling stage, immediately before the flue-mouth is sealed, carbonizes and remains as a layer of abundant charcoal fragments and black ash.

Material sealing the junction of the flue and stokehole in the last firing of a kiln also requires careful observation and recording. It may comprise anything from waste pots, broken furniture and kiln debris to raw clay of various types. As already stated (p. 34), one function of this blocking was to exclude oxygen from the oven during the cooling stage and obtain a reducing atmosphere for the wares by sealing the flue completely. In some instances it was probably not air-tight but, like a baffle, was meant to prevent a sudden rush of cold air into the kiln at the cooling stage. The position of such material within the stokehole/flue gives some indication of the height to which ash and other debris had accumulated during the life of the kiln. At Lower Sloden (unpubl.), the stratigraphy sealed below the latest flue-blocking of Kiln I indicated alternating phases of use and non-use.

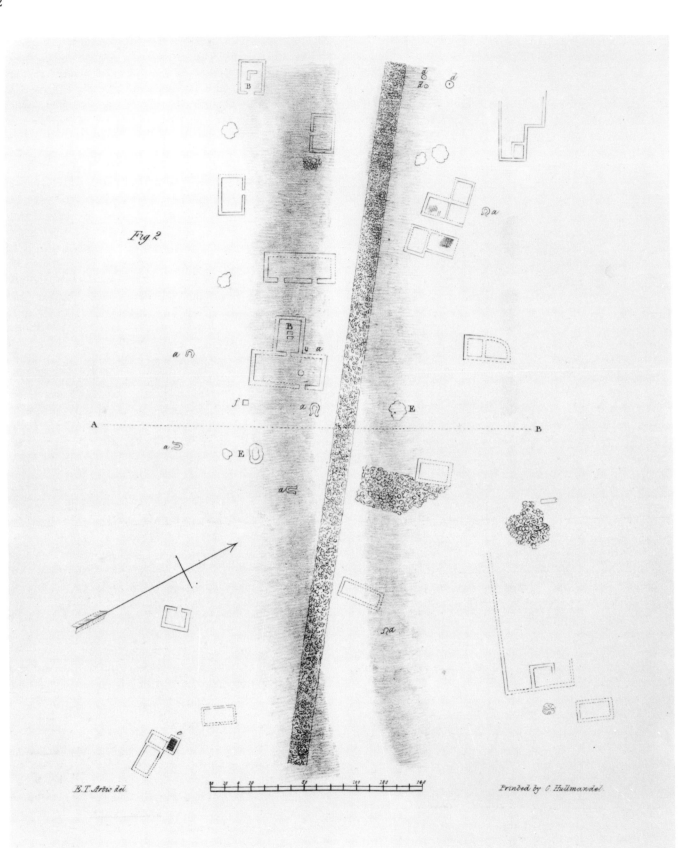

Fig 2

A B

E.T.Artis del.

Printed by C.Hullmandel.

A Plan of that part of the Pottery through which the old Roman Road passes showing the site to have been occupied by the Potters previous to the Formation of the old Roman road or forty footway Fig 1 section of the line A B a marked upon the plan Fig 2 a a a a a a a a Ovens B B Stoves C Baking hearth d.d.d stones for grinding E E clay in a prepared state f a square well.

CHAPTER 4

Kiln sites and their associated features

Apart from the building and operation of the kilns, the manufacture of pottery involved a number of other essential processes. Raw materials such as clay, tempering, water and wood had to be acquired, stored and prepared. Vessels had to be formed, decorated, dried and stored after firing. Many of these activities can be linked to features discovered on some of the more extensively-excavated sites. It is, however, a sad reflection of the current state of kiln studies that, of numerous sites investigated, very few have been extensively excavated. For most, only the kiln itself, or a very small adjacent area, has been studied. Even so, some of the earliest and most limited digging, aimed merely at the location of kiln structures or the collection of pottery, has provided tantalizing glimpses of the results possible from extensive stripping (Wise 1863, 220). In the present state of pottery studies, however, substantial benefit is unlikely to be derived from further small-scale excavation involving kiln structure alone. More large-scale area-excavation is essential (cf. Nida-Heddernheim: *G.R.II* (1924), pl. xxxviii) to redress the present imbalance, and to provide information on the character and layout of all the various components making up a factory.

Raw materials: treatment and storage

Although some of the larger Romano-British industries working on a long-term basis drew supplies of clay and temper from as far as 10 km away (Young 1977, 16), many potteries obtained raw materials from their immediate vicinity. The resulting large clay pits must have resembled small quarries when in use. After abandonment, many of them apparently reverted eventually to ponds and, as such, can still be readily located near a number of sites. Examples include the 'Fish-ponds' 140 m ENE of the Cantley Estate kilns, Dale Pond 800 m E of the West Stow kilns, Bitham Pond in Savernake Forest, Pond Hole at Lea, Lincs., and probably the Lincoln Swanpool itself, converted into fish-ponds in the Medieval period. Systematic programmes of fieldwork, and the scrutiny of place-names, old maps and other documents, would no doubt locate many more examples.

In a number of places, clay and sand were apparently obtained from small delves within the potteries themselves. It is, however, not always possible to determine whether pits of more regular shape were primarily for storage, or for the extraction of raw materials. Pits of varying size and shape cut in the natural clay were excavated among the kilns at Hadham, Herts. (inf. K. F. Hartley), Rettendon, Essex (Tildesley 1971, 37), and Brampton and Scalesceugh, Cumberland (Bellhouse 1971, 39 ff.). At West Stow and Rushden, Northants., concentrations of pits for clay and sand were on the peripheries of the complexes (inf. S. West and P. Woods).

Once dug, the clay had to be weathered before use. It was spread on the ground and turned from time to time to allow the sun, wind, frost and rain to break down the particles, thus increasing its plasticity. Dumps of clay at various stages of weathering or preparation have sometimes been found on Romano-British kiln sites. Wise, digging in the 1860s in the New

Plate 10. *opposite*: Normangate Field, CASTOR, Hunts.: plan of workshops, kilns and allied features fronting on Ermine Street, as excavated by Artis. The superimposed earthwork (*centre*) is a build-up of plough-soil, resulting from use of Roman road as a headland in the Medieval open fields: *after* Artis (1828, pl. XXXIX).

Forest at Pitts Wood, recorded 'two distinct heaps of white and fawn-coloured clay and red earth placed ready for mixing, and a third of the two worked together, fit for the immediate use of the potter' (1863, 220). In the Nene Valley, a large dump of white clay and ironstone, almost 2 m across, apparently intended for preparing colour-coats, was excavated adjacent to a kiln at Sibson (Hartley 1960, 15, 18). A special stone platform served as a probable base for a clay dump at The Churchill Hospital, Headington, Oxon. (Young 1977, 16).

Clay kept for long periods in a cool, damp place, that is 'soured', improves in plasticity. This stage must also have required extensive storage facilities on Romano-British potteries. Some pits recorded on kiln sites must almost certainly have been used for this purpose, for example the clay-lined pit near Kiln 4 at Norton (Hayes and Whitley 1950, 13), that at Common Barn, Rickinghall Inferior, Suffolk, and that containing prepared clay on the London GPO site (Norman and Reader 1912, 282–6). Others possibly used for storage were subsequently infilled with waste material, such as prepared potting-clay and kiln debris as at Shaw, Berks. (inf. J. Greenaway) and Verulamium, Herts. (Frere 1961, 82; 1983, *forthcoming*).

Temper

The tempering most commonly used for pottery was sand, presumably also extracted from pits. A large quarry was recorded 275 m S of the Hill-top Café kiln site at Brockley Hill (Suggett 1954, fig. 1), and a smaller probable sand-pit, ultimately back-filled with rubbish, occurred near the kilns at Radlett (Castle 1976b). Sand was presumably stored in bulk near workshops until required. Scoops containing non-local sand were noted on the Higham Marshes, Kent (inf. R. Hutchings) and London GPO kiln sites, and a pile of special white sand occurred on that at Perry Barr, Birmingham (Hughes 1959). Some varieties of temper must have been extracted from the clay or other local deposits by washing them, and then crushing or grinding the larger particles which sank to the bottom of the flotation tank. Flints had to be calcined by burning before they could be crushed. Evidence of this comes from Rettendon, where flint-tempered pottery was made (Tildesley 1971, 38), and in the New Forest (Swan 1973, 121), where the mortaria had trituration grits of flint. Large quantities of shells, especially oyster, found in association with kiln debris in Sharfleet Creek, Upchurch (OS Records), probably relate to the production of shell-gritted wares. Potsherds and charcoal, freely available as waste on every kiln site, were also sometimes used for tempering.

Wood (for sources and supply *see* p. 7 ff.)

The results of kiln experiments at both Barton-on-Humber and Swanpool have indicated that fuel must be thoroughly dry and preferably stored for a while before use (Nicklin 1979, 447). That little evidence of this survives is hardly surprising. Any structure erected to cover wood would hardly be distinctive and may, indeed, have been very insubstantial. One exception is the presumed wood-store at Holt, a works-depot so far unique in Britain. Some stores may well have been positioned where they could utilize residual heat from the kiln.

Water

Many kiln sites were supplied with water from wells near the workshops or kilns, as at Sheepen, Colchester (Dunnett 1975, 128, n. 17), and on the Oxfordshire sites (Young 1977, 16–17). At Mancetter, a network of channels from one or more wells took water to various parts of the site (*Archaeol. Excav. 1971*, 22–3).

Clay

In addition to weathering, the raw clay required much preparation before it could be used for building kilns, making kiln-furniture, and throwing, slip-coating, and decorating vessels. To cleanse it of unwanted impurities such as grit or stones, that is to levigate it, the clay was mixed with water to form a slurry and left to stand. Coarser particles would sink to the bottom. Any lighter organic debris immediately floating to the surface could be skimmed off, enabling the clean clay slurry to be separated and dried ready for use. For coarse wares, less separation was required. The addition of water would indeed have made the clay easier to blend with any temper, to make it pliable and ready for wedging and throwing. The most basic levigation system comprised a series of pits with interlinking narrow channels. A gully could be dammed up with clay and other debris to allow larger inclusions to settle in an adjacent pit. It would then be breached, allowing the slurry of finer clay in suspension to be drawn off and channelled into the next pit. The process could be repeated if necessary. The slurry would eventually be dried out either by evaporation, only possible in hot dry weather, or by allowing all the clay particles to settle completely and then draining away excess water via the exit channel. Such interconnecting gullies are well attested at Verulam Hills Field, St Albans (Anthony 1968, 21–2), at Bromham, Beds. (Tilson 1973, 27), and Trent Vale, Staffs. (Fig. V; Mountford *et al.* 1968, 23). Fragments of partially excavated probable systems, not always recognized as such, are distinguishable on numerous other sites.

An excellent impression of how these Romano-British arrangements possibly worked is gained from levigating systems still in use in the 1950s and 60s in various parts of the Mediterranean area (Hampe and Winter 1962; 1965). One Cretan pottery used wodges of straw to block the gullies linking a chain of puddling pits (ibid. 1962, Abb. 15). In Sicily and Greece, small dams of clay and soil separated the various troughs (ibid. 1965, Taf. 20, Taf. 57). Cipriano Piccolpasso illustrated a similar arrangement of troughs used in the manufacture of earthenware (Rackham and Van de Put 1934, pl. 4). On the island of Rhodes, Hampe and Winter (1965, Taf. 56.3) photographed a sequence of sub-rectangular levigating pits terminating in a large stone-revetted settling tank at the bottom of a gentle slope. Large balls of clay nearby, of a type also described by Piccolpasso (Rackham and Van de Put 1934, 17 ff.), are reminiscent of those found near the

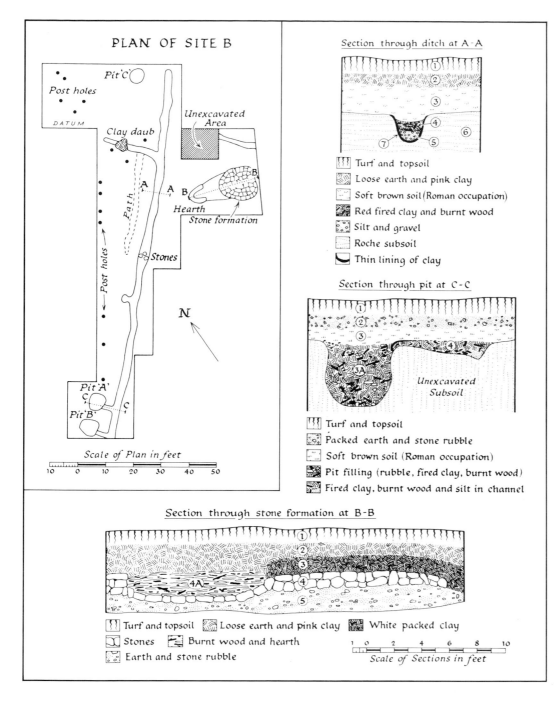

PLAN OF SITE B

Pit 'C'

Post holes

DATUM

Clay daub

Path

Post holes →

A

A B

B

Hearth

Stone formation

N

Pit 'A'

C

Pit 'B'

C

Stones

Unexcavated Area

Scale of Plan in feet

10 0 10 20 30 40 50

Section through ditch at A-A

⊞ Turf and topsoil
▨ Loose earth and pink clay
▦ Soft brown soil (Roman occupation)
▨ Red fired clay and burnt wood
▨ Silt and gravel
▦ Roche subsoil
◗ Thin lining of clay

Section through pit at C-C

Unexcavated Subsoil

⊞ Turf and topsoil
▨ Packed earth and stone rubble
▦ Soft brown soil (Roman occupation)
▨ Pit filling (rubble, fired clay, burnt wood)
▨ Fired clay, burnt wood and silt in channel

Section through stone formation at B-B

⊞ Turf and topsoil   ▨ Loose earth and pink clay   ▨ White packed clay
▨ Stones   ▨ Burnt wood and hearth
▨ Earth and stone rubble

Scale of Sections in feet
1 0 2 4 6 8 10

Fig. V.

TRENT VALE, Staffs.; system of pits and gullies for clay levigation, and stone platform probably for mixing clay: *after* Mountford *et al.* (1968, fig. 3).

Romano-British settling system at Bromham. In Roman Britain, the more elaborate flotation tanks, sometimes rectangular and lined with clay or clay and tile, tended to occur within specialist factories, for example those on some of the Oxford kiln sites (Young 1977, 17, fig. 4, 18), and at Brockley Hill, near Kilns 3, 4 and 8 (Castle 1972a, Site A; Castle and Warbis 1973).

Puddling, that is mixing and blending clay with temper, water and sometimes other substances, was often done with the feet, sometimes on a flat surface. Small stone-paved platforms covered with clay, such as those excavated on two Oxford kiln sites (Young 1977, 16), on two sites in the New Forest (Hawkes 1938, 121), at Colchester (Fig. XXIII; Hull 1963, 141, fig. 9), and at

Trent Vale (Fig. V; Mountford *et al.* 1968, 23, fig. 3), closely resemble clay-mixing areas in relatively recent use inside peasant workshops in Greece and Southern Italy (Hampe and Winter 1965, 5, Abb. 2 and 4; 135–6, Abb. 124–5, Taf. 34.4 and 5). On one South Italian site, this process was carried out in a funnel-shaped pit (ibid. 1965, 27, Abb. 16), a practice which excavators of Romano-British sites should bear in mind.

Wedging, the last stage of fabric preparation, involved the cutting, beating and reversing of the clay to expel air and ensure an even and pliable texture. This was also probably carried out on platforms, using the feet, as well as on benches, in small amounts, by hand and with a knife, immediately before potting.

Workshops

In Britain, the forming of vessels, their storage before and after firing, and probably kneading, would necessarily have taken place under cover. A number of potters' workshops have now been recorded, including several of rather flimsy character, but few have been published. There is, nevertheless, fragmentary evidence of many more, partially-excavated, probable examples in the form of isolated post-holes, cobbled, paved, beaten earth or clay surfaces, and stone foundations. They were rarely far from the actual kilns which, as the Swanpool experiment has shown (Wood, unpubl.), presented no particular fire-hazard, and some seem likely to have been sited within workshops or other buildings. The structure apparently covering Kilns 19, 20 and 22 at Warren Fields, Sheepen, Colchester, was a case in point (Fig. XXIII; Hull 1963, 15 ff., fig. 10). In recent excavations at Alice Holt (AH52, phase 2), the kiln apparently occupied one side of a building and was stoked from the outside (inf. M. Lyne).

Of varying size, most potters' huts as excavated comprised a single room. At least one at Arlington, Sussex (Holden and Holmes 1980), however, had a fragmentary wooden partition screen, possibly separating a bay or room with a hearth for drying and storage from the workshop proper. This arrangement is tentatively suggested for another building in complex A at The Churchill Hospital (Young 1977, 24–6). Although only one emplacement for a potter's wheel has been found *in situ* in such a building, a flagon-neck set in the ground at Alice Holt, Binsted (AH52), Hants., Basil Brown suggested the possibility of another at Garden House, Rickinghall Superior, Suffolk (Fig. VI). This survived as a small piece of decayed iron in the centre of a roughly circular dished area of white prepared clay in the corner of a probable potter's hut. It appeared to Brown that the clay had accumulated on the workshop floor from surplus 'thrown off' by the rotating potter's wheel.

In buildings, fully excavated on several different sites, other elements have been recorded. Rectangular or square, stone-lined chests or troughs, apparently used as containers for clay ready for immediate use, occurred in buildings at Mancetter, at Stibbington in the Lower Nene Valley (Wild 1973, 136–7; Wacher 1978, 200, fig. 40), at Whitehill Farm, near Swindon, Wilts. (Anderson 1979, fig. 6), and Vicarage Garden, Norton (Pl. 11; inf. R. Hayes). In the latter workshop, a large storage jar set in the floor was probably for the potter's immediate use as a container for water for wetting the hands (cf. Rackham and Van de Put 1934, 16 n. 37, pl. 72) or perhaps for slip. Similar jars set into the ground with clay occurred at Rushden (inf. P. J. Woods), Oakleigh Farm, Higham, Kent (Catherall 1983, *forthcoming*), Cherrry Hinton, Cambridge (Hughes 1903) and at Clonmore, Linwood, in the New Forest (Hawkes 1938). How many of these had lain within buildings, however, is not clear. A good example of the internal layout of a potter's workshop of the mid to late 3rd century has been uncovered at the Titelberg, Luxemburg. It comprised a kiln, troughs, the emplacement for the potter's wheel, a possible drier and other features (Metzler and Weiller 1977, Abb. 15).

It is worth comparing the workshops illustrated by Piccolpasso (Rackham and Van de Put 1934, pls. 15, 23, 27) or the general layouts of buildings in several primitive potting establishments still operating in the Mediterranean area in the 1950s and 60s (Hampe and Winter 1965, 135–6, Abb. 124–5). In the latter, the workshop itself normally had a wheel with an adjoining raised slab for the final kneading of small amounts of clay for immediate use. There was also a pile of clay on the ground beside a small paved wedging or mixing surface, and planks or other emplacements on which to stand the green ware fresh from the wheel. Adjoining it were the living quarters, a storeroom, a yard with a dump or trough of drying clay, and a covered wood-store. Close by, either under cover or outside, was the kiln itself. The whole

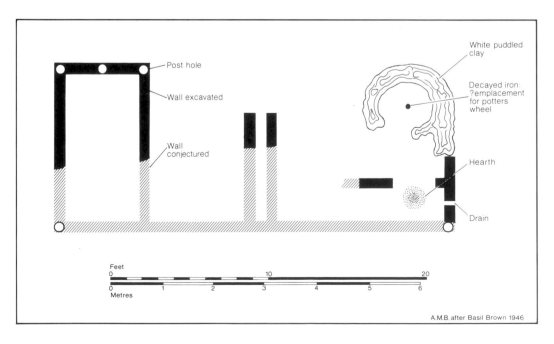

Fig. VI.

Garden House kiln site, RICKINGHALL SUPERIOR, Suffolk; probably potters' workshop excavated by Basil Brown: based on unpubl. records by B. Brown.

Plate 11.

Vicarage Garden, NORTON, Yorks. East Riding: (*top left*) Stone-paved floor of possible workshop in potting quarter of industrial *vicus*; dark area in *centre foreground* represents surviving base of one of two jars set into floor; *centre background*, a stone box also set into ground. (*bottom left*) Detail of stone-lined box. (*top right*) Stone trough found reused in inverted position in paving of floor. (*bottom right*) Large storage or water-jar found set into floor.

establishment took up an area of no more than 400 sq m. The ephemeral character of some potters' buildings in the Mediterranean area leaves little doubt that in Britain many workshops, with any adjoining quarters, have disappeared without trace. Others may yet be recorded on kiln sites where large areas are carefully excavated.

Drying

The general arrangement still found in the Mediterranean area might be expected in a Romano-British workshop, but with the addition of some source of heat. Before firing could take place, vessels had to be gently dried to drive off the free water. Because of vagaries of the British climate, this must normally have taken place indoors using artificial heat. An efficient drying-plant would have been vital for any major producer, since a regular and systematic turnover of products independent of the weather was no doubt a prime factor underlying his prosperity. For this reason, presumably, the more sophisticated drying-systems tend to occur more often on the sites of the larger or more specialist industries. Even so, it cannot necessarily be assumed that lesser manufacturers worked only seasonally, in summer. Potteries making containers for agricultural produce needed to be stocked up by harvest-time. If hired workmen were involved, the period of maximum activity in a workshop might have been arranged to

coincide with slack seasons on the land (Cockle 1981, 92 ff.). Here again some sort of drying system would have been necessary. The most elaborate drying-plant known in Roman Britain was at Holt. It occupied one end of a rectangular building and resembled a normal hypocaust system (Grimes 1930). Its purpose may have been orientated more towards the special drying needs of tiles (Leach 1976, 99). At Mancetter, a 2nd-century large, roofed drying-shed had an integrally-constructed elaborate system of flues retained by stone kerbs. Its second phase was designed so that one half could be fired separately or both halves together (*JRS* lvi (1966), 206, pl. vi.i).

The type of pottery-drier most frequently recorded comprised a T-shaped channel. Examples occur in close association with kilns at The Churchill Hospital (Young 1977, 20–22), at Hamstead Marshall, Berks. (Pl. 12), Norton (Hayes and Whitley 1950, 15–18), and Crambe, Yorks. N.R. (King and Moore 1975). Until recently it was considered to have been connected primarily with the drying of grain (Goodchild 1943) or with malting (Reynolds and Langley 1979). There seems little doubt, from grain found in many driers on kiln sites, that they often served a dual purpose. There is much to be said for Young's suggestion (1977, 20) that T-shaped driers in Britain were initially pottery-driers, and only much later did their exclusive use for drying grain or malting become widespread.

A variety of other probable forms of drier are known. Most of

Plate 12. HAMSTEAD MARSHALL, Berks.: tile-lined T-shaped drier found within kiln site.

those listed by Young (1977, 20–23) from the Oxfordshire kilns involved a long trough or channel with an expanded rectangular, ovate or lobe-shaped end, a variant of the T-shaped drier. The general type is not unlike one still used in Britain in the vernacular pottery at Wrecclesham, near Farnham, Surrey. Sited within a building, this comprises a long, tiled, slow-burning, horizontal channel with a flue at one end. Its warm air percolates to a loft above, where the unfired vessels are stacked on a slatted wooden floor. Their positions in relation to the source of warmth are rotated according to their progress in drying. In the Nene Valley, some dumb-bell-shaped ovens found within buildings near kilns in Normangate Field, Castor, Northants. (unpubl.) were possibly used for drying vessels, but this is not yet proven. Not all pottery-driers were sited within buildings, but a substantial proportion apparently were. Extra care is clearly needed in excavating the immediate surroundings of such features to ascertain the facts. The stone paving surrounding the Norton driers is reminiscent of the hut floors elsewhere within that complex, possibly suggesting their operation under cover (Hayes and Whitley 1950, 15–17, fig. 5).

Several other kiln sites have produced 'hearths' or ovens of uncertain use, which may have been for drying, for example Cleavel Point, Ower, Dorset (unpubl. inf. P. Woodward). At Alice Holt, Binsted (AH52), the floor of a 2nd-century probable drying-shed had several rectangular or circular burnt patches where successive fires had been lit. There were also indications of the former positions of struts against the walls, perhaps to support shelves (inf. M. Lyne). One of two buildings excavated within the West Stow pottery (inf. S. West), and a building 10 m from the kiln at Garden House, Rickinghall Superior, both contained a 'hearth' (Fig. VI). Leach (1976, 94) illustrates a primitive potter's hut in Korea where, in winter, drying still proceeds on a gently-heated platform in one corner.

In Italy, Hampe and Winter (1965, 4, Abb. 1) recorded a primitive rural pottery, still working in the 1950s and 60s, with its kiln inside a workshop. To utilize its residual heat, the drying

pottery was stacked on racks covering the walls and even forming several shallow tiers across the roof-space of the building. Examples may, indeed, have existed in Roman Britain, and more attention could be paid to the three-dimensional potentialities of potters' workshops already known.

There has occasionally been confusion between simple kilns and drying-ovens. The structures claimed as drying-ovens in Wapsey's Wood, Bucks. (Oakley et al. 1937, 266 ff.), were grey inside, that is reduced, which is more consistent with their use as kilns proper. Driers tend to show signs of oxidation and appear orangey in colour. Some excavators have been inclined to class as ovens kiln-like structures whose clay lining was not substantially hard-fired. Kiln experiments at Alice Holt (inf. M. Lyne) have shown that a single firing may result in only a very thin burnt crust on the interior of the chamber. When exposed to frost this rapidly crumbles, leaving only a lining of soft clay. Possible ovens of a distinctive type, and at present of unknown function, have been recorded at Brockley Hill, beside Kilns 2 and 4 (Suggett 1953; Castle 1972a, Site A), and at Colchester, adjoining Kilns 30 and 32, and inside a building adjoining Kiln 20 (Fig. XXIII; Hull 1963, 15, 168, fig. 10). Each had a small tiled platform and a clay lining integral with or close to the wall of a normal kiln. They were apparently designed to utilize the heat from this kiln or at least to be fired from the same stokehole. The apparent absence of such ovens from other sites in Britain may further emphasize the similarity of traditions at Brockley Hill and Colchester (p. 98). Such ovens, however, possibly had no connection with any manufacturing process, merely being used for baking food by potters living on the site. In 1958, Hampe and Winter recorded, in a vernacular pottery in Orei, Greece, a domestic oven of generally similar form attached to a kiln in like manner (1965, 136, Abb. 125, feature 11). A small open fire noted near each of several of the Longthorpe kilns (Dannell 1975, 18) may have fulfilled such a function.

Many sites lack evidence for the drying of pottery. This could, however, have been carried out very slowly in a standard kiln, as the initial heating stage in a continuous firing process. The hardening of portable kiln-furniture before use may also have taken place there. Peter Woods (pers. comm.) has, however, suggested that some of the long, sunken ovens found at Rushden may have been involved in the firing of kiln-bars.

Access to communications

Many kilns were sited relatively near major roads and rivers (see p. 8). Several potteries, however, apparently provided their own means of access to main lines of communications. For example, special service roads were built from the Mancetter kilns to Watling Street and from the Hadham complex to the main Harlow–Braughing road. A service road and trackways from the Brampton, Norfolk, workshops led to a timber wharf beside the River Bure (Knowles 1977, 211). At Stanground (South) Sluice, in the Lower Nene Valley, the discovery of a wharf and a 'road covered with pottery' is recorded, presumably hardcore derived from the nearby kilns.

Kilns in their immediate locality

Hitherto there has been relatively little discussion of the precise siting of kilns in relation to individual settlements and other industries. The well-known clause in the Urso, now Osuna, Spain, charter forbidding tile and pottery works within that *colonia* (Johnston *et al.* 1961; Bruns 1909, pt. I, 128, Lex Ursonis LXXVI) was possibly partly a precaution against fire. Judging from the rest of the charter, however, it probably also stemmed from the fact that part of a colony's revenue would have been derived from municipal, as opposed to private, potteries and tileries. Private rivals could thus not be tolerated within the city boundary. As Mark Hassall has pointed out (per. comm.), Roman colonial and municipal charters often have stereotyped phrasing. It is, therefore, possible that the *coloniae* in Britain, and perhaps the *municipia,* possessed similar restrictive laws. Certainly most Romano-British towns had their potteries on the outskirts.

In the past, however, several of these workshops were thought to lie within towns or *coloniae.* Of these, the Caistor St Edmund, Norfolk, kilns have recently been shown to have operated before the formal laying out of the town on that site (Swan 1981). At Canterbury, the land which the Dane John kiln occupied was not incorporated within the town defences until long after the kiln had ceased production (Webster *et al.* 1940). At Verulamium, the Hadrianic-Antonine pottery manufacture in Insula V (Wheeler and Wheeler 1936, Pit 6, 111–12, 186–90, figs. 30, 31, pl. CXX; Corder 1941; Frere 1961, 82; 1983, 45–6) occurred at a time when the city apparently lacked formal defences, since the early defensive earthwork had become obsolete and filled in. Only at Gloucester was a kiln, the 'Telephone Exchange' kiln (Hurst 1972, 41, fig. 9), apparently working within the *colonia* defences in the first decade of the 2nd century. There could be several explanations for this. Its plot was possibly already being used for other industrial purposes at a time of transition from fortress to *colonia.* During this period there may well have been some irregularities. If the pottery was owned by the *colonia,* possibly in the hands of a veteran, or had been handed over to the urban authorities from military control, it might initially have been exempt from a restrictive clause such as applied at Urso. The latter, however, may just have been ignored.

Due to the general dearth of substantial excavations in the suburbs of *vici* and towns, it is difficult to assess what arrangements there might have been for the allocation of land to potteries and other industries. In the Norton *vicus*, the kilns apparently lay within enclosed plots separated by ditches. A seemingly similar arrangement has been noted at the Great Holme Street site just outside Leicester (inf. J. Mellor).

Even in rural areas, it is difficult to cite a kiln which definitely lay within the residential area of a settlement. Several types of situation recur. Some potteries were sited within a special ditched enclosure delimiting the industrial or working area attached to a settlement, such as the probable kilns in Prae Wood, St Albans (Wheeler and Wheeler 1936, pls. XI, XVI) and a number in Northamptonshire, including those at Hardingstone (Woods 1969) and Wakerley (Jackson and Ambrose 1978). It may reasonably be presumed that the practice dated back to before the Conquest, and large-scale area-excavation of more rural settlements might indicate that this was normal. There are, indeed, numerous surface indications of kilns lying just outside the main nucleus of individual settlements.

A number of kilns are known to have been sited on the edges of fields, often partly overlapping the boundary ditches, as at Mucking (Jones and Rodwell 1973). There they have been interpreted as those of peripatetic potters. If such craftsmen worked very infrequently on the site, there was possibly no designated industrial space available. As all agricultural land also was presumably in use, they had to operate in very small areas within the most peripheral land available. Generally similar sitings occur at Ash, Kent, South Ockendon (Chaplin and Brooks 1966), Kelvedon, and probably Palmer's School, Thurrock, Essex. It seems likely that, wherever possible, kilns were built on land unsuitable for other purposes. Those at Dragonby, Lincs. and Rushden were thus set up on an abandoned part of the adjacent settlement. Excavations on a number of sites have revealed apparently cramped conditions, implying a definite shortage of available space. The superimposition of successive kiln structures one upon another and the siting of furnace-chambers in the stokeholes of disused kilns were commonplace, even on rural sites. This would, of course, sometimes have saved digging as well.

There is clear evidence from numerous kiln sites that pottery production was not the only industrial activity within the area. Iron-smithying seems to have been the most common adjunct. This was particularly so in the industrial compounds, enclosed or otherwise, immediately adjacent to smaller towns and rural settlements. It has also been noted in Gaul (Duhamel 1975, 14). Presumably such industries would have supplied the surrounding area as well as the adjacent settlement. It would, indeed, have been an economic advantage to exploit jointly sources of raw materials such as wood and to transport mixed loads of goods to markets and other points of sale. The Lincolnshire Wold-edge iron and pottery industries of Claxby, Owersby, Tealby and Walesby may have shared their service road to Owmby in just this manner (Whitwell 1982, 66). The evidence for bronze-working alongside pottery manufacture is much more sparse. Apart from military contexts, it tends to be associated with urban or more important settlements. From Mancetter there is rare evidence for glass manufacture within the pottery.

On the North Kent and North Somerset Marshes and in South Dorset, pottery production and salting apparently took place side by side, both requiring quantities of clay for kiln-furniture, oven-linings or brine-evaporation vessels. The potteries presumably supplied containers for the storage and transportation of the salt. The conjunction of these industries poses problems of identification, particularly in Kent and Somerset, since some items of their prefabricated clay furniture were probably substantially similar. In the past few decades, in fact, there has been a tendency to dismiss as salting briquettage the fired-clay furniture and other material found in the Upchurch Marshes in the late 19th and early 20th centuries, and doubt has been cast on claims of a substantial pottery industry there. A more balanced view of the simultaneous operation of both industries is now emerging, thanks to recent careful and persistent observation and salvage excavation (Jackson 1975a; Miles 1975).

In the *vici* attached to early forts, an exceptionally wide range of items was frequently manufactured alongside pottery. Enamelling, bronze-casting and beating, iron-smithying and pottery production, all for the military market, are well exemplified at sites such as Chapel Street, Chichester (Down 1978), Longthorpe, and Camulodunum, Colchester (Dunnett 1975, 43–4, 128–9). Whether the compounds in which these activities took place were military works-depots proper or merely used by civilian contractors is sometimes uncertain. It is however interesting, and perhaps significant, that on being abandoned many were systematically cleared up. Pits and ditches were infilled, kiln structures carefully dismantled, and the area completely levelled, possibly for return to civilian use. A similar procedure may have pertained on leased sites. The terms of an agreement from Egypt stated that at the end of the lease period the pottery was to be handed over 'free from ash and sherds' (Cockle 1981, 90).

Tileries and potteries are a logical combination, since they could have shared supplies of clay, fuel, etc. Apart from military examples mainly of Trajanic date (p. 87), they are not, however, frequently found together. In Romano-British civilian contexts, little more than a dozen examples are known at present.

One aspect of kiln excavations deserving comment is the repeated occurrence of later burials on kiln sites. This may well be pure coincidence, since burials, like potteries, tended to be sited on the edges of towns and settlements. It is likely, however, that once a pottery was abandoned, the site itself with its waster and ash heaps, clay dumps, pits, etc., would have become 'industrial waste-land', being of little use for agriculture or much else. Thus, where cultivatable land or pasture was at a premium, a derelict pottery would have been an obvious place for a cemetery.

Tools and other portable equipment

This subject has, as yet, received relatively little attention from excavators. Young (1977, 19–20) briefly discussed this aspect of the Oxfordshire industry, but was inevitably hampered by the lack of material evidence. It cannot be claimed that all Romano-British potteries taken together provide a vast number of relevant artefacts. The infilling of some abandoned kilns and their stoke-holes with rubbish from adjacent domestic sites, moreover, means that such non-ceramic material should always be treated with caution. Nevertheless, enough objects recur on kiln sites for a preliminary statement to be attempted.

For digging clay, sharp tools such as spades would undoubtedly have been required. Their absence so far from Romano-British kiln sites may, however, reflect a lack of excavation of clay quarries. An iron pick found near Brockley Hill, Kiln 2, may have been used for this purpose. Many tools, however,

were possibly wooden and thus have failed to survive. In Crete in the 1950s, potters working in the traditional manner dug clay with wooden picks and beat it with wooden flails to break it down (Hampe and Winter 1962, Taf. 1.2 and 18, Abb. 16, Taf. 1.1).

Querns are a very common find on kiln sites, often in quantity. Many broken ones were incorporated in the paving of some of the Norton potters' workshops. Their prime purpose was presumably to grind up temper to the requisite size, and to reduce to powder the ingredients for slip-coats. At Rushden, several large stones found near the kilns had worn cup-shaped areas, considered by the excavator to have resulted from pulverizing slip or other paint constituents in them.

A little evidence is known for some of the components of Romano-British potters' wheels. Possible socket-stones for the spindle were found at Wilderspool, Shotover, Oxon. (Young 1977, fig. 4, D1), and Highgate Wood (Brown and Sheldon 1974, 224). Among potters' refuse dumped in a well, near a workshop at Stibbington School, was a stone with four socket-holes on one side and three on the other (Pl. 13). The symmetrical and relatively deep wear-pattern on the sockets does not appear consistent with the stone having served as the pivot for a door. It

Plate 13.

Stibbington School, SIBSON CUM STIBBINGTON, Hunts.: pivot-stone possibly for potters' wheel, found dumped with rubbish (including probable potters' kick-wheel, Pl. 14) in well adjacent to a Nene Valley potters' workshop.

is more suggestive of its use as the bearing for a pole which had pivotted full-circle, causing such heavy wear that the socket had needed to be repositioned repeatedly. This stone must surely have formed the emplacement for a potters' wheel. At Alice Holt (AH52), a flagon-neck sunk in the workshop floor apparently formed the setting for the wheel-pivot. Immediately adjacent to it was a slot possibly for the potter's bench. The suggestion (Wild 1973, 137) that some quern-stones from kiln sites possibly fulfilled the role of kick-wheels is worth investigating. Some relatively large examples, from Crambe, Alice Holt (AH52), and elsewhere, would have been suitable for this purpose. They differ little from fly-wheels from other kiln sites in the Roman world (Rieth 1960, 50–54), for example at Speicher (Loeschcke 1922, 5, Abb. 8) and the Titelberg (Metzler and Weiller 1977, Abb. 14 and 15), and from primitive potteries working recently in the Mediterranean area (e.g. Hampe and Winter 1962, Taf. 42.1). The Rushden kiln site had a fragment of a probable stone kick-wheel. A complete but broken kick-wheel was also found in the well just outside the potters' workshop at Stibbington (Pl. 14). At some stage in its life, several holes had been carefully drilled in its

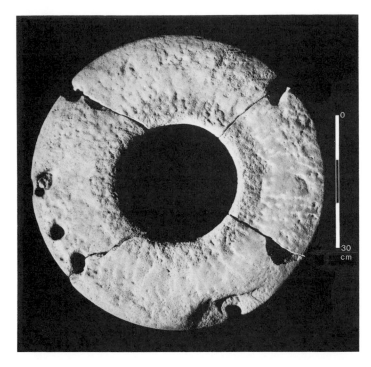

Plate 14. Stibbington School, SIBSON CUM STIBBINGTON, Hunts.: probable potters' kick-wheel found dumped in well adjacent to a Nene Valley potters' workshop: (*top*) upper side showing drilled holes filled with lead for balance, and concentric dished area of wear superimposed on pattern of concentric 'pecked' grooves; (*bottom*) underside showing relatively unworn grooving.

upper side and into these lead had been poured to balance it. Superimposed on a pattern of tooled grooves, it has a concentric area worn smooth by the action of the potter's foot. It has been suggested that it had originally been manufactured as a commercial millstone. The collar, however, seems exceptionally large and the concentric furrows, clearly visible on the underside, would scarcely have enabled it to function as such. It may have been dressed deliberately for use as a potters' wheel, since the pecked concentric grooves would have afforded a certain amount of grip for the potter's foot, without causing the juddering that might have occurred with the radial furrows typical of millstones and querns. A thorough examination of the surface dressing of all 'millstones' may result in the identification of other probable kick-wheels. Wooden kick-wheels, however, as described by Piccolpasso (Rackham and Van de Put 1934, 14 ff., pls. 11–15), may have been more normal in Roman Britain. This could well explain the apparent dearth of evidence.

While the basic shaping of the vessels on the wheel was probably done by hand, a sharp tool would have been required for shaving 'leatherhard' vessels and for other finishing processes. Iron knives must have been ideal for this purpose. A number of small ones associated with kiln material from Rushden, and several individual examples from other sites, tend to confirm this. Kiln sites at Rickinghall Superior, Somerton, Suffolk, Brunswick Road, Gloucester (Rawes 1972), Horningsea, Harrold, and Slayhills Strayway, Upchurch, have produced other iron 'tools', perhaps for a similar function, which might repay study. From the last site came a 'large flanged file'. From Water Newton, an unpublished tanged iron object is very similar to a modern 'modelling tool'. A Bronze-Age gouge may have been reused in pottery manufacture at Rushden. Such items are not unlike the iron shaving tools used by modern craft-potters (Leach 1976, 83). From Alice Holt (AH52), a large, broad knife would have been more suitable for wedging clay or chopping wood.

Styli would have made admirable implements for the detailed decoration of pottery. In form, they do not differ substantially from late Iron-Age bone modelling tools, from Gussage All Saints, Dorset, used for shaping and decorating clay moulds for bronze-casting (Wainwright 1979, 131, fig. 98), and similar implements for decorating moulds in lamp-factories in Germany (Fremersdorf 1922, 39, Abb. 44). Several styli occur on kiln sites but none is yet unequivocably associated with pottery production and all could be strays from settlement.

Flint flakes occur repeatedly on kiln sites. They would have made good trimming blades and possibly had other functions. A nodule with a worn tip from Oakleigh Farm, Higham, could have been used as a burnishing or incising tool. Flints should, of course, be treated with caution. Some may be residual from earlier periods, but they occur too frequently for that to be universally applicable.

From a few sites, such as Holt (Pl. 15a), have come bone gouges, gravers, or other pointed tools, most presumed to be used for producing incised decoration. Bone items on kiln sites deserve close examination. Young has suggested (1977, 19) that a length of rib-bone from The Churchill Hospital, cut at one end to a right-angled point, could have been used as a template for setting correctly the angle of flange to body on a mortarium (cf. Chenet 1941, pl. II, 8). From Cantley, and so far unique (Buckland *et al.* 1980), is a ceramic handle with holes for bristles or teeth, for making combed decoration, or for painting on slip. It is comparable to a modern one illustrated by Leach (1976, 118). Among the most common artefacts on kiln sites are pebbles or stones showing signs of wear. Most were probably used for burnishing or smoothing the surfaces of vessels. Some stone artefacts, however, such as those from Bagber, Dorset (Farrar 1973b, fig. 10) and Holt (Pl. 15b and c), may have been modelling tools

Plate 15. HOLT, Denbigh.: (a) bone tool perhaps for making incised decoration; (b) and (c) stone templates or modelling tools.

or templates, generally comparable in form to wooden ones illustrated by Piccolpasso (Rackham and Van de Put 1934, 20, pl. 20). It is interesting that on at least three British sites, namely Rushden, Hevingham, Norfolk, and Derby Racecourse, Neolithic stone axes were apparently reused for this purpose, a phenomenon also recorded in the samian industry in Central France (inf. B. R. Hartley).

The items already discussed might be expected on most kiln sites. From the specialist potteries, however, come a number of more sophisticated aids for forming and decorating vessels, such as a cylindrical roulette from Eccles, Kent (Detsicas 1974, 306). The clay dies for forming *appliqué* medallions, or for impressing vessels with a potter's name or decorative motifs are well attested within the various mortarium industries, in the Colchester colour-coated industry (Hull 1963), and in early military-orientated workshops at Holt (Grimes 1930) and Eccles (Detsicas 1974, 306; 1977). Some variation in the form of such die-stamps is discernible between the various factories. Loop-handles were normal at Hartshill/Mancetter, and cylindrical ones at Holt and Colchester. At Brockley Hill, the stamp of the mortarium manufacturer Matugenus comprised a simple rectangular tablet without a handle, with the lettering on the narrow faces (Suggett 1955). On the evidence of impressions on vessels, many die-stamps must have been of wood and thus have not survived.

Most Romano-British stamps were impressed directly on to the vessel and consequently produced sunken lettering or designs. For moulded wares, however, master dies with decoration in relief (*poinçons* or punches) were often used to impress a decorative scheme into a mould which was subsequently lightly fired. Such dies have been found in the Colchester samian factory and, for moulded lamps, at Holt. These 'biscuited', that is slightly porous clay moulds for vessels, occurred in the samian factory at Colchester, and on the sites of allied industries at Pulborough, Sussex (*PSAL* xxiii (1909–11), 127–8, fig. 5; Webster 1975), Littlemore, Oxon. (Young 1971), Water Newton, and in North-west Wiltshire (Anderson 1978). Those from the last three centres were not stamped but scribed, presumably with a stylus or similar sharp implement. Decorated samian and its close imitations were made by pressing clay into the 'biscuited' mould and allowing it to dry until it shrank away from the mould walls. The base and rim of the vessel were then added on the wheel. A clay mushroom-shaped tool from Colchester presumably aided the initial pressing of the clay into the mould (Hull 1963, 108–9, fig. 50.3). Face-masks on many jugs were also moulded, and a number of moulds for these have been found, including some from Horspath, Risinghurst, Oxon. (Hassall 1953), Homersfield, Suffolk (Smedley and Owles 1965), Hadham (*JRS* lv (1965), 211), and Stibbington.

The need for a greater knowledge of potters' tools provides yet another argument for a more extensive excavation of kiln sites than has been usual hitherto.

CHAPTER 5

The early development of kiln structures

The late Iron Age to first century AD

Evidence for the making and firing of pottery in Britain before the Roman Conquest is relatively meagre, presumably because of the very ephemeral character of 'kilns' at this period. Probably much of the pottery of the Iron Age or earlier was fired either in a 'clamp' type of pit or in an above-ground clamp or bonfire.

Surface clamps or bonfires

In the technique of clamp-firing, pre-dried vessels are stacked close together, upside-down on the ground, and surrounded with fuel which is then set alight (Fig. II.i). Probably the bottom layer of vessels would have been raised on a layer of spaced-out logs, blocks of clay, or even stones if the local rock was of a type, such as sandstone, unlikely to crumble or explode when heated. This would have allowed a draught to circulate upwards through the load, and also permitted sticks to be poked under the bottom tier of vessels. Logs in particular would have prevented the rims of the lowest vessels from remaining under-fired, but would not have burnt out fast enough to make the pottery-stack unstable. Experimental surface bonfire-firings (O'Brien undat.; Coleman-Smith 1972) and anthropological observations (Shepard 1954, 75 ff.) have shown that firing with a surface clamp is quite practical. To the inexperienced, however, the greatest problems are in controlling the rate of burning and in achieving an even combustion throughout the fire, particularly with larger clamps. Because of this and the fact that vessels are often subjected to the direct impingement of the flames, the surface of clamp-fired wares is sometimes uneven in colour. They are rarely fired to more than 700–900 °C.

Primitive potters in general preferred a sheltered position for the bonfire and avoided gusty days for firing. A surface clamp-firing would usually leave little more than an ashy deposit and sometimes an ill-defined area of burning on the natural soil or subsoil. With heavy ploughing such as is normal in Britain, these would be among the first features to be eradicated. Occasionally a few burnt stones might survive. Because the vestiges of surface clamp-firings are difficult to detect archaeologically and interpret convincingly, it is hardly surprising that for the Iron Age very few examples have yet been claimed by excavators.

One of the most convincing, in the Trent Valley at Willingham, Derbyshire, comprised an irregularly-shaped hearth (F56) sited on the top of a partially silted pit (Wheeler 1979, 80–84). Within this hollow and around its edge, clay blocks of a type sometimes termed 'loom-weights' had been set at irregular intervals; on these had been placed pottery vessels which had broken *in situ* and appeared distorted and overfired. These unevenly-fired clay blocks, and other similar contemporary ones from the adjacent late Bronze-Age/early Iron-Age settlement, ranged in shape from a truncated pyramid or cone to a rectangle (approx. 10 cm² by 12–18 cm). At about one-third of the distance from the top of each was a horizontal perforation, which showed no sign of wear; some blocks had a small hole or shallow groove in the top. Although it was suggested that, as found, they were being used as makeshift clamp-furniture or were in the process of being deliberately fired, they were assumed to have had another ultimate but unknown purpose. Among the parallels discussed by Elsdon (1979, 197–9), a similar group of blocks from Badwell Ash, Suffolk had clearly been used in a comparable manner in a clamp-firing (Winbolt 1935). There seems no reason why blocks of this type should not have been intended primarily as clamp-furniture, although a dual function cannot be totally dismissed. A horizontal perforation would have helped to prevent heat-shattering; its position in the upper part of a block, probably above the ash level in the early stages of a firing, would also have facilitated the passage of hot air. A groove or hole at the top of a block would have aided the stability of the superimposed vessel and allowed hot air to pass beneath its rim at that point. Elsdon's preliminary list of comparable blocks (ibid., 208–10) includes many apparently discarded in pits as rubbish. A thorough survey, however, of all surviving examples with known contexts, and a careful reassessment of features described as hearths in excavation reports might reveal evidence for a number of possible sites of Iron-Age surface clamp-firings.

For the Romano-British period, at least one possible site of repeated surface bonfire-firings has been recognized and partially excavated at Ridge, near Wareham, Dorset (Farrar 1975). It comprised a shallow scoop in the hillside containing dense black sooty deposits interleaved with lenses of brilliant tile-red earth, probably the result of heavy burning *in situ*. The feature occurred within one of the many Durotrigan sites producing black-burnished ware, an industry whose ceramic traditions, and in some instances manufacturing centres, were a continuation of those of the pre-Conquest late Iron Age, with only slight changes in vessel-forms (Gillam 1976, 57; Farrar 1973a). Its technology never embraced the use of the potter's wheel but perpetuated the practice of hand-forming and hand-burnishing vessels throughout the Roman period. Firing methods also seem likely to have remained unchanged, and the use of surface clamps was thus probably normal for this industry during the Romano-British period as well as in the Iron Age.

It seems reasonable to assume that this bonfire technology would not have been confined to the Durotrigan industries. In much of Southern England, S of the Thames and excluding Kent, it would probably have been the most frequent method of firing pottery throughout the Iron Age and in many places even for much of the Roman period. This would help to explain why no Iron-Age and relatively few Romano-British kilns have been recorded in a region, densely populated throughout those periods, where pottery had been in use continuously since the Neolithic. Even the indirect evidence of unassociated kiln-furniture is absent.

Pit clamps

Identification of traces of pit-clamp firings on archaeological sites is almost as problematical as that of bonfire-firings. In general technique the process would have differed little from that of surface-firing. The siting below ground of all, or most of the clamp, however, would have afforded greater heat-retention and better shelter from sudden draughts (Rhodes 1969, 3–8). In experiments on the chalk lands of Butser Hill, Hants., Reynolds (1977, 35; 1979, 15; undat., and unpublished inf.) found that repeated shallow pit-clamp firings on the same spot broke up the subsoil. This resulted in the conjoining of adjacent pit-clamp sites into one large, irregular depression. Features of this general character have, in fact, been excavated within classic Iron-Age chalkland settlement-enclosures, such as Little Woodbury, Wilts., in positions peripheral to the living area. There they have been classed as 'working areas' or 'working hollows' (Bersu 1940, 69 ff.), and undoubtedly may have had a range of functions, such as providing shelter for threshing. Their ashy fill too could indeed represent the dumping of rubbish from elsewhere. Meticulous excavation, nevertheless, might sometimes establish a positive link between such hollows and small-scale pottery production (Reynolds 1977, 35). Clearly, as much attention always needs to be directed to the areas peripheral to the living quarters as to the huts themselves. It is in these areas that pottery manufacture and other semi-industrial processes seem to have been frequently sited in the Iron-Age and Romano-British settlements of the East Midlands and elsewhere, as at Rushden, near Irchester, Northants.

A possible site of pre-Conquest Iron-Age pit-clamp firings has been recorded at Pear Tree Farm, Wattisfield (Ipswich Mus. Records). Its identification is not certain, since it was excavated under less than ideal conditions. It comprised a large irregular scoop, 5.2 m by 1.8 m across narrowing to 0.45 m at one end and 0.75–1 m deep, with evidence of burning *in situ*. It was filled with ash and sherds, perhaps the result of numerous successive firings. The site lies very close to the earliest nucleus (late 1st-century) of the important 'Wattisfield' Romano-British pottery industry, suggesting possible continuity of production there. Two other sites of repeated pit-clamp firings recently salvaged at Alice Holt, Binsted, may also indicate similar continuity (inf. M. Lyne). One was perhaps dated to shortly after the Roman conquest of the area and the other was immediately pre or just post-Conquest (p. 119). Although damaged and originally of irregular shape, their diameters were probably approximately 1.60 m and 1 m.

The only possible pit-clamp site of definite Romano-British date to be recognized was excavated at West Stow, just 22 km WSW of Wattisfield (West 1955, 42). The roughly-circular, flat-bottomed, steep-sided pit, 1.4 m across and 0.36 m deep, was filled with ash and reduced sherds, with indications of burning *in situ*. It occurred within a mid-Flavian to Hadrianic pottery production centre, whose early ceramic and later kiln traditions had close links with the Wattisfield industry. This centre utilized sunken single-chambered clay-lined kilns, themselves perhaps ultimately derived from pit-clamps (p. 114).

La Tène III-derived kilns

Clamps were not the only means of firing pottery in the late Iron Age in Britain. During the past decade increasing evidence has been recorded for the existence of distinctive types of simple up-draught kiln, beginning in the pre-Conquest period and surviving until at least late in the 1st century AD. From them a multitude of more elaborate offshoots can be traced. The sequence may be discussed under three headings: La Tène III-derived surface kilns; La Tène III-derived semi-sunken kilns; and sunken kilns with some La Tène III-derived features.

Surface kilns

The main characteristics of this most rudimentary type comprised a circular or oval furnace-chamber on the surface or near-surface with a flue and a stokehole similarly sited (Figs. II.iii, VIII). Sometimes, but very infrequently, there were two flues and stokeholes. Neither the furnace nor oven had any substantial permanent walling or lining. Turves must have been the main material used, sometimes sealed internally with a thin coat of clay. The false or raised temporary oven-floor, of reusable bars, spanned all or most of the furnace-chamber. Sometimes it had supplementary prefabricated flooring components such as perforated plates and it rested on one or more reusable prefabricated clay pedestal-support(s). The outer ends of the bars would have been incorporated into the temporary kiln-walling or, less likely, propped up with further supports arranged along the circumference. Occasionally the bottom of the furnace-chamber was plastered over with a skim of clay. This coating, however, never formed an essential component in the kiln structure as did the clay lining-wall of more sophisticated kiln types. Prefabricated kiln-furniture occasionally lined the flue (Fig. VIII). The advantages of this simple type of up-draught kiln are obvious. The fire could be controlled better in the flue. Hot gases and flames from the fire effectively circulated the heat directly to the wares, and the kiln-walls retained the heat.

In the Nene Valley, Woods (1974) divided kilns of this general type into a number of minor local variants, according to the shapes, sizes and relative depths of the furnace-chambers, flues and stokeholes (Types IA, IB, IC, IIA, IIB, IIC, IIIA and IIIB). An important point to emerge from his discussion is that the stokehole or stoking area might sometimes have been sited above the level of the furnace-chamber. On a ploughed site, therefore, an excavator may be faced with a shallow bowl-shaped scoop with a little burning *in situ* and no trace of the related stoking area. In the frequent absence of associated kiln-furniture, this poses serious problems of interpretation. In excavations, the most widely encountered superficial indication of a surface kiln is the characteristic 'dumb-bell'-shaped area of burning, a feature diagnostic enough to make possible some reinterpretation of published material, particularly when associated with fragments of portable furniture, such as bars, props and perforated plates. Prae Wood is a case in point (Wheeler and Wheeler 1936, 44, pls. LVI, LXXVIA, 178 ff.). Woods also noted the frequent siting of such kilns close to earlier partly back-filled ditches, which had been utilized as ready-made stoking areas. This phenomenon was not confined to the Nene Valley. An exceptional kiln in the Nene Valley (Woods's Type IIB) apparently had a double furnace. Only one vaguely similar example elsewhere has been recorded, at Mucking (Jones and Rodwell 1973, fig. 3). There must have been difficulties in heating both chambers adequately and in controlling draught, which can be clarified only by experimental firings.

In the area in which surface kilns were concentrated, reduced wares, usually grey to black, predominated throughout the Roman period. This was despite the fact that before the Conquest many such kilns produced mainly oxidized pottery, red or orange in colour, and few if any of their wares were fully reduced. Subsequently, however, there was a trend towards sunken kilns (*see* p. 57) and a simultaneous tendency towards reduced pottery. This is not to say that reduced wares were never made in surface kilns. Nevertheless, in such kilns, wholly above ground and made of temporary materials, the problems of maintaining the sealed atmosphere necessary for proper reduction must have been considerable. Surface kilns were thus inherently more suitable for oxidizing pottery.

Semi-sunken kilns

This related type was probably a development of that just described. It utilized similar props and bars, but had a shallowly-sunken vertical-sided furnace-chamber, sometimes lined with clay, and an above-ground oven, apparently walled with temporary materials such as turves. The false oven-floor spanning all or most of the furnace-chamber was sited exactly at ground level (Fig. III.ix), so that the outer ends of the kiln-bars rested on the rim of the furnace-chamber, as at Earl Shilton, Leics., and Lincoln Racecourse. For this purpose, the rim of a combustion-chamber with a clay lining was often flattened and expanded outwards into a 'lip', a feature which would also have aided the stability of any turf oven-walling superimposed on it. The flue and stokehole were usually larger than those of surface kilns and normally sunken, but sometimes utilized an existing ditch, depression or natural fall-away in the ground.

The advantage of this kiln over its surface-built contemporaries lay in the greater shelter, and thus ease of control, which it afforded for the fire in the flue and furnace-chamber. Both types, however, shared the disadvantage of the poor insulation inherent in an oven wholly above ground.

Sunken kilns with La Tène III-derived features

These, apparently evolving directly from the two types previously discussed, were usually clay-lined. They were however deeper, the furnace-chamber, the oven-floor and part of the oven being below ground. The circumference of the raised oven-floor, again spanning all or most of the furnace-chamber and usually of bars, could thus no longer rest on the kiln-lip. It had to be supported by some additional method, such as a ledge

Plate 16.

Spong Hill, NORTH ELMHAM, Norfolk: holes for seating flooring-bars, poked in back wall of first-century kiln while clay still wet. *Foreground*, small rectangular clay pedestal, originally one of two, broken off at top (scale in cms).

(Figs II.ii, vii, IX; Pls. 18, 20), or moulded recesses part way up the kiln-wall, or by bars positioned in holes poked in the kiln-lining while the clay was still wet (Fig III.viii; Pl. 16). Loose pedestals, bars and plates sometimes remained in use, as in the more rudimentary kilns. In other, mostly later examples, more substantial pedestals were built into the kiln structure. Bars also tended to be secured in position and were thus rendered less re-usable. It is probable that the siting of these permanent supports reflected the earlier arrangements of the temporary props. The clay walls in these kilns had the advantage of retaining heat better and reflecting it back into the kiln as their surfaces became red hot.

Origins

Exactly when the most rudimentary kiln technology became established in Britain is not yet certain. Out of a small group of possibly pre-Roman kilns, the number definitely so is minimal. In most instances it is impossible to determine whether a pre or immediately post-Conquest dating is appropriate. Of the surface-built kilns, the most securely dated pre-Conquest excavated examples were connected with the second phase of activity (Cii) on the 'Rushden' site. On the basis of associated imported pottery and metalwork, these ought to belong to about the third decade of the 1st century AD. Others which may pre-date the invasion include one at Milfordhope East, Upchurch, and possible examples now recognized at Prae Wood (Wheeler and Wheeler 1936, 44, pls. LVI, LXXVIA, 178 ff.). A single, possibly pre-Conquest, semi-sunken kiln was excavated at Barksore Farm in the Upchurch Marshes (Jackson 1972). On ceramic grounds it was most likely in use within the two or three decades

before the Conquest, although arguably it might just be Claudian. At Mucking, a series of near-surface or semi-sunken kilns within this general range includes undifferentiated examples of both immediately pre and post-Conquest date (inf. M. U. Jones). Loose pedestals, bars and other furniture indicative of the probable existence of such rudimentary kilns have been found in contexts which might be pre-Conquest elsewhere on the Upchurch Marshes (Hume 1954; inf. I. Jackson), at Camulodunum (Hawkes,and Hull 1947, 282), and at Welwyn, Herts. (Rook 1965, 65; 1970, 34, 36).

How did these rudimentary kilns emerge in Britain? Were they a spontaneous development, or the innovation of immigrant craftsmen from the Continent, or the result of a diffusion of ideas, such as Romanizing influences from Gaul in the period shortly before the Conquest, as suggested by Dr Hugo Thoen (pers. comm.)? Their products, where known, are almost always associated with wares of late La Tène ('Belgic') character, usually wheel-thrown but sometimes handmade. The overall distribution of these early kilns, and of prefabricated furniture indicative of them (Map 8), coincides very closely with the main concentrations of pre-Conquest wheel-thrown La Tène III ('Belgic') pottery in Britain, that is around the Thames Estuary and its hinterlands, the Upper Thames Valley, and the valleys of the Trent and some of its tributaries, and of the rivers converging on the Wash. There may also be a link between this simple technology and that of salt production. That industry, whose furnaces and kiln-furniture have much in common with the earliest kilns, burgeoned mostly in the 'Belgic' areas of Britain in the late Iron Age.

Portable bars and other kiln-furniture would presumably have formed as much a part of a potter's specialist equipment as the wheel. The arrival of the potter's wheel marked a substantial intensification of the professional, as distinct from the mainly domestic element in pottery manufacture (Childe 1940, 252; Frere 1967, 23; Harding 1974, 92), and an increase in pottery production on a much larger scale. Hodges (1970, 60–61) has suggested the probability of a link between this innovation and the development of the proper levigation of clay by settling it out at the bottom of a pit (*see* p. 44). This process was designed to make the clay smoother than had been normal hitherto, and thus easier to use on the wheel. It would, therefore, be logical to expect a more efficient firing technology to emerge at the same time as the development of such specialist manufacturing techniques. In short, the potter's wheel, late La Tène ('Belgic') pottery, and rudimentary kilns were quite probably introduced simultaneously into Britain from the Continent.

Evidence to support this theory is not easy to find on the Continent. The unreliable character of much excavation and recording in the past in France, the preoccupation there with only the more sophisticated pottery industries, and the relative lack of publications of kiln sites in Germany probably explain this dearth of information. It should be remembered, however, that until the late 1960s surface kilns of the type described were still unrecognized in Britain. Evidence comes from the 'Rushden' site (Phase Ciii), where potters, apparently from the Continent, arrived soon after the Roman Conquest. Their products were in an exotic La Tène III tradition. The kiln type which they introduced was slightly larger than, but otherwise virtually identical to the surface kilns already current on the site. If it is accepted that migrant craftsmen would have retained both their native ceramic styles and the kiln technology with which they were familiar, then this evidence might suggest that surface kilns were still in use in their Continental homeland. Unfortunately its location has so far defied identification, but was surely within the North-western provinces of the Roman Empire.

Similar surface-built kilns, alongside more developed sunken La Tène III types, were the main type used by another group of probable immigrant potters, perhaps from the Rhineland to judge from their products. These worked from about the late 40s to the early 60s AD E of Longthorpe Roman fortress in the Lower Nene Valley (Wild 1974, 160; 1977). The evidence from Longthorpe and Rushden and the discovery at Clermont-Ferrand of an 'ultimate La Tène' sunken kiln with a movable, composite, central pedestal and tapering bars (Duhamel 1979, fig. 29; Daugas et Malacher 1976, fig. 5:4) encourages the belief that surface kilns with portable furniture will eventually be found and excavated on the Continent. A thorough search of archaeological literature and museums in Europe might well reveal examples of loose bars and other prefabricated items found out of context, as on many British sites.

Development

The general classification of these La Tène III kiln types shows the normal trend in Britain to have been one of gradual increase in the depth and, to a lesser extent, in the area of the furnace-chambers and stokeholes. Isolated exceptions, such as some 2nd and 3rd-century surface-built kilns in the Doncaster potteries (Buckland and Dolby 1980), seem to have been determined by geological factors. In the Upper Nene Valley, the general trend is clearly exemplified by the sequence at Rushden. The earliest kilns and stokeholes belonged to the second phase of activity on the site (Cii) *c.* AD 20/30 +. They had portable supports and floors and were either surface-built or sited in relatively shallow scoops. The third phase (Ciii), probably lasting less than a year in the mid 40s AD, saw similar kilns there associated with immigrant potters, presumably reintroduced by them. In the indigenous fourth phase (Civ), the late 40s AD, the kiln-furniture was similar. The chambers, however, comprising vertical-sided pits sunk approximately 0.4–0.6 m into the ground, were generally larger in diameter than hitherto and sometimes thinly lined with clay. Because of ploughing, and the semi-salvage nature of the excavation, it is often impossible to decide whether such pits were semi-sunken or relatively shallow sunken kilns. As Woods has pointed out (1974, 274), however, the latest kilns in the Rushden sequence form a local link between the most rudimentary surface versions and the very solidly-built, deeply-sunken Lower Nene Valley kilns of the 2nd, 3rd and 4th centuries.

These general developments are echoed in the Nene, Ouse and adjacent valleys. Although no other pre-Conquest kilns have yet been excavated in the area, numerous surface kilns were clearly present in the immediate post-Conquest period. These were increasingly superseded by sunken varieties, and scarcely appear to have survived into the Flavian period. The apparent relative abundance of such kilns in the middle of the 1st century must surely reflect the economic impact of the Roman Conquest on local pottery production, and the huge demands of the garrisons for ceramic supplies. Northampton, for instance, has been suggested as the possible region for the site of a vexillation-fortress (Frere and St Joseph 1974, 38, n. 55). Only in rare cases, as at Rushden and probably at Longthorpe, do these demands appear to have been met by immigrant craftsmen from the Continent. At Longthorpe, however, they may have worked in association with local craftsmen. Clearly, local potters would have made strenuous efforts to increase the quality, quantity, and overall range of their output. It is also possible that potters working in multifarious La Tène-derived traditions in other areas, particularly South-east England, migrated to the Nene Valley and elsewhere, perhaps to Thorpe St Andrew, Norfolk (Gregory 1979), with an eye on new outlets for their wares. In the Upper Nene Valley, such an instance has been suggested at Hardingstone (Woods 1969, 1, 9). Clearly the Roman advance must have done much to speed up the changes in existing La Tène-derived kiln technology in England. It also resulted in its rapid spread to other areas, particularly those which hitherto had been aceramic (Maps 4, 8, 13), or had been using only simple handmade wares, fired by primitive techniques.

Outside the Nene Valley, the Ouse valleys and their periphery, only a handful of Conquest-period La Tène-type surface or near-surface kilns have so far been recorded. There are examples at The Churchill Hospital (Young 1977, 31, 33, fig. 8), at Kelvedon (unpubl.), Gun Hill, Tilbury, Essex (Drury and Rodwell 1973, 62–4) and Mucking, probably at Welwyn (Rook 1965; 1970) and Prae Wood (Wheeler and Wheeler 1936, 44), at Cherry Hinton (Hughes 1903), and in the North Kent Marshes (Jackson 1962; 1972).

For most of these sites, the excavated evidence is rather fragmentary or, in a few cases, not yet fully processed. It is thus more or less impossible to pinpoint clear regional kiln characteristics such as appear to exist in the Nene Valley (Fig. VIII). The exotic late Neronian-early Flavian products in a 'Belgic'-type fabric at the Cherry Hinton site may indeed represent another rare instance of immigrant potters from the Continent working in La Tène-derived traditions of kiln technology.

As yet, only the La Tène-derived kilns in North Kent seem to possess regional characteristics unlike those of the early Upper Nene Valley kilns (Fig. IX). The forms and arrangement of the kiln-supports and bar-floors, in particular, were apparently quite different. The relationship of these kilns to the early Nene Valley kilns was as that of 'cousins'. No definite surface kilns have yet been excavated in North Kent, although a dumb-bell-shaped area of burning with bars nearby, at Milfordhope East (inf. I. Jackson), could be relevant. The discovery of a possible pre-Conquest semi-sunken kiln at Barksore Farm (Jackson 1972) may imply that this type either emerged here earlier, or arrived in the area already evolved from surface kilns. This, together with the differences in kiln-furniture, may suggest that the North Kent kilns were inspired or introduced directly from the Continent, perhaps from a source distinct from that which influenced the Nene Valley and its hinterland.

In North Kent, semi-sunken kilns apparently continued to be built until the second half of the 2nd century, as at Slayhills

Salting, Kiln 1 (Jackson 1975b and unpubl.). By the early to mid 2nd century onwards, however, the larger, deeper kilns had developed from them. These, sometimes possessing some form of integral support as at Iwade (inf. A. Miles), still at first used loose bars and occasionally some portable furniture. In the mid to late 2nd century, there was a gradual change to permanent, and thus more stable, floors as well as built-in supports, for example at Cooling (frontispiece, Pl. 1) and Oakleigh Farm, Higham (Pl. 17; Catherall 1983, *forthcoming*). This probably coincided with the peak of North Kent's share in the important black-burnished ware (BB2) industry of the Thames Estuary (Map 17; Williams 1977). It presumably reflected the improvements associated with the emergence of exceptionally large-scale production and very widespread distribution to consumers, including the garrisons of the northern frontiers.

Elsewhere in Britain, a few sporadic semi-sunken kilns were used in isolation until the mid to late 2nd century, as at Earl Shilton (Clarke 1950) and Lincoln Racecourse (Corder 1950a). In the main, however, fully sunken kilns with La Tène III-derived furniture seem to have replaced surface kilns quite suddenly, soon after the Roman Conquest. There is little evidence that the semi-sunken type ever formed a chronologically clear-cut transition between the two.

La Tène III portable kiln-furniture

As the same ranges of furniture occur in surface, semi-sunken, and developed-but-related early sunken kilns, they have been treated together. The essence of this furniture was its portability. This does not necessarily indicate a system of itinerant craftsmen, carrying pedestals around in the way that modern farriers often transport portable anvils. It meant that a kiln structure could be rapidly assembled and, after firing, any furniture surviving intact could be salvaged for later reuse.

This almost certainly accounts for the total absence of furniture *in situ* in many of these early kilns. In the past this has often hampered the recognition of surface kilns, and sometimes led to their identification as hearths or cooking-ovens, as at Welwyn (Rook 1965, 55, 65; 1970, 31, 34, 36). A thorough search of reports on the excavation of late Iron-Age sites might, indeed, reveal more examples of such kilns, described as ovens. The reuse of kiln-furniture also explains why, in Kiln 3 at Slayhills Salting (Fig. IX) where most of the furniture had been abandoned *in situ* after the firing, the bars were not homogeneous but apparently made by more than one hand and at different times. This reuse inevitably renders pointless any attempts to reconstruct kiln-floors by matching up loose bars scattered over a site.

Kiln-furniture that was reused included broken pedestals, bars, and plates. They were sometimes incorporated into the linings of these early kilns as reinforcing material, as at Camp Hill, Hunsbury (Shaw 1979, Kiln 25) and Massey Close/St Martin's Lane, Hardingstone, Northants. (inf. R. Turland). In later kilns at Sibson, Hunts., in the Lower Nene Valley (Hartley 1960, 14) and at Great Casterton, Rutland (inf. C. Mahaney), large

Plate 17. Oakleigh Farm, HIGHAM, Kent: Kiln C, semi-sunken, with central built-in pedestal and permanent solid-clay raised oven-floor vented in bar-like pattern; viewed from damaged rear. On *right*, behind ranging pole, part of expanded lip of kiln-wall survives intact at ground level; 'domed' flue protrudes at *top right*. The kiln was making black-burnished ware (BB2) within the period *c.* AD 160–80 (ranging pole in 20 cm divisions).

quantities of bars were used as core material for tongue-supports.

The main disadvantage of prefabricated kiln-furniture was its inherent instability. For this reason, a portable pedestal would sometimes be secured in position with a light luting of clay at the foot. It was still sometimes removed for reuse, even when this involved serious damage to the clay at the bottom of a furnace-chamber. Careful examination can occasionally locate the scar whence a support has been wrenched out, thus providing an indication of the internal arrangement of the kiln-furniture, as at Kelvedon. Such problems, involving the stability and strength of portable furniture, must have stimulated the gradual development of permanent in-built supports and floors. These would have been essential when kilns tended to become larger as many local pottery industries expanded and adopted more sophisticated techniques.

Before the late 1st century AD portable furniture was almost always of prefabricated clay, usually a coarser variety of that used in the fabric of the vessels fired in the kiln. Occasionally vegetable fibre was added. Calcite-tempered kiln-furniture almost always reflects the fabric of at least some kiln products, and is thus informative when these are in doubt. On this basis, the possible manufacture of Huntcliffe-type wares at Norton may be deduced. At Cherry Hinton, the fine, pale fabric of some of the kiln-furniture enables these simple 'ovens' to be linked with the manufacture of the sophisticated table-wares from the site, as well as the ordinary kitchen-wares. The colour of kiln-furniture may also indicate the firing conditions normal in a kiln, whether oxidizing or reducing. At Weekley, Northants. (inf. R. Rattray), several bars, oxidized and predominantly orange in colour, were grey at one end, perhaps where they had been overlain by the (?)turf kiln-wall and thereby reduced.

Portable oven-floor supports

Pedestals

Before the late 1st century AD these were mostly of prefabricated clay. Although some regional variation exists, Woods's description of the Nene Valley types (1969, 34; 1974, 275) still forms an excellent basis for further discussion. He distinguished at least two prefabricated clay pedestal types, dumb-bell and slab.

Dumb-bell-type pedestals. These comprised a square, rectangular, or circular column, expanded at both ends, occasionally with a lateral perforation (Fig. VIII). The ends were usually flat. An example from Billing Aquadrome, Northampton (Johnston 1969, fig. 9, no. 7), however, is slightly recessed at the centre of one end, possibly to accommodate a fire-bar with a hooked end. It is rarely possible to determine the height of these props because they are so often found broken. A probable average would be about 0.25–0.4 m, but it must in any case have varied according to the intended height of the furnace-chamber. This variety was the most common portable support in the Upper Nene Valley, where its introduction at Rushden certainly preceded the Conquest (*contra* Young, *in* Sturdy and Young, 1976,

63). Most excavated examples, however, just post-dated the Conquest. Its distribution, though primarily concentrated in the NE Midlands, had outliers in Oxfordshire, for example at Hanborough, perhaps as a result of copying rather than potter-migration. This pedestal-type was apparently also transmitted beyond the traditional La Tène ('Belgic') cultural areas of Britain by potters probably from the territory of the Coritani. Moving in the wake of the Roman army, they set up kilns near Little Chester, Derbyshire, in the Trajanic period, perhaps in association with potters from elsewhere (Brassington 1971; 1980), and introduced their native vessel-forms at the same time (*see* p. 125). The kilns with such supports, Derby Racecourse Nos. 1e, 1f, 2c, and possibly 4b and 6, were sunk well below ground. Their very small size, the shape of their pedestals, here well plastered into position, and the use of bars and circular plates as flooring elements (*see* p. 124), clearly point towards their probable ancestry. The earliest known kilns at Hartshill appear to have originated in such circumstances, from a generally similar source (p. 100).

How were such dumb-bell-shaped props normally arranged in these early kilns? Only very few have been recorded *in situ*. The position of the slightly later, in-built, 'waisted' pedestals derived from them may, however, reflect their original dispositions. Several arrangements seem to have been favoured:

(i) A single, centrally-placed pedestal (Fig. VIII), as in Kiln IV at Hardingstone (Woods 1969, 5), at Kelvedon, and later at Derby Racecourse (Brassington 1971). It is probably no coincidence that the Upper Nene and adjacent valleys have the greatest known concentration of portable dumb-bell-shaped supports as well as the greatest frequency of integrally-built, central, circular, 'waisted' pedestals.

(ii) Four pedestals forming the corners of a square, as at Ise Village, Kettering, Northants. (Foster 1976, fig. 5).

(iii) A number of pedestals arranged in a circle, possibly around a central prop or a circle of props, as at Hunsbury Hill, Northants. (Dryden 1885, 58, 61), and in Kiln IV at Elstow, near Bedford (Pl. 18; inf. G. Dring).

(iv) Three pedestals on the apices of a triangle, as in Hanborough Kiln 2, Oxon. (Sturdy and Young 1976), and much later in Hartshill Kiln 8 (inf. K. F. Hartley).

(v) Two pedestals on the flue axis, as in Hartshill Kiln H (Hartley 1973a, fig. 2).

'Slab-type' pedestals. These comprised a near-rectangular, prefabricated, fired-clay block, slightly expanded on the edge of at least one of the longest sides to aid stability (Fig. IX). Some were perforated, as in Wellingborough Kiln 4, Northants. (Foster *et al.* 1977). This would have helped to prevent the fabric of the pedestal from cracking unduly during use, by ensuring that it was pre-fired evenly throughout. It would also have facilitated the free movement of hot gases in the furnace (Woods 1974, 276). Such a pedestal would have been easier to remove from the

furnace-chamber before cooling, for immediate use elsewhere. It could be carried by two men, by means of a strong stick passed through one of the holes.

Unperforated, rectangular, slab-pedestals occurred most consistently in the North Kent Marshes. At present they are the only type of portable support known there, for example at Barksore Farm, in Slayhills Salting Kilns 3 and 4, from other allied features at Slayhills, and possibly at Milfordhope 'Site B',

Upchurch (inf. I. Jackson). They varied substantially in length from roughly 0.25 m in the Barksore Tiberio-Claudian kiln (Lower Halstow 1) to at least 0.5 m in Slayhills Salting Kiln 3. Sometimes they tended to be more pronouncedly wedge-shaped than most of such pedestals elsewhere in Britain (Fig. IX). At Cherry Hinton the 'long wedge-shaped bricks' (Hughes 1903, 235), 'rectangular blocks $11 \times 5\frac{1}{2} \times 1\frac{3}{4}$ inches ... some perforated with holes ... not laid to form a floor or built into the side (of the

Plate 18.

Mile Road, nr. Elstow, BEDFORD: Kiln IV: (*upper*) detail of oven-floor of prefabricated cigar-shaped bars *in situ*, overlying portable rectangular clay pedestals; (*lower*) furnace-chamber with bars removed showing supporting ledge and temporary rectangular pedestals clustered around a larger, more permanent, circular central pedestal (scales in ins).

furnace), but as if rammed in with clay' (ibid. 3, 474), seem likely to represent slab-pedestals. This could also apply to an unpublished fragment, approximately 0.16 m by 0.07 m thick and more than 0.16 m long, in Cambridge University Museum. Some of the thicker fragments of pre-Roman 'bricks' associated with 'ovens' in Prae Wood (Wheeler and Wheeler 1936, 44, 178 ff. pls. LVI, LXXVI) may be derived from such pedestals. Following the Prae Wood report (1936), other excavators have published 'Belgic bricks'. A reconsideration of more of these may well result in the identification of further simple kilns, as at Welwyn. Not all the 'pierced bricks' from the other sites mentioned by the Wheelers (ibid., 180) necessarily derive from pottery kilns. Each needs to be reassessed in its context. At Prae Wood, the shape and general character of the ovens, and the presence of bars or props as well as perforated and unperforated bricks collectively suggest their probable use as pottery kilns.

Unfortunately no information is available on the more recent Prae Wood Farm kiln discovery. Photographs of this salvage excavation (in Verulamium Mus.) suggest a cluster of several 'block'-like pedestals collapsed inwards in the centre of the furnace-chamber. This arrangement possibly resembles that used in Kiln IV at Elstow (Pl. 18). There the excavator, G. Dring, found slab-pedestals *in situ,* in a central rough circle, set on their short edges to supplement a larger, mushroom-shaped, central, more permanent pedestal in supporting many radiating loose bars. The North Kent kilns show their own distinctive internal arrangements. Two pedestals were arranged in a blunt 'V'-formation at Barksore, Lower Halstow (Jackson 1972) and at Slayhills (Fig. IX). In Wellingborough Kiln 4 (Foster *et al.* 1977, fig. 4), one slab-pedestal apparently lay parallel to, but slightly to one side of the flue axis. Unfortunately evidence of the arrangement of the other supports was lacking but originally there may have been two parallel ones, as was probable at Spong Hill, North Elmham, Norfolk (Pl. 16; inf. R. J. Rickett).

Hollow cylindrical pedestals. Few are known: at Harrold (Kiln 2), two were probably positioned on the line of the flue axis (inf. A. Brown); at Lincoln Racecourse (Corder 1950a) and Longthorpe (inf. J. P. Wild), a single centrally-placed pedestal of this type seems likely.

Simple slightly tapering pillar-like props. The relatively unstable character of some of these items may imply their use in larger quantities than the more stable pedestals proper, perhaps grouped together. Alternatively, they may have played a supplementary role alongside more substantial pedestals in supporting the floors. It may be significant that other furniture occurring with such props often comprises unusual or less standard varieties, such as the flat bars and flat clay ring at Wood Burcote, Northants. (Pl. 23; Woods 1974, fig. 6, A and C). In a later kiln at Norton (No. 3), at least two pillar-like props were found side by side in the centre of the furnace-chamber, in conjunction with four banana-shaped props resting against the kiln-wall (Hayes and Whitley 1950). At Cherry Hinton, Hughes found four generally similar 'pyramidal blocks... apparently almost in their

original relative position', set vertically and arranged in a square. His reconstruction (Fig. VII; 1903, 475, fig. 36) shows these clay 'pillars', with their superimposed bun-shaped clay 'levelling-pads', acting like table-legs. They alone supposedly shouldered the full weight of the kiln-floor (comprising a large flat clay disc) and its load, a rather unsteady combination. Hughes (1903, 475) did, however, admit that there were other objects 'in

Fig. VII.

War Ditches, Cherry Hinton, CAMBRIDGE: prefabricated clay 'pyramidal' blocks, bun-shaped pads and flat plate: as illustrated by McKenny Hughes (1903, fig. 36).

that... fireplace' which were 'hard to explain'. It is possible that slab-pedestals from this site were also involved somewhere in the internal arrangements. Alternatively, the props may have rested against the wall of the kiln like the banana-shaped props in the Norton kiln (Pl. 39). In Hughes's reconstruction-drawings, some props do have a hint of curvature. Unfortunately not all the kiln-furniture survives for reassessment.

Banana-shaped props. The only definite examples of this type were from Norton Kiln 3 (Pl. 39; Hayes and Whitley 1950, fig. 8, pl. II). These may never have been used in conjunction with a raised oven-floor (*see* p. 100) and their relationship to La Tène-derived kiln-furniture is, therefore, in doubt. This is further emphasized by the 3rd-century date of the Norton kilns, which are substantially later than most kilns in Britain with temporary prefabricated supports and flooring.

Impromptu supports. Waster vessels on kiln sites would have been eminently suitable for reuse as impromptu temporary central supports for bar-floors. Evidence suggests that they sometimes fulfilled this role, as at Sheringham, Norfolk (Howlett 1960). Storage-jars or large cooking-pots were apparently found to be most suitable (Fig. III.i), presumably because of their height and the greater durability of their more coarsely-tempered, often thicker walls.

Composite prefabricated pedestals. As surface-built kilns gradually developed into sunken structures, so more elaborate composite pedestals emerged. Taller, portable, prefabricated pedestals, necessary for the deeper furnace-chambers, were presumably less easy to construct strongly in one piece and inherently more unstable. The simplest, and some of the earliest, composite pedestals comprised a single column of large stones, luted together with clay. These were not always heavily over-plastered and, theoretically, the components could often have been reused. At Weston Favell, Northants. (Bunch and Corder 1954), the top of the pedestal had been levelled up by super-imposing on it a loose, flat, circular clay 'plate'.

Where stone blocks were not readily available, another solution was sometimes adopted to enable portable clay pedestals to be used. Into the kiln was built a permanent raised platform, upon or into which a temporary pedestal could be superimposed or set. The central raised area in the mid 1st-century kiln at Caldecotte, Bucks., and the impression in the central mound of Hanborough Kiln I (Sturdy and Young 1976) may probably be interpreted in these terms.

A more sophisticated type of early composite pedestal was recorded at Longthorpe (Wild 1977). Positioned in the deeper, more developed of the two kiln types, it comprised a central column of prefabricated circular clay bricks, bonded together with clay. No parallel to this exists in Britain. In view of 'exotic' affinities of most of the kiln products, however, it may have been introduced by craftsmen from the Continent. Composite circular pedestals of segmental-shaped tiles are known in late Republican kilns in Italy (inf. Prof. J. Mertens).

Portable flooring materials

Bars

Of all kiln-furniture, bars are most frequently encountered. They can be easily recognized on excavations, even in non-kiln contexts, from relatively small fragments. As surface finds on unexcavated sites, they are often the sole indicators of the probable former presence of kilns (Map 8). Like all prefabricated clay kiln-furniture, bars were shaped by hand but were some-times knife-trimmed, particularly if tapering at the ends. Occasionally they were formed around a stick, twigs, or small bundles of straw, for reinforcement and to minimize shrinkage and discourage cracking during the drying and firing processes.

0   5   20 cm

Plate 19. Wood Burcote, TOWCESTER, Northants.: detail of fragmentary kiln-bar showing method of manufacture, by wrapping clay around a stick.

This technique can be seen in examples from Bakehouse Lane, Mears Ashby (Johnston 1969, 94, fig. 9, 3), Wood Burcote (Pl. 19; Woods 1974, 277, fig. 6, C) and Weekley, Northants. (inf. D. Jackson and R. Rattray).

The arrangement of kiln-bars was largely determined by the positioning of the pedestal(s). From the limited evidence,

however, the most popular was apparently one in which they radiated from a central pedestal (Fig. VIII; Pl. 20). Differing arrangements must have been made in kilns with more than one portable pedestal, but only one example, Slayhills Salting Kiln 3, has been found with all, or almost all, of its bars *in situ* after a firing. Figure IX shows how bars of different lengths were used to accommodate the different spans within the kiln. In the front of the kiln-chamber, just inside the flue-arch, a substantial area remained without any raised floor, similar to that in the Sheringham kiln. There the holes for the bar-ends terminated roughly half-way along the sides of the furnace-chamber (Howlett, 1960). Both the Slayhills and the Sheringham kilns had very short flues and were producing reduced wares. The gap in the floor at the front of the oven might, therefore, have had the advantage of allowing room for extra fuel to be pushed into the chamber itself, especially when it had to be amply stoked immediately prior to the sealing of the dome and flue and the final reduction of the kiln-load.

Like portable pedestals, loose kiln-bars were liable to rock or shift. Improvements on the earlier rudimentary arrangements, therefore, inevitably involved attempts to fix them more securely. One method, only possible as kilns became deeper, was to thrust the ends of the bars into the clay kiln-wall while it was still wet, as at Spong Hill and Weston Favell (Pl. 16; inf. R. Rickett; Bunch and Corder 1954). This technique was probably best suited to tapering bars with narrow ends (Fig. III.viii). Another, more gradual, overall tendency was for bars to be permanently secured to the support(s) and kiln-wall, or its ledge, by luting their ends with clay (Fig. XII). Sometimes the overplastering was extended to cover virtually the whole of the bars. This often made the gaps between them so small that superficially the oven-floor appeared to be of the solid-clay vent-holed type. Such bars were inevitably more or less impossible to reuse. A late variant of this method was to construct a bar-floor *in situ*. Sticks positioned in the kiln, usually thrust into the wall, were wrapped around with clay and fired. Subsequently the bar-system was completely over-plastered, leaving only vent-holes. This technique was en-countered in the late 2nd to early 3rd-century Nene Valley Kiln A at Water Newton (Hartley 1960, 13) and early 2nd-century kilns at Northwich, Cheshire (Curzon and Hanson 1971) and Piercebridge, Co. Durham (inf. P. Scott).

The simplest methods of securing the ends of bars, by luting or by coating the whole bar-systems with clay, scarcely occurred much before the end of the 1st century. Isolated Claudio-Neronian examples of bars totally overplastered, as those near the military sites at Longthorpe (inf. J. P. Wild) and Trent Vale (Mountford *et al.* 1968, pl. IV), seem more likely to represent the presence of immigrant potters than to reflect normal native practice at this early date (Map 8). Many of the earliest of these more elaborate stabilized bar-systems occur in Trajanic contexts closely linked to army supply (p. 87), for example in Brampton Kiln 3, Cumberland (Hogg 1965), at Northwich (Curzon and Hanson 1971), and in a number of the kilns on Derby Racecourse (Brassington 1971; 1980). It is as though the greater pressure of army demand, and possibly contact with incoming craftsmen from more sophisticated backgrounds, forced native British potters, moving into aceramic areas in the wake of the army, to become technologically more professional by updating and streamlining their kiln structures, in order to make their firings more reliable and their kiln loads larger.

In Germany, La Tène-derived kiln technology possibly developed along similar lines, hand in hand with the military conquest of the area, but inevitably a little earlier than in Britain. At *Novaesium* (Neuss), one of the late Augustan kilns (Gechter Kiln 26), circular and with a long flue, had a circular central pedestal from which multiple overplastered and vented bars radiated. Its associated wares were a mixture of Roman vessels, such as flagons, and late La Tène-derived forms (inf. Dr M. Gechter). Another kiln at Bonn of similar shape and mode of flooring, but with a rectangular pedestal, was probably in use in the Tiberian period (*BJ* cvii (1901), 221–2: pottery in the Rheinisches Landesmuseum, Bonn, examined by the author with Dr M. Gechter). Its products too comprised a generally similar mixture of native La Tène and Roman, probably military-orientated, forms. Possibly some of the kiln-types transmitted to Britain by potters from the Continent were themselves still at this interim stage of development.

In Britain, loose bars continued to be employed sporadically throughout most of the 2nd century, as in the kiln at Lincoln Racecourse (Corder 1950a) and at Slayhills (Fig. IX). Thereafter they were usually secured in position or overplastered. Kilns which used bars after the middle of the 2nd century almost always occurred, within or close to, areas where bar-floors were normal in the previous century. This is clear from their distribution (Maps 5–8, 13, 14, 17). It is as though the new Roman technology, introduced from the Conquest onwards, never completely submerged the already established La Tène 'bar'-tradi-

tions. This is most obvious in the Nene Valley, a region with abundant evidence for 1st-century kilns with loose bar-floors. The use of bars, albeit secured or overplastered, was embodied in the technology of the major specialist pottery industry which developed there in the second half of the 2nd century. Indeed, despite numerous indications of external, often Continental, influences both on the pottery and on kiln structures (p. 96), bars continued to be employed in the oven-floors of the majority of known kilns there until the demise of that industry early in the 5th century.

The shape, size, and character of kiln-bars varied quite substantially, often within the same site, as at Perry Barr (Hughes 1959), and sometimes slightly within the same kiln, as at Slayhills Salting (Fig. IX). The latter phenomenon probably resulted from their perpetual reuse. In the past, disproportionate attention has been paid to an estimation of the length of base not found *in situ*. The intact, loose bar-floor found *in situ* at Slayhills clearly shows that substantial differences in the lengths of bars were essential for satisfactory arrangement in a single kiln. Individually, therefore, they are not helpful indicators of kiln size. No doubt many potters would have kept a stock of bars of varying lengths, since no two kilns would have been likely to conform to exactly the same dimensions.

Tapering 'cigar-shaped' clay bars (Fig. III.i, vii–ix). This is the only bar-form with a clearly concentrated distribution pattern. It is mainly confined to the middle Trent Valley and the river valleys radiating from the Wash basin, namely South Lincs., Notts., Leics., Rutland, Northants., Hunts. and Peterborough, North-west Norfolk, North-east Bucks. and Beds. (for example kilns at Elstow; Pls. 18, 20). The few outliers are mostly found in adjacent areas to the W and NW which produced little or no

Plate 20.

Mile Road, nr. Elstow, BEDFORD: Kiln VI, showing *in-situ* oven-floor of cigar-shaped bars resting on internal ledge and permanent central pedestal; flue at *top* of picture (scale in ft).

pottery before the Conquest. The technology was probably transmitted to those regions by migrant potters following in the wake of the Roman army. Woods (1969, 33; 1974, 276–7, fig. 6) has recorded considerable variations in the sizes of such bars. Some were perforated; examples in two sizes occurred at North Hykeham gravel pit, Lincs. (Thompson 1958, 18). In the Nene Valley a possible general chronological tendency for tapered bars to become more substantial is not yet securely proven.

Bars were presumably deliberately tapered in the first place so that more could radiate from a small central pedestal (Pl. 20). Their near-pointed ends would also have been easier to thrust into the turf and, later, clay kiln-walling. The surface of several from Weekley showed a clear colour change from orange to grey at the tapering end, where it was probably tucked between the turves of the kiln-superstructure (inf. R. Rattray).

Untapered clay bars (Fig. IX). Bars generally comparable in size to the cigar-shaped range, but with no significant taper at either end, were apparently commonest in the Thames Estuary, as at Gun Hill, Tilbury (Drury and Rodwell 1973, 89, fig. 19), at Mucking (inf. M. U. Jones), and particularly in North Kent, as at Barksore Farm (Jackson 1972) and various Upchurch Marsh sites (Map 17). There may be definite reasons for this. Wider-ended bars would have sat better on the flat lip of a kiln-wall such as occurred in some of the semi-sunken kilns of the Upchurch area. As two or more long slab-pedestals were used in that region, a sufficient number of such bars could be fitted on them. It follows that non-tapering bars would seem more likely to occur in areas lacking the tradition of a single central pedestal. The arrangements pertaining on sites where both tapering and non-tapering bars have been found, as at Hackleton, Northants. and Perry Barr, have yet to be resolved. Perhaps one variety served as flue-roofing (*see* p. 67).

Clay slab bars. A third type of early bar had a flattish, roughly rectangular section and a slab-like appearance. Tapering and rectangular versions, sometimes perforated, have been recorded in 1st-century contexts in the Upper Nene Valley, for example at Wellingborough (Foster *et al.* 1977) and Rushden (Woods 1969, 33; 1974, fig. 6, D and E). In the 2nd-century semi-sunken kiln at Lincoln Racecourse (Corder 1950a), the bars were wedge-shaped, the ends being 0.05 m and 0.23 m respectively. This modification gave them stability on the flattened kiln-lip and left adequate room on the central pedestal for all their ends. Slab-like clay bars may have anticipated the use of stone slabs as kiln-flooring material in areas with suitable local geology.

Hooked clay bars. A few examples of bars hooked at one or both ends are known from the mid 1st century onwards in such widely separated areas as Grendon, Weekley, and Ecton, Northants. (Johnston 1969, fig. 9, no. 4), Fulmer, Bucks. (Tarrant and Sandford 1972, 187, fig. 9, bar 2), and Norton (Hayes and Whitley 1950). They were presumably mostly used in conjunction with a narrow rim or ledge, or perhaps a pedestal recessed at the top. No coherent pattern is yet discernible.

Curved clay bars. A number of sites have produced the occasional fragment of curved clay bar but none in a very useful context. Those at Pakenham (Kilns 22 and 147) and at Biddlesden, Bucks. (Fig. XVI) appear to be quite unrelated to La Tène kiln-traditions (p. 111 ff.). Curved bars were possibly sometimes used not for oven-floors but in flue-arches (*see* p. 67). They could also have been positioned, while still pliable and unfired, to cope with a variety of impromptu situations where supplementary support was needed.

Anomalous clay bars. A number of unique bars defy classification, among them the perforated 'arrow-shaped' examples from Pakenham, Suffolk, Kiln 22 (Smedley and Owles 1961b, fig. 37). These, unfortunately, occurred in positions suggestive of reuse and their original role within the kiln is not clear.

Stone bars or slabs. These occurred only in areas with suitable geology, but even there they were not common. In the Upper Nene Valley region, they were used from the late 1st century onwards, for example in the Ise Village Kiln, Kettering (Foster 1976), and later at Wakerley (Jackson and Ambrose 1978, 150–51). Their incidence elsewhere was usually very localized, as at Wappenbury, Warwicks. (Stanley and Stanley 1964, 99).

Clay Plates

Evidence for the precise use of these is tenuous. At least some of the larger ones, however, must have been employed as portable components in oven-floors, either alone or with bars. They could also have been used as spacers for separating layers of pots in the kiln. Most, however, seem rather too large for this purpose, averaging 0.15–0.3 m across, and would have obstructed the upward flow of heat. Substantially smaller, but otherwise identical objects have been considered as spacers (*see* p. 41). The larger plates are most often represented by fragments only, posing their own problems of interpretation. At present the following varieties may be distinguished.

Unperforated plates of circular or subrectangular form. It is important to distinguish these from the so-called 'dome plates' (p. 37). In general the former are more carefully made, having properly defined edges and an even thickness of at least 0.025–0.051 m. Like dome plates, they may occasionally be tempered with grass or marked with superficial grass impressions, but are generally of much more regular shape. Such plates as are known in the Nene Valley, from Hardwick Park, Wellingborough (Woods 1974, 277, fig. 6B), and Blandford Avenue, Kettering, Northants., were normally very well finished, averaging 0.17 m in diameter and 0.03 m in thickness. Rougher-surfaced grass-tempered examples occurred in the kiln at Sheringham (Howlett 1960, 213, fig. 5) and in one kiln at Derby Racecourse. In the latter (Brassington 1971, Kiln 1e) three were found arranged in a trefoil form, radiating from a central dumb-bell-shaped pedestal and resting slightly against the kiln-wall. Their use like this, without the addition of bars, is uncertain but they seem rather thin to have supported any very substantial weight. Small straw-tempered bars, which may be relevant, were found among the waste dumped into an adjacent kiln (1c). The kiln with which the plates were associated, however, is only 0.51 m in diameter, too small to have contained a very large, weighty load. Some of the thinner 'Belgic bricks' from Prae Wood (Wheeler and Wheeler 1936, pl. LVIA) may have been fragments of flooring plates. Unlike perforated plates, however, they were not found in direct association with the 'ovens' but in more scattered locations. They may, therefore, have had a different function (inf. P. Barford). The use of unperforated plates was not, apparently, confined to kilns with La Tène affinities. They were associated with the kiln at Little Munden (Saunders and Havercroft 1977, fig. 15, 263), but here could represent the involvement of native potters.

Circular plates with a central perforation (Pl. 21). The best known example of this type, 0.22 m in diameter and almost 0.03 m thick, comes from Weston Favell. It was found *in situ* at

Plate 21.

Wood Burcote, TOWCESTER, Northants.: clay plate, originally roughly circular with central perforation.

0   5   15cm

the top of the kiln-pedestal (Bunch and Corder 1954) which it presumably served to level up. A similar situation was presumed in kilns at Ecton and on Lincoln Racecourse. There is, however, no reason to assume that such plates were used solely in this position. Slightly smaller examples, such as one from Highgate Wood, 0.13 m in diameter, would have been equally suitable for spanning gaps between the bars.

Plates of varying shape, perforated with multiple holes (Fig. VIII). Only a few of these are recorded. The publication of some from Blackmore Thick, Southwick, Northants. (Smith and Todd 1974, 9–10), however, may stimulate the recognition of others. In the past, perforated pieces of fired clay from kiln sites tended to be interpreted, automatically, as shattered fragments of permanent, vent-holed, raised oven-floors. Where such material occurs in conjunction with bars and/or portable supports, it may well be derived from portable, perforated plates. As with the material from Camp Hill (Shaw 1979, 23–4), a 'finished' edge is often a good clue to their recognition. Evidence indicating the possible role of such plates occurred in Kiln IV at Elstow. There, virtually the whole raised oven-floor, of many radiating loose bars, had been abandoned *in situ* (Pl. 22). Several perforated-plate fragments were found above the bars, resting randomly against two jars, the *in-situ* residue of the kiln-stack (inf. G. Dring). Perhaps the plates had been used higher up in the oven to span gaps between vessels and generally aid the stability of the load. From there possibly they had slipped down or had been subsequently thrown back into the chamber during unloading.

At Blackmore Thick, two distinct varieties of multi-perforated plates occurred in association with clay bars. One type was long and oval, approximately 0.2 m by 0.1 m by 0.03 m thick, and perforated with two or three holes, unparalleled elsewhere. The

Plate 22.

Mile Road, nr. Elstow, BEDFORD: clay plates with multiple perforations, thrown back into Kiln IV on its abandonment. Inverted pots comprise residue of kiln-load *in situ* on bar-flooring (scale in ins).

other was wider and subrectangular or oval with more perforations, rather similar to those at Elstow, and averaged 0.3 m by 0.25 m by 0.05 m thick. Some had a notch on one edge, the purpose of which is unclear. It may have enabled them to be linked together by the unique, and otherwise unexplained, prefabricated clay 'links' found on the site.

Perforated plates were apparently not confined to the Welland/Nene and Ouse valleys. In Hertfordshire, fragments of 'pierced bricks' from Belgo-Roman 'hearths' at Prae Wood (Wheeler and Wheeler 1936, 178 ff., pl. LVIB) and Grubs Barn, Welwyn (Rook 1970, 34) may derive from such plates.

At a later date, perforated, often roughly triangular plates were used, possibly for a similar purpose, in several of the specialist Lower Nene Valley kilns, for example at Sibson (inf. B. R. Hartley). Their role is discussed elsewhere (p. 96), but they may well have derived ultimately from the much earlier types in the region.

Heavy Clay Rings

These, averaging 0.2 m in diameter and from 0.01 m to 0.05 m thick, are much larger than the stacking-spacer rings from such sites as Crambeck (Corder 1928, fig. 18). Because of their size,

Plate 23. Wood Burcote, TOWCESTER, Northants.: *right* and *left*, fragments of heavy clay stacking-rings; *centre*, tapering kiln-props.

they may not always have fulfilled precisely the same function as the smaller rings, although there was possibly some overlap in use. They could have been used to supplement bar-flooring in virtually the same way as the perforated plates. Bars and such rings were certainly present among the loose kiln-furniture at Wood Burcote (Pl. 23; inf. R. Turland). There was clear evidence that two or more rings had been superimposed during their firing, either before or in actual use. Possibly they were deliberately designed to key in with one another for stacking, when required.

Flue furnishings

The flue was one of the most vulnerable parts of a kiln structure. It lay at the point of greatest heat and was also exposed to constant wear and tear from the pushing-in of fuel and raking out. In surface-built kilns of temporary materials, turves in the flue region would have required additional protection, being too crumbly for use on their own. They may have been overplastered with clay. A better method, however, was to employ prefabricated clay cheek-pieces as in modern fireplaces (Fig. VIII). As furnace-chambers became sunken or semi-sunken, so often did the flues which served them. Portable flue-cheeks were thus gradually rendered obsolete since it was easier to line the side of a flue-hole or tunnel with clay. Where the subsoil was firm, little or no clay coating was necessary, nor clay roofing if the flue was tunnelled. The transition from portable prefabricated flue-linings to those of clay, plastered *in situ*, was apparently not always immediate and loose cheek-pieces lingered on in some sunken kilns. Prefabricated kiln-furniture was also sometimes incorporated into the clay grouting of the flue. In Kiln VI at Elstow, semicircular clay plates reinforced the lining of the sunken flue (Pl. 24). A pedestal was reused on one side of the flue-lining in the late 1st-century kiln at Great Holme Street, Leicester (inf. J. Mellor).

As with other reusable furniture, portable flue-cheeks are rarely discovered loose *in situ*. The few exceptions comprise 'pedestals' identical to those normally used in kilns for other purposes. This implies some ambiguity over the original role of such items when not found *in situ*. In particular, 'pedestals' more heavily burnt on one side than the other are more likely to have been derived from the flue than the furnace-chamber. Items recorded in use as portable flue-cheeks include prefabricated

Plate 24.

Mile Road, nr. Elstow, BEDFORD: Kiln VI: (*left*) flue with prefabricated clay cheek-plate set into clay lining on each side, and stone blocking stoking-passage; (*right*) detail of semicircular cheek-plate (scales in ins).

dumb-bell-shaped clay pedestals (Fig. VIII) from Wellingborough Kiln I (Foster *et al.* 1977, fig. 8), clay slab-type pedestals at Barksore Farm (Jackson 1972, 288–9) and stone slabs in Grendon Kilns II and III (unpubl. inf. A. McCormick).

Portable flue-roofing *in situ* is even more elusive. Cigar-shaped bars were found over the flue of the kiln at Weston Favell (Bunch and Corder 1954), and in the extension of a flue in Derby Racecourse Kiln 3 (Brassington 1971). This could provide a clue to their possible role on other sites. For example, they occurred in concentration in the flue of a kiln at Iwade (inf. A. Miles), and at Mucking several were incorporated into the clay blocking of a flue (inf. M. U. Jones). Were they used on their own for roofing flues or to support a turf roof? The question is insoluble on present evidence, but nevertheless ought to be considered by future excavators of kilns (*see* Fig. VIII).

A more sophisticated version of prefabricated roofing is to be seen in the thick, curved, clay arch-bar found at Corby, Northants. (Thompson 1902). It may, indeed, have been fitted and fired *in situ* and was thus barely portable. Like stone slab-flooring, stone slab-roofing has been recorded sporadically but not in contexts earlier than the end of the 1st century. It is found bonded with clay more often than on its own.

Late La Tène-derived ('Belgic') surface-built kiln with turf lining and portable prefabricated furniture as in the Upper Nene Valley (plan and elevation after Woods 1974)

Approximate scale of the perspective illustration 1:24

Scale of plan 1:48

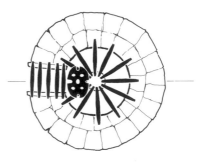

Fig. VIII.

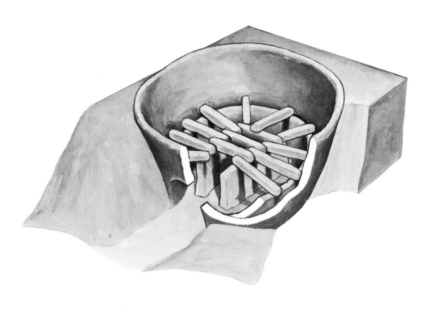

La Tène-derived sunken kiln with clay lining, integral ledge, portable prefabricated furniture and open-topped superstructure as in the Upchurch Marshes (based on Inf. from I. Jackson)

Approximate scale of the perspective illustration 1:24

Scale of plan 1:48

Fig. IX.

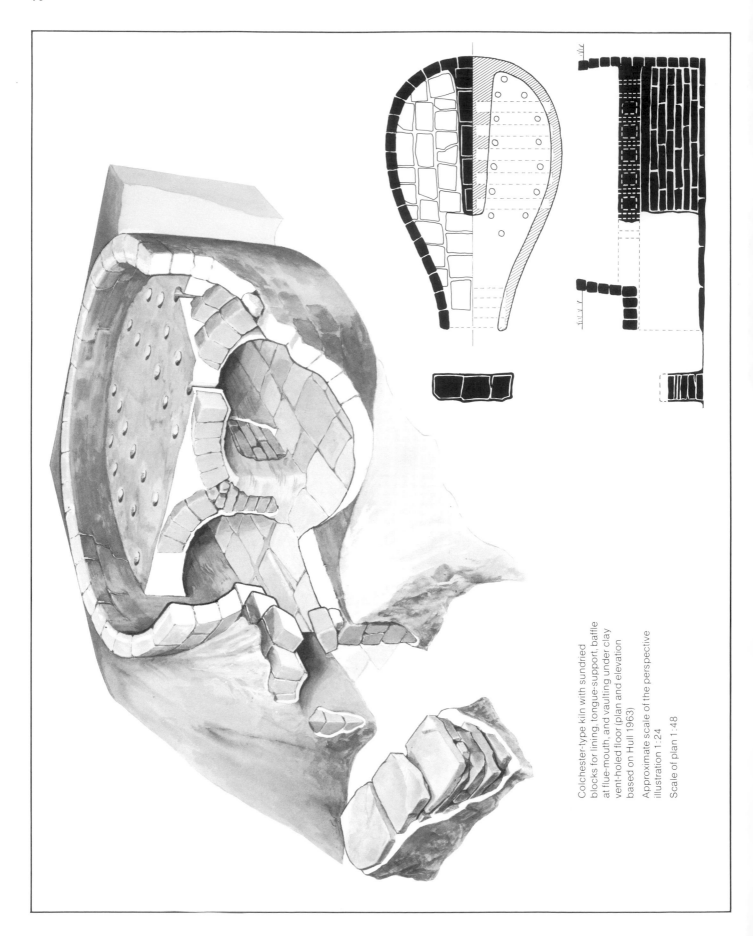

Colchester-type kiln with sundried blocks for lining, tongue-support, baffle at flue-mouth, and vaulting under clay vent-holed floor (plan and elevation based on Hull 1963)

Approximate scale of the perspective illustration 1:24

Scale of plan 1:48

Fig. X.

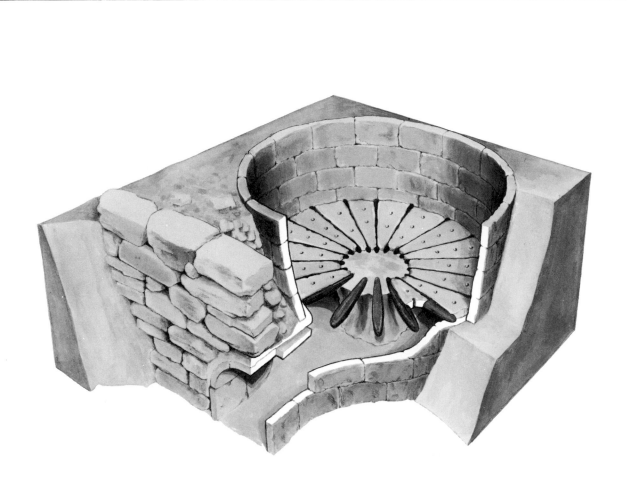

Lower Nene Valley-type kiln of curved blocks, with oven-floor of bars and wedge-shaped perforated plates, a flue of prefabricated components and a coursed stone façade to the flue-mouth (after Artis 1828 and Inf. B.R. Hartley).

Approximate scale of the perspective illustration 1:24

Scale of plan 1:48

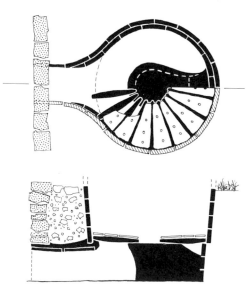

Fig. XI.

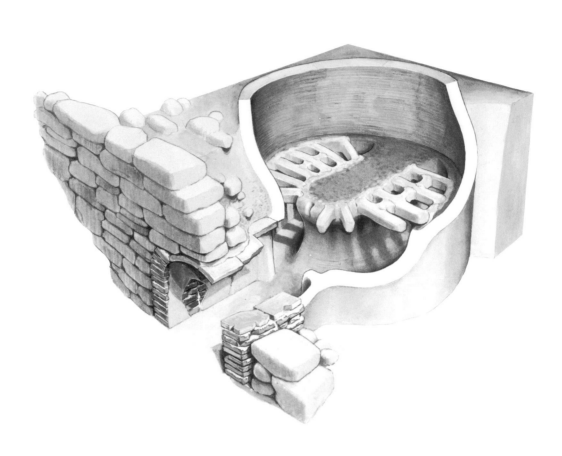

Lower Nene Valley-type kiln with clay lining, integral tongue and ledge, oven-floor of prefabricated bars and spacers overplastered with clay, and coursed stone façade to flue-mouth (plan based on Wild 1973)

Approximate scale of the perspective illustration 1:24

Scale of plan 1:48

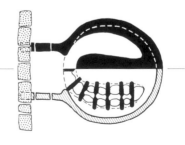

Fig. XII.

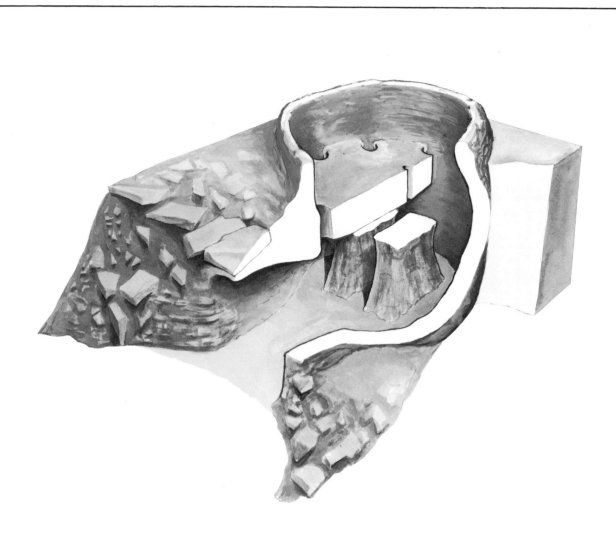

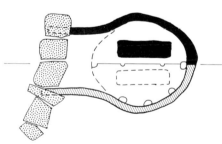

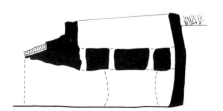

Hartshill/Mancetter third century-type clay-lined kiln with massively built integral pedestals, heavy solid-clay oven-floor, open-topped superstructure and flue of clay incorporating stone pieces (plan and elevation after Hartley 1973a)

Approximate scale of the perspective illustration 1:24

Scale of plan 1:48

Fig. XIII.

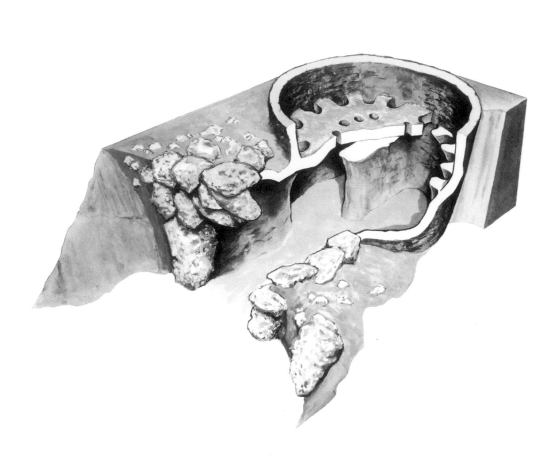

Oxfordshire fourth century-type clay-lined kiln with narrow integral tongue and corbels, solid-clay vent-holed floor and clay-lined flue incorporating stones (plan and elevation based on Young 1972 and 1977)

Approximate scale of the perspective illustration 1:24

Scale of plan 1:48

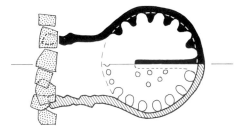

Fig. XIV.

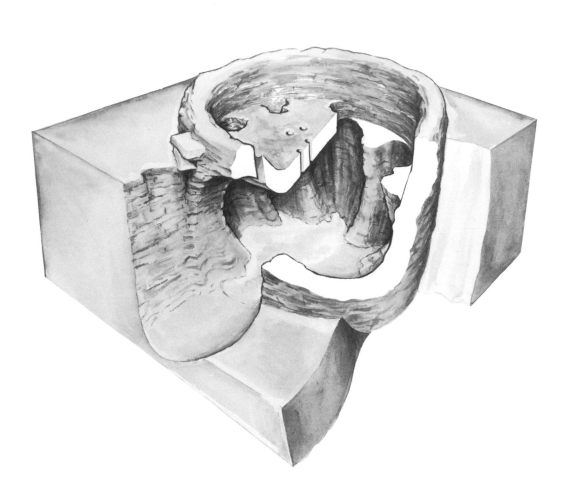

New Forest-type clay-lined kiln with deep furnace-chamber, integral pilasters, solid-clay vent-holed floor and very short flue (plan and elevation based on Swan unpubl. records)

Approximate scale of the perspective illustration 1:24

Scale of plan 1:48

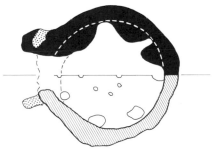

Fig. XV.

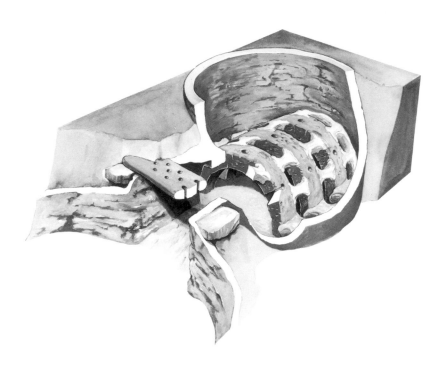

Biddlesden, Bucks, clay-lined kiln with
a barrel-vaulted oven-floor of
prefabricated clay bars and spacers,
positioned while flexible, then luted in
place with clay, and hardened *in situ*
(based on Inf. from R. Turland)

Approximate scale of the perspective
illustration 1:24

Scale of plan 1:48

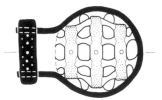

Fig. XVI.

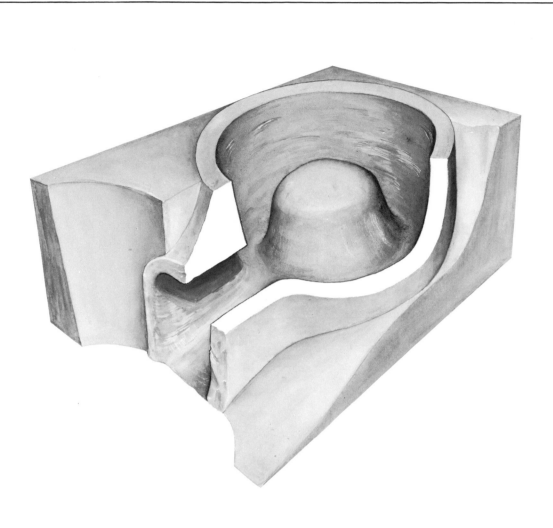

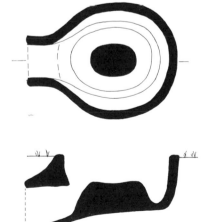

Wattisfield-type (East Anglian) single-chambered single-flued kiln with clay lining and integral 'bollard'-type pedestal (plan and elevation based on B. Brown unpubl. records)

Approximate scale of the perspective illustration 1:24

Scale of plan 1:48

Fig. XVII.

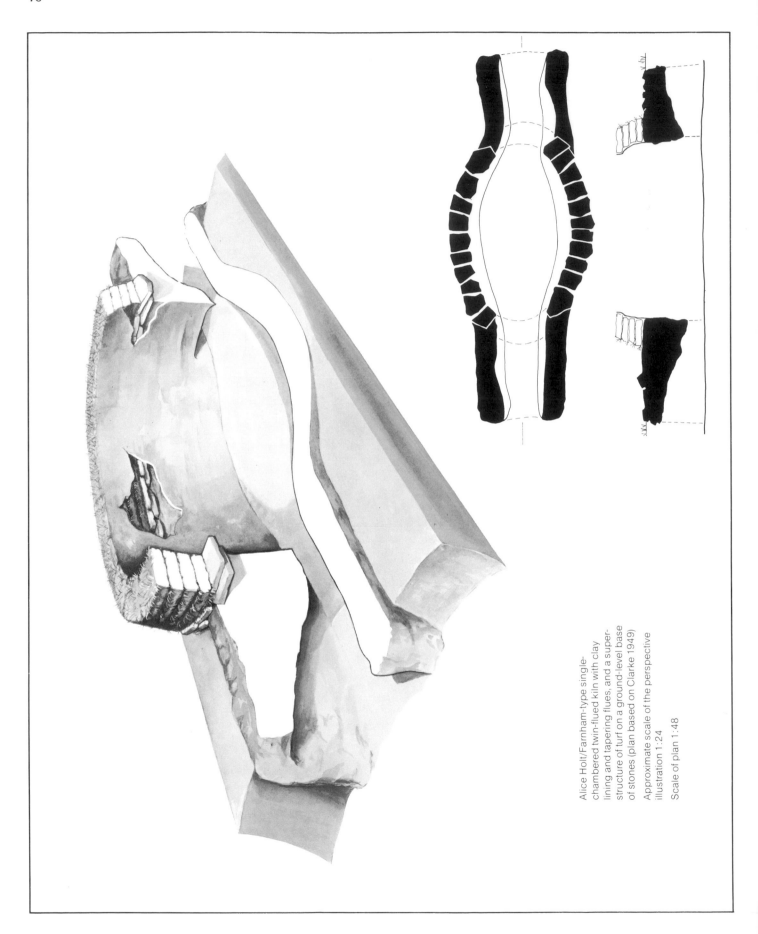

Alice Holt/Farnham-type single-chambered twin-flued kiln with clay lining and tapering flues, and a super-structure of turf on a ground-level base of stones (plan based on Clarke 1949)

Approximate scale of the perspective illustration 1:24

Scale of plan 1:48

Fig. XVIII.

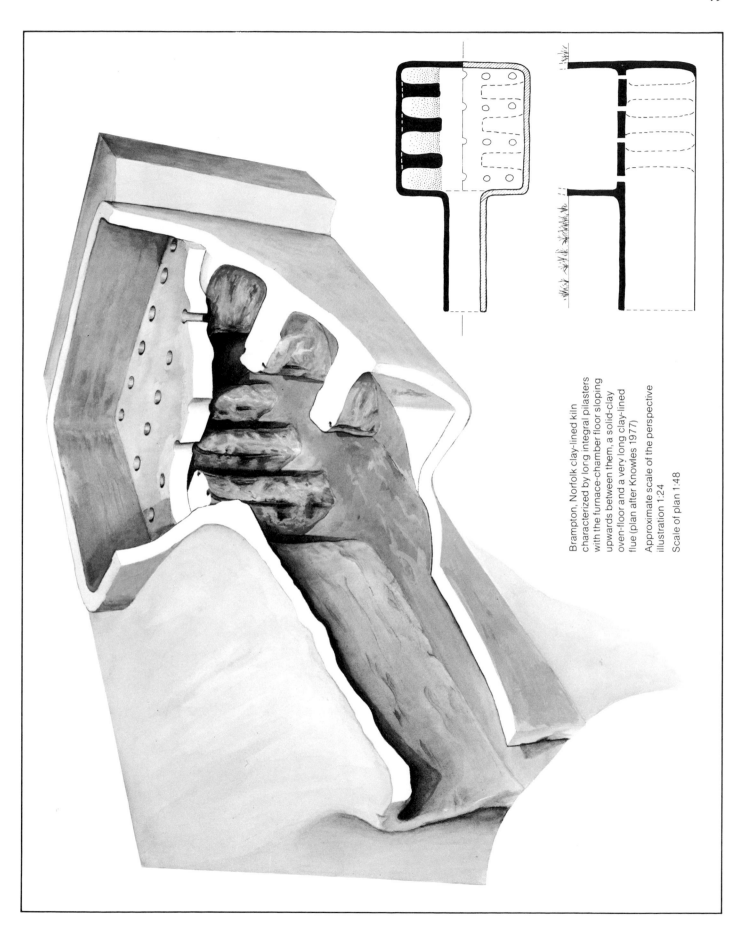

Brampton, Norfolk clay-lined kiln characterized by long integral pilasters with the furnace-chamber floor sloping upwards between them, a solid-clay oven-floor and a very long clay-lined flue (plan after Knowles 1977)

Approximate scale of the perspective illustration 1:24

Scale of plan 1:48

Fig. XIX.

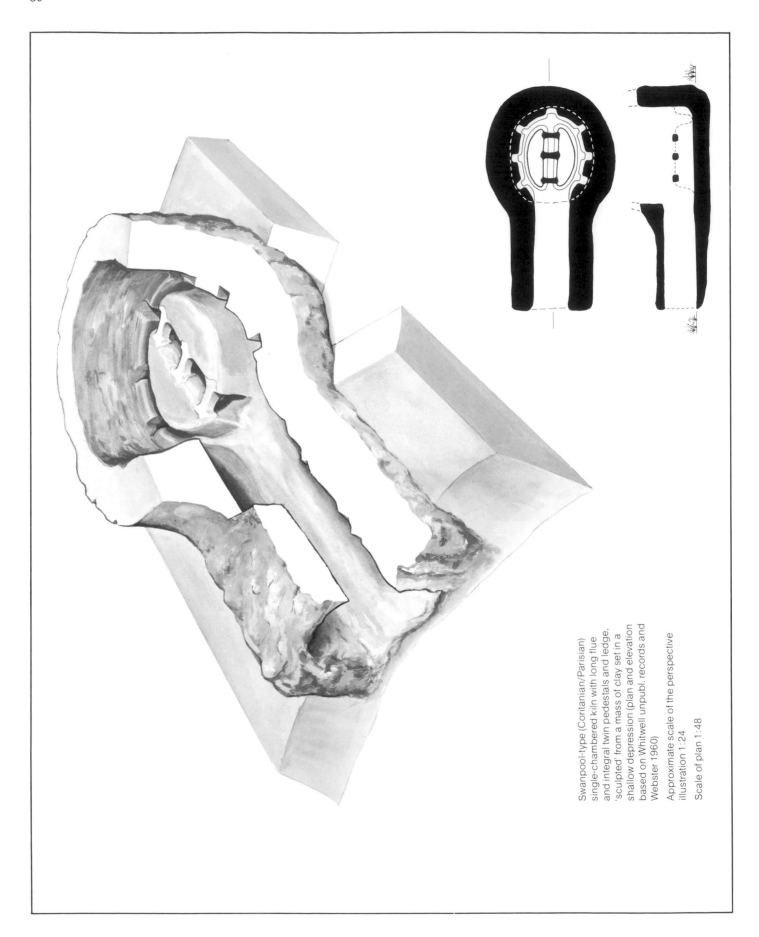

Swanpool-type (Coritanian/Parisian)
single-chambered kiln with long flue
and integral twin pedestals and ledge,
'sculpted' from a mass of clay set in a
shallow depression (plan and elevation
based on Whitwell unpubl. records and
Webster 1960)

Approximate scale of the perspective
illustration 1:24

Scale of plan 1:48

Fig. XX.

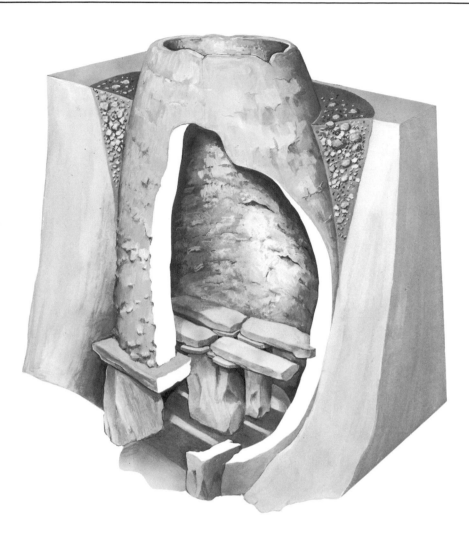

Derbyshire-type deeply-set kiln with
clay lining, stone pedestals, bars, flue-
cheeks and flue-arch, and chimney-like
superstructure (plan and elevation
based on Kay 1962)

Approximate scale of the perspective
illustration 1:24

Scale of plan 1:48

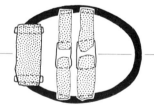

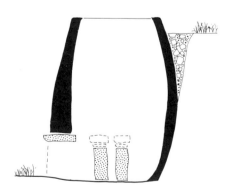

Fig. XXI.

CHAPTER 6

The Conquest period: new kiln types

The initial impact of the Roman Conquest on pottery production from AD 43 onwards was substantial. Not only did the Roman garrisons require pottery in vast quantities, but also classes of vessels not hitherto produced in Britain, and fine table-wares of a quality scarcely achieved by more than a handful of native 'Belgic' potteries mainly in the South-east. Most British workshops apparently continued to manufacture indigenous ranges of vessels in the traditional manner, with little change for several decades (Swan 1981, 130). Some potteries, however, re-orientated their output to satisfy the demands of the Roman army and in the process inevitably tended also to advance their kiln technology more rapidly. Immigrant craftsmen from a variety of sources on the Continent set up a number of other centres, sometimes perhaps encouraged by the army. A very few of them, as a last resort, involved army potters. Their technology ranged from rudimentary kilns and fabrics in late La Tène III traditions, as at Rushden, Longthorpe and possibly Cherry Hinton, to totally Romanized wares and highly sophisticated kiln structures with ultimately Mediterranean origins.

Early centres gearing their production to army consumption may mostly be distinguished by the special character of their output. This is not to say that they never supplied civilian markets. As forts in the South and Midlands were gradually evacuated, many ultimately became dependent on the burgeoning Flavian and later towns for their trade. Almost always, however, a military presence nearby had been the reason for their initial establishment and their distinctive output. Vessel-forms most favoured by the army in the Claudian to early Flavian period include ring-necked or 'Hofheim'-type flagons, two-handled honey-jars, hemispherical or carinated bowls with reeded rims, flanged and wall-sided mortaria, tazze, cheese-presses, lamp-holders, lamp-fillers, imitations of Italian, Gallo-Belgic or samian forms, tripod-vessels, campanulate cups with handles, segmental bowls with lug-handles, spouted jars, storage-jars with folded-back rims (Gillam 100) and copies of Lyon and allied fine-ware cups and jars (Greene 1979, 13–105). Careful assessment of kiln groups with a reasonably high percentage of these forms aids the identification of military-orientated workshops, even when forts which they supplied have not been located. From this, distinctive types of kiln structures may be singled out for study. Many of these vessel-forms reflected popular contemporary ranges in the Rhineland, whence much of the initial Roman invasion force was drawn. It is, therefore, reasonable to expect that some of the kilns in which they were made should exhibit similar relationships.

Rectangular kilns

This small, but distinctive, Claudian to early Flavian group comprises clay-lined kilns, usually large and square, rectangular, or near-rectangular. They had a permanent raised oven-floor supported by lateral, often rectangular pilasters (cf. Fig. III.v; Fig. XIX) and/or a long rectangular tongue projecting from the back of the kiln (Map 9). Most of the raised oven-floors were apparently of solid clay and vent-holed as at Colchester in Kilns 23 and 26 (Hull 1963, 147–9) and Kiln 34 (inf. B. P. Blake); and

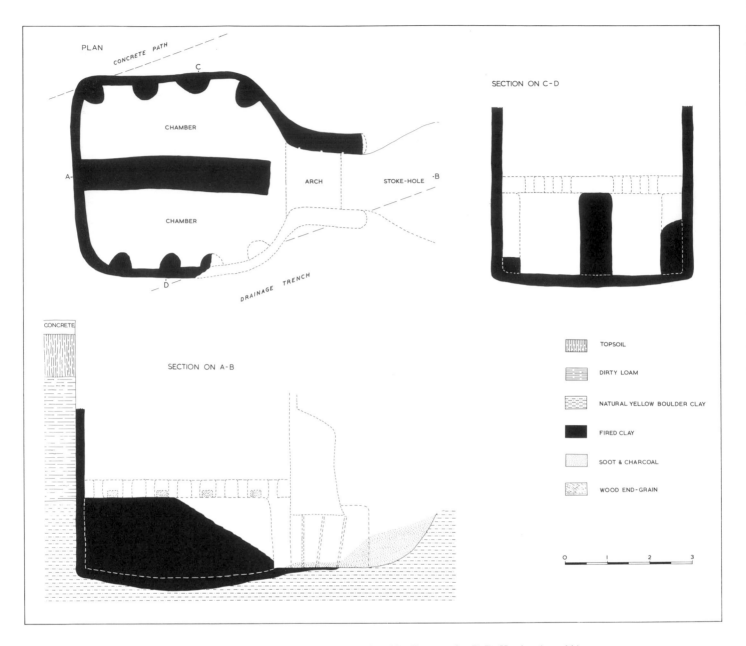

PLAN

CONCRETE PATH

C

CHAMBER

A

CHAMBER

ARCH

STOKE-HOLE

B

D

DRAINAGE TRENCH

SECTION ON C-D

CONCRETE

SECTION ON A-B

TOPSOIL

DIRTY LOAM

NATURAL YELLOW BOULDER CLAY

FIRED CLAY

SOOT & CHARCOAL

WOOD END-GRAIN

0   1   2   3

Fig. XXII. Kiln 1, MORLEY ST PETER, Norfolk: an early rectangular kiln with pilasters: *after* D. R. Howlett (unpubl.).

in Norfolk at Caistor St Edmund, Kilns 1–3 (Atkinson 1932), and Morley St Peter, Kiln I (Norwich Mus. Records; Fig. XXII). Two may have utilized broad bars, of stone at Otford, Kent (Pearce 1930) and clay at Little Munden (Saunders and Havercroft 1977). These possibly served only as an underflooring element which was plastered over with clay and vent-holed. Two kilns, Colchester Kiln 26 and Little Munden, utilized super-imposed tiles in their structures and/or supports. In Kiln I at Morley St Peter, prefabricated sun-dried clay blocks were found loose in the kiln-chamber and one had been incorporated in the kiln-wall (*see also* p. 85). This, combined with the use of pilasters, tends to emphasize the probable ultimate ancestry of this class of kilns, a kiln type with long cross-walls (Pl. 28) which, in Britain

and often on the Continent, is associated with the production of tiles and often mainly constructed of them (*see* p. 87; McWhirr 1979). The evolution of such pilasters, by shortening the kiln cross-walls, is not difficult to envisage. Such a modification would have enabled larger quantities of fuel to be raked into a kiln furnace-chamber, thus facilitating firing-temperatures higher than were necessary or customary for tiles.

Whether with pilasters, or with a tongue-support, these early rectangular kilns clearly belong to the same general family. Moreover, the overall ranges of vessel-types produced in them suggest that they were probably primarily geared to military supply or possibly, as in the case of the Colchester kilns, to the needs of an urban community with military origins and

Romanized tastes. Their relatively large dimensions and great capacity were particularly suitable for the greater quantities of pottery required by the army and for the many larger vessels involved, such as mortaria, storage containers and flagons. The flagons were particularly space-consuming since they could not be stacked inside one another. Many of these vessels were very heavy and the generally more robust character of the kilns, with their long broad tongue and/or pilasters set at close intervals, was thus well-suited to them. The generally greater thickness of such vessels, particularly mortaria, would, as with tiles, have made necessary a long, slow firing. It would indeed be useful to establish by experiment whether the design of pilastered and cross-walled kilns is particularly appropriate for this need. All of them seem to have been intended to produce oxidized pottery, a feature again emphasizing their ultimate link with tile kilns. The firing of oxidized pottery in them may have been partly tradition. To some extent, however, it may also have derived from the fact that square or rectangular kilns were probably more difficult to roof, dome, or seal satisfactorily for reducing wares than circular or oval kilns. When in use they may, like tile kilns, have resembled open-topped boxes.

In the Rhineland, the close links between such kilns and military establishments are unequivocal. This is particularly evident at *Novaesium* (Neuss), the base of *Legio* XX before its move to Britain at the Conquest. Of the twenty Augustan to Claudian kilns excavated on the site (mostly unpublished, but for which records survive at the Rheinisches Landesmuseum, Bonn), five of the six rectangular or square ones appear to be Claudian in date, and the sixth is uncertain but possibly Augusto-Tiberian. The other six Claudian ones are oval or round. None of the eight definitely or probably Augustan kilns is rectangular. Of the rectangular or square Claudian kilns, three had pilasters (Filtzinger 1972, Taf. 97.4) and the other two, although fragmentary or incompletely recorded, seem likely to have been similar. The undated kiln had a long, heavy tongue-support. Another feature of the *Novaesium* kilns also found in some of these rectangular kilns in Britain was the frequent use of sun-dried bricks and/or tiles. In Germany the use of sun-dried bricks at this date tended to be confined to military constructions such as defences (Oelmann 1931, 227 ff.; *R.E.* 8A, 1820; inf. Dr M. Gechter). This provides an additional reason for linking their use in kilns with the presence or influence of the Roman army. Without a full study of Continental kilns it is impossible to judge how common square or rectangular kilns were in the mid to late 1st century. Preliminary work, however, suggests that they were almost exclusively on military sites. In Pannonia, for example, the introduction of square pottery kilns, late in the 1st century, to sites such as *Aquincum* seems to be linked with the presence of the army (Fitz 1980, 329; Bónis 1980, 363 ff.).

Such kilns may not always have been operated by the army itself, but were perhaps sometimes constructed by closely associated civilian potters, working in the military tradition. On occasions, however, soldiers did make pottery (Haalebos and Koster 1981, 70). It has been suggested (Swan 1981, 131) that in

Plate 25. HEVINGHAM, Norfolk: Kiln III, a Flavian to Trajanic sub-rectangular structure, with solid-clay vent-holed floor and tongue-support (scale in ft).

Britain, in the late Neronian to early Flavian period, the building of square or rectangular pottery kilns may have spread from Colchester to the Icenian territory, including sites at Morley St Peter and Caistor St Edmund (the published dating of the latter kilns has recently been reconsidered and is now placed earlier than hitherto). The sub-square Flavio-Trajanic kiln at Hevingham (Kiln III; Pl. 25) may be a slightly later local copy (Norwich Mus. Records). At Colchester, no immediately post-Boudican square or rectangular kilns have been found. Mid to late 2nd-century kilns of these shapes can be shown to represent later reintroductions from the Continent (p. 95). The Antonine square kilns at Brampton, Norfolk (Fig. XIX; Knowles 1977, Kilns E, FI, G, and DII) may, therefore, have been copying the contemporary Colchester ones at this date (p. 122).

Of the much-quoted rectangular late 1st-century mortarium kiln of the potter Vitalis at Lincoln Technical College, the structural evidence as recorded (Baker 1937, and unpubl. photographs in Lincoln City Mus.) is insufficient to support a rectangular chamber. Whether it is an actual kiln is uncertain, though pottery was undoubtedly produced in the immediate vicinity. No kiln structures have been excavated at the several Claudian to Flavian centres producing similar wares and apparently geared to army supply, such as at Eccles (Detsicas 1977) and Hoo, Kent (Blumstein 1956), Nayland with Wissington, Suffolk, Minety, Wilts. (inf. M. Stone), Exeter (inf. P.Bidwell), the St Cuthbert's site in York (King 1974), and the southern side of Field 410 SW at Brockley Hill (Castle 1973a). Square or rectangular pottery kilns could well be found on any of these sites.

Circular or oval kilns with pilasters

Circular or oval kilns with pilaster-supports also first appeared in Britain in the early Conquest period (Map 10). They produced a range of products similar to those made in the contemporary rectangular kilns. Their floors, where known, were of solid clay with vent-holes, but the pilasters varied in shape, number, and constructional technique. In Kiln III at Morley St Peter (unpubl.) and in Kiln 4 at Dragonby (May 1970, 229, pl. xxxb), the rectangular pilasters were built of prefabricated, sun-dried clay blocks (Pls. 26, 27). The latter's products seem likely to have been destined for the fort at Brough across the Humber. At St

Plate 26. MORLEY ST PETER, Norfolk: Kiln III, a late Neronian to early Flavian structure, with rectangular lateral pilasters of prefabricated sun-dried blocks (scale in ft).

Plate 27. Dragonby, SCUNTHORPE, Lincs.: Kiln 4, a circular, Neronian to early Flavian structure, with square pilasters incorporating prefabricated sun-dried bricks (scale in ft).

Stephen's (Area II), Canterbury (Jenkins 1956), broken tiles were used in the raised oven-floor, in the four triangular pilasters and in the later supplementary free-standing rectangular pedestal-support. These constructional techniques may link these kilns with contemporary rectangular ones such as those at Morley St Peter and Little Munden. The two types are probably related. The occurrence of a pilastered rectangular kiln immediately adjacent to an apparently contemporary pilastered oval or circular one at Colchester (Kilns 34 and 35) and at Morley St Peter (Kilns I and III) may support this suggestion.

Circular or oval kilns may have been easier to roof and seal for a satisfactory reducing atmosphere than rectangular ones. By having a rectangular and an oval kiln side by side, potters perhaps had the option of producing either oxidized or reduced wares. There may, however, have been other reasons.

Like their larger rectangular 'cousins', these kilns were apparently introduced from the Continent at the Conquest, presumably by potters following in the wake of, or organized to supply the Roman army. This again tends to be supported by the unpublished evidence from *Novaesium*. Of the twenty excavated kilns in the complex adjacent to the fortress, five are circular or oval, with pilaster-supports and solid-clay vent-holed floors. One is probably Augustan, but the rest are either definitely or almost certainly Claudian (e.g. Filtzinger 1972, 52, Abb. 3). Sun-dried bricks were used in the construction of at least one of the latter kilns.

As with the contemporary rectangular kilns, there is little indication that these early circular or oval kilns with pilasters had any very lasting impact on kiln technology in Britain. Apparently only at Canterbury did this type continue in use in the same location for half-a-century or more after its introduction. Two examples post-dating the Conquest-period have been recorded there, at Whitehall Gardens, Kiln 1 (Jenkins 1960, 59, 60) and North Lane (Bennett 1978). They were of very similar structure and made some of the same general classes of products. Presumably the later ones were geared to the more sophisticated tastes of an expanding urban population. There is no evidence that other kilns with pilasters of Trajanic to Hadrianic and later date have any close relationship with the Conquest-period ones. The products of several of them, particularly those at Paternoster Row, London (Marsden 1969) and Wiggonholt, Sussex (Evans 1974), included very sophisticated and even exotic wares. These may represent a reintroduction of the kiln type from the Continent. They occurred at a time when, after a temporary lull in the Flavian period, there was a marked upsurge in the production of fine wares in Britain. This has been attributed to the possible presence of immigrant potters following the decline of the Lyon and other Continental factories and the slump in the exports to Britain of samian from South Gaul (Marsh 1978, 206–8).

The significance of the circular pilastered kilns at Brampton, Norfolk (Knowles 1977, Kilns H, A5, A6, F and F4) and other Icenian sites must remain uncertain until a full study has been made of their sequence and products (p. 121). Nevertheless, at Brampton they occurred alongside contemporary rectangular kilns with pilasters, in an industry producing both oxidized specialist products and reduced local-type kitchen-wares. Perhaps, as on the earlier sites, their role was complementary.

Circular or oval kilns with tongue-supports

This was a particularly common type over most of the western provinces of the Roman Empire. Its advantages are obvious. The tongue afforded support to the central, weakest part of the floor and lessened its overall span. Its attachment to the back of the kiln made it more stable than a free-standing pedestal. It was also sometimes easier to build since a spit of natural soil could simply be left *in situ*, if the subsoil was of a firm material such as brick-earth. This method occurred in St Stephen's, Canterbury, Area I Kiln (Jenkins 1956, 46) and others. The inherent disadvantage of the tongue-pedestal was its tendency to leave a colder region in the back of the kiln, where the load might have remained underfired. Sometimes this could have been partly offset by a vent at the back of the kiln-superstructure (p. 38; Fig. II.v).

In the main, circular kilns with tongues were apparently a Roman introduction to Britain and their products are always Romanized in character. Rather surprisingly, unlike the rectangular kilns with tongues, none appears to be earlier than Neronian to Flavian. The earliest examples occur at Trent Vale, in association with bar-flooring (Mountford *et al.* 1968), at Caistor St Edmund (Kiln IV), possibly at Morley St Peter (Kiln II) and at Cherry Hinton (Lethbridge 1948). The type was most universally popular in the Flavian and Trajanic periods, for example at Middleborough Cattle Market, Colchester (Kiln 36); in Norfolk, at Brampton (Green 1977, 37 ff., Kiln B17), Hevingham (Kilns 1–3), and Lyng (Norwich Mus. Records); at Derby Racecourse (Brassington 1971, Kilns 1b, 3, 4a, 8a, 8b); in St Stephen's, Canterbury, Area I Kiln; at Brampton, Cumberland (Hogg 1965, Kilns 3 and 5); at Northwich (Curzon and Hanson 1971); at Ardleigh, near Colchester (VCH, *Essex* iii (1963), 36, fig. 8); and in some of the kilns within the industry of the Verulamium area (Brockley Hill/Radlett; p. 97). Thereafter it tended mainly to be confined to a few major centres and their satellites, for example Brampton, Norfolk, the Verulamium area (p. 98) and Hartshill/Mancetter (p. 99), and the colour-coated industries of Colchester (p. 92), Oxfordshire (p. 102), and the Nene Valley (p. 96). Of these, it was already established in the first four, and possibly five, by the end of the first decade of the 2nd century AD. In all of these places, except Hartshill/Mancetter, this general form continued in use through the life of the industry.

Other early kiln introductions to Britain

Several other kilns, apparently occurring in isolation, seem likely to have been innovations at the Conquest or shortly after. The oval or circular kiln at Stowmarket (inf. S. West and J. Plouviez), with its two horseshoe-shaped pedestals and solid-clay vent-holed floor, is difficult to fit into any indigenous kiln sequence, despite the La Tène III ('Belgic') character of some of its output. The

probable presence of flagons among its products is also anachronistic at this date and the possibility of relatively local craftsmen working alongside immigrant potters should be considered. Similarly, at Chichester there is an exotic single-chambered kiln, of sun-dried bricks, with a range of products probably geared to military supply (*see* p. 118; Down 1978, 53, 56 ff.).

Trajanic kilns near military establishments

In the North Midlands and North, the Trajanic period yields a substantial body of evidence for large groups of kilns producing pottery for adjacent military garrisons (Maps 4, 5). Potteries established at about this period which fall into that category include Holt (Grimes 1930), Grimscar Wood, near Slack, Yorks. W.R. (Purdy and Manby 1973), Quernmore, Lancs. (Leather 1973), Brampton, Cumberland (Hogg 1965), Scalesceugh (Richardson 1973) and possibly Muncaster, Cumberland (Bellhouse 1960; 1961) and Manchester (unpubl.), also Derby Racecourse (Brassington 1971; 1980), Piercebridge (inf. P. Scott), and probably Aldborough, Yorks. W.R. (Jones 1971, 53 ff.). The kiln at Northwich, which just post-dates the first phase of military occupation on that site, must surely also represent the residue of a similar industry formerly serving the garrison. Of these potteries, the first six and possibly seven also made tiles. Within the group as a whole, several kilns manufacturing pottery alone were generally similar. They were circular or oval with a raised oven-floor of bars, subsequently overplastered, thus giving the superficial impression of a solid-clay vented floor (*see* p. 62).

Wales, most of the North Midlands and North of England lacked strong indigenous ceramic traditions at the Conquest. Pottery, handmade and of very poor quality, was manufactured there only in small amounts, mostly on a domestic basis, and very little circulated from adjacent areas. Kilns in those regions must therefore represent the immigration, in the wake of military conquest, of potters from other parts of Britain, particularly the East and North-east Midlands, areas where such kilns, under the stimulus of army demands, had already been rapidly evolving.

In some of the tileries/potteries in this group, particularly Holt, there are difficulties in distinguishing between kilns used for pottery and those for tiles. It should be emphasized that in Britain, unlike on much of the Continent, particularly in Italy and the Mediterranean area (Cuomo 1979), this distinction is generally quite clear-cut. On only two known British sites, Harrold (Kiln 7) and Arbury, Warwicks. (Scott 1975), was a structure of a type usually associated with pottery manufacture apparently used for firing tiles. The basic kiln type most characteristic of tileries, particularly military ones in Britain, was normally large and rectangular. It was often lined with tile or stone and had multiple parallel lateral cross-wall supports interrupted only by the arched opening of the central axial channel running from the flue (cf. Fig. III.iv; Pl. 28). The raised oven-floor was either of specially-made perforated tiles, sometimes overplastered, or of vent-holed solid clay. The heavy

ELEVATION

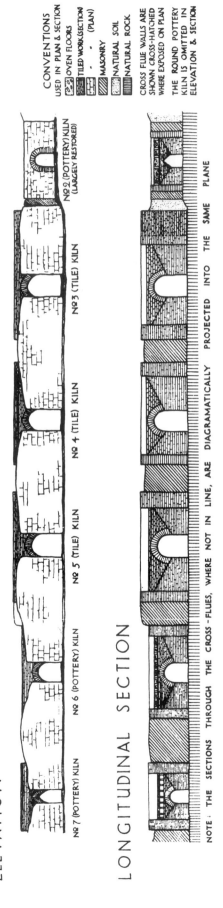

No 2 (POTTERY) KILN
(LARGELY RESTORED)

No 3 (TILE) KILN

No 4 (TILE) KILN

No 5 (TILE) KILN

No 6 (POTTERY) KILN

No 7 (POTTERY) KILN

LONGITUDINAL SECTION

NOTE : THE SECTIONS THROUGH THE CROSS-FLUES, WHERE NOT IN LINE, ARE DIAGRAMATICALLY PROJECTED INTO THE SAME PLANE

GENERAL PLAN

CONVENTIONS
USED IN PLAN & SECTION

OVEN FLOORS
TILED WORK (SECTION)
" · - (PLAN)
MASONRY
NATURAL SOIL
NATURAL ROCK

CROSS FLUE WALLS ARE
SHOWN CROSS-HATCHED
WHERE EXPOSED ON PLAN

THE ROUND POTTERY
KILN IS OMITTED IN
ELEVATION & SECTION

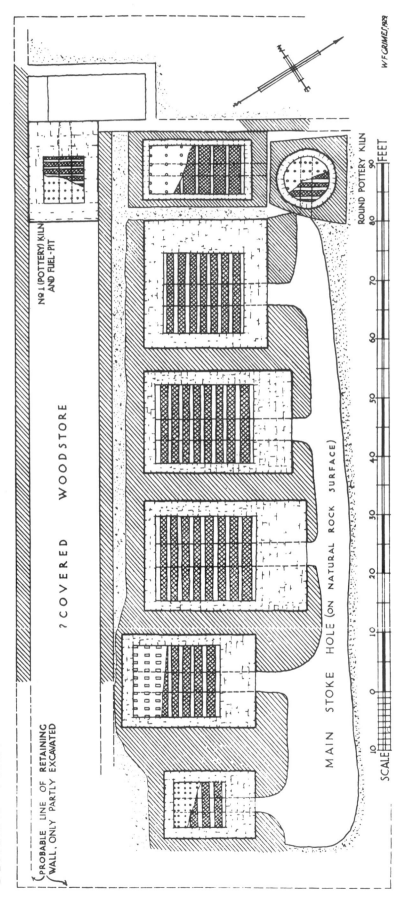

W.F.GRIMES/1928

No 1 (POTTERY) KILN
AND FUEL-PIT

? COVERED   WOODSTORE

PROBABLE LINE OF
RETAINING
WALL, ONLY PARTLY EXCAVATED

MAIN   STOKE   HOLE   (ON   NATURAL   ROCK   SURFACE)

ROUND POTTERY KILN

SCALE

FEET

Plate 28. HOLT, Denbigh.: battery of military tile and pottery kilns showing the substantial cross-walls built to support the raised oven-floors: *after* Grimes (1930, fig. 19).

weight and size of tiles undoubtedly dictated the need for substantial floor-supports at such frequent intervals. Because of the space these occupied, fuel presumably could not be pushed under the raised oven-floor. To accommodate extra fuel, therefore, a long flue was usually provided or, occasionally, two parallel flues. These kilns were apparently Graeco-Roman in origin and common throughout the Roman world, particularly in Eastern Europe and the Mediterranean area (e.g. Fletcher Valls 1965; Rădulescu 1969). They were well suited for other thick, heavy items requiring slow firing, such as mortaria which, in the late Republic and early Empire, were manufactured alongside tiles in the brick-fields near Rome (Hartley 1973d), amphorae and large flagons. It is thus hardly surprising that this type was most favoured by legionary and auxiliary works-depots such as Holt, where Raetian and Eastern Mediterranean traits in some of the vessel-types, and in the use of saggars for firing lead-glazed wares, have been suggested. By tradition, however, such kilns produced oxidized goods, which may be why military or so-called 'legionary' pottery tends to be orange or buff. Presumably this oxidizing tradition had been extended to the related kilns with pilasters (p. 83 ff.).

Circular versions of such kilns, with similar cross-walls (Fig. III.iv), are also well attested in the Empire. As yet only one has been found in Britain, at Holt (Pl. 28), where it was considered to have been used for pottery (Grimes 1930, Kiln 2). Of the rectangular kilns there, the excavator (T.A. Acton) linked four (1, 7, ?2, ?6) to pottery manufacture and the remainder to tile production. Unfortunately, difficulties surrounding the compilation of the excavation report after Acton's death make it impossible to assess the reliability of these interpretations. The abundant pottery found in Kilns 1 and 7 could have been dumped there as waste from the circular kiln, which was clearly an afterthought. Pottery manufacture on this site may, therefore, have been only a secondary activity, begun after some of the tile kilns had gone out of use. Unfortunately, the Continental evidence for a correlation between the function and shape of such kilns with cross-walls is not helpful. At the contemporary military depot at Holdeurn near Nijmegen, Holland (Holwerda and Braat 1946), the reverse applied. The circular or oval kilns with cross-walls were assigned by the excavator to tile production, while adjacent rectangular kilns of similar substructure were linked to pottery manufacture. There were also smaller, more usual types of pottery kilns within the same complex. The probability thus remains that at such works-depots there was no marked distinction between kilns for pottery and those for tile. Perhaps the composition of the loads alternated. Even the possibility of mixed loads cannot be discounted until experiment has shown it to be impractical.

Such considerations apply at Grimscar Wood, where wasters, attesting pottery as well as tile production, were found near a rectangular kiln with normal 'tile-kiln' characteristics. At Muncaster, a complex in which pottery production may also be reasonably surmised, one of two presumed tile kilns (Kiln I) has slightly foreshortened cross-walls, like long pilasters, and a short tongue-like back support. It could be viewed as a hybrid between a normal tile kiln and one of the rectangular types of pottery kilns (see p. 84). This problem occurs at Lythe Brow, Quernmore, where both pottery and tile wasters occurred near a fragment of a possible tile kiln. At York, also at this date, waste legionary tiles and rejects of pottery in so-called 'legionary' tradition occurred in very close association, although no kiln structures survived in the area excavated (King 1974).

90

Plate 29. Normangate Field, CASTOR, Hunts.: E.T. Artis's 1822 kiln excavation: *after* Artis (1828, pl. XL).

CHAPTER 7

Kilns of the major industries

Perhaps the most significant point to emerge, even from a brief survey of kiln types in the major industries, particularly Colchester (Essex), the Nene Valley (Hunts., Peterborough and Northants.), and Hartshill/Mancetter (Warwicks.), is that while for any given period one or two kiln types tend to predominate, a few completely different kilns were apparently in use simultaneously. How should this observation be interpreted in cultural, technological, and socio-historical terms?

From the study of potters' stamps on several wares, it is well established that a great deal of continuous movement occurred within the pottery industries of the Western Empire in the 1st and 2nd centuries AD. Although such evidence begins to fail towards the end of the 2nd century, it is probable that the migrating habits of potters continued during the 3rd and 4th centuries. The phenomenon is particularly well attested in the samian industries of Gaul (Hartley, B.R. 1977). In Britain evidence is growing for the movements of mortarium manufacturers (Hartley 1973b, 41; 1973a, 144; Hartley and Richards 1975), all of it not yet assessed collectively in a single publication. Some of them are known to have migrated as many as three times during their working lives.

Such movements sometimes resulted in the foundation of entirely new factories, as often happened when potters migrated northwards. In Britain, there was a tendency in the 1st and 2nd centuries for mortarium manufacturers in particular to move from the South to the Midlands and North, namely towards their most important markets, the great concentration of troops on the northern frontiers. Sometimes, however, a migrant potter transferred his workshop not to a completely new site, but to an established pottery, presumably attracted by the success of its products, the ready availability of raw materials such as wood and clay, the particular quality of the clay, for example the superb 'pipe clay' of the Hartshill/ Mancetter area, and not least, by the ease of access and proximity to good consumer outlets such as towns or forts. Even when potters' stamps are lacking, it is sometimes possible to detect the presence of a newcomer on an existing site by the non-local style of his products. Sometimes, however, a migrant potter, attracted by the success of an industry, might have set up his workshop within a pre-existing complex and copied its best-selling products.

Technology in the ancient world seems to have been inherently conservative and less prone to change than were the ranges and styles of such manufactured goods as pottery. Moreover, kilns of different structure can often produce identical or near-identical products, if fired under the same atmospheric conditions. Granted these facts, it seems unlikely that most newcomers to a pottery centre would suddenly change the kiln structure already familiar to them, merely to fire different vessel-forms. Non-standard kilns within a large pottery-manufacturing complex may thus reasonably be ascribed to incoming potters with alien kiln traditions. No doubt immigrant potters sometimes gradually absorbed elements of the standard kiln technology of the centre to which they had migrated, and on occasions may have shared kilns, workshops and other facilities with established potters. In other instances, there are hints that they may have influenced that technology. Clearly, in a complex of kilns with mixed traits, it is often difficult to decide who influenced whom!

Colchester, Essex

Colchester's prominent position in the 1st century, successively as legionary fortress and *colonia*, is amply reflected in the number and sophistication of the Claudio-Neronian kilns (Hull 1963, 147–8, 157–61 and unpubl.; Maps 4, 15). The products of the exotic rectangular kilns, Nos. 23, 26, 34, with tongue or pilaster-supports, and of the circular pilastered kiln No. 35 (*JRS* li (1961), 185, pl. XIV.4) must have been geared particularly to the needs of Colchester's military consumers (Dunnett 1975, 128; Wacher 1978, 117). There are similarities between some of these kilns and some of the Tiberio-Claudian kilns at *Novaesium* (Neuss), North Germany, the previous base of *Legio* XX before its departure for Britain in AD 43 (*see* pp. 85, 86). It may not be coincidence that at least part of this legion was at Colchester until *c*. AD 49 (Frere 1974, 87). Some of its veterans were also probably settled there when the *colonia* was founded in AD 49 (ibid., 95). Whether any of these excavated Claudio-Neronian kilns were operated by the army itself, as elsewhere on the Continent (Haalebos and Koster 1981, 70), or were linked more indirectly, is uncertain. The existence, however, of a pre-Flavian mortarium from Colchester, inscribed 'IVSTI SVPERI' before firing, may at least imply a military pottery-making establishment in the general vicinity (Frere 1974, 87, n.18). Most, and possibly all of these early kilns apparently ceased operating at the time of the Boudican revolt and sack of Colchester in AD 61, if not before. There is no indication yet that these distinct traditions of kiln technology continued after that period.

The evidence, particularly that of potters' stamps on mortaria, suggests that Colchester's pottery industry flourished in the Flavian period (Birley 1980, 132–4; inf. K. F. Hartley). Only one contemporary kiln, however, is known, Kiln 36 (inf. P. Crummy). Its situation, at the Middleborough Cattle Market Site immediately outside the NW corner of the city's defensive circuit, supports Wacher's tentative suggestion that the industry may have been moved nearer to the *colonia* in its immediately post-Boudican phase (1978, 117). The kiln had a long oval chamber, a long tile-built tongue-support, and a solid-clay vent-holed floor. Although late Flavian, structurally it would not have appeared out of place among many of Colchester's Antonine kilns. This basic form (Fig. X) was to predominate at Colchester for at least a century and a half. It may, therefore, have been established there during the late Flavian period or shortly before. Another relatively early kiln of this typical 'Colchester form', found at Ardleigh within a few miles of the city, is dated to within the late 1st to early 2nd century (VCH, *Essex* iii (1963), 36, fig. 8).

The 2nd century was the heyday of Colchester's pottery industry. The manufacture of colour-coated wares which closely imitated Lower Rhineland products had already begun by or during the Hadrianic period. Rough-cast cornice-rimmed beakers of Colchester origin occurred in small quantities in early contexts on Hadrian's Wall (Anderson 1980, 37). The distinctively Rhineland character of these vessels could well indicate the arrival of immigrant potters from that area. Whether any of the excavated kilns may be linked to the production of these wares at such an early date, however, is problematical. All of those belonging to the large complex producing colour-coated wares (*inter alia*) at Warren Fields, Sheepen (Colchester Kilns 15–22 and 30–31), appear on balance to be probably Antonine. Only a limited part of the pottery site, however, was explored (Fig. XXIII). The published report (Hull 1963, 13–147) lacks full details of stratigraphy and the specific provenance of material, and proportionately little pottery survives in Colchester Museum for reassessment. The situation is complicated by the close proximity of many of the kilns to one another. Frequently wasters from one kiln-firing had been dumped into an adjacent earlier kiln, or pits had been levelled up with wasters from elsewhere, a perennial problem for kiln excavators. Hull did however record evidence, probably from the NW corner of the site, of Hadrianic activity around a well (Well 5), near which waster flagons of late 1st to early 2nd-century date had been dumped (1963, 142, pl. XX). It is thus near there that earlier kilns should be sought.

The one kiln, No. 21, long accepted as indicating the presence of intrusive potters, excavated in the Warren Fields complex, was connected with the manufacture of samian ware. It probably belonged to shortly after the middle of the 2nd century and a date of *c*. 160 seems most likely, for reasons too complex to discuss here. Largely demolished in antiquity, it was massive, almost 2.5 m diameter externally, with a very long tile and clay-built 'flue' extending to the back of the furnace-chamber. It also had a wide range and quantity of associated rings, tubes, stoppers, discs and similar objects of fired clay. These elements clearly mark it out from the adjacent kilns. It is not proposed to discuss it in detail or illustrate its structure and technology, the only known example of that type in Britain. The limited evidence and its problems have been detailed by Hull (1963, 20–34). Kilns of this general type are well known from several of the East Gaulish samian factories, for example at Heiligenberg, Alsace (Forrer 1911, 31, fig. 8, 33, figs. 8–10), at Blickweiler and Eschweiler (Knorr and Sprater 1927, Tb. 37–40 and Taf. 102–4), and at Cannstatt (Paret 1932, 184, Abb. 85). At Sinzig on the Middle Rhine, only the characteristically long flue remained of a similar kiln, otherwise stripped of its tubes and structural components (Hagen 1917, Taf. XXVIII, Kiln 1). At least fourteen, and probably twenty, potters were apparently involved in samian manufacture on the Warren Fields site. The evidence of the dies of potters' stamps shows that several of them were immigrants (Hartley, B. R. 1977, 256–7). Two, Lipuca and Miccio, who had possibly originally worked in the samian factory at La Madeleine (East Gaul), had migrated to Colchester from the Sinzig samian pottery. Another, Minuso, had previously worked at Trier, possibly elsewhere in the Argonne, and at Sinzig. The Continental affinities of two brooches and a bead in the potters'

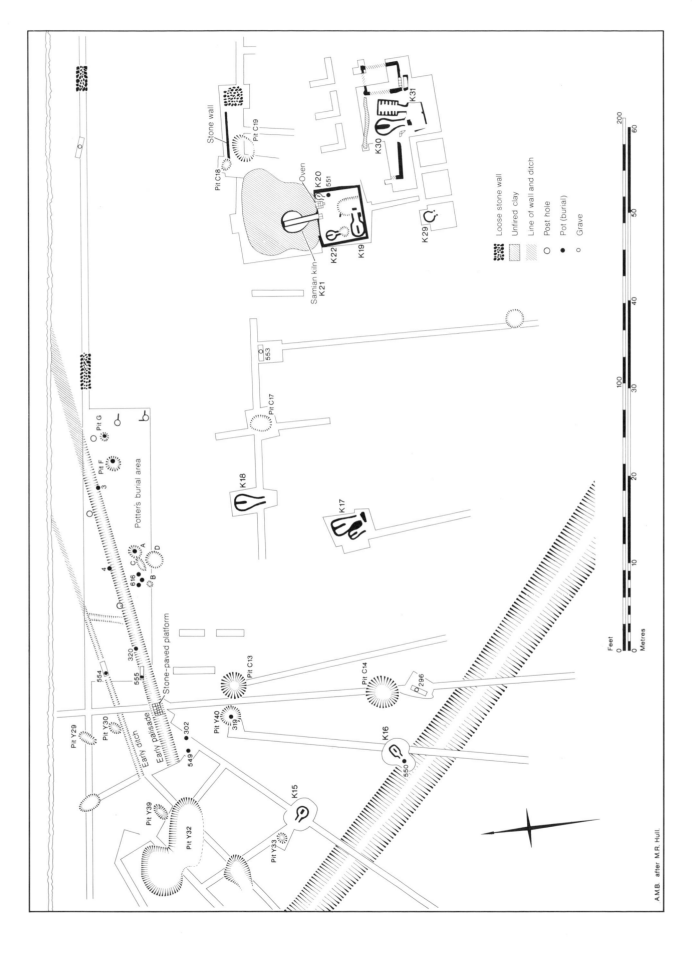

Fig. XXIII. Warren Fields, COLCHESTER: layout of kiln-complex excavated in 1933 and 1959: based on plans by M. R. Hull.

A.M.B. after M.R. Hull.

Stone wall

Pit C19

Pit C18

K31

K30

Samian kiln
K21

Oven

K20
551

K22   K19

K29

Pit C17

553

K18

K17

Pit G

Pit F
3

Potters burial area

A
C
616   B   D
4

554
555   320

Stone-paved platform

Pit C13

Pit C14

296

Early ditch

Early palisade

Pit Y29
Pit Y30

302
549

Pit Y40
319

K16
550

Pit Y39

K15

Pit Y32

Pit Y33

Loose stone wall
Unfired clay
Line of wall and ditch
Post hole
Pot (burial)
Grave

Feet
0   100   200

Metres
0   10   20   30   40   50   60

burial area near the Warren Fields kilns also emphasizes the immigrant status of their owners (Hull 1963, 144–7, Graves 302, 553; inf. S. Esmonde-Cleary). Some of these craftsmen no doubt introduced their own kiln technology with their pottery.

All or most of these Continental samian workshops were probably involved in the production of other types of fine ware, including colour-coated beakers (Hartley, B.R. 1977, 257), and even sometimes mortaria. At Colchester the potter Acceptus (ii) stamped samian, colour-coated 'hunt cups', and mortaria of Cam. 501B, almost certainly an exotic form (Hull 1963, 85). Unfortunately, his origins cannot yet be traced back to the Continent with any certainty. Some of the potters who moved from the East Gaulish samian factories to Colchester thus probably made several classes of pottery. The resulting fresh infusion of techniques and ideas was presumably grafted on to Colchester's pre-existing Rhineland-derived colour-coated industry. Its products thus continued to resemble closely their Continental prototypes in the second half of the 2nd and into the 3rd century (Anderson 1980, 35–7). This point has implications for the kiln structures of that period.

Of the kilns situated immediately adjacent to the samian kiln, most appear to have been more or less contemporary with it (Fig. XXIII). Some were certainly used for the firing of colour-coated wares, notably Kilns 20, 30, possibly also 19 and (?)31. Less certain is the chronological relationship to it of Kiln 17. This was associated with colour-coated wares but was not immediately adjacent. Certain elements in the design and constructional techniques of some of these kilns suggest that they reflected the innovations of their immigrant builders. The method of building kiln-walls, oven-floor supports or vaulting with shaped clay blocks, whether raw, pre-fired or sun-dried, as in Kilns 19, 20, 29, 30 and 31 (Fig. X), is particularly characteristic of structures in the samian and colour-coated industries of Gaul and the Rhineland, as at Xanten (Heinberg and Rüger 1972, figs. 3, 4), Sinzig (Hagen 1917, Taf. XXVIII), Rheinzabern (Ludovici 1905, 151, fig. 7), Waiblingen-Beinstein in Würtemberg (Paret 1932, 139, Abb. 88), Trier (Loeschcke 1928, 68, Abb. 1), and Lezoux (Chenet and Gaudron 1955, fig. 40). It is perhaps significant that in the Warren Fields complex, the technique occurred only in kilns near the samian kiln; these comprised Kilns 19, 20 and 22 (all immediately adjacent to and obviously closely associated with it), Kiln 29 (immediately post-dating it), and Kilns 30 and 31 (possibly post-dating it). Such blocks were absent in Kilns 15, 16, 17 and 18. Scattered well to the W of the samian kiln and not obviously linked to it as satellites, they might thus just pre-date it. This can be no more than speculation on the limited available evidence. None of the pottery known to be associated with them need necessarily be later than that of the other kilns.

Elsewhere in Colchester, of the six kilns utilizing block construction, Kilns 7, 13a & b, 24 and 25 were certainly in production later than the samian kiln group, and Kiln 1 and Oaks Drive Kiln 3 were probably so, but on more limited evidence. All, except possibly Kiln 1, were connected with the manufacture of specialist products such as colour-coated wares or mortaria. In the 2nd and 3rd centuries in Britain, the technique of block-construction is known otherwise only in the Lower Nene Valley potteries (p. 96; Fig. XI). That industry has, for some time, been considered to have had close connections with the colour-coated production centres of East Gaul and the Rhineland (Dannell 1973, 141; Hartley 1960, 21). The use of clay block-construction in some of the Colchester kilns, therefore, was apparently probably a direct result of the arrival of craftsmen perhaps associated with the immigrant samian potters from those areas.

A similar link could well be reflected in the use of a 'baffle' immediately in front of the kiln-flue, as recorded in Colchester Kilns 17, 19, 30, 24 and 25 (Fig. X). Hull (1963, 16) considered that this was intended to aid the control of the draught and, if necessary, actually to assist the closure of the flue entrance instead of using a stone. Such an immovable block must have proved a hindrance to the stoking and raking out of the flue. Much extra material, moreover, would have been needed to ensure the total flue sealing necessary for a proper reducing atmosphere. All the Colchester kilns with such a feature were used for firing colour-coated wares. Elsewhere in Britain, the only kiln known to have had a similar baffle, at Pakenham, site 147 (Smedley and Owles 1961b; 1964), also produced colour-coated beakers in the same general traditions (p. 111). Many of the Colchester colour-coated vessels were sold with an oxidized, or only partially reduced, surface finish. The kilns producing them may, therefore, never have been intended to be totally sealed for a fully reducing atmosphere. The prime purpose of the baffle may thus have been to combat sudden draughts, or a sudden rush of air at the cooling stage in kilns generally larger than average and therefore more prone to temperature fluctuations, but needing particularly careful control because of their finer and more specialized products.

What of the basic form of the Warren Fields and other 2nd and 3rd-century Colchester kilns? Kilns used predominantly for colour-coated wares were characterized by a solid-clay vent-holed floor and a long tongue-support or, in a few examples, a long rectangular pedestal with only a narrow gap between it and the back wall. They also had a rather elongated pear or bottle-shaped chamber (Fig. X), sometimes with a tendency to squaring-off at the back. Kilns with these features are also particularly characteristic of the contemporary colour-coated and allied industries of East Gaul and the Rhineland, for example at Xanten (Heinberg and Rüger 1972, fig. 3), at Rheinzabern (Ludovici 1905, 155, figs. 22–3, 157, fig. 33), and at Trier (Loeschcke 1928, 68, Abb. 1). As already indicated, pear-shaped kilns with a tongue and a solid-clay vent-holed floor, as a general type, were already in use in the Colchester area by the late Flavian period (e.g. Kiln 36). This form, however, may well have been reintroduced in the first third of the 2nd century, with the establishment of a Rhineland-derived colour-coated industry, and again in the middle of that century when the samian potters and their associates arrived. Additionally, the second time, baffles and block-construction techniques may have been used. This ensured the continuous usage of this kiln type in Colchester well into the 3rd century, perhaps until the demise of the colour-coated industry.

A less common, but distinctive kiln type is worth discussion. Near the samian kiln at Warren Fields was a rectangular five-pilastered structure (Kiln 31), lined and vaulted with pre-shaped blocks. It had been used to fire stamped mortaria and possibly also colour-coated wares. Certainly, its operation was closely linked with that of Kiln 30 immediately adjacent, which was used for colour-coated wares. In the Sussex Road area, Kiln 7, a similar but larger, rectangular, block-built, 'pilastered' structure was also associated with mortaria, but of a slightly later date. Colour-coated wares of probable contemporary date were produced in the immediate vicinity, if not in this kiln. Hull (1963, 3) was uncertain whether or not to link it to tile production because of the general similarity of its form to that of a tile kiln. To do so is unnecessary. Against a background of Continental pottery industries allied to samian production, however, neither this, nor Kiln 31, was out of place. Both seem best related to rectangular or square, pilastered, block-built pottery kilns of the East Gaulish samian and colour-coated ware production centres such as those at Heiligenberg (Forrer 1911, 24, fig. 5, 39, figs. 15–17, Taf. IV & V, 42, figs. 18–21, Taf. VII, 50, figs. 26–9), Rheinzabern (Ludovici 1905, 151–2, figs. 8–10) and Sinzig (Hagen 1917, Abb. 3, Taf. XXVIII, Oven II). They are much too late to be related to Colchester's Claudio-Neronian rectangular, pilastered kiln structures (Map 15).

Not all of Colchester's 2nd and 3rd-century kilns produced exotic fine wares and mortaria. The Warren Fields site produced evidence for the production of black-burnished ware (BB2) and other allied local-type grey kitchen-wares (Hull 1963, 137). These were possibly fired in Kilns 15 and 16, or in their immediate vicinity. Elsewhere in Colchester, kilns associated with such products, certainly Nos. 27, 28 and possibly Nos. 9, 10, 11 (Hull 1963), were unlike those of the colour-coated industry. They comprised clay-lined single-chambered, single or double-flued structures without raised oven-floors (p. 113 ff.) or the use of blocks. Some had bollard pedestals. All were structurally most at home in the regional grey-ware industries of South Suffolk, particularly Wattisfield (Fig. XVII) and South-west Essex. In fabric, technique and in some of the vessel-forms, the contemporary Colchester grey wares would not have looked out of place on any of these native sites. They did, however, include copies of roller-stamped or rouletted beakers (Cam. 391), and flasks and flagons (including Cam. 281), all hitherto forms normally made in colour-coated ware there.

These Colchester kilns all belonged to the 3rd century, when the production of colour-coated wares was well past its prime. They possibly represented attempts of native potters from the countryside to set up workshops within Colchester's industrial area. This was perhaps to augment grey-ware production there, by then carried out on a relatively small scale, at a time when there was a sharp run-down in the manufacture of colour-coated and allied wares upon which the population had relied very substantially.

The Lower Nene Valley and its vicinity
Northamptonshire, Huntingdonshire and Peterborough

The Nene Valley had been an important area of continuous pottery production from before the Conquest (Maps 4, 14). Almost every known kiln structure of the early 1st to mid 2nd century involved one or more free-standing pedestals, and a raised oven-floor of prefabricated clay bars, usually unsecured (p. 114 ff.; Fig. VIII).

Around the middle of the 2nd century or soon after, an important colour-coated industry was established in the Lower Nene Valley, with its nucleus near the Roman town of *Durobrivae* (Water Newton) but spreading westwards into Northamptonshire and eastwards along both sides of the river as far as Stanground South, SSE of Peterborough town (Map 14). It had probably been grafted on to the existing indigenous pottery manufacture of the region (Howe *et al.* 1980, 6 ff.). The latter's products in the first half of the 2nd century had included well-made table-wares in Belgic-derived techniques, among them the so-called stamped 'London wares' (Perrin 1980). This clearly indicates a local demand, already, for finer quality pottery. The initial manufacture of Nene Valley colour-coated wares (formerly called Castor ware), however, almost certainly represents the presence of immigrant potters. These perhaps emanated from the Lower Rhineland, since some of the earliest colour-coated beakers are very close to their Cologne/Rhineland prototypes in form, fabric, decoration and finish. Nevertheless, the substantial overall diversity in colour-coated products between the middle of the 2nd century and the first third of the 3rd, and the attempt to make moulded samian early in the 3rd century, may imply the arrival of immigrant craftsmen at different times, and possibly from several sources, perhaps including Trier as well as the Rhineland (Dannell 1973; Howe *et al.* 1980, 7 ff.).

To what extent is this situation reflected by the character of the kiln structures? The lack of excavated kilns firmly datable to earlier than the end of the 2nd or early 3rd century is one of the greatest obstacles to an understanding of the transition from the production of indigenous wares alone to that of colour-coated and local-type grey wares side by side. The pottery from the kiln salvaged at Sulehay, Yarwell, Northants., for which an earlier date has been claimed (Hadman and Upex 1975), in the opinion of the author and others (R. Perrin pers. comm.), is a mixed deposit mostly of the late 2nd century or later. Hartley (1960, 9) has suggested that the earliest nucleus of the colour-coated industry may have lain on the N bank of the River Nene, in Normangate Field, Castor, which became the industrial suburb of *Durobrivae* on the opposite bank (Pl. 10). Evidence for early to mid 2nd-century production of grey 'Belgic'-derived vessels, pre-dating the manufacture of Nene Valley colour-coated wares and possibly using surface-built kilns, was recorded there in 1968–9 and 1973 during the excavation of pits and later buildings, but no permanent early kiln structures (*BNFAS* iii (1969), 9; ibid. v (1971), 8; *Northamptonshire Archaeol.* ix (1974), 87).

It is tempting to see the well-known kiln excavated there in

1822 (Pl. 29) and beautifully drawn by Artis (1828, pl. XL) as possibly one of the earliest in the development of the Nene Valley colour-coated industry, but this is impossible to prove. The pottery published from it (ibid., pls. LIII, LIV) was not all contemporary and probably included rubbish survivals back-filled into the chamber well after its abandonment. This kiln is among the most elaborate and sophisticated of those excavated in the area. It was circular and had been lined with pre-fired, curved, clay blocks specially made to fit its circumference exactly (Pl. 30). The interior of its relatively short flue

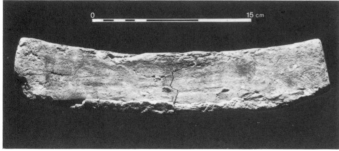

Plate 30. Prefired curved block of the type used for lining kilns in Lower Nene Valley: (a) side view; at each end are finger-marks where the block was removed from its mould while still soft; (b) view from top.

was also faced with shaped tiles and/or other prefabricated clay components; at its junction with the stokehole was a coursed stone retaining façade (Fig. XI). As in most Lower Nene Valley kilns the raised oven-floor was sited well below the contemporary ground level. This undoubtedly improved insulation and probably facilitated the attainment of the high temperatures to which Nene Valley colour-coated wares were usually fired. The raised oven-floor rested on a clay tongue-support with a rounded end. Problems relating to the character of the oven-floor, as illustrated by Artis, are discussed later (p. 97).

The structure of this kiln as a whole and several of its individual components are unparalleled in Britain outside the Lower Nene Valley. A number of its more unusual and distinctive features, however, when considered individually, can be identified on various sites in Gaul and Germany. Curved fired-clay blocks were also used in the Nene Valley, at Sibson (Kilns B

and F) and Stibbington (Kiln W), and rectangular but otherwise similar blocks, at Chesterton (Kilns P and R) and Stanground South (Kilns I and II). The Continental parallels for the use of such blocks for lining kilns have been discussed in connection with Colchester (p. 94). This is the only other factory in Britain where the technique has been recorded, and its links with contemporary Rhineland and East Gaulish potteries are well attested (p. 92). The use of a stone retaining-wall flanking the flue-mouth, extremely common in the Lower Nene Valley but not recorded elsewhere in Britain, has been found in conjunction with block-construction in the specialist kilns of the Trier potteries (Loeschcke 1928, 68, Abb. 1) and in the Central Gaulish samian industry (Vertet 1979, figs. 10.1, 11, 18; Duhamel 1974, 66). At Cannstatt, Germany, it occurred in a circular kiln with a long tongue-support perforated by diagonal vents (Paret 1932, 137, Abb. 86, Taf. XII, 1). Both elements were present in a large circular kiln excavated at Stibbington (Hartley 1960, fig. 2, Kiln A). The technique of diagonal vents is as yet unparalleled elsewhere in the Nene Valley industry and, indeed, anywhere in Britain. An integral tongue-support, rounded at the end, sometimes of concave elevation and often of solid clay or clay incorporating reused kiln material, was however particularly characteristic of the Lower Nene Valley industry (Figs. XI, XII). In Chesterton Kiln P and possibly Sibson Kiln B, a large aperture had been made at the top of the back of the tongue to facilitate the circulation of hot air directly under the floor, in the coldest part of the kiln (Fig. XI). This may also be why the tongue of Water Newton Kiln A (phase II) had not been luted to the back wall of the kiln-chamber. The very restricted occurrence of a tongue-support in Britain after the early to mid 2nd century (Map 10) and its frequent use in contemporary Continental colour-coated industries have also been mentioned in connection with the Colchester kilns (p. 94).

The oven-floor depicted by Artis in his two kilns, at Normangate Field and Sibson (1828, pl. XL; 1847, 164), comprised a circle of perforated wedge-shaped tiles radiating from the centre of the kiln. These are unparalleled in Britain and a preliminary search of the relevant Continental literature also failed to locate any examples. In the Lower Nene Valley itself, moreover, no floor of this kind has been recorded in any of the numerous kilns excavated since Artis's work. The type of oven-floor most characteristic of the industry comprised prefabricated clay bars, of varying shape but often quite massive (Pl. 31). These were usually positioned with one end resting on the tongue and the other on an internal ledge, or in holes made in the kiln-wall; they were often secured with clay or overplastered with a vented clay over-floor, and the whole was subsequently fired prior to loading (Fig. XII). A few minor variants of the method are known; only one definite and one possible example of the use of a solid-clay oven-floor have been recorded (Sibson Kiln B; Hartley 1960, 10–11; and Chesterton Kiln P). There consequently seems good reason to doubt the validity of Artis's interpretation of kiln-floors.

During excavations by B. R. Hartley at Water Newton (1958) and at Sibson (1959), the latter probably in the vicinity of the kiln published by Artis (1847, 164), a number of pieces of roughly-made perforated clay plates were found in addition to the usual fragmentary kiln-bars. Several plates appeared to have been originally more or less wedge-shaped, with a thickened spine through which holes had been poked, and tapering edges. Their sintered condition suggested that they had been exposed to repeated firing or overfiring in the kiln. B.R. Hartley has suggested to the author that such plates could perhaps have been used in the kiln as flooring, their longer, thinner edges resting on and just overlapping the bars in order to bridge the wedge-shaped gap between them (Fig. XI). Their constant reuse would explain their fragility when found. These may well be the items which Artis depicted as perforated wedge-shaped flooring tiles, but whose employment in conjunction with bars he failed to appreciate. The probable joint use of such perforated plates and bars is reminiscent of the occurrence of clay bars and perforated plates of varying shape in 1st and early 2nd-century kilns of the Upper Nene and adjacent valleys (Fig. VIII; p. 65). These could, indeed, be ancestral to those of the colour-coated industry.

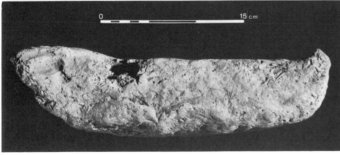

Plate 31. Prefabricated wedge-shaped clay bar of a type used for oven-floors in Lower Nene Valley kilns: (a) underside; (b) side view.

It is probable that just as the range of pottery produced in the Lower Nene Valley was a blend of native and exotic, with both coarse and colour-coated wares fired in the same loads, so the kiln structures may represent a compromise between the earlier native traditions (i.e. circular kiln-chambers, bar-floors and reusable perforated plates) and the more sophisticated techniques introduced from outside (i.e. tongue-supports, shaped clay block-linings, and coursed stone flue-façades). Because pottery manufacture had been widespread in the region since the Conquest, and probably before, with firmly established native (La Tène-

derived) traditions of kiln-building, the survival of the pre-existing in face of an influx of new and more sophisticated methods and products was presumably ensured. This could explain why the Nene Valley potteries, unlike most other colour-coated industries in Britain, never fully adopted solid-clay vent-holed floors but instead employed a compromise.

The only other British workshop producing colour-coated wares and using kilns with tongues and bar-flooring akin to those characteristic of the Lower Nene Valley potteries, was at Great Casterton only approximately 17 km N of Water Newton, along Ermine Street (Map 14). Though its production may have commenced marginally earlier than that of the Nene Valley, or perhaps have stemmed from a slightly different source, its ranges were mostly very similar, with the exception of the rough-cast beakers. This suggests a possible relationship between the two industries (Corder 1961, 50–53 and unpubl.; inf. C. Mahaney).

South Carlton, Lincs., 65 km to the N, was another production centre for colour-coated and other specialist wares founded shortly before the middle of the 2nd century (Map 13). Here, however, the character of both the kilns, with their integral solid-clay floors vented in a bar-like pattern, and their distinctive products (mortaria and flagons as well as rough-cast, stamped and painted vessels) suggests the presence of manufacturers from another Continental source as yet undefined but perhaps North Gaul, for example Jaulges-Villiers-Vineux (Jacob and Leredde 1975). The British market at this date clearly offered substantial opportunities to specialist potters and there is undoubtedly great scope for research into the relationships between the contemporary fine-ware industries of Britain and the Continent.

The Verulamium area
Hertfordshire and Middlesex

In the Flavian and Trajanic periods, the industry producing at least half of the mortaria in Britain was concentrated in five, possibly seven or more, centres on or near Watling Street, just S of the Roman city of Verulamium, St Albans (Map 14). The best known were Brockley Hill (Harrow and Hendon), Middlesex (Castle 1972a, b; 1973a, b; 1974; 1976a; Castle and Warbis 1973; Suggett 1953; 1954; 1956) and Radlett, Aldenham, Herts. (Page 1898; Castle 1976b). All of these factories may have formed a single industry, since their products are similar and have the same general date-range. Moreover, some of the potters who stamped mortaria are known to have had kilns in more than one of them, perhaps simultaneously (Hartley 1976b, 222; Castle 1976b, 149).

Production had certainly begun in the area about AD 50. Mortaria characteristic of this industry occurred in deposits pre-dating AD 60 at Verulamium (Frere 1972, fig. 102), and a pit on the southern edge of the Brockley Hill complex, in field 410 SW, contained potters' clay, kiln debris and numerous wasters of the decade AD 50–60 (Castle 1973a). Unfortunately, no associated kiln structure was found. The relative scarcity of local types of vessels in the pit, and the technique and generally exotic character of most of its contents, strongly suggest immigrant potters, attracted there by the military consumers along Watling Street. The earliest recorded kiln, dated to the late Neronian to early Flavian period, was found at Little Munden, St Stephens (Saunders and Havercroft 1977). It was associated with an assemblage of vessels, including Hofheim-type flagons, characteristic of army supply, and mortaria stamped by Oastrius such as have been found on a number of military sites. The kiln-chamber was shallowly-set and rectangular, with a rectangular tongue and side piers, all of tiles bonded with clay. Its flue was walled and possibly corbelled with tiles, and its stokehole floored with tiles in the final phase of use. Structures of this general type and date have been discussed in their wider British and Continental settings (p. 83 ff.). No other example has yet been recorded on the kiln sites of this industry, although mortaria of similar form and technique were made at Brockley Hill by other potters. The extensive use of tiles in kiln structures was common in the other factories of the Verulamium industry throughout the last quarter of the 1st century and into the early 2nd century. Whether the tiles were made with the pottery or in nearby tile factories is not known. Several tile kilns or sites of tile production have, however, been recorded in the adjacent region (McWhirr and Vyner 1978, 373). The identification of tile kilns there, from surface indications alone, is made difficult by the extensive use of tiles in pottery-kiln structures. To the field-walker, a plough-damaged kiln with a tile-vaulted oven-floor, as at Radlett (Page 1898), may appear mainly as a surface spread of tiles. The presence, moreover, of wasters from adjacent tileries, no doubt considered adequate for building into the structure of pottery kilns, could also be misleading. Two sites, at Elstree and at Aldenham School, undoubtedly pose such problems of interpretation.

The only other late 1st to mid 2nd-century, civilian-dominated pottery industry employing tiles in comparable quantities in kiln construction was at Colchester. Characteristic of both this and the Verulamium industries was the random use of irregularly-shaped fragments of broken tile bonded with clay for the fabric of kiln-walls, and sometimes for underfloor supports and oven-floors (*see also* p. 86). From the evidence of potters' stamps on mortaria, Mrs K. F. Hartley concluded (Frere 1967, 258; Hartley 1972, 373 ff.) that several manufacturers had moved their workshops from Colchester to the Verulamium area. Sextus Valerius Ius., one of the five linked 'Sexti Valerii' whose total working-life spanned the period AD 70–100, left Colchester in *c.* AD 80–90. Aprilis, producing within the period *c.* AD 60–90/95 was probably in the Veralumium region in *c.* AD 80–90/95. G. Attius Marinus moved from Colchester, and set up at Radlett in *c.* AD 95. 'T.M.H.', whose total career spanned the period *c.* AD 100–140, was working in the Verulamium region in *c.* AD 100/120–40 (inf. K. Hartley). What impact, if any, these manufacturers had on the technology of the Verulamium industry is at present uncertain. In terms of output alone, most were relatively minor potters there.

Our overall knowledge of the relevent kiln structures is surprisingly limited, in proportion to the amount of excavation,

particularly at Brockley Hill (Castle 1976a, 223 ff.). This is partly because much of it has been of a rescue or salvage nature, and also because many of the kilns at Brockley Hill seem to have been demolished during the life of the industry, perhaps *inter alia* for the reuse of tiles from their structures in other kilns. Another probable reason is that at least some were very shallow, more or less surface-built, like the Little Munden kiln. Unlike sunken kilns, they could not be levelled simply by back-filling but had to be totally dismantled to prevent obstruction of subsequent activity on the same site. This may imply that, at the height of pottery manufacture, space was at a premium along the Watling Street frontage of Brockley Hill's industrial complex. By the Hadrianic to Antonine period, however, production may have contracted to the northern part of the site. This theory tends to be supported by the recent analysis by X-ray fluorescence of the fabrics from the various kiln sites (research by and inf. from D. Devereux).

The limited evidence suggests that the main kiln type of the Verulamium industry in the late 1st and 2nd centuries was oval or circular with a relatively narrow tongue-support and a solid-clay vent-holed floor. Whether the similarities of form and constructional techniques within the potteries of the early Colchester and the Verulamium industries reflect the close links between the two, or merely a common, ultimately Continental ancestry, cannot yet be assessed. Clearly consideration should be given to this problem in any future work on both industries and their products.

Why the Hadrianic-Antonine Kilns I and II of *c.* AD 130–65+, immediately S of Verulamium itself (Anthony 1968), are structurally so different from those on the predominantly earlier sites at Radlett and Brockley Hill, also requires explanation. The Verulamium town kilns were active at a time of great change within the Verulamium industry, when the regular stamping of mortaria was gradually being discontinued and stamps in general were far more illegible than hitherto. At this period, AD 130–65+, the Verulamium potteries were rapidly becoming purely a local supplier. Already within the first decade of the 2nd century, one major producer, G. Attius Marinus, and at least two other potters had migrated to the Hartshill/Mancetter region (p. 99). Other potters also probably left the area within the first quarter of the 2nd century to set up potteries in the Oxfordshire region (p. 102). The Verulamium town kilns with their structural deviations thus may not be representative of the mainstream technology of the industry. As already indicated, the potter 'T.M.H.' did not migrate to the area until *c.* AD 110–20. Perhaps, therefore, these kilns reflect ideas introduced very late in the history of the industry.

Hartshill/Mancetter, Warwickshire

The large concentrations of kilns recorded at Hartshill and Mancetter, both well known for their mortaria, lie about two miles apart. For several reasons, however, they are best considered as a single industry. Excavations by Mrs K. F. Hartley (1973a and unpubl.) have indicated that the date range and character of products from both sites were similar. A number of mortarium manufacturers who stamped their wares can also be shown to have had kilns in both areas.

The beginning of pottery production there has often been assumed to be the direct result of the immigration of mortarium manufacturers from the Verulamium area in c. AD 100–105. The industry, however, may well have had a more complicated history. From the earliest excavated kilns onwards, two continuous but very different traditions can be discerned. These are distinguishable in the character of the kiln structures and in the wares associated with each.

Hartshill and Mancetter lie in a region whose pre-Conquest ceramic traditions, if any, are virtually unknown. This may be partly due to the very limited amount of excavation on the local ultimate Iron-Age sites. In the adjacent areas to the E, in Northamptonshire, and particularly in the Upper Nene Valley and its vicinity, handmade and wheel-thrown pottery of La Tène III ('Belgic') ancestry was manufactured and used in quantity in the decades immediately preceding the Roman Conquest (Map 4). To the S and W, in the valley of the Warwickshire Avon, and in the Welsh Marches and their immediate environs, relatively small amounts of very simple, coarse, handmade wares circulated, mostly from a few specialist centres, for example Malvernian ware (Peacock 1967a). In the Hartshill/Mancetter region at this date pottery of any kind rarely occurs in quantity, little or none being manufactured on a regular domestic basis. Although a very few vessels from both adjacent sources may have been brought there, in general the area apparently lacked strong indigenous pre-Conquest ceramic traditions. On present knowledge, it may be considered to have been virtually aceramic.

The 1st to 4th-century Romano-British settlement at Mancetter (*Manduessedum*, ultimately a *burgus*) almost certainly owes its origin to the existence of a legionary or vexillation-fortress to the W of Watling Street, in the Claudio-Neronian period (Webster 1978, 111–12; 1980, 165; 1981, 47–9), or possibly several successive early military establishments in the vicinity. The adjacent *vicus* would have developed to service the garrison(s). Pottery suitable for the army's wide range of requirements would not have been readily available in the immediate vicinity and, in consequence, potters from elsewhere would have been attracted to the site. The nearest and most obvious source for such immigrants was immediately to the SE, particularly the Upper Nene Valley, where a wide range of table and culinary-wares was already being produced. A distinctive group of vessels occurring frequently at Mancetter in Neronian to Flavian deposits onwards, and considered to have been local products (Mahaney 1975, 35, fig. 7, nos. 35–7 and 41–6; O'Neil 1928, pl. xxv, nos. 29, 30), resembled the lid-seated or channel-rimmed jars so common at this period in the Upper Nene and Ouse valleys (Friendship-Taylor 1979, fig. 36, no. 56; Woods 1972, fig. 25, no. 188; Tilson 1973, fig. 23, no. 198). Other types, often present in Claudio-Neronian and subsequent phases in various locations at Mancetter, were also closely similar to La Tène III-derived vessels common in the 1st century in that same general area to the E. These included cordoned carinated bowls (Oswald and Gathercole 1956, 44–5, fig. 10, no. 48, fig. 13, nos. 75 and 78, 47; Mahaney 1975, 34, fig. 7, nos. 27–9, described as possibly a local-type), and 'necked' bowls or wide-mouthed jars (Mahaney 1975, 35, fig. 7, nos. 30, 31; Oswald and Gathercole 1956, 45, fig. 11, nos. 65, 47, fig. 12, no. 79).

The Coritanian and North Catuvellaunian potters of Northamptonshire and Bedfordshire to the E and SE, making such wares at this date, used La Tène-derived kilns with circular, often portable, prefabricated pedestals, and raised floors of loose clay bars (cf. Fig. VIII; p. 114 ff.). If it is accepted that in the Claudio-Neronian period such potters probably introduced simultaneously their own native pottery and their kiln technology to the Mancetter area to meet a military demand, then when the army departed, perhaps in the late Flavian period, some pottery production would most probably have continued nearby. This would presumably have been in the same tradition but perhaps on a reduced scale. It would, however, be interesting to know if the potters were supplying other legionary bases in the West Midlands, such as Wall, Kinvaston, Leighton and Wroxeter. There is evidence to show some occupation from AD 60/65 on the site of the later potteries adjacent to *Manduessedum* (inf. K. F. Hartley). In c. AD 100–105, mortarium manufacturers from the Verulamium area arrived, attracted no doubt by the existing industry and the white clay source. From this background it is clear that, from the early 2nd century onwards, there were two distinct threads of tradition in the Hartshill/Mancetter potteries, that of the SE Coritanian territory and that of the potteries S of the Verulamium region.

One of the immigrant mortarium manufacturers was Gaius Attius Marinus, from Radlett (Hartley 1972, 373–4). He is unlikely to have moved alone and stylistic evidence suggests that the die-cutter of his name-stamps went with him. Other migrants probably included a potter called Doccus, Doccas or Dollas (Hartley 1973c, 58–9, fig. 24, no. 1). One or more of the migrants would almost certainly have been experienced in kiln construction. The career of Gaius Attius Marinus has been mentioned elsewhere (p. 98). In the very late Flavian period he was producing at Colchester, and subsequently had a workshop at Radlett (Hartley 1972, 373–4; 1976b, 213). There, two kilns which he shared with several other potters have been uncovered (Page 1898; Castle 1976b). The kiln structures of the regions most familiar to him would have had a relatively short tongue-support, a solid-clay vent-holed floor, and an oval chamber incorporating tile fragments.

Unfortunately, despite the attribution of G. Attius Marinus to Hartshill and the discovery of two of his stamps there, his kilns have not yet been located. At Mancetter, Mrs. Hartley found that many of the kiln structures, and often the oven-floors, had been seriously damaged by ploughing. Even so, the majority of those pre-dating AD 160 for which adequate evidence survived (Kilns 6, 7C, 7D and possibly 8) were shallowly-built and oval, with a short tongue-support and probably a solid-clay vent-holed floor. There was, furthermore, no distinct angle at the junction of the kiln-chamber and flue, but a gradual merging of the two (Hartley 1973a, Kiln A). The character of the mortaria and other associated products also indicates a link with the Verulamium factories. Most of these earliest Mancetter kilns, and others particularly up to the end of the 2nd century, were built of clay incorporating lumps of local quartzite and diorite and, occasionally, fragments of mortaria. These might be interpreted as substitutes in the kiln structures for the traditional chunks of tile more freely available and used in similar fashion in the areas from which these potters had migrated. Mrs. Hartley has drawn attention to the relatively small size of these early kilns at Mancetter (1973a, 147). They were, indeed, generally smaller than the smallest similar contemporary mortarium kilns at Colchester, Brockley Hill or Radlett, and usually contained mixed loads of mortaria and kitchen-wares. This perhaps reflected the relatively small, less certain markets in the earliest decades of the Hartshill/Mancetter industry, which at first had to compete with the supremacy of the Verulamium producers. However, it more likely stemmed from the current working arrangements within the various firms.

The contemporary evidence recorded by Mrs. Hartley from the Hartshill complex is more detailed, because the excavated kiln structures were much better preserved. Unfortunately, many more in the vicinity must have been lost through quarrying. It is possible, but by no means certain, that kilns were already operating at Hartshill before the establishment of mortarium production. Two of the earliest known kilns, Hartshill 12 and 24, making 'local-type' kitchen-wares such as dishes, jars and beakers of 'Belgic' Coritanian affinities, were not associated with either mortaria or kitchen-wares of Hertfordshire type. They were characterized by one, or more, cylindrical removable pedestal(s), oven-floors of unsecured tapering clay bars, dome-plates, an internal ledge moulded into the wall of the circular kiln-chamber, and a circular shape with a clear-cut angle where the flue joined the furnace-chamber (Hartley 1973a, Kiln H). Such features are all typical of early Coritanian kilns within the period late 1st to early 2nd century, but these Hartshill kilns, unfortunately, cannot be dated with any precision. It is, therefore, impossible to determine whether they pre-dated mortarium manufacture or were merely specializing in kitchen-wares when kilns elsewhere within the complex were already concentrating on the production of mortaria.

Several kilns provisionally dated to within the first three or four decades of the 2nd century show an interesting possible sequence of developments in the interplay of Coritanian and Verulamium traditions. Hartshill Kiln 32, contemporary with mortarium potter Vitalis IV (c. AD 115–145), had Upper Nene Valley constructional characteristics. It, too, specialized mostly in SE Coritanian-type kitchen-wares, but possibly also produced Hertfordshire-type carinated bowls with reeded rims. Was this an example of a local potter copying the newly-introduced kitchen-wares but retaining his traditional kiln technology? Another contemporary kiln (Hartshill 22) had the cylindrical chamber, internal ledge, probable loose bars, stone-capped flue, and

composite but permanent circular central pedestal, which all reflected contemporary Upper Nene Valley technology. This kiln had been used by Vitalis IV, whose mortaria are so similar to those of the Hertfordshire-derived G. Attius Marinus that he could have been an ex-apprentice or associate of his. Vitalis IV was using it for firing mortaria and kitchen-wares of Brockley Hill/Radlett type only. Clearly, at this stage, social and economic arrangements within the industry must have been very fluid.

Another potter, Cevanos, was working within the same period at Hartshill and Mancetter, making mortaria closely similar to those of G. Attius Marinus, as well as kitchen-wares mainly within Verulamium traditions. One of his kilns (Hartshill 14a; Pl. 32) was also small and circular, with a built-in, circular central pedestal, but in contrast had an integral solid-clay vent-holed floor, sited at ground level. It was, however, built in a technique and arranged in a 'spoked' pattern reminiscent of radiating bars with a circle of elongated holes between. This may well represent the fusion of the normal Hertfordshire solid-clay vented oven-floor technology and the Coritanian bar-flooring traditions. It was the hallmark of Hartshill and probably Mancetter kilns from shortly before the middle of the 2nd century until the late 2nd–early 3rd century, with one doubtful exception thereafter, Hartshill Kiln 3. Such a venting pattern in an integral solid-clay floor appears elsewhere in Britain only in industries whose earliest kilns had contained prefabricated bar-floors, as in North Kent (cf. Oakleigh Farm, Higham; Pl. 17) and at Wilderspool, where two of the kilns may perhaps be indicative of a probable link with Hartshill/Mancetter in the early Antonine period (p.105).

From shortly before the mid until the late 2nd century, most excavated kilns at Hartshill had a single, central, circular or oval pedestal, an integral clay, often bar-like, vent-holed floor, and an oval, as distinct from the earlier circular, chamber. They were roughly built, often incorporating lumps of stone. The last two features both perhaps reflected the influence of Hertfordshire kiln technology. A trend towards a single free-standing pedestal-support is just discernible at Mancetter (e.g. Hemsley 1959), where the use of a tongue-support ceased around the middle of the 2nd century (Hartley 1973a, 144). From then onwards Hartshill and Mancetter kilns exhibited very similar developments in technology. Was this shift of preference at Mancetter towards a free-standing pedestal a reflection of the dominance of local Coritanian-derived kiln-building traditions? It may simply have been found to have had a particularly apt technological advantage in helping to eliminate the cold spot at the back of the kilns with a tongue, at a time when, between c. 140 and early in the 3rd century, their overall size was increasing. The simultaneous tendency for an apparent increase in the firing temperature of the products must undoubtedly reflect these technological changes. These clearly went hand in hand with the maximum growth period of the industry (Hartley 1973a, 144). Soon after c. 160, as a secondary development in this 'streamlining' process, kilns with one free-standing pedestal were gradually superseded by larger ones with two or three pedestals,

Plate 32.

HARTSHILL, Warwicks.: Kiln 14a (c. AD 100–130), a circular, semi-sunken structure, with integral raised oven-floor of clay incorporating lumps of stone, and pottery arranged in a bar-like formation. The clay lining, apparently terminating level with oven-floor, must have been continued above ground level with a temporary turf superstructure (scale in ins).

as in Mancetter Kilns 1 and 2, and Hartshill Kilns 18, 31 and 33. Like their smaller immediate predecessors, however, they were still relatively roughly built.

By the beginning of the 3rd century, a more or less standardized Hartshill/Mancetter kiln type had crystallized (Fig. XIII). It was large and oval, and carefully and massively built, with two parallel, elongated, often rectangular, free-standing pedestals, and a thick floor with widely-spaced vents of a shape and arrangement less bar-like and more regular than hitherto (Hartley 1973a, Kiln E). Such kilns were the hallmark of the 3rd century. From the end of that century single pedestals again became more commonly used, but the general character of the kilns otherwise remained the same. Almost all of these massive 3rd and 4th-century kilns were fired at temperatures higher than any in the 2nd century, and were used for firing mostly or solely mortaria instead of the very mixed loads common hitherto.

Alongside this relative uniformity of products and kilns in the 3rd and 4th centuries, one kiln unique to the industry, Hartshill No. 6, stands out as indicative of an alien potter (Hartley 1973a, fig. 2, Kiln G). It had a thin, heavily fired, tongue-support, sixteen small clay corbels along its circumference, and an integral solid-clay floor, evenly vented at close intervals. Unlike contemporary Hartshill/Mancetter kilns, it was associated with grass-marked dome-plates. Both its structure and products, colour-coated beakers and late 'imitation samian' wares, were closely paralleled within the 4th-century industry of the Oxford region (Fig. XIV; p. 103) and leave no doubt about the source of the migrant potter (Bird and Young 1981, 306 ff.). Three other non-standard kilns could perhaps represent immigrant influences.

They may, however, be seen as a general copying of selected features found elsewhere in Britain since they exhibit typical Hartshill/Mancetter constructional techniques, such as the use of random lumps of stone in their structures. A case in point is Hartshill Kiln 19, used by Gratinus (c. AD 135–60). In addition to the roughly rectangular central pedestal usual at this date, it had six small prefabricated cylindrical pilasters fixed to the kiln-wall. Mancetter Kiln 19a (Hartley 1973a, fig. 1, Kiln C), which fired kitchen-wares, could be the only example of a single-chambered kiln in the whole industry (p. 115). It had a central 'bollard' but no trace of any ledge or raised oven-floor. There were pot-rim impressions on parts of the bottom of the kiln-chamber, which had been replastered with clay; pots found *in situ* there, around the pedestal, had presumably formed the bottom layer of the load. Another kiln, Hartshill No. 15, had a circular central pedestal and an integral bar-like, clay vent-holed oven-floor which spanned only the front half of the furnace-chamber (Hartley 1973a, fig. 2, Kiln F). At the bottom of the back of the chamber, the remaining D-shaped area comprised a slightly raised, solid-clay platform on which pots would have been stacked direct. This loading arrangement is reminiscent of that found in the Derbyshire-ware kilns 50 km to the N (Fig. XXI). This unique kiln, probably dating to the late 2nd or very early 3rd century, apparently fired kitchen-wares only, and may have been an experiment at a time when substantial technological changes were taking place within the industry. On the other hand, the close link which had existed between Hartshill/Mancetter and the Derbyshire potteries early in the 2nd century (p. 125) may also have been a relevant factor.

The Oxford region

The history of the development of the potteries and their kilns in this region is apparently a classic instance of the superimposition of an intrusive specialist industry upon pre-existing indigenous production. The resultant blend of the two traditions, in both the final products and their underlying technology, is therefore not without interest.

Excavation and research in the Upper Thames Valley over the past fifty years suggest that there must have been a substantial amount of pottery-making there in the late pre-Roman Iron Age (Harding 1972). There is, however, no evidence yet for the use of proper kilns at that date. The earliest known kilns in the area, at Hanborough and at The Churchill Hospital (Phase 2), fall within the mid to late 1st century and were supplying purely local needs. The former apparently relate to La Tène traditions, having portable pedestal(s) and bars. They are not, however, identical to those of the same date and affinities in adjacent areas; for example, the Hanborough pedestals were not fired sufficiently hard to be truly portable. They have thus been interpreted by Young (1977, 32; Sturdy and Young 1976, 63) as the result of a general imitation of a La Tène-derived technology, rather than its direct introduction by immigrant potters. At The Churchill Hospital (Phase 2), the 1st-century kilns were unlined and found without any internal fittings. Whether these had existed but had been removed for reuse elsewhere cannot be determined with any certainty. There was, however, a complete absence of any 'scars' or ghost-marks where portable kiln-furniture might originally have rested (Young 1977, 31). If none had been used, then these kilns and those at Overdale, Sunningwell, Berks. (Harris and Young 1974), on the SW fringes of the later main Oxfordshire pottery-making area, may represent outliers of the North Wiltshire group of single-chambered kilns, single or twin-flued, whose greatest concentration lay on the fringes of the valleys of the Rivers Kennett and Ray (Maps 11, 12). Both of these tributaries of the Thames could have provided links with the region in which lay the nucleus of the early Oxfordshire industry.

All the 1st-century Oxfordshire kiln sites and that at Overdale, just slightly later, were making indigenous La Tène III-derived ('Belgic') kitchen-wares or, occasionally, simple Gallo-Belgic-derived table-wares such as the platters at Hanborough. During the first quarter of the 2nd century, however, the character of pottery-manufacture in the region radically changed. Specialist wares such as flagons and mortaria, presumably intended for wider markets and more sophisticated tastes, were now also produced. Thereafter, kilns which confined their output to the former wares were the exception, such as that at Foxcombe Hill, Berks. (Willett 1948).

The forms and generally very sandy-textured fabric of several of the earliest of these newly-introduced products, particularly the ring-necked flagons and flanged mortaria, clearly resemble those of vessels manufactured in the Verulamium area at that period. Several mortaria within Young's (1977) type 2, with the top of the flange above the level of the top of the rim, correspond very closely to the profiles of those stamped by the potter Melus, who was working at Brockley Hill between c. AD 95 and 130/135. Like the late Verulamium craftsmen (p. 98), some of the early Oxfordshire potters used trade-stamps, albeit of a rather low standard and most of them illegible. In the Verulamium industry, however, it was precisely the early 2nd century when the legibility of stamps in general was deteriorating and many potters were discontinuing the stamping of all their products. Moreover, elsewhere in Britain few newly-established potteries, other than those ultimately related to the Verulamium industry, regularly stamped their mortaria in the manner of some of the earliest Oxfordshire potters. For these and other reasons, it seems likely that the emergence of a specialist industry near Oxford resulted from the migration of potters from within or close to the Verulamium industry. Perhaps they were former apprentices or associates of well-known potters whose status had hitherto barred them from stamping their own mortaria.

For a short while after its establishment, the Oxfordshire mortarium industry may possibly have continued as a branch of the Verulamium area potteries. The evolution of types of mortaria in the latter, shortly before the middle of the 2nd century, was marked by a change from small rims and outward-hooked flanges, characteristic of the products of Melus and others, to high, upstanding rims and flanges pointing downwards. The Oxfordshire industry was the only other centre in Britain whose mortaria showed this particular evolution in the second half of the 2nd century. This cannot be purely coincidental. Young (1977, 61) has not favoured a direct link between the two industries but there seems to be good reason for believing that one existed during at least the first few decades of specialist production in the Oxfordshire region.

To what extent is this possible relationship substantiated by the character of the kilns belonging to this new phase? Of the kilns whose structural details are known, only Overdale, and Rose Hill, Cowley, belonged to the 2nd century. Only Rose Hill included specialist wares such as mortaria among its products (Harden 1936). Its dating is not entirely secure, but it probably belonged to about the middle of the 2nd century. If this is correct, then it implies that the type of kiln to predominate in the industry for the next one-and-a-half to two centuries was already in use there by that date. Its structure comprised an oval or circular chamber, with an integral, narrow, relatively short tongue-support, and a solid-clay, vent-holed, raised oven-floor. In the 1st and 2nd centuries, almost all of the few kilns of this type throughout Britain were clearly associated with the production of specialist wares. Could the type have been in operation in the Oxfordshire potteries since the early decades of the 2nd century, after having been introduced simultaneously with the first production of mortaria and flagons? It was used in the Verulamium area in the early decades of the century but has not been recorded in any other region near Oxfordshire at a comparable period. If a possible link between the two industries is accepted on ceramic grounds, then similarities in kiln morphology would be a logical concomitant. Clearly, certainty is not yet possible but it is difficult to see from where else this combination of vessel and kiln types could have originated.

Once introduced, such kilns remained the dominant type throughout the life of the Oxfordshire industry (Young 1977, 35–40). This contrasted sharply with developments at its main competitor, Mancetter, also related to the Brockley Hill/Radlett potteries and the nearest generally similar industry. There, the use of kilns with a tongue-support, relatively common before the middle of the 2nd century, declined sharply thereafter and ceased altogether before the end of that century, having been superseded by those with free-standing pedestals (p. 100). Within the Oxfordshire industry, only a few variations on the basic kiln type have been found (Young 1977, 34–42). All but one are of a relatively minor character and none appears to relate to differences in the range of wares produced. Kilns occurred both with or without proper flues. Several were of stone, rather than of clay, and one was narrow enough for the oven-floor to span the furnace-chamber without a tongue-support. A single 4th-century kiln at Allens Pit, Dorchester on Thames, was of prefabricated clay blocks, plastered in the interior with a skim of clay (Harden 1936). This might suggest some contact with the Lower Nene Valley. The tongue-supports, oven-floors and flues of that industry were, however, totally different in character from those of the Oxfordshire potteries.

More important was a structural innovation appearing late in the life of the Oxfordshire industry. Clay corbels, springing from halfway up the furnace-chamber wall, were used to add support to the oven-floor, supplementing that provided by the tongue (Fig. XIV). The limited number of excavated kiln structures of this period, and a lack of precision in their dating, make it impossible to determine whether the distribution of this later type reflects chronological factors or merely individual preferences. Certainly it does not appear in some 4th-century centres, for example at Foxcombe Hill, Dorchester on Thames and Shotover, and at late 4th-century Cowley. Neither was it used by the Oxfordshire potters who migrated to Harston, near Cambridge, in the second quarter of that century (Bird and Young 1981). On the other hand, all the kilns of The Churchill Hospital complex, dated to late in the 4th century or to some time within it, had corbels. The Oxfordshire potter making colour-coated wares, who migrated to Hartshill in the second quarter of the 4th century, was also using this type (Hartley 1973a, fig. 2, Kiln G). It may, therefore, be expected at other contemporary centres within the industry. Whether the addition of corbels to the basic Oxfordshire kiln type was developed simultaneously to improve efficiency when the industry was reaching its peak, or was copied from elsewhere, is uncertain. It would however be surprising if, at this date, it was purely fortuitous. The New Forest potteries, the industry's main rival in the S, had been successfully using kilns without a tongue or free-standing pedestal-support, but with corbels or pilasters alone, since shortly after the middle of the 3rd century (Fig. XV). It was the only British specialist pottery industry to do so at that date (p. 108).

How did the emergence of a specialist industry in the Oxfordshire region, early in the 2nd century, affect the indigenous single-chambered kilns and their regional culinary-wares? No single-chambered kiln there can be dated to later than the middle of the 2nd century. By then, the type seems to have been completely superseded by the new, more sophisticated double-chambered kilns. Perhaps the local producers were rapidly absorbed into the workshops of the incoming potters. From the start of specialist production, it was apparently normal practice to make oxidized and reduced local-type kitchen-wares alongside items such as mortaria and flagons. After the middle of the 2nd century, only one kiln is known to have been used solely for regional non-specialist reduced wares. This was the 4th-century kiln at Foxcombe Hill, Berks., sited far from the industry's nucleus (Willett 1948). It was double-chambered, with a tongue and vented clay oven-floor, even though it occurred in the very area where single-chambered kilns had been used for local-type wares up to the middle of the 2nd century. Only one indigenous technical legacy to the superimposed industry can be distinguished, the use of 'dome-plates' presumably for covering the kiln-load. These occurred in association with the early La Tène-related kilns at Hanborough, and in the early Oxfordshire single-chambered kilns. They were used in many of the more sophisticated double-chambered specialist kilns of the Oxford industry and also in those of its migrant potters at Harston, Cambs. They were not used traditionally in all kilns in specialist industries. At

Plate 33. HAMSTEAD MARSHALL, Berks.: Site F, Kiln 5, showing small, narrow tongue-support characteristic of Oxfordshire pottery industry: probably fourth-century (ranging pole in ft).

Hartshill/Mancetter, they occurred only in a very few kilns of individual craftsmen, such as that of the Oxfordshire potter who set up workshop there.

By the 4th century, the kiln-form dominating the Oxfordshire potteries had spread to, or was being copied by, local non-specialist potters within an adjacent area of about 40 km to the S. In Berkshire, the structures of Compton Kilns I and II (Harris 1935; Hardy 1937), of kilns at Foxcombe Hill (Willett 1948), and of Kiln 5 at Hamstead Marshall (Pl. 33; Connah 1964), all very closely resembled those of the Oxfordshire industry. In particular, they had the very distinctive short, narrow tongue-support, coupled with a solid-clay vent-holed oven-floor. Elsewhere in Britain at this date, this precise structural combination occurred only in the kilns of those Oxfordshire potters who migrated to Hartshill and Harston.

At Hamstead Marshall, a native-type single-chambered twin-flued kiln was in use apparently in the same general phase of production as the Oxfordshire-type kiln (inf. late D. B. Connah). This juxtaposition of traditions perhaps reflects the limit of the technological sphere of influence of the Oxfordshire specialist potteries, at the peak of their prosperity, on their rural regional counterparts.

Wilderspool, Cheshire

The kilns at Stockton Heath, near Wilderspool, Warrington, fall within that small group of pottery industries which were either founded by potters from major workshops elsewhere, or suddenly expanded their existing range and volume of production as a result of such immigrants.

There had been settlement and industrial activity in the vicinity since at least the Flavian period (Thompson 1965, 81). This perhaps initially stemmed from military occupation in the area, although evidence for this is lacking as yet. No 1st-century kilns have been found, but several of the vessels published as Wilderspool products ought, typologically, to belong to this early period (Hartley and Webster 1973, fig. 2, nos. 1 and 2, and possibly fig. 6, no. 48).

The ceramic evidence for pottery manufacture from the early 2nd century onwards is more substantial. Production of a wide range of oxidized vessels, including unstamped mortaria, many of them of so-called raetian type, began then. These, among the earliest mortaria produced, dating from c. AD 110, were characterized by a red slip on the upper surface of the flange and on a limited zone immediately below the rim. They were unlike contemporary mortaria in South, East or central Britain but comparable with mortaria made in the military potteries at Holt and Chester, and also at Wroxeter and elsewhere in the North-west (Hartley and Webster 1973). Initially the tradition had stemmed from Raetia and Upper Germany. Such a link is further emphasized by the production of tablewares with red stripes and other distinctive painted decoration at Holt and Wilderspool (Hartley 1981), as well as in the Continental workshops making raetian-type mortaria at Straubing (Walke 1965, 42–3, Taf. 141), Weil im Schönbuch and Welzheim (Bersu et al. 1911, 119–25, 128–35). These centres seem to have been primarily geared to supplying the garrisons of adjacent forts. No doubt 'raetian' traditions arrived in Britain via the army, perhaps initially through men trained in pottery-manufacture on the Continent in the Flavio-Trajanic period. The workshop at Wilderspool may, therefore, have been a secondary offshoot of the process. Unfortunately, none of the kilns found there can be positively

Plate 34.

Wilderspool, WARRINGTON, Cheshire: Kiln 2; open-topped superstructure, apparently intact up to kiln-lip.

ascribed to a particular phase within the total known period of production.

In the Hadrianic-Antonine period, a number of new potters seem to have set up workshop at Wilderspool. They introduced the practice of stamping names or trade marks on the mortaria, but otherwise seem to have kept the character of their wares within the existing traditions of the industry. At least one of them, C.C.M., apparently came from the Wroxeter area but no structural details were recorded of a probable mortarium kiln found there. Another Wilderspool potter, Nanieco (stamping NANIIICO), had previously worked in the Midlands, probably in Hartshill/Mancetter potteries in the late Hadrianic to early Antonine period. In profile and in the use of a red-brown slip on the flange, his Wilderspool mortaria follow pre-existing Wilderspool traditions, differing markedly from his Midland products. He is the only Wilderspool potter whose stamped vessel was recorded on the Stockton Heath kiln site. Although it is uncertain whether any of the kilns recorded there were his, an attempt at comparing them with contemporary structures in Hartshill/Mancetter potteries seems reasonable. Certainly, they do not resemble any of the Holt kilns, nor indeed the two other roughly contemporary kilns known within the Cheshire Plain at Northwich (Curzon and Hanson 1971) and Manchester (unpubl.). Of the three Stockton heath kilns excavated by May (1904, 57–8; Hartley and Webster 1973), Kilns 2 and 3 were circular (Pl. 34), with a central, probably circular pedestal and a solid-clay vent-holed floor, and were not particularly large (May 1904, 57–8; Thompson 1965, fig. 19). Apart from minor details, their structure and the general venting pattern of their oven-floors would not be out of place at Hartshill itself in the Hadrianic-Antonine period, when solid-clay floors in a 'spoked' pattern and with a single circle of vent-holes had superseded prefabricated bar-flooring, but kilns were still relatively small and circular, usually with circular central pedestals. Such a kiln type could have been transmitted to Wilderspool from elsewhere, but at present no other known regions provide possible links in both kiln types and potters or pottery.

The first kiln excavated by May (1904, 54–7) was different from Kilns 2 and 3. Although it had been partly destroyed at the front before excavation, May was able to ascertain its plan from the colour of the burnt subsoil. It seems to have been large, with straight sides and a subrectangular or bottle shape. A pair of long rectangular pedestals parallel to the flue axis supported the clay oven-floor, which apparently had fewer vent-holes than the circular kilns. The back of the kiln structure was 'partly conjoined' with Kiln 2, but unfortunately May's sections did not indicate which was the earlier. Kiln 1 is without precise parallel in Britain but its very size and robust character may link it to the production of mortaria.

Of the four published Continental kilns associated with the production of 'Raetian' mortaria and allied wares, two at Welzheim were bottle-shaped (that is rectangular or near rectangular) with a long tongue-support (Bersu et al. 1911, 129, Abb. 63). One in the S vicus of Straubing fort was rectangular, probably with side and rear pilasters (Walke 1965, 43, Abb. 13).

A fourth, at Weil im Schönbuch, appeared to be subrectangular or bottle-shaped, with a tongue-support, but was illustrated at a very small scale (Bersu et al. 1911, 119, Abb. 58). All had solid-clay vent-holed floors. Bottle-shaped, rectangular, or subrectangular kilns were rare in Britain at any period. As has been shown elsewhere (pp. 85, 95), they were almost always associated with the production of vessel-types with close Continental connections, either by military-linked or immigrant civilian enterprises. It is, therefore, tempting to explain the large size and bottle shape of Wilderspool Kiln 1 as indicative of raetian-derived kiln technology. Perhaps the use of free-standing pilasters, instead of a tongue-support, was a tradition adopted from Wilderspool's Midland potters. Unfortunately, without a full record of their structures and associated finds, discussion of the Wilderspool kilns must necessarily remain speculative.

The need now is for excavation of more kilns at Wilderspool and in the NW Midlands, as well as the discovery and exploration of the potteries near Carlisle or in SW Scotland which were founded by migrants from Wilderspool around the middle of the 2nd century. These potteries gradually took over the Wilderspool industry's long-distance markets, its status becoming merely that of a local pottery after c. 165 until its demise late in the 2nd century (Hartley and Webster 1973, 103).

The Doncaster area, Yorkshire, West Riding

Potteries immediately E and SE of Doncaster, within the parishes of Auckley, Cantley and Rossington, constitute one of the largest excavated regional kiln concentrations in Britain, and may be considered as a single industrial entity (Map 13).

Their immediate area, on present evidence, was apparently essentially aceramic in the pre-Roman Iron Age, with little pottery being made there or circulated from outside the region. To the E, however, the Lower Trent Valley and NW Lincolnshire had strong ceramic traditions in the late Iron Age, continuing into the Roman period. This is particularly well exemplified by the sequence of pottery from the late Iron-Age/early Romano-British settlement at Dragonby (May 1970, figs. 92–4; 1976, figs. 7–9).

The origins of pottery production in the Doncaster area are not yet clear. The first potters at Rossington might well have worked near the pre-Flavian vexillation-fortress, as did those of its counterpart at Longthorpe (Wild 1977). No kilns of this date however are known, nor has the vexillation-fortress itself been excavated yet. Like Longthorpe, it was possibly too short-lived for its associated potters to have established adequate permanent civilian markets or influenced subsequent local developments.

The most likely stimulus for the establishment of a permanent industry was probably the foundation of the early Flavian fort at Doncaster itself, and its continuing occupation, both military and civilian. No kiln sites of Flavian date have been recorded. The distributions of the potters' stamps CEN, REDITAS, and SACE, on a group of vessels of generally similar technique

(Gillam form 30, and Gallo-Belgic-derived form, Gillam 337), which centre on the Doncaster area in that period (Rigby and Stead 1976, 187), however, suggest possible Flavian production nearby. Another clue to the possible existence of local pottery production late in the 1st or early in the 2nd century is the presence of cooking-pots with a shoulder-groove and linear rusticated decoration among the products of the Antonine kilns at Cantley Estate and Rossington Bridge (Buckland *et al.* 1980, 152, fig. 3, 19). This particular type was essentially pre-Hadrianic, and in the North was primarily associated with supplies to military consumers. As a defunct fashion, it would hardly have been introduced *de novo* in the Antonine period. It must surely have survived as an integral part of the repertoire of a pre-existing local pottery industry.

Whatever the nature of pottery manufacture in the late 1st and early 2nd century in this area, an enormous expansion in production must have begun in the early Antonine period. The major impetus was possibly the establishment of workshops by one or more potters from the Hartshill/Mancetter industry (p. 98 ff.). Their earliest known kilns were sited at Rossington Bridge Pumping Station (Pl. 35). Evidence of potters' stamps suggests that at least one workshop, operating there between *c.* 135 and 170, was a branch of the Hartshill/Mancetter firm of Sarrius. Sarrius himself apparently continued production at Mancetter, but perhaps sent probable associates or former apprentices, Setibogius and Secundua. Potters from regions adjacent to Doncaster were also apparently involved in the enterprise; rusticated jars, parisian stamped wares probably traditional to Lincolnshire (Elsdon 1982), and other local Romanized vessel-types were closely associated with it. The firm apparently also attracted one or more potters skilled in the production of Durotrigan-type black-burnished wares, presumably from Dorset (Buckland *et al.* 1980). The products of these kilns reached as far as the Antonine Wall and other northern military sites. Their main markets, however, lay within the adjacent region, particularly the Doncaster fort, reoccupied in the Antonine period. After the late 2nd century, however, their wider distribution apparently ceased. This change resulted in a readjustment of the ratio of different vessels produced, with more jars and wide-mouthed bowls than hitherto, presumably for local rural consumers. Thereafter, the Doncaster industry remained of purely local status until its demise in the mid to late 4th century.

Many of the characteristics of the early kilns of Sarrius's branch at Rossington Bridge Pumping Station reflect closely those of his Mancetter kilns, as well as those of Junius, his close associate there (Hartley 1973a, 146, fig. 1, Kiln D; Mancetter Kilns 1, 3, 3a, 4 and 19b). These had either one central pedestal, or two to three pedestals usually set parallel to the flue axis. Roughly oval to rectangular, they were not always very carefully constructed. Another feature held in common was the relatively shallowly-set, often oval kiln-chamber, of clay frequently incorporating lumps of stone or pebbles (Pl. 35). A possible difference between Sarrius's kilns at Mancetter and those at Rossington Bridge was in the construction of the raised oven-floors. At Mancetter, though damaged by ploughing, they seem to have

Plate 35. Rossington Bridge Pumping Station, CANTLEY, Yorks. West Riding: *Foreground*: Kiln 1; note roughly-built structure incorporating lumps of stone, and two elongated pedestals. *Background*: Kiln 2. Both kilns date to within *c.* 135–70 AD (ranging pole in ft).

been of the solid-clay vent-holed variety (p. 99). At Rossington Bridge, they were similarly destroyed, but the pedestal-tops were often apparently 'finished off' and showed no roughness where an integrally-built floor might have been demolished. This may suggest floors of prefabricated clay bars secured or overplastered with clay. *In-situ* bar-floors of the mid 2nd century onwards on other sites within the industry may confirm this. They occur fragmentarily at Rossington Bridge Farm, frequently on the Cantley Estate (Annable 1954; 1960; Gilmour 1955) and at Bessacarr (inf. P. Buckland).

Bearing in mind the predominantly La Tène III (Gallo-Belgic) traditions probably underlying parisian-ware forms, the use of bar-flooring is not surprising. Moreover, in the nearest essentially ceramic region, Lincolnshire to the SE, bars were a frequent flooring medium in the non-specialist kilns of the 1st and 2nd centuries, and in a modified form later. Perhaps in the Doncaster potteries bar-flooring should be seen as the surviving element of adjacent native technology in an industry which, at least in its earliest decades, was mainly of an immigrant specialist character.

The method of firing the Rossington black-burnished ware (BB1) has not yet been fully resolved. As Buckland has pointed out (1980, 157), from the close association between the BB1 and rusticated ware, parisian ware, and the mortaria of Sarrius in the Rossington kilns, it was apparently fired in kilns rather than in the surface clamps or bonfires postulated, and more recently recognized, for some BB1 in its Dorset homeland. He also noted, however, extensive waster-tips containing much soot and black sand, down the side of the Torne Valley. These could indicate bonfire-firing W of the known kilns, but may represent the debris of temporary turf superstructures and coverings involved in the reduced firings of the kilns proper.

At Cantley Estate, specialist pottery-production seems to have begun very soon after that at Rossington Bridge Pumping Station. One kiln, Cantley 24, apparently used by the potter Virrinus, working within *c.* AD 150–80, was associated with stamped mortaria of early hammer-head and wall-sided types (Cregeen 1957). Both forms were characteristic of the Hartshill/Mancetter potteries, but typologically slightly later than those of Sarrius's Rossington Bridge workshop. Perhaps Virrinus migrated from the Midlands a little after Sarrius's immediate associates. He could well have been an associate of Sarrius's Mancetter partner Junius, whose working life ended about a decade later than that of Sarrius, and whose products included similar early hammer-head and wall-sided forms. Unfortunately, the structure of Virrinus's Cantley kiln is unknown. Most of the

Plate 36. Sycamore School, CANTLEY Estate, Yorks. West Riding: Kiln 32, a late third to fourth-century structure, with raised oven-floor of prefabricated bars overplastered with clay and supported by circular free-standing central pedestal; flue in *right foreground*. Note niche in back wall of kiln, perhaps to aid process of stacking or to stabilize kiln-load (scale in ins).

Plate 37. Sycamore School, CANTLEY Estate, Yorks. West Riding: Kiln 31, a late third to fourth-century deeply-sunken structure, with two large, roughly rectangular free-standing clay pedestals (scale in ins).

other surviving structures probably dating to within the 2nd century, because of their association with parisian and/or rusticated wares (Cantley Estate Kilns 2 and 6 and Rossington Bridge Farm Kilns 1 and 2), are generally similar to or variants of those within the early Rossington Bridge Pumping Station complex. Only one could be different. Evidence suggests that Cantley Estate Kiln 6, however, may have operated as a single-chambered kiln (Annable 1960, 19 ff.).

At the Blaxton and Branton centres, surface or near surface-built kilns with temporary turf linings were apparently normal between the late 2nd and early 4th centuries. Such arrangements are unknown elsewhere in Roman Britain as late as this. There is no evidence that the products or date-ranges of these kilns differed from those of the sunken ones in the Doncaster industry. The Blaxton and Branton kiln sites were, however, several hundred metres from their clay source. Turf, therefore, was possibly considered a more convenient or more economical alternative to clay.

Unfortunately, most of the other Cantley Estate kilns, except those of the late 3rd century and later, cannot be closely dated. This is because their wares were very regional in type, were inadequately recorded or survived only partially. Most apparently had floors of prefabricated bars overplastered with clay (Pl. 36). Some, however, had two parallel, massive and carefully-built, rectangular clay pedestals (Pl. 37), generally comparable with those typical of the Hartshill/Mancetter industry from towards the end of the 2nd century onwards. Whether links between the two industries continued after the late 2nd century is uncertain. Nevertheless, throughout the life of the Doncaster potteries, even in the 4th century, the mortaria tended to resemble contemporary Midland products rather than those produced by the neighbouring Lincolnshire industries. On the other hand, the types and forms of the kitchen-wares fell firmly within the local ceramic traditions of the North-east.

Among the relatively few Cantley Estate kilns datable to within the late 3rd to mid 4th century and making mortaria as well as kitchen-wares, Nos. 33 and 38 and possibly No. 34 were structurally distinct. They were characterized by very small, cylindrical, solid-clay pedestals, probably prefabricated, from which radiated clusters of bars overplastered with clay. Kiln No. 33 had three of these (Pl. 38), No. 38 four, and No. 34 one. At this date, kilns of this type were exceptional in Britain. Only Hartshill has produced similar ones, Kilns 8 and 17, with very small cylindrical pedestals arranged in a triangle as in Cantley Kiln 33. As yet their dating is tentative but one at least probably

Plate 38. Goodison Boulevard, CANTLEY Estate, Yorks. West Riding: Kiln 33, a distinctive late third to fourth-century structure, with three small cylindrical pedestals supporting clusters of radiating fire-bars overplastered with clay. Due to subsidence during use, two cuboid pilasters (*centre right* and *left*) were placed in furnace-chamber as supplementary supports (scale in ins).

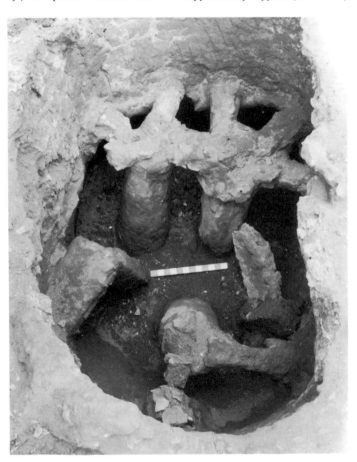

fell within the second half of the 3rd century. At Hartshill they were clearly not mainstream types, although at least one had a solid-clay vent-holed floor. Clearly, further research is needed to establish their true relationship, if any, but the mutual similarity of their structures and mortaria seems unlikely to be pure coincidence.

The New Forest, Hampshire

The New Forest pottery kilns lie scattered in clusters over an area of 60 sq km, E of the River Avon with one exception, and away from major roads (Map 18). This industry, producing colour-coated wares, painted parchment wares, mortaria and grey local-type kitchen-vessels, was apparently established soon after the middle of the 3rd century. There is no evidence of any earlier specialist production in the region. Earlier pottery-making in the vicinity is known only from a small, probable 1st-century, twin-flued kiln found at Gorley (Sumner 1917, 50, plan IXA), which produced local-type kitchen-wares. On present evidence, the area does not seem to have supported a large population in the Roman period. This was probably because intensive prehistoric settlement, forest clearance, and cultivation, particularly in the late Neolithic – Bronze Age, had resulted in soil deterioration (Tubbs 1969, 30–32). These conditions may have aided the growth of a substantial new Roman pottery industry with kilns spread over a wide area, since good clay and sand were plentiful but the land was not particularly valuable for agriculture.

Until a reassessment within the last decade (Swan 1971), many of the New Forest kiln structures had been misunderstood. This arose from Heywood Sumner's misinterpretation of the results of his kiln-excavations in the 1920s, described and illustrated in 1927 in his attractive book, *Excavations in New Forest Roman Pottery Sites* (Fig. I). Excavation in the 1950s and 60s, including the re-excavation of one of Sumner's kilns, however, made possible a reinterpretation of his work. It established without doubt the existence of a standard type of New Forest kiln (Fig. XV). This was oval or circular, with a fairly short flue. It had a solid-clay vent-holed floor, supported by integrally-moulded, roughly subrectangular, oval or subtriangular pilasters, occasionally a hybrid between a pilaster and a corbel. In the absence of a local pre-existing industry, the kiln structures and their specialist products were presumably derived from elsewhere. Yet there is no obvious link between them and contemporary kilns elsewhere in Roman Britain. After the middle of the 2nd century, only the territory of the Iceni had kilns of generally similar type, but the pilasters there were different and the flues were normally relatively long (p. 121). Moreover, none of them was associated with the manufacture of colour-coated or parchment wares, and their mortaria and the local-type kitchen-wares were totally dissimilar to the New Forest products. In the Oxford region, at a late stage in the industry, well into the 4th century, corbel-supports were adopted for use in the kilns in conjunction with the tongue (p. 103; Fig. XIV), probably imitating this feature in New Forest kilns. There is thus no evidence that the Oxfordshire kiln structures influenced those in the New Forest. An origin for the latter ought, therefore, to be sought outside Britain.

The character of the pottery in the earliest New Forest kilns, particularly those excavated at Lower Sloden in 1966 (almost certainly dated too late by Fulford, 1975, 40), tends to support this (Swan, *forthcoming*). A comparison of products shows that the Oxfordshire industry did not exert a strong influence on New Forest vessels until the middle of the 4th century. Nor is there more than a very distant relationship between New Forest wares and some of the contemporary Nene Valley products. This is not the place for a detailed discussion on the subject. It is, however, worth pointing out that the character of some of the fabrics, the forms and the decoration on the earliest New Forest vessels find their closest parallels among the mid/late 3rd-century wares (published and unpublished) of pottery-industries in the Argonne and Forêt de Compiègne, North-eastern France, and the Eifel district of West Germany, including Speicher (Chenet 1941, Types 302, 304, 306, 309, 310, 317, 324, 326, 343, 345, fig. 21, no. 2; Gose 1950, Types 14, 95/6, 100/101, 172, 187, 194, 206/207, 209, 270/271, 462 and 563; Holzhausen Types D92, F837, 1233, 1330–42 and F1485, and Niederbieber type 69 (in precise detail)). Moreover, some material collected by the author from the Speicher kiln sites is remarkably similar in character and technique to the New Forest sandy parchment wares, an observation worth pursuing in greater detail. Unfortunately, little is known of the structures of the pottery kilns of the Speicher factories at this period. A thorough search through records deposited in museums, and through the more local literature on potteries in North-eastern France, the Moselle and the South Eifel, might well produce close parallels to the structures of the New Forest kilns.

Technologically the New Forest kilns are not without interest. Not all the structural features of those illustrated by Sumner are comprehensible in the light of modern knowledge (Swan 1971). The poor quality of his excavations may cast doubt on the interpretation of some of those features which are inconsistent with the structures of kilns excavated within the past few decades. In particular, the solid-clay step illustrated by him at the back of Sloden Enclosure Kilns 1 and 2 was possibly misunderstood (1927, 57–67), but this cannot be ascertained without a re-examination of these kilns.

Except for the latest known kilns in the industry, for example at Amberwood (Fulford 1974), most New Forest structures apparently had a relatively deep furnace-chamber. They were also characterized by a short or virtually negligible flue-passage, and a small or very narrow stokehole. Because no tongue or other support protruded into the centre of the furnace-chamber, substantial quantities of bulky fuel could be fed into it. This rendered a longer flue unnecessary. New Forest colour-coated wares were normally fired to very high temperatures, about 1,000–1,250 °C. This was at least as high as or even higher than any of such wares elsewhere in Britain and often to the consistency of stoneware, producing highly lustrous surfaces. The deep and capacious furnace-chamber, which allowed ample room for both draught and fuel, may have largely contributed to these high firings. It is perhaps significant that, in general, the latest New Forest colour-coated wares of the late 4th century, such as those from Amberwood, seem to be less lustrous and more matt in appearance, probably having been fired at slightly lower temperatures. They tended to be associated with smaller, shallower, more ephemeral kilns which could not perhaps achieve the high temperatures possible in the earlier, deeper structures.

Norton and Crambeck
Yorkshire, East and North Ridings

The Romano-British settlement at Norton, on the E side of the River Derwent (Map 13), developed primarily as the industrial sector of the *vicus* of Malton Roman fort, which lay on the opposite bank (Robinson 1978).

When the fort was founded, probably in the early Flavian period, small quantities of coarse native Iron-Age pottery were already being made in the region. These consisted of very simple handmade mineral-calcite-gritted cooking-pots, orange or sometimes black in colour, and presumably fired in clamps within or near the native settlements, as at Knapton (Corder and Kirk 1932, 96–9). During the late 1st and the 2nd century, however, the native potters improved and extended slightly their range of forms, apparently to meet some of the garrison's demands. Their wares and general potting techniques, nevertheless, remained almost unchanged and they supplied only a fraction of those needs. The cooking-pots are often termed Knapton ware, after a probable production site.

Despite the early establishment of Malton fort, there is no evidence for kiln structures in the vicinity before the 3rd century AD (Hayes and Whitley 1950). Nevertheless, grey wares in the same Romano-British tradition as the products of Norton's 3rd-century kilns (*see* p. 110) have been found in the *vicus* immediately outside the fort, in a deposit dating to the late 2nd century (Mitchelson 1964, fig. 12, nos. 125 ff.). The excavated 3rd-century kilns may, therefore, have been part of an existing industry, possibly established in the wake of the Antonine re-occupation of the fort shortly after the middle of the 2nd century.

The character of these kilns and their wheel-thrown products of Romano-British fabric and type are quite distinctive (Hayes and Whitley 1950). This suggests the presence at Norton of non-local potters and their descendants. The kilns each had a small, circular or oval furnace-chamber and a long, proportionately wide flue, usually of stones, or stones bonded with clay. Their highly individual internal arrangements possibly comprised a temporary raised oven-floor or partial floor, involving prefabricated, rectangular, square-sectioned, often perforated, clay bars, and supports of various types. One kiln-chamber contained banana-shaped props, resting against and luted to the kiln-wall

Plate 39. Howe Road, NORTON, Yorks. East Riding: Kiln 3, showing *in-situ* prefabricated banana-shaped clay prop luted to kiln-wall, and typical long stone-lined flue in *foreground* (length of scale probably two ft).

(Pl. 39), and free-standing oblong blocks or bricks of roughly rectangular section. Occasionally, extra support was provided by protruding fragments of pottery incorporated in the furnace-chamber wall as in Kiln 3 (ibid., 23), or by slots cut into the kiln-wall as in the Grove Bungalow kiln. Flat clay plates may sometimes have been used to bridge the bars or act as 'setters' (p. 41).

Corder, using available evidence, discussed in detail the probable disposition of the furniture in the kilns, concluding that this must have varied (1950b, 20–25). It may be that the banana-shaped props and the bars were not intended for use in conjunction with one another as he envisaged (ibid., fig. 8). On analogy with arrangements in some Medieval kilns, for example in the 15th-century kiln at Cheam, Surrey (Jope 1957, 297, fig. 285), banana-props may have been used alone and positioned to lean against the kiln-wall to prevent the stacking of vessels in that region. This would have allowed the unimpeded circulation of hot air along the kiln's internal circumference. The load would have been stacked on the bottom of the more central part of the chamber and fired, without a raised oven-floor and separate oven-chamber. The relatively long flue was presumably designed to prevent fuel having to be fed into the kiln-chamber, thereby displacing portable furniture or vessels stacked in it.

The Norton potters obviously did not come from the immediate locality. Similar, but always slightly later, examples of the same general vessel-types are present among the products of the various kilns of the Throlam industry of Yorkshire, East Riding (p. 123). The closest parallels to the Norton forms, however, come from kiln sites in North-west Lincolnshire, such as Roxby, Dragonby and Thealby (Rigby and Stead 1976, figs. 64, 66–8). They include slightly earlier versions of vessels identical to Norton types 4a, b and c, 5, 6, 7a and 10b. Some of these North Coritanian products also share the same decorative techniques, for example repetitive fine comb-stamping. Antecedents of, or parallels to the Norton kiln structures should thus be sought in North Lincolnshire. Aside from essentially exotic kiln-types at Dragonby, Scunthorpe, few 1st or 2nd-century kiln sites in that area are known in detail (p. 85). Many kilns there, however, apparently had long, stone-lined or stone-roofed flues, as at Thealby, Burton Stather (Dudley 1949, 203, 213–14), Elsham (Samuels 1979), and Conesby Mine (Dudley 1949, 176–7). Probable clay props also occurred at Thealby (ibid., 213–14). Square-sectioned clay bars, sometimes perforated, are common on many Lincolnshire kiln sites, mostly N of Lincoln, for example at Elsham (Samuels 1979, fig. 3), near Caistor, and in the Claxby/Walesby area (unpubl.; Bryant 1977a). Corder (1950b, 21, n. 2), in fact, remarked on the close similarity between the Norton bars and those *in situ* in Linwood Kiln I (Pl. 44; *JRS* xxxii (1942), 110) and near the Colsterworth 'furnace' (Pl. 45; Hannah 1932). The latter can now be reinterpreted as a kiln (p. 122). Clearly, further excavation in this area is needed to define more precisely the details of other kilns.

Most of the pottery associated with the Norton kilns consisted of wheel-thrown grey wares in Romano-British fabric. Nevertheless, the evidence of calcite-gritted 'stackers' and wasters suggests that handmade native jars (Knapton ware) were also fired on the site, possibly in the same kilns. At about this period, Knapton wares apparently ceased to be predominantly orange, that is oxidized, and thereafter were almost always dark grey or black in colour, that is fired in a reducing atmosphere. Perhaps this represents a radical innovation in firing technology, such as a change from clamps or bonfires to proper sunken kilns. These allowed closer atmospheric control and reduced firings were traditional in them. The establishment of Romano-British pottery workshops at Norton could well have advanced the technology of the native industry by introducing proper kilns. It could also have made it more centralized, by attracting indigenous rural potters to move their workshops into the Norton industrial complex and share raw materials and drying facilities (Hayes and Whitley 1950, 15–19).

If native calcite-gritted wares were fired in the Norton kilns, were the same temporary raised kiln-floor arrangements used for them? Corder (in Hayes and Whitley 1950, 24) noted that the condition of some of the calcite-gritted jars suggested their possible use, in an inverted position, at the bottom of the furnace-chamber. This, he presumed, was to support a bar-floor. Bearing in mind probable traditional firing techniques, these vessels could well have been fired in structures without a raised oven-floor. They could have been superimposed on a layer of reusable, or expendable, inverted pots at the bottom of the furnace-chamber, as in some single-chambered kilns, with or without banana-props, but with clay plates or rings to aid stacking.

Some time during the 330s or 340s, pottery production began at Crambeck, 7.5 km SW of Norton (Corder 1928), and at other sites nearby, Crambe (King and Moore 1975), Mount Pleasant (Corder and Birley 1937), and N of Welburn Village. This development almost certainly involved potters from Norton. Crambeck is best known for its cream-buff mortaria and painted table-wares. Large quantities of grey kitchen-vessels, in a tradition identical to that of Norton products, were however also made there, apparently as well as small quantities of the calcite-gritted Huntcliffe-type cooking-pots, derived from Knapton ware. Undoubtedly, Norton potters had been attracted to the Crambeck area primarily by the discovery of a seam of white clay. This enabled them to produce quality table-wares and mortaria for the first time. It was instrumental in their rapid expansion and ultimate dominance of northern ceramic markets in the last third of the 4th century. In the Norton *vicus*, the manufacture of native Huntcliffe-type wares, and possibly also of grey regional kitchen-wares, apparently continued simultaneously with that at Crambeck (Robinson 1978, 8–9).

The kilns at Crambeck and its satellite sites resemble very closely those excavated at Norton in having small circular or oval chambers, with long, proportionately wide flues involving the use of stone. Corder (1928, 16 ff.), and Corder and Birley (1937, 394–7), followed by King and Moore (1975), assumed that the Crambeck and Crambe kilns had each originally had an integral, self-supporting, solid-clay, vent-holed, raised oven-floor. None, however, was found *in situ*, nor were there any convincing associated fragments of flooring. That illustrated by Corder (1928, fig. 16) was very rough and could have been derived from the kiln-superstructure. Corder was clearly puzzled by the absence of any indication of where a floor might have sprung from the interior walling of the kilns (ibid., 18).

It could be assumed that the same type of temporary prefabricated flooring-components had been used as those found in the Norton kilns, and that none had been left *in situ*, presumably because of their reuse in other Crambeck kilns. There was, indeed, a certain amount of evidence for such items on the main Crambeck site. Unfortunately, at Crambe the areas excavated were too small for their apparent absence to be significant. At Crambeck, Corder (ibid., 43, 21) mentioned 'roughly hand-made bricks of various sizes', possibly bars or props, and 'fingered clay fragments', possibly luting for such prefabricated components. In the 1950s and 60s, as a result of further quarrying and the subsequent tidying up of Crambeck quarry-face, the stokeholes of two kilns and a section across an earlier ditch were exposed and recorded (Dent 1966, fig. 1; Hayes 1966, fig. 3). Their contents included perforated square-ended kiln-bars of the type known at Norton in association with cylindrical saggars and Crambeck-type wasters. Clearly more extensive excavation, particularly on the important main Crambeck site, is greatly needed. This might

not only clarify the suggested internal arrangements within the kiln structures, but could also tackle the many outstanding problems relating to the products and the chronology of the industry as a whole.

Two small specialist industries Pakenham and Biddlesden

Pakenham, Suffolk

At Pakenham, an industry making colour-coated vessels, mortaria and other specialist wares was established in the first half of the 3rd century (Smedley and Owles 1961b). Non-specialist kitchen-wares, however, were produced on the site early in the 2nd century (Map 15; Smedley and Owles 1964), during the 3rd century, and possibly also in the intervening period. Significantly, there was no tradition of making colour-coated wares anywhere in that area. It, therefore, seems reasonable to assume that the impetus for production, if not the actual producers, must have come from elsewhere.

The colour-coated wares produced were in the same general tradition as Lower Rhineland/Moselle wares of the mid 2nd to mid 3rd century and, therefore, generally similar also to the colour-coated products of Colchester and the Nene Valley. The mortaria, however, did not closely resemble those made at Colchester. Most of them had a reeded flange vaguely reminiscent of contemporary Norfolk products, but with closest parallels within the Nene Valley industry.

The affinities of kilns present great problems. Superficially their circular furnace-chambers, with oval tongues and vented floors, were like those of the Nene Valley (p. 96), but there the resemblance ends. The Nene Valley-type stone façade to the flue-mouth was absent and, instead of a sub-floor of straight prefabricated bars overplastered with clay, a series of curved bars was used on either side of the tongue, giving the appearance of two spans of vaulted under-flooring. Though the technique was different, this may have been an attempt to copy the vaulted under-flooring of some of the Colchester kilns (Fig. X; p. 94). Moreover the presence of a baffle in the flue of Kiln 147 is paralleled in Britain only in the Colchester colour-coated industry. On the other hand, the double-span bar-sequence might represent a modified version of a structural phenomenon known in Gaul, Italy and elsewhere (Cuomo 1972, 435, Tav. V.II/c). The four pilasters of Kiln 22, two on each side of the tongue, are however more reminiscent of the structure of contemporary kilns in Norfolk (p. 121).

These mixed affinities are generally similar to those suggested for the pottery. Moreover, the structures form a stark contrast to those of the contemporary Pakenham kilns making kitchen-wares alone. The latter, single-chambered, single-flued, with pedestals (Fig. XVII), are entirely typical of the native industries of Suffolk and Essex (p. 115). Possibly the workshop making colour-coated wares at Pakenham belonged to potters of mixed origins, Continental and British. Alternatively, it could have involved Norfolk potters, who had briefly worked in or seen the Colchester and Nene Valley factories and were trying to produce similar products, copying technologies of which they were not fully cognizant. The evidence available at present permits no more than speculation.

Biddlesden, Buckinghamshire

Of four kilns recently recorded in the Great Ouse Valley at Biddlesden, 10 km SSW of Towcester, three (Kilns II, III and IV) were operating in the second half of the 2nd century (Map 14). They made colour-coated beakers of Continental affinities, and grey wares of local and more universal British type. The colour-coated wares again reflect the same general traditions as the Lower Rhineland/Moselle potteries and are also ultimately comparable with contemporary Colchester and Nene Valley products. There is, however, no evidence for the earlier production of such types in the Biddlesden area. The fourth kiln on the Biddlesden site (Kiln I) was in fact Flavian in date and had been producing a distinctive, quite unrelated range of highly decorated vessels but not colour-coated wares. Its structure had apparently involved prefabricated cigar-shaped fire-bars entirely in keeping with the kiln types characteristic of the Ouse and Upper Nene Valleys at that date.

In contrast, the remarkable structure of the three later Biddlesden kilns has not yet been recorded elsewhere in Roman Britain (Woods *et al.* 1981). This applies particularly to the 'barrel-vaulted' raised oven-floor, of perforated curved clay bars separated by prefabricated clay spacers. The bars had been positioned while still flexible and hardened *in situ* (Fig. XVI). Single-span prefabricated bar-vaulting of the same general class occurs in a number of kilns on the Continent (Cuomo 1979, fig. 5.2) but, so far as is known, is usually used to support a superimposed oven-floor, as at Morgantina, Sicily (Cuomo 1972, Tav. VIII, 418–21). At Biddlesden no such over-floor existed. The vaulting itself thus constituted a raised oven-floor. No attempt, however, was made to level its curvature on the upper side by overplastering the bars with clay near the kiln-wall. Extra precautions must, therefore, have been necessary in setting the pottery load. This element also distinguishes these Biddlesden structures from other Romano-British specialist kilns, all of which had level raised oven-floors.

For these reasons, it is tempting to explain away the type as having been introduced by migrant potters from the Continent at a time when Rhineland-derived colour-coated industries were being set up or augmented by immigrant craftsmen elsewhere in Britain. This theory, however, is not easy to prove, mainly because of the relative dearth of detailed publications of kilns in Gaul and Germany. Only one almost exact parallel is known to the author, a specialist kiln found at the Fürstenberg, Xanten, in Germany, but unfortunately this is Augustan (Hagen 1912, 344, fig. 1, ofen 2 and Taf. XLIX). It does, however, indicate that single-arched bar-floors lacking a level over-floor were in use in Rhineland kilns at an early date. There seems no reason, therefore, to doubt that the tradition could have continued there for several centuries and subsequently spread elsewhere. It is, perhaps, significant that some of the early Medieval Pingsdorf (Rhineland) stonewares of the 9th to 12th centuries were fired in kilns of this nature (Jope 1957, 295). Kilns of very similar structure, dating to the early 11th century, have been excavated at Thetford, Norfolk (Davidson 1967, 192–3, figs. 54, 55). These may imply the continuous survival of this tradition on the Continent from the Roman period, and its eventual reintroduction into Britain in the late Saxon period.

Clearly the relationship of the Biddlesden kiln structures must remain conjectural at present. There is, however, a distinct possibility that other minor colour-coated industries were situated not far away in the Upper Nene Valley/Towcester area. If this is so, and kilns are located, further light may well be shed on the true affinities of the industry at Biddlesden.

CHAPTER 8

Non-specialist regional kiln types

Single-chambered single-flued kilns

An awareness of the existence of kilns lacking a proper raised or false oven-floor is of comparatively recent origin. Grimes omitted such kilns from his classic appendix on Romano-British kiln structures in the Holt Report (1930). The astute recognition of one version of the type at Hedgerley, Bucks., by Oakley, Vulliamy and Rouse, who usefully discussed the problem (1937, 259–60), was apparently overlooked by subsequent excavators until Corder drew attention to the phenomenon in 1957.

Corder (1957) considered such kilns (his type 'C') as having a makeshift temporary floor, which he defined as having no fire-bars or other prefabricated furniture, but being formed of unfired pots or wasters. This description now requires modification. Such an internal arrangement barely deserves the term 'floor', and the whole phenomenon would be better completely redefined. It is preferable to class such kilns as lacking a temporary or permanent raised oven-floor spanning all or most of the furnace-chamber but having, instead, a 'kiln-chamber', combining 'furnace' and pottery-chamber (Fig. II.ii). To facilitate the passage of a draught upwards through the kiln and allow the heat of the fire to circulate below the lowest tier of vessels, thus preventing them from being under-fired, temporary portable props, wasters, or permanent inbuilt features were often utilized. Pots were normally superimposed directly upon these. Both clay vent-holed 'false' floors and true flooring-bars are always absent from such kilns.

The recognition of these kilns from excavation reports is not always straightforward. In the past, many excavators, finding no raised oven-floor *in situ*, naturally assumed its former existence. They sometimes suggested that it had disintegrated during use, or had been destroyed on the abandonment of the kiln, or had subsequently been ploughed away. Frequently, no careful examination of kiln debris was made for fragments of bars or perforated clay floor. Of the very little clay debris reaching museums from such 'problem' kilns, even less now survives for scrutiny. In excavations confined to the structure alone, such kilns may indeed be indistinguishable from La Tène-derived sunken kilns from which the supports and bar-furniture have been removed. Despite such problems, a clear-cut group of single-flued kilns which never had raised floors can be recognized with some certainty. The validity of the grouping is apparently confirmed by a certain coherence in their distribution, which centres on Suffolk and Essex but also includes South Norfolk, East Herts. and North Kent, with outliers in Warwicks., South Bucks., South Oxon., North Wilts. and Monmouthshire (Map 11). It is interesting that the nucleus of this distribution, together with that of the probably related single-chambered twin-flued kilns (Map 12), largely excludes those areas of Britain with strong pre-Conquest La Tène III ('Belgic') traditions of pottery manufacture. Kilns peripheral to the main concentration comprise those which, from the late 2nd century onwards, had probably been spread thither from adjacent areas. This could mean that single-chambered kilns ultimately derived from, or represent the Romanization of, a firing technology already in existence in

Britain before the introduction of late La Tène III kilns. Such a technology was apparently used in Gaul until the end of the Bronze Age, if not later (Duhamel 1973b, 145).

In many ways these single-chambered single-flued kilns are little more than sophisticated, enclosed, vented, sunken bonfires (Rhodes 1969, 9). The lack of a separate raised oven-compartment and presence of a single chamber both for the fire and the pottery serves to link them technologically to clamp-firings. They differed from these in possessing a clay-lined chamber and a proper stokehole. As with that technique, the vessels were not sufficiently elevated to be out of contact with the fuel and flames of the fire, but only enough to allow the passage of a draught beneath them, and to enable combustible material to be pushed into the bottom of the furnace-chamber. In all, it would be logical to expect single-chambered kilns to have evolved directly from pit-clamp techniques.

This type of kiln may be considered under three headings:

(1) kilns with specially-made portable prefabricated furniture to facilitate stacking and the circulation of the draught within the load;

(2) those with one or more permanent inbuilt 'platform(s)' designed for the same purpose;

(3) those with neither element but in which a bottom layer of vessels, sometimes rejects, must have been arranged to fulfil a similar role.

Single-chambered single-flued kilns with prefabricated portable furniture

This variety, among the simplest within the class, shows one of the closest relationships to bonfire-firings. In it, temporary prefabricated clay blocks were positioned at intervals at the bottom of the sunken clay-lined furnace-chamber. The vessels were then stacked directly on top of the blocks, which were just high enough to enable a draught to circulate beneath the load, and for fuel to be raked in and out. The general arrangement was thus very much akin to that of positioning stones, logs or clay blocks at the bottom of a primitive clamp or bonfire (Fig. II.i; O'Brien 1980 and undat.). The kilns at West Stow (West 1955 and unpubl. inf. S. West) could well show a relationship between the technologies. One feature found there, best interpreted as a pit-clamp (the 'smother pit'), was near to and roughly contemporary with several late 1st-century single-chambered kilns. The Iron-Age possible 'pit-clamp' (Ipswich Mus. Records) found at Pear Tree Farm, Wattisfield, only c. 22 km to the E (p. 34), also suggests an indigenous Iron-Age background of bonfire-pit technology. Such a technology may, ultimately, have lain behind the marked concentration of single-chambered kilns in the region.

Whether the transition from pit-clamps to permanently-lined, single-chambered kilns was a spontaneous development in Britain, or represented the post-Conquest impact of either late La Tène ('Belgic') or Roman influences on the earlier native technology, cannot yet be determined. Perhaps the adoption of substantial permanent clay linings reflected the impact of Rome, while prefabricated portable clay kiln-furniture, more elaborate than in early Iron-Age clamp-firings, may suggest late La Tène ('Belgic') influences. Indeed, at West Stow and Hedgerley, the only sites in which kilns of this sub-type have been recognized, the forms of a substantial proportion of the vessels, though in a Roman fabric, had La Tène III ('Belgic') ancestry. The firing technique itself, however, was so simple that it seems more likely to have been a survival than the result of external stimuli. The practice of arranging bricks beneath, and distributing waster tiles throughout a kiln-load, to ensure ample circulation of hot gases, is indeed still used in Britain by rural potters for firing such items as flower-pots.

The Hadrianic–early Antonine kilns of this group at Hedgerley (Oakley et al. 1937) were associated with clay 'bricks' of at least two types. These were obconical blocks about 0.23 m high and 0.15–0.2 m in diameter, and large rectangular blocks, sometimes perforated, one measuring 0.18 by 0.13 by 0.08 m. Three blocks, two obconical and one rectangular, were found in situ in Kiln 1, in an arc formation near the wall and parallel to it. This arrangement echoes the general dispositions of the blocks in the Iron-Age clamp-sites at Willingham and Badwell Ash (p. 53 ff.) and particularly that in Kiln 5 at West Stow, where a ring of up-ended bricks was found on the bottom of the furnace-chamber. The clay blocks associated with the latter and with several other kilns on that site were more varied in form. At least some of the less symmetrical ones were apparently also used in the related, but slightly later kilns of that complex in conjunction with an inbuilt stacking platform. Most blocks were cylindrical, rectangular, or square, generally not more than 0.30 m on the longest axis, and sometimes perforated. At least one variety was expanded slightly at the top and bottom. Symmetrically-shaped blocks would have been suitable for use both on the bottom of the furnace-chamber and distributed throughout a load to aid stacking.

Additionally, however, at West Stow perforated clay plates were apparently used between at least some of the lowest blocks, and perhaps were positioned elsewhere among the pots being fired. In the absence of bars from the site, such plates seem scarcely likely to have functioned alone as a proper floor. They are perhaps best seen as just a component in the 'scaffolding' network which supported and spaced out the kiln-load. At the bottom of the load, they possibly aided the stacking of vessels whose diameter was insufficient to bridge the optimum gap between two blocks. Their occurrence at this period might have represented another borrowing from contemporary La Tène III kiln technology. Certainly they seem to have been linked with only the earliest kilns at West Stow. On some kiln sites 'loom-weights' were thought to have been used in single-chambered kilns, as in Kiln 3 at Dragonby (Stead 1976, 96–7, fig. 46) and at Tottenham House site, Great Bedwyn, part of the Savernake industry of Wiltshire. In the absence of their full publication, however, it is uncertain whether or not they resembled the perforated blocks associated with Iron-Age clamp-sites (Elsdon 1979).

Single-chambered single-flued kilns with one or more permanent inbuilt 'platform(s)'

Within this type three clear-cut sub-groups may be distinguished:

(A) kilns with a single, solid, circular or oval central 'bollard' or 'pedestal';

(B) kilns in which this feature was perforated or divided into two distinct segments;

(C) kilns with bollards or pedestals of individual form.

(*A*) The central pedestal or bollard within this sub-group frequently occupied a substantial proportion of the kiln-chamber, with a relatively narrow, sometimes 'V'-shaped gully around it (Fig. XVII). Large pottery vessels or, more rarely, 'stacking furniture' could be wedged into this, leaving ample room below for the circulation of air and, if necessary, for the raking in and out of fuel. Experiment has shown that this system operates very satisfactorily (Watson 1958).

Aside from the general requirement that a 'pedestal' should take up most or much of the space within the bottom of a kiln-chamber, its character seems to have been greatly flexible. Most were either of solid clay or of soil overplastered with clay. The exception, of stone, at Overdale (Harris and Young 1974), was an outlier in the overall distribution of the group. They might often have resembled a flattened hump, with vertical or slightly-splayed sides and a shallowly-domed or near-flat top. The precise form, however, does not seem to have been of critical importance. Kilns at Wattisfield, West Stow and elsewhere apparently continued in normal use even after the upper side of the pedestal had broken away and become irregularly concave.

Within the range, certain local, minor structural preferences can be detected. Around the Thames Estuary (Maps 11, 17), a group of such kilns had pedestals which tended to be of lower elevation than elsewhere and to have occupied less of the kiln-chamber, features shared with the segmental pedestals there (*see* p. 116). Several were little more than a slight step, as in Kiln F368 at Moulsham Street, Chelmsford, Essex (inf. P. Drury) and Kiln B at Oakleigh Farm, Higham (Catherall 1983, *forthcoming*). In North Suffolk, pedestals were generally taller and took up a larger area. Such kilns were especially characteristic of the 'Wattisfield' industry – numerous kilns with similar products, spread over the parishes of Botesdale, Hepworth, Hinderclay, Market Weston, Rickinghall Inferior and Superior, and particularly Wattisfield itself (Map 16; Maynard *et al.* 1936). They are thus often termed 'Wattisfield-type' kilns (Fig. XVII).

The very few single-chambered 'pedestal kilns' which also used prefabricated stacking furniture seem to have occurred early in the sequence. At West Stow, several near wedge-shaped blocks were found in the channel of a kiln of this type. They were apparently carefully proportioned to fit between the central bollard and the slope of the kiln-wall (West 1955, 41). These Trajanic-Hadrianic pedestal-kilns were the immediate successors, on the site, of the Flavio-Trajanic kilns which used portable blocks alone. This may imply that the single-chambered 'pedestal-kiln' developed from the block type, the blocks being no longer essential to their operation but merely a survival in usage. At Mucking, the earliest single-chambered 'pedestal-kiln' (No. I), dating to within the late 1st–mid 2nd century, contained fragments of tapering clay 'bars' in its back-fill (Jones and Rodwell 1973). There was no low ledge or recess in the kiln-wall on which their outer ends could have rested. They too may, therefore, have been jammed in the relatively wide gap between the pedestal and the kiln-wall and/or incorporated in the stacking of the pottery load. It is perhaps no coincidence that the earliest kilns of any type on this site, probably operating within the immediately pre-Conquest to Flavian period, were of the late La Tène type which also utilized bars. As at West Stow, these bars were probably a survival of usage from earlier kilns. They were absent from the similar single-chambered kilns of the 3rd and 4th centuries there (Kilns II, III, IV and V), and occurred only in the two predominantly 2nd-century ones (Kilns I and VI). One of these had a single and the other a segmented pedestal (*see* p.116). The tiny integral lumps, so-called 'draught-stops', in the channel of two of the Icklingham, Suffolk, pedestal-kilns (Frere and Clarke 1945, 213) may represent later inbuilt versions of earlier portable bridging furniture.

Most kilns seem likely to have been fired with pots wedged or stacked in the gap between the pedestal and kiln-wall. Little evidence of their exact positioning has survived. At Beech Tree

Plate 40. CALDICOT, Mon.: Kiln 2, a single-chambered single-flued structure, with central pedestal, probably mid to late third-century. Some of the vessels positioned around pedestal possibly comprise the *in-situ* expendable bottom of kiln-load (scale in ft).

Farm, Wattisfield, several possible waster vessels laid on their sides around the bollard appeared to be *in situ*. At Mancetter in Kiln 19a (Hartley 1973a, 146, Kiln C) and at Caldicot, Mon. (Pl. 40), however, the stacking appeared to have been more random.

Although kilns of this type first appeared in the early 2nd century, and were apparently most frequent in the 3rd, they continued to be built without visible structural differences into the second half of the 4th century, as at Market Weston (inf. D. Compton). Their distribution, centred as it was on Suffolk and South-west Essex, changed little throughout that period (Maps 11, 15, 17).

(*B*) In this sub-group the oval or circular central 'pedestal' was of similar overall proportions to that in group (A). It differed, however, in being either perforated or divided into two distinct segments by a narrow channel on the line of the flue axis. Occasionally such segments were independently shaped and

Plate 41. ICKLINGHAM, Suffolk: Kiln I, a single-chambered single-flued structure, with perforated central pedestal, probably mid to late third-century; stokehole in *foreground*.

spaced sufficiently far apart to warrant the term twin or double-pedestal. They, nevertheless, appear to be sufficiently closely-related to merit inclusion in this group. The mode of stacking in such kilns must have been identical to that in the single-bollard ones. The perforation, and more particularly the complete division of the pedestal into two, would have assisted the circulation of hot air in the centre of the oven, which must always have been a localized cold spot in the solid-pedestal kilns of group (A). The modification thus apparently represented an improvement. At West Stow, there is indeed evidence to suggest the development of one from the other. Kiln 4, the only one there with a perforated pedestal, seems to have been chronologically the latest, probably dating to the Hadrianic period (inf. S. West). Despite their evolution, perforated or two-segment pedestals continued, generally, to be far less common than the solid type in Suffolk and Essex. The overall distribution of both types, however, differed little (Map 11).

Within this general type, distinctive regional clusters can be recognized. In South Norfolk and North Suffolk, in Needham Kiln 2 (Frere and Clarke 1945, 209 ff.) and Icklingham Kiln I (Pl. 41), there was an axial perforation through the pedestal. When eroded by ploughing, or otherwise damaged, such a kiln might appear to have had a segmental rather than a truly perforated pedestal. This possibility is worth remembering in future excavations.

At Mucking (Jones and Rodwell 1973), of six single-chambered kilns, beginning in the late 1st or early 2nd century and spanning a total period of at least two centuries, three had single and three had twin pedestals. The earliest of the latter type dated from well within the 2nd century and, like its single-pedestal predecessor, was associated with clay bars. A larger than average gap between the pedestal and kiln-wall also tended to distinguish the Mucking twin-segment kilns from their Norfolk and Suffolk relatives. The central channel between the twin 'pedestals' was spanned by a small impromptu clay 'bridge' in two of them.

A completely separate group of kilns with split or twin pedestals occurred in Lincolnshire and Yorkshire, East Riding in the 4th century. Their relationship to the rest is uncertain since their probable evolution and many of their other characteristics were quite different. They are therefore discussed elsewhere (*see* p. 122 ff.).

(*C*) A few kilns with bollards or pedestals of unusual form existed. Several within the Savernake, Wilts., industry were 'U'-shaped (Annable 1962). The remainder occurred in Suffolk, within the area with the greatest concentration of solid-pedestal kilns (Map 11). None appears to reflect any outside influences. Arrangements such as the two sausage-shaped 'islands' in a 3rd-century kiln in Field II at Hacheston (Ipswich Mus. Records), and the horseshoe-shaped 'pedestal' in the mid to late 3rd-century kiln at Homersfield (Smedley and Owles 1961a), seem best interpreted as experiments or idiosyncrasies of individual potters, and of no wider significance.

Single-chambered single-flued kilns without portable furniture or inbuilt 'platforms'

A number of kilns in Britain apparently had neither a raised oven-floor nor furniture, nor any internal structure to aid draught circulation and/or stacking stability. Large pottery vessels such as wasters, stacked at the bottom of the kiln-load, probably fulfilled this function. There are indeed difficulties in distinguishing such featureless kilns from La Tène-derived sunken kilns which have had their floor bars and props totally removed after use, or from single-chambered kilns with the floors stripped of portable bricks. The problem is especially acute where a kiln structure alone has been excavated, to the exclusion of any adjacent features. These might well have contained fragments of discarded furniture, or other items capable of shedding light on the technology of the adjacent kiln. This applies particularly to the kiln at Martlesham, Suffolk (inf. S. West). Its early date, mid to late 1st century, sets it apart from the other kilns in this group, all of which post-dated the late 2nd century and most of which probably belonged to the late 3rd and 4th centuries.

The general distribution of these single-chambered kilns without furniture, though not quite as cohesive as that of the corresponding pedestal-kilns, nevertheless covered the same general area. It suggests that in most instances the types were probably related and perhaps even interchangeable in use (Map 11). This tends to be confirmed at Needham, where within a limited area of the site at least one, and possibly two kilns of this type (Nos. 1 and 3) and one with a perforated pedestal (No. 2) seem to have been operating at approximately the same date (Frere and Clarke 1945). Other groups, in East Hertfordshire at Hadham, and in West Essex at Moulsham Street, Chelmsford (Feature 322), Rettendon (Tildesley 1971), and possibly Halstead (inf. J. Smallwood) and Inworth (inf. C. Going), are also connected by close similarities in many of their products. In the last and latest of these kilns, two pots found inverted on the bottom of the kiln-chamber were presumably the residue of the expendable supportive layer of vessels.

Single-chambered twin-flued kilns

Kilns belonging to this group also lacked a raised oven-floor but included two diametrically opposing and usually identical flues (Fig. XVIII). The majority had an oval furnace-chamber with which the flues often tended to merge gradually, rather than forming an abrupt angle. The major variants within the type involved the same general range of internal structures and furniture as those found in single-chambered single-flued kilns. Corder (1957, 23–4), following Grimes (1930, 61), erroneously classified these twin-flued kilns as horizontal-draught kilns. He thereby implied that the fire was sited in one flue while the opposing flue acted as a chimney or vent, drawing the heat horizontally through the pottery. As Bryant has shown (1973,

149), a true horizontal firing can only be achieved when a kiln-chamber has a solid permanent dome and when its exhaust flue terminates in a proper chimney. There is no indication of such a technology being used in Roman Britain. Examples of a possible variant are discussed on p. 120. Most Romano-British twin-flued kilns have been found with indications of burning in both flues. Evidence of this from the three kilns at Overwey was published as early as 1949 (Clark 1949, 44), but in 1957 Corder had failed to grasp the full implications of Clark's discussion. As Bryant has pointed out (pers. comm.), evidence for the use of horizontal-draught kilns by peasant potters is singularly lacking anywhere in the world.

At Chichester (Gunn 1971), Alice Holt (M. Lyne, pers. comm.) and Barton-on-Humber (Bryant 1977b), experiments in firing copies of Romano-British double-flued kilns with fires burning simultaneously in both flues have shown the method to be practicable, holding few snags for an experienced potter. These kilns worked on an updraught principle like almost all other Romano-British types. Their advantage lay in their rather elongated form which allowed a generally greater overall size of kiln-chamber, at the same time avoiding a cold spot at the back of the oven. This must have been a perpetual problem in single-flued kilns, particularly those with a large single chamber. The Alice Holt experimental firings have, however, shown that single-chambered twin-flued kilns tend to develop a colder spot in the centre of the oven. The very careful loading of inverted vessels in vertical stacks or, alternatively, the use of a platform or expendable vessels in the middle of the kiln-chamber helped to combat this.

Single-chambered kilns with double flues seem to have been closely related to those with a single flue. Like them, they had presumably developed from clamps or bonfire-kilns. The probability of this close relationship may be reinforced by the fact that both occasionally used portable stacking elements or a substantial central 'pedestal'. Several potters apparently used both single and double-flued varieties simultaneously, or at least in the same phase of production, as at Chichester (Down 1978, 56 ff.), in Kilns 1, 2, 4, 5 and 6 at Column Ride, Savernake (Annable 1962), at Overdale (Harris and Young 1974), at Hadham (inf. B. Barr and K. F. Hartley), possibly also at Tottenham House, Great Bedwyn, and in Kilns 9, 10, 11 at Colchester (Hull 1963, 3 ff.). Like single-chambered single-flued kilns, most double-flued kilns were used to produce reduced grey or black regional kitchen-wares, rather than fine or colour-coated wares. Exceptions comprised Hadham, where colour-coated wares proper were clearly a minority product (inf. K. F. Hartley), and the Chichester kilns, whose immediate origins were probably entirely exotic in character.

There is, at present, no conclusive evidence of single-chambered twin-flued kilns in Britain before the Conquest. This, however, does not mean that they were never used, since there is so little evidence for pre-Roman kilns of any type. Isolated 'ultimate La Tène' examples of twin-flued kilns, probably without raised oven-floors, have been found in Gaul (Duhamel

1979, 73, fig. 43). Two were recorded at Villedieu-sur-Indre, Central France, one certainly having a central pedestal (Ferdière 1975, 91–2, 101), but a preliminary examination of the literature suggests that they were either relatively uncommon there or that few have so far been recognized. Whether the establishment of twin-flue technology in Britain resulted from its introduction by immigrant potters before or around the time of the Conquest, or was a spontaneous and independent development, must remain

uncertain for the time being. The mid 1st-century single-chambered twin-flued 'pedestal'-kiln at Chichester (Down 1978, fig. 7.8) may, with reasonable certainty, be linked to the presence of immigrant Gallo-Belgic potters, perhaps from Gaul, who were supplying the army. The precise range of vessel-forms, the finish of their products and the elaborate method of lining this kiln, using small, curved, rectangular-sectioned, unfired or sun-dried bricks arranged to give a 'basket-weave' effect, are alien to Britain at this period. The latter technique is, indeed, without precise parallel among Romano-British pottery kilns of any date. It is unlikely that such a kiln made any significant impact on the development of twin-flued kilns in Roman Britain. Only limited numbers of 1st-century kilns of this type have been recorded but, even so, their main concentration lies nowhere near Chichester (Map 12). Their character, furthermore, is very different from the deeply-set circular example there. Almost all other 1st to early 2nd-century Romano-British twin-flued kilns are quite shallow or even surface-built, although later they tended to become deeper. Unlike the Chichester kiln, they were also very elongated, often almost boat-shaped, lacked a sharp angle between flue and kiln-chamber, and had relatively wide flues (Pl. 42). Their products too, although ultimately with La Tène III ('Belgic') affinities, had little in common with the sophisticated Gallo-Belgic-derived table-wares from the Chichester kiln.

If no links existed between that at Chichester and the subsequent twin-flued kilns elsewhere, does the distribution of the normal 1st and early 2nd-century examples provide any hint of their origin? Their concentration is in North Wiltshire, in Savernake Forest (Annable 1962), at Great Bedwyn, Brooms-grove near Pewsey, Purton (Anderson 1980) and Whitehill Farm, near Swindon (Anderson 1979). There are additional scattered examples at Gorley, South Hants. (Summer 1917, 50, plan IXA), Overdale, and in the Highgate Wood complex, where they comprised the earliest excavated kilns (inf. P. Tyers). This produces a distribution-pattern (Map 12) in marked contrast to that of the earliest La Téne-derived kilns with bars (Map 8). Given the relatively ephemeral character of most early

Plate 42.

(*upper* and *lower*) Whitehill Farm, LYDIARD TREGOZE, nr. Swindon, Wilts.: Kiln 6, a shallowly-built, single-chambered twin-flued boat-shaped structure, probably of Antonine date (ranging pole in half metres).

double-flued kilns, some examples of pre-Conquest date may yet be found. It would be unwise to draw firm conclusions from the limited yet reasonably cohesive evidence available from the distribution-pattern. One interpretation, however, might be that this reflects the impact of Continental immigrants, as distinct from 'kiln-bar' users, who settled in the Thames Valley and central Southern England in the late Iron Age. Alternatively, and perhaps preferably, early single-chambered double-flued kilns may represent the localized Romanization of a long-standing indigenous bonfire or clamp technology. This tradition had possibly survived in these areas until the Conquest because, unlike its counterpart in Eastern England, it had not been influenced or superseded immediately before then by the arrival of late La Tène kiln technology.

It is unfortunate that in the Alice Holt/Farnham industry, with which single-chambered twin-flued kilns have long been associated (Fig. XVIII), no preserved kiln structures proper earlier than the very late 2nd century have been located. This is despite the fact that evidence from earlier waster heaps suggests that production commenced around the middle of the 1st century AD (Lyne and Jefferies 1979). In 1981, however, two pit-clamps, the sites of repeated firings, were salvage-recorded by M. Lyne (pers. comm.) in a pipe-trench at Binsted, Alice Holt. One, associated with the manufacture of Iron-Age saucepan-pots, has a radiocarbon date of between AD 30 and 60 (corrected according to Shriver's recent unpublished calibration table; inf. M. Lyne and A. J. Clark). This, complemented by the author's unpublished research material from Iron-Age/Romano-British settlements in Hampshire, suggests that at least in some areas saucepan-pots probably continued in use until the Conquest, later than hitherto supposed. The other clamp produced handmade cordoned, lattice-decorated, 'necked' jars, of which wheel-thrown versions are associated with the earliest phases of the Alice Holt industry. It may, therefore, date to immediately after the Conquest. This new evidence may indicate continuity of pottery production in that area, reinforcing the possibility of development from pit-clamps to single-chambered twin-flued kilns. The first use of proper kilns in that industry possibly coincided with the introduction of finer fabrics for some of the products. Thereafter, clamps may indeed have continued in use for considerably longer, but only for firing the coarsest wares (inf. M. Lyne).

The 3rd and 4th centuries saw the peak not only of the activity of the Alice Holt/Farnham potteries, but of the use of twin-flued kilns throughout Britain (Map 12). Evidence suggests that at this time industries in East Anglia and the North-east Midlands were changing over to such kilns, as at Harrold (inf. A. Brown), or at least supplementing single with double flues. During this period also, the type seems to have occurred for the first time in areas where, hitherto, single-chambered single-flued kilns had generally dominated in the production of local-type wares. Examples are known at the Bandlefield site, Wattisfield, and at Hacheston, and possibly also at Colchester (Hull 1963, Kilns 10 and 11), and at Hadham. The precise phasing of the last two within their respective industries is not yet fully established. The cause of this change is not clear, but it is just possible that the greater capacity and efficiency of double kilns were gradually becoming more widely appreciated. The apparent trend, in Roman Britain at this date, towards the concentration of pottery manufacture in the hands of fewer producers may not be unconnected.

Single-chambered twin-flued kilns with prefabricated furniture

The prefabricated furniture was presumably placed beneath the lowest stack of vessels to allow warm air from the furnaces to pass freely beneath the whole load. Although a wide but ill-assorted variety is known, no item is exactly comparable with those recorded in the single-chambered single-flued kilns. A large 'loom-weight' and a 'cubical object' found together in the earliest double-flued Savernake-ware kiln at Great Bedwyn are reminiscent of objects associated with Iron-Age clamp-sites (p. 53 ff.), and presumably functioned as described above. In a similar category were the coil-built clay rings and perhaps the perforated 'clay sheeting' occurring on the earliest Alice Holt/Farnham kiln dumps (Lyne and Jefferies 1979, 17) and possibly, but less certainly, the 'bricks or tiles with rounded edges' from Oare, Wilts. (Swan 1975, 38). It is difficult to see what other function could have been served by the nearly-squared, baked slabs, 0.04 m thick and resembling bricks, in Kiln II at Overwey. A slight 'step' at the junction of the side-walls with the floor of this kiln could have complemented their use (Clark 1949, 39–40). Unfortunately, presumably because of the reuse of furniture, none has been found definitely in situ. The 'shadows' of rectangular blocks on the bottom of a late 2nd to early 3rd-century Alice Holt Kiln (AH52), however, give some possible indication of their original arrangement. Evidence suggests that subsequent rebuilds of the same kiln, into the middle of the 3rd century, may well have been fired without furniture. This practice apparently accords with a probable general tendency to discontinue its use. The body of evidence is not yet very large, but prefabricated furniture tends to occur mostly in earlier kilns, and is absent from definite 3rd and 4th-century sites, as with single-chambered single-flued kilns (Maps 11, 12).

Single-chambered twin-flued kilns with pedestal or other integral internal feature

These occur much less frequently than the corresponding single-chambered single-flued kilns with integral support(s). Such as are known, however, have a similarly wide chronological span, ranging from the late 1st to the 4th century. The internal features are also more diverse in character, much more so than those associated with single-chambered single-flued kilns. They include, however, a large flat-topped central pedestal, as in Savernake Kiln 4 and Hamstead Marshall Kiln 2. Another variation comprised a small pedestal near each flue-mouth, later replaced by two sausage-shaped platforms, in the kiln in 'Field IV' at Hacheston (inf. E. Owles). At the same settlement, the latter arrangement was also recorded in the kiln in 'Field II'. The pedestals near the flues represent types of 'baffles' intended to deflect sudden rushes of cold air into the kiln at the cooling stage (inf. R. Coleman-Smith). It may be significant that, in those areas of Eastern England where a large central solid-clay pedestal occurs frequently in single-flued kilns, it is totally lacking in the double-flued kilns. In many places both types belong to the same industries, which adopted twin-flued kilns at a late stage in their history.

Single-chambered twin-flued kilns lacking internal features

Potters operating these kilns presumably managed to maintain a good draught without the use of furniture, by the judicious stacking of large waster pots or fragments of vessels at the bottom of the load. Such vessels have been discovered apparently *in situ*, as at Broomsgrove. Where no props are found, it is impossible to identify kilns which had portable furniture, subsequently removed for reuse. This may apply particularly to some of the earlier kilns and those on sites where the area excavated was very restricted. Except at Hacheston, however, none of the more easterly sites with 3rd or 4th-century single-chambered kilns of both double and single-flued type have produced evidence of any furniture (Maps 15, 17). The majority seem to form a distinct regional group, comprising Bandlefield, Wattisfield, Colchester, Much Hadham, and possibly Harrold. On ceramic grounds, however, Hacheston seems to have been working in isolation, with rather idiosyncratic traditions.

Sloping or cross-draught kilns(?)

Excavations on at least one site have uncovered kilns which might perhaps best be described as sloping-draught. These are distinguished by having one 'flue' at a higher level than that of its counterpart. As Bryant has pointed out (pers. comm.), provided that the oven-superstructure was proportionately low and the floor slope sufficient, they might have functioned rather like oriental bank-kilns, such as the climbing kilns of Japan (Rhodes 1969, 18 ff.; Leach 1976, 183 ff.). Although without a chimney, these nevertheless develop a strong draught because the entire kiln, from the stokehole, through the flue and oven, is built on an upward slope. This may account for an uphill opening, or back exhaust-vent, opposite the stokehole in the Romano-British kilns. This allowed hot air from the fire to be drawn across the oven towards the back of the kiln. It contrasts with the normal Romano-British updraught type in which the oven-superstructure tended to be much taller, with an exhaust-vent or vents at or near its top.

Features apparently conforming to this sloping-draught arrangement were noted in several examples from seven superimposed or modified kiln structures at the Savernake-ware factory at Great Bedwyn. The excavator, E. H. Steele, recorded that 'The ovens . . . in each modification, had a pronounced slope to the floor, the opening to the fire-pit at the lower end being slanted and curved around the wall of the oven. By contrast, the openings at the upper end were rectangular in shape, having horizontal lintels. In the final version, this opening had been carefully blocked and the inner face lined with saggars [i.e. setters] of circular shape . . . The upper openings (in all phases) revealed little sign of stoking operations' (*WAM* 1x (1965), 136). If of a temporary nature, the final blocking of the 'flue' may be explained by the fact that reduced wares were being produced at the last firing.

At Alice Holt (AH52), a similar structure, possibly but less certainly of this type, was found built into a waster dump. It comprised the latest of five superimposed kilns spanning the late 2nd to mid 3rd century. The excavators recorded that 'one of the two flues, apparently the more up-hill one, had its outer end blocked off with kiln waste, so that the flue was deflected upwards into the base of a pit thus created, and looked more like a chimney' (Lyne and Jefferies 1979, 18). The function of this latter feature is difficult to understand. It may merely represent a 'fire-box' arrangement to stop wind gusting directly into the kiln.

Only testing by experimental firings will show whether all these structures can operate successfully as sloping or cross-draught kilns. Other advantages may be inherent in their design. Indeed, until more of them are carefully excavated, the existence of Romano-British sloping-draught kilns must remain no more than a very tentative idea.

Icenian kilns

The northern part of East Anglia N of the River Waveney, esssentially the territory of the Iceni, on present evidence had no strong pre-Conquest ceramic traditions, either in wheel-thrown or handmade wares. This was in sharp contrast with the Trino-vantian, Catuvellaunian, and Coritanian neighbours to the S and W. The initiative for the production of quality wares must, therefore, have come from outside, perhaps with the arrival of the Roman army.

In the Neronian to early Flavian period, some of the newly-established pottery-manufacturing centres may have involved immigrant craftsmen from other Roman provinces. This is probably implied by the rectangular structures and exotic nature of products from the earliest kilns at Caistor St Edmund (Swan 1981) and Morley St Peter (Fig. XXII; pp. 83–5). These may have emanated directly from the Continent or have been set up by immigrants initially working at Colchester (Swan 1981, 131). Perhaps about the mid and late 1st to early 2nd century, native potters also moved into the territory (Map 15), working mainly in British La Tène-derived ('Belgic') traditions and using kilns with prefabricated bars as at Thorpe St Andrew (Gregory 1979), Spong Hill, North Elmham (Pl. 16; inf. R. Rickett), possibly at Snettisham (inf. A. Gregory), and later at Sheringham (Howlett 1960).

Mrs K. Hartley (pers. comm.) has remarked on similarities between the late 1st-century mortaria produced in Norfolk, for example at Hevingham and immediately S of the Roman town of

Caistor St Edmund (inf. J. Webb), and those made by potters working in the vicinity of Colchester. This may suggest that the traditions of the Colchester region continued to exert a strong influence on pottery manufacture in Norfolk. The structures of four late 1st to early 2nd-century kilns at Hevingham, two circular and two roughly rectangular, each with a narrow, rectangular tongue-support and solid-clay vent-holed floor, may also imply some sort of continuity in technology.

The most important factory in the 2nd century was undoubtedly that at Brampton (Knowles 1977). The nature of the surface material from W of the main complex suggests that its origins, possibly geared to military supply, may go back to the late Neronian to early Flavian period. The earliest excavated kiln, oval with a narrow rectangular tongue-support and solid-clay vent-holed floor, is probably Flavio-Trajanic, with the emphasis on late Flavian since its back-fill incorporated much later intrusive material (e.g. Green 1977, fig. 27, no. 23). A full-scale study of the Brampton kilns and their products has yet to be accomplished so that any conclusions are still tentative. The peak of production, however, apparently occurred in the mid to late 2nd century, with activity thereafter on a reduced scale, perhaps until the mid 3rd century.

Of the various types of kilns found at Brampton, two major categories stand out: those of circular form with rectangular and/or triangular pilaster-supports, solid-clay vent-holed floors and long flues (Pl. 43; Knowles 1977, Types II A–C, Kilns A5 and 6, F and F4, and H); and very large, rectangular or square kilns, with longish lateral, rectangular or near-rectangular pilasters, solid-clay vent-holed raised oven-floors and very long flues (Fig. XIX; Knowles 1977, Types I A and B, Kilns D2, E, F1 and 2). The origin and date-span of the former are uncertain, but one of the smallest, Kiln H, seems to belong, provisionally, to the early/mid 2nd century. Such a relatively dense concentration creates difficulties in determining whether the pottery in the kiln-chambers or stokeholes related to the kilns in which it was found. It could have been redeposited from dumps or even thrown in during the unloading of other kilns.

Contemporary circular kilns with pilaster-supports alone and solid-clay vent-holed floors are very rare elsewhere in Britain in the 2nd–early 3rd century (Map 10). The only generally similar examples, Kiln I at Whitehall Gardens, Canterbury (Jenkins 1956; Trajanic-early Hadrianic) and a recently excavated kiln at Hedgerley Lane, Gerrards Cross, Bucks., have little else in common to suggest a relationship with the Brampton examples, in either their products or method of construction. Whatever their origins, circular kilns with pilasters seem to have formed a small but distinctive regional group in Norfolk from the early to mid 2nd century onwards (Map 15). Apart from at least five at Brampton, there were 3rd-century examples at Shouldham, one (inf. J. Smallwood), Pentney, at least two (inf. A. Gregory), and Witton, one, and an oval late 3rd to 4th-century one at Hevingham, all primarily producing reduced local-type kitchen wares. A late 2nd to early 3rd-century example at Ellingham (inf. A. Rogerson) had a long narrow tongue as well as pilasters. It

Plate 43. BRAMPTON, Norfolk.: Kiln F: (*upper*) solid-clay vent-holed raised oven-floor (ranging pole in ft); (*lower*) furnace-chamber with oven-floor removed showing rectangular and triangular clay pilaster-supports, and flue on right.

occurred on a site, however, where at least one Colchester potter, Regalis, had a workshop specializing in mortaria of Norfolk type, flagons and mica-dusted wares and, like those products, may indicate some hybridization. A possible relationship with the pilastered kilns operating in the late 2nd–3rd century at Horningsea (Walker 1912) may be worth consideration. It is, however, uncertain whether they originally had a raised oven-floor, or were of an unusual single-chambered type with pilasters effectively preventing the stacking of vessels along the kiln's circumference, thus allowing the unimpeded circulation of hot air in that region.

Structurally, the very large rectangular or square kilns at Brampton, with the furnace-chamber floor sloping downwards between relatively long pilasters, resembled tile kilns (Fig. XIX). There is, however, no doubt of their primary association with the manufacture of oxidized wares, including very large, buff, double-handled flagons, medium and small ring-necked flagons, and mortaria of Norfolk type. Some of the latter were stamped with herringbone trade marks or the names of potters, including

AESVMINVS. These potters were exporting small quantities of mortaria, and probably flagons, to Lincolnshire and North-eastern military sites within the mid to late 2nd century (inf. K. F. Hartley).

Rectangular pottery kilns with pilasters were extremely rare in Britain after the Northern 'military' ones of the Trajanic period (p. 87 ff.; Map 9). It is difficult to believe that the Brampton examples represent a regional survival from that date, particularly as they differed morphologically. Two certain later examples are known elsewhere, both at Colchester, Kilns 26 and 31, where they may have been reintroduced from the Continent (p. 95). Like those at Brampton, these were large, with an inward-sloping or raised furnace-chamber floor between pilasters. They were of the mid to late 2nd century, and also apparently connected with the manufacture of mortaria, often impressed with name-stamps or 'herringbone' trade marks. The Colchester potteries were at their most progressive, cosmopolitan, and successful at this precise period and the Brampton potters may have copied their newest technology in an attempt to compete in the East Anglian and northern markets. Brampton's production of jars with moulded appliqué face-masks might also represent a contemporary challenge to Colchester's more elaborately-moulded or barbotine-decorated table-wares. Alternatively, and perhaps less likely, one or more Colchester manufacturers may have been involved at Brampton. There are elements of similarity in several of the flagon-forms. At Ellingham, in the Waveney Valley, the manufacture of mortaria impressed with the stamp of the potter Regalis shows that at least one Colchester craftsman thought it worthwhile either to migrate to or open up a branch factory in Icenian territory.

If a possible link between Brampton and Colchester is rejected, extensive research further afield, that is on the Continent, will be required to establish the immediate origins of these kilns. Clearly, such distinctive pottery kilns seem hardly likely to have been a spontaneous development in such an area. It is ironic that despite the apparent tremendous efforts of the Brampton potters to achieve large-scale production of specialist wares, only a very small proportion of these was exported outside East Anglia, their main markets lying within Icenian territory. Perhaps for this reason, the manufacture of such wares as mortaria and flagons at Brampton seemingly lasted only until the late 2nd century, when the use of this type of rectangular kiln was also possibly discontinued.

Coritanian and South Parisian kilns

The non-specialist kilns in these areas can be classified into distinct regional types (Map 13). During the 1st and 2nd centuries, the kilns found in the South Coritanian territory, comprising Rutland, Leicestershire, Nottinghamshire, North Northamptonshire and South Lincolnshire, had similarities with those typical of the valleys converging on the Wash, namely La

Tène-derived ('Belgic') circular kilns with a raised floor of portable tapering bars, often a short flue, and a portable clay, sometimes central, oven-floor support (Map 8). The group as a whole has already been discussed (see p. 55 ff.). Its most northerly outliers in Lincolnshire seem to be those at North Hykeham gravel pit (Thompson 1958) and Lincoln Racecourse (Corder 1950a).

Another small but distinctive group lay within the North and West Coritanian and the South Parisian territories. Typologically, the earliest kilns within it are perhaps best termed 'Linwood-type', from the place where such structures were first recognized. On only four sites are they identifiable with certainty from excavations, at Linwood (Kiln I and possibly Kiln II) and Colsterworth in Lincolnshire, at Hasholme, Holme upon Spalding Moor, Yorks. E.R. (Hicks and Wilson 1975, Kiln 1) and at Ravenstone, Leics. (inf. H. Clamp and A. Hurst). There are, however, several possibly related variants in North Lincolnshire, at Claxby (Bryant 1977a), and less certainly at Dragonby (Kiln 2) and Thealby, Burton Stather (Dudley 1949, 203, 213–14). In any case, few of the many kiln sites in the region have been excavated. 'Linwood-type' kilns were characterized by two

Plate 44. LINWOOD, Lincs.: Kiln I, with twin rectangular clay pedestals of typical 'Linwood-type', spanned by short, square-ended 'bridging-bars' (length of pedestals 0.7 m approx.).

long, roughly parallel clay or stone blocks positioned centrally on the flue axis, approximately 0.18 m–0.3 m apart, and usually occupying a substantial part of the kiln-chamber (Pl. 44). The gap between these was normally spanned by stone slabs or square-sectioned, roughly rectangular clay bars, sometimes perforated and occasionally slightly curved, but invariably blunt-ended. At Colsterworth, in the late 1st or early 2nd-century kiln formerly thought to be an iron-furnace (Pl. 45; Hannah 1932), and later at Ravenstone, such bars were overplastered with clay, and mere vent-holes had been left between them. In Linwood Kiln I, possibly mid to late 4th-century (JRS xxxii (1942), 110), clay luting secured them in place at the ends. No bars have been found spanning the gap between pedestal and kiln-wall, except

Plate 45. COLSTERWORTH, Lincs.: 'Linwood-type' kiln, formerly considered to be an iron-furnace: (*upper*) bars, spanning the two central pedestals, overplastered with clay; (*lower*) the two central pedestals with surrounding kiln-wall, and some 'bridging-bars' removed. Note rectangular bar-fragment in *foreground* (scales probably 2 ft in length).

possibly in Ravenstone Kiln 2, where several roughly-rectangular pieces of stone rested on jar-bases wedged in the front of the kiln-chamber, adjoining the flue. Such a gap, not more than 0.3 m at its widest point, could indeed have been spanned easily by larger vessels. At Ravenstone, inverted vessels were found at the bottom at the back of one kiln-chamber, apparently *in situ* where they had been fired (inf. A. Hurst). In three kilns in this group where the flue survived intact, two at Ravenstone and in Hasholme Kiln 1 (Hicks and Wilson 1975), it was relatively long, over two-thirds of the length of the kiln-chamber long axis.

It is not clear what relationship these kilns had with the earlier Coritanian La Tène-derived examples, which also used prefabricated bars though mostly tapered. Their chronologies are as yet too uncertain to establish a positive link between them. Moreover, those La Tène III-derived kilns in Britain with the nearest pedestal arrangements, but with proper raised oven-floors, occurred not in South Coritanian territory but mainly in North Kent (Fig. IX). One example is known in Icenian territory, at Spong Hill. The recent discoveries at Ravenstone may indicate some link between these Coritanian structures and the Derbyshire-ware kilns (p. 124). Certainly the general character and dispositions of pedestals and bars, and vessel-stacking arrangements were similar (Fig. XXI). It is evident that excavations on early kiln sites in the Trent Valley are needed before any reliable assessment can be made.

Perhaps during the first half of the 4th century, the so-called 'Swanpool-type' kiln (Fig. XX) seems to have evolved from the Linwood twin-pedestal type. At this stage apparently, the rectangular pedestals of the generally earlier kilns had evolved into two integral D-shaped clay pedestals, occupying most of the furnace-chamber. In possibly the earliest examples, the narrow gully, between the pedestals along the flue axis, was still occasionally spanned by clay bars or small clay bridges, as at Rookery Lane, Lincoln (Webster 1960). The surrounding channel, rarely more than 0.15 m across, was probably normally bridged by large vessels. The development of these pedestals in Lincolnshire could perhaps have been influenced by kilns with a central 'split' or segmental pedestal in East Anglia and Essex (p. 116). Like them, as well as probably the Linwood group, Swanpool-type kilns ought to be classed as single-chambered.

Unlike those East Anglian kilns, the method of construction of the Swanpool-type was highly idiosyncratic. A large, shallow, oval scoop was dug, into which raw clay was dumped, and from this the whole kiln, chamber, pedestals and flue, was constructed, or 'sculpted', *in situ*. The lower parts of the walls of both the furnace-chamber and the characteristically long flue thus have a very thick appearance, particularly when ploughed examples are excavated, as at Oak Farm, Swanpool, Lincoln (Pl. 46). Normally, the chamber lay almost entirely above ground, explaining why few have survived up to the pedestal top.

It is difficult to determine precisely when 'Swanpool-type' kilns emerged. At Hasholme, on the same site as the late 3rd–early 4th-century Linwood-type kiln already mentioned, two slightly later kilns had been constructed in a clay-filled scoop using an identical technique. They had long flues, but lacked the Swanpool-type integral segmental pedestals, the original portable internal furniture possibly having being reused elsewhere. They may thus represent a transitional stage in the development of that type. Possibly the earliest known fully-developed Swanpool-type kilns, with D-shaped pedestals, occurred in the Trent Valley at Knaith, Lincs. (Fig. XX). They have been tentatively dated by the excavator, B. Whitwell, to within the period late 3rd to mid 4th century. Square-ended bars found near them may suggest the presence of the possibly ancestral Linwood-type kilns within that extensive complex. At Linwood, however, one Linwood-type kiln was apparently in use until after the middle of the 4th century. Swanpool-type kilns clearly

124

Plate 46. Oak Farm, Swanpool, LINCOLN: Kiln 1 (*foreground*), badly eroded by ploughing, showing typical Swanpool-type construction, with kiln-chamber and two massive D-shaped pedestals 'sculpted' out of a dump of clay. Kiln 2 (*background*), sited in its stokehole (scales in ft and ins).

painted wares, made in such kilns (Webster and Booth 1947). Some of these vessels resemble those made at Crambeck, where the kilns may, ultimately, have had an ancestry similar to that of the Linwood-type, but had developed along different lines in the succeeding two centuries (p. 110).

A number of other, unexcavated, sites in Lincolnshire possibly had kilns of the Linwood/Swanpool class. Several rural locations have produced surface concentrations of grey pottery within the range outlined, together with kiln debris and bars. These include Buslingthorpe, the Navigation Lane and Mill Dam sites near Caistor, Market Rasen (inf. K. Hunter), Risby Moor and Walesby Moor, Walesby (inf. J. Mostyn Lewis), and possibly Woolsthorpe. Other unusual but possibly related kiln structures utilizing bars could, however, have been involved, as at Barnetby Top (Samuels 1979), possibly at Little London near Torksey, at Bourne, and in the major factories of the Doncaster area to the NW (p. 105 ff.). The kilns of the last centre, with its Harts-hill/Mancetter links, were perhaps non-local in origin. In the middle of the 2nd century, however, they may have embraced local Coritanian traditions in the use of bars for flooring, albeit spanning the whole combustion-chamber and permanently secured. Clearly, there is great need for a proper programme of excavation and research on many of these probable kiln sites, particularly in North and West Lincolnshire, Leicestershire and Nottinghamshire. As yet, discussion of their origins and relationships must remain very tentative.

Derbyshire kilns

There were essentially no strong ceramic traditions in the Derby area immediately before the Roman Conquest. The origins of Romano-British pottery production in that region probably date back to the Flavian period, when the establishment of a fort at Little Chester apparently attracted potters to set up workshops in its industrial *vicus* immediately to the E, in the area now occupied by Derby Racecourse Playing Fields. Subsequently production continued on the same site, reaching its peak in the Trajanic and early Hadrianic periods (Maps 4, 5). Evidence published in excavation reports (Brassington 1971; 1980) suggests that in the Antonine period this derelict industrial area was apparently levelled and much rubbish, including pottery from old waster dumps, was back-filled into the abandoned kilns. This resulted in much mixing of pottery types from the various phases of activity. The dumping of wasters from kiln loads into adjacent disused kilns during earlier pottery manufacture compounds the problems of interpretation. The only sealed and relatively uncontaminated Flavian or Flavio-Trajanic deposit was found in a well. Although overlaid by a Trajanic-Hadrianic kiln, this ought to relate to earlier kilns on the site.

Careful reconsideration of the published evidence suggests to the author that probably the earliest excavated kilns were the

continued until the end of the Roman period at Swanpool itself (Webster and Booth 1947). Their known distribution (Map 13) is confined to sites N of, or adjacent to Lincoln, such as Rookery Lane, Swanpool itself, Knaith (Fig XX), possibly Walesby, Lincs., and Throlam, Holme upon Spalding Moor (Corder 1932), the industry to which the Hasholme kilns belonged. Few 4th-century kilns, however, have been excavated on the Lincolnshire Wolds or in the West Coritanian territory.

The products of both Linwood and Swanpool-type kilns were normally grey, with areas of burnishing and often burnished line-decoration. Although differing slightly in profile between sites, they had a certain regional unity in both their technique and in the basic range of vessel-types involved. They included cooking-pots of so-called Swanpool and Dales-types (Gillam 1951; Loughlin 1977), large S-profiled bowls, jars with lug or, later, counter-sunk handles, narrow-mouthed jars with loop-handles, and copies of black-burnished ware flanged bowls. Only at Swanpool were specialist products, mortaria, colour-coated and small, or relatively small, Kilns 1e, 1f, 6 and 7. These were characterized by a small, portable, clay or stone central support, loose clay radial bars and, sometimes flat stacking or flooring-plates. Their structural affinities seem to lie with the La Tène-derived kilns of the valleys converging on the Wash basin, including the Upper Nene Valley (p. 55ff.). Of the Little Chester products which appear typologically to be the earliest, some forms, such as the carinated bowls, Brassington Nos. 9–11, and 'necked' bowls, Nos. 526–7, would not be out of place in mid to late 1st-century deposits from other sites in that area, for example at Irchester. Others, such as everted-rimmed jars, Nos. 159–60 and 212–4, closely resemble in form vessels which Todd (1968) defined as Trent Valley ware, a regional type of pottery current in the Middle to Lower Trent Valley primarily in the mid to late 1st century. Unfortunately, nothing is known of the structures of kilns producing such wares in the Trent Valley, and there is great need for their location and excavation. The possible presence at Little Chester of potters from the Upper Nene Valley or its vicinity seems to be reinforced by the occurrence in the back-fill of the Derby Racecourse kilns of non-local, rilled, lid-seated, shell-gritted jars, typical of Northamptonshire in the mid to late 1st century (Brassington 1971, Nos. 137–42). Copies of such vessels were also made in a gritty fabric on the Derby Racecourse site. These, termed pre-Derbyshire ware (Brassington 1971, 59–60), developed into the true Derbyshire ware characteristic of the middle of the 2nd century onwards.

During the Trajanic to early Hadrianic period, other potters were apparently drawn to the Little Chester *vicus*. The later kilns there were generally larger and more elaborate than hitherto. Even so, they often utilized bars in their raised floors, now normally overplastered with clay and vented. New vessel-types appear to have been introduced at the same time. At least two mortarium potters may have migrated to the site from the Midlands or opened up a branch workshop there (Brassington 1980), although the possibility of their movement to Hartshill/Mancetter from Little Chester, on its decline in the early Hadrianic period, should not be discounted. Kiln 2a on Derby Racecourse, apparently associated with the Mancetter manufacturer Septuminus, was remarkably like an improved version of Kiln 22 at Hartshill. It had a cylindrical chamber and roughly circular, central pedestal, composed of a core of stones overplastered with clay. The evidence of black-burnished ware (BB1) from Derby Racecourse may imply that potters familiar with its manufacturing technique, presumably Durotrigan, were also operating there (Brassington 1980, 39–40). At some stage, other immigrant potters must have brought to the site the technique of lead-glazing. The method of firing lead-glazed wares at Little Chester was simpler than that at Holt (Grimes 1930). Unlike Holt, there was no evidence recorded for the use of saggars or special props in the Derby kilns.

It is uncertain when the Derby Racecourse kilns ceased operation, but some time within the mid to late Hadrianic period seems probable. This possibly resulted from the removal of all or most of the Little Chester garrison in the early Hadrianic period

(Webster 1961, 109). The ceramic evidence from Chesterfield fort, *c.* 33 km to the S and not evacuated until *c.* AD 140, however, indicated a steady decline in its supplies from the Derby Racecourse kilns after *c.* AD 120 (inf. A. C. Anderson).

During the mid-Antonine period, the re-garrisoning of Little Chester may well have occasioned the taking over and clearing up of the old industrial *vicus* area and the back-filling of the kilns. In about the mid–late Hadrianic period, the local potters apparently moved out from the *vicus*, probably to sites in the adjacent valleys such as Holbrook (Kay 1962). About this time too, the more characteristic Derbyshire ware (Gillam 1939; Jones and Webster 1969) seems to have developed from the less highly-fired, lid-seated jars produced by the Little Chester kilns. The latter, termed pre-Derbyshire ware, were not fired as hard as true Derbyshire ware. It is difficult to chart from existing evidence the precise transition from one ware to another. This seems to be integrally linked with a radical change in kiln type, no doubt at about the same time. Of course, the latest kilns at Little Chester or the earliest kilns in the adjacent valleys may still be undiscovered. A large percentage of distorted sherds of Derbyshire-ware jars in a dumped deposit, itself comprising 40 per cent Derbyshire ware (Brassington 1980, Puddling pit C), could perhaps indicate the production of Derbyshire ware on Derby Racecourse itself. The excavator has however suggested, possibly less plausibly, that these, forming the bulk of the Derbyshire ware in the assemblage, were watertight seconds sold for industrial purposes from Derbyshire-ware kilns elsewhere, such as those in the Hazelwood/Holbrook area.

Derbyshire-ware kilns proper (Kay 1962) were characterized by twin, roughly rectangular, stone pedestals, set centrally side by side (Fig. XXI). On either side of these were two stone bars, each with one end resting on the pedestal and the other plastered into the kiln-wall, leaving a D-shaped area at the back of the kiln-chamber without a raised oven-floor. Here wasters or expendable vessels were apparently positioned on the furnace-chamber floor, a practice paralleled in some peasant potteries still operating in the Mediterranean area (Hampe and Winter 1965, 234, Abb. 150). The most striking feature of Derbyshire-ware kilns was their overall height, which was not merely an accident of survival. Because each kiln was normally sunk 2 m or more below ground, the oven itself could be constructed much taller than if it had been free-standing above ground. The typical Derbyshire-ware kiln, thus, probably looked and functioned like an underground chimney, whose strong draught must have induced very high temperatures. This was undoubtedly reflected in the very hard 'stoneware' characteristic of Derbyshire-ware cooking-pots, often fired to the point of vitrifaction.

Only the loosest links can be discerned between the structures of typical Derbyshire-ware kilns and those of the Derby Racecourse kilns. The prefabricated bars and clay central pedestals in the latter had possibly been superseded by stone in the former because the necessary gritstone was readily available on the sites NW of Derby. Tall oven-chambers emerged perhaps because it was found to be easier to sink kilns deep into the steep hillsides where many of these potteries were sited. It is, however, difficult to see why the Derbyshire-ware potters positioned oven-bars on each side of the kiln only, when their presumed ancestors on Derby Racecourse used oven-floors with bars spanning the whole furnace-chamber. The twin rectangular pedestals and the practice of stacking vessels at the bottom at the back of the kiln-chamber could perhaps indicate a relationship with the contemporary 'Linwood-type' kilns of Lincolnshire and Leicestershire (p. 122). There, however, the resemblance ends.

A break or unknown additional factor may, in fact, have been involved in the development of Derbyshire ware and its kiln technology. J. P. Gillam pointed out to the author that: (1) the form and fabric of Derbyshire-ware cooking-pots and Mayen-ware lid-seated jars from Germany are very similar; (2) the technological change necessary to produce true Derbyshire ware is more likely to have been a deliberate rather than an incidental process; and (3) similar deeply-sunken Romano-British kilns are absent elsewhere in Britain. Clearly the problem is insoluble on evidence available at present in Britain and on the Continent. These questions must, nevertheless, continue to be asked.

CHAPTER 9

Kiln studies: current techniques and future research

Discussion in this volume should have heightened awareness of the inadequacies existing in the present information about the kilns of the Romano-British pottery industry. Higher standards of excavation, archive preparation and publication are clearly desirable. Perhaps this study will help to initiate a carefully planned national research policy.

The kilns and kiln sites recorded here probably formed only a small percentage of those once existing in Roman Britain. Systematic field-walking of selected areas would undoubtedly pinpoint the locations of more. In the 1960s, such a programme in the Upper Nene Valley in Northamptonshire added dozens of kiln sites to the then existing maps. It also provided a new and invaluable insight into the social and economic development of the area at the time of the Roman army's advance. Field-workers and air-photographers covering areas adjacent to Romano-British kiln sites should also bear in mind the possible former existence of irregular earthwork compounds relating to coppicing.

On sites of suspected pottery production, field-walking can be supplemented by geophysical prospecting techniques to establish the precise position of kiln structures, and to define the limits of the complex as a whole. Magnetic surveying is particularly apposite on kiln sites (Tite 1972, 9 ff.). Baked earth structures such as kilns are weakly magnetic, and thus produce a localized increase in the magnetic field intensity. Additionally, pits and ditches with burnt or decaying organic fillings frequently produce weaker detectable magnetic anomalies. In Britain, such principles were first exploited in 1958 by the Oxford University Research Laboratory for Archaeology and the History of Art, using the proton magnetometer to locate pottery kilns near Water Newton in the Nene Valley in advance of road works (Aitken *et al.* 1958). In the past two decades, this instrument has been superseded by Plessey's fluxgate gradiometer (Philpot 1973; Clark 1975). Much faster to use, it gives continuous, as opposed to 'spot'-readings, and also has the advantage of an automatic plotting attachment. For kilns, this can outline the oven-walls and the position of the stokehole. A memory attachment enabling the 1,000 readings taken for each 30-metre square to be processed by computer is currently being developed by A. J. Clark at the Ancient Monuments Laboratory of the Department of the Environment.

Electro-magnetic surveying with a soil conductivity meter, such as the pulsed induction meter or 'banjo' (Alcock 1968, 8–10), is generally less helpful in the location of sunken kiln structures (CBA 1970; Tite 1972, 32 ff.). As yet the method has proved disappointing in its depth penetration. Its usefulness in the examination of topsoil for burnt features or concentrations of burnt material, however, might be exploited with benefit on sites with exceptionally shallow topsoil or on ploughed sites where surface-built kilns or clamp-firings are being eroded. Unfortunately, the surface remains of recent agricultural bonfires cannot be distinguished from ancient burning by this technique and readings need to be checked by excavation. Electro-magnetic surveying could, however, also prove useful on sites where topsoil has already been stripped by machine.

It could also help archaeological directors with restricted time or finances in deciding on excavation priorities. The study of rural sites, in particular, might benefit substantially from such locational work. Excavation of the internal features of rural settlements has often been preferred to work on the periphery where industrial activity usually occurred. The use of electromagnetic surveying could well result in a more efficient use of excavation resources and a substantial increase in the recorded number of rudimentary kilns. This is particularly desirable in the South of England, where there is much pottery, but where few production centres have been found. The same approach might be equally productive in areas adjacent to military establishments. At present only a handful of kiln sites can be linked directly to fortresses and forts and, in consequence, the sources of pottery supplied to the army in the 1st century are still relatively unknown.

The Excavation of Kiln Sites

Suggestions for future work could include consideration of the following points:

1. There is a great need for the excavation of much larger areas, with the aim of stripping whole factories in order to study their spacial organization. It would be useful to know of any differences in working-methods between the major and minor producers. It is no coincidence that most of the kiln sites providing the more significant and wide-ranging information, such as The Churchill Hospital and Mancetter, are those where considerable areas have been excavated. Apart from the greater chance of locating ancillary structures and features, extensive excavation also enables the products to be more reliably associated with particular kilns, and pottery densities and variations at different parts of a site to be recorded. Stratified but mixed assemblages may also be studied with greater confidence, since the pattern of waste disposal on the site can be assessed *in toto*. The application of statistical methods (p. 129), essential for the analysis and ordering of such data, can only provide potentially sound results when large pottery groups from a reasonable number of archaeological features, preferably over a large area, are available for comparison.

2. All excavators require a thorough understanding of the workings of kilns and their associated structures. This should enable the right questions to be posed and useful deductions to be made during the recording of structures which are often fragmentary and, in some cases, have been deliberately and extensively dismantled. Excavators have often drawn the wrong conclusions, especially in failing to distinguish single-chambered kilns from those with raised oven-floors which have been destroyed.

3. Higher standards of recording, involving more detailed and coherent drawings of kiln structures, are highly desirable. Whilst data for the perspective illustrations in this volume (Figs. VIII–XXI) were being compiled and collated, the inadequacy of the kiln drawings in many excavation reports became obvious. A plan and two sections are insufficient for what is, so often, a completely asymmetric structure. All too rarely are loose kiln-furniture, demolished or broken fragments of kiln structure and other fired clay debris adequately described and illustrated.

Kiln structures are, of course, difficult to represent visually by conventional means, particularly in plan. Different techniques need to be devised, such as contouring by photogrammetry or other means. The importance cannot be overestimated of a continuous section, drawn across the structure and its infill, from behind the centre of the back wall of the chamber to beyond the edge of the stokehole. This necessarily involves cutting through the kiln-wall, support(s), oven-floor, and flue(s). It is, nevertheless, essential for the accurate recording of the initial processes of construction and subsequent remodelling, renewal or repair. Another *desideratum* is a section across the deposited layers in the flue, in addition to one through the solid kiln structure at right angles to the flue axis. The assertion, in one excavation manual, that 'it is very unlikely that there will be any stratification to study' is somewhat misleading. If followed, this could lead to the loss of critical information. At a kiln excavated in 1966 in Sloden Enclosure in the New Forest, for example, over 0.6 m of stratified levels survived in the kiln-flue. These included several layers of ash separated by silt representing firings with periods of disuse between; a layer of debris representing the relining of the walls, the replacement of the raised oven-floor and repair to the flue; and raw clay indicating the blocking of the flue during the last firing. Such potential information may well have been lost through inadequate excavation and recording techniques in other cases. When excavating the interior of a kiln 'the most difficult problem', as Webster has wisely pointed out (1974, 63), 'is that of determining whether each piece of structure is collapsed debris, or part of the kiln *in situ*. Sometimes each piece has to be carefully isolated to make quite sure it is not attached to a standing fragment'.

4. Essential scientific procedures now include sampling of kiln structures for an independent determination of age by magnetic dating. A clay structure fired to $c.$ 700 °C or over acquires a weak permanent magnetism, the direction of which is parallel to the earth's magnetic field at the time of firing. By comparing the calibration of the fired clay samples from kiln structures with a reference curve indicating the changes in direction of this magnetic field, they may be dated independently (Aitken and Weaver 1962, 6; CBA 1970). Measurements (by A. J. Clark) can now be made on samples so small that damage to the kiln structure can be almost invisible (Clark 1980, 9). For the Roman period, however, the dating of Romano-British pottery by normal archaeological means almost always has greater precision than that possible from geomagnetic sampling, but future improvements in the detail and reliability of the geomagnetic curve are dependent on an increase in the number of samples collected from securely-dated fired structures. Geomagnetic

sampling of a kiln structure is therefore desirable in itself, irrespective of whether its date is known.

5. Radiocarbon (^{14}C) dating of charcoal samples from kilns may now prove useful in determining their age. The basis of this method (Tite 1972, 58–61, 79–90) depends on the concentration of radioactive carbon in dead organic material which decreases continuously at a slow but slightly variable pace. A recently revised calibration curve indicating the variations in this rate of decay has been established by Shriver (unpubl.). It now has particular relevance to the late Iron Age and Roman periods and, at best, can give probable dates to within ± 12 years (inf. A. J. Clark). Charcoal samples produce some of the most reliable measurements for radiocarbon dating. As suggested elsewhere (*see* p. 7), much of the wood used in firing kilns was probably young coppiced material and unlikely to involve the more ancient inner rings of a slow-growing tree. Where several ^{14}C dates are obtained, preferably from charcoal derived from a sequence of features such as stokeholes, radiocarbon dating may be more precise and reliable on Romano-British kiln sites than hitherto supposed. This applies particularly to the 3rd and 4th centuries, for which the dating of pottery is least precise.

6. In general there is a notable lack of palaeo-environmental information on kiln sites. The sieving, flotation and scientific examination of the contents of stokeholes, pits, and deposits sealed by waster-heaps could be informative on the types and age of fuel used, the former existence of turf superstructures, and the many aspects of the contemporary environment. A knowledge of the sampling requirements for such material would be useful to any intending excavator.

Kilns and their Products

While this volume has necessarily avoided the ceramic aspects of kiln sites, the function of a kiln was nevertheless to produce pottery. Indeed, the importance of kilns for pottery studies cannot be overstated. The excavation of major workshops often enables dates already assigned to their more widely-traded products to be applied to their locally-distributed ranges, intrinsically more difficult to date. Kiln sites also yield valuable information on the sources of wares not otherwise assignable. They aid the understanding of distributional patterns, of the marketing of pottery, and of the social, economic and technological development of a region. For these reasons it is essential that, wherever possible, excavation reports on kiln sites should be accompanied by information on their products and a discussion of their dates.

Those archaeologists who have never excavated a Romano-British kiln site may find it difficult to appreciate the vast quantity of pottery which may be recovered, and the very considerable amount of post-excavation work required for publication. It follows that such excavation should not proceed without the assurance of adequate post-excavation resources. The amount of unpublished pottery from kiln sites deposited in museum stores by archaeologists unable to deal with this problem is a sobering warning to any would-be kiln excavator.

The procedures for processing and publishing Romano-British pottery in general have recently been described in full (Young 1980), but several points are particularly relevant to kiln assemblages (Freke and Craddock 1980, 15–17). It is important that excavators should appreciate that pottery found on a kiln site will include many rejects. The surface colour, finish, hardness and sometimes shape of these, by their very nature, will not therefore necessarily conform to the traded output of the factory. In publishing such material, a detailed account of the colour, finish, decoration and fabric of each individual sherd is unnecessary. The report should, however, include descriptions of the wares as marketed. This will help other excavators to recognize more easily the source of the pottery they find. 'Alien' sherds not made on the kiln site, often strays from domestic occupation, need to be isolated and treated separately.

A number of scientific and statistical methods can aid the study of kiln products and their contexts. It should, however, be remembered that many of such techniques are expensive and their practitioners scarce.

Statistical analysis of the spacial distribution of vessel-types or fabrics across a site (e.g. trend surface analysis) may be necessary to define the patterns of waste disposal there and sometimes to highlight residual material (Orton 1970; Hodder and Orton 1976). Additionally, the relationships of deposits may be clarified. The proportions of vessel-types or fabrics within assemblages at various times may also be evaluated by statistical means (Orton 1975; 1978) and the results published as incidence matrices, cumulative percentage graphs, histograms or pie charts (Orton 1980, 161 ff.). Kiln sites sometimes produce many vessels of generally similar but not identical forms, and others of unusual profile. The difficult classification of such vessel-shapes may require the aid of more sophisticated statistical analysis (Doran and Hodson 1975). Specialist advice is essential for this. Allied techniques have also been used in an attempt to reconstruct possible vessel-shapes from sherds (Orton 1974). The extent to which vessel-forms and sizes were standardized in samian and other factories has already been examined (Rottländer 1966; 1967; 1977; Orton 1980, 208–10). Similar statistical work on more Romano-British kiln groups would also be valuable.

It is particularly interesting to determine the original firing temperature of kiln products. This is possible by means of thermal expansion measurements taken when the pottery is reheated steadily (Tite 1969; 1972, 298–300). Ceramic material, reheated beyond the point reached during its original firing in antiquity, begins to shrink, thereby providing an indication of the original firing temperature. The method is particularly appropriate for pottery fired at relatively high temperatures, that is 700–950 °C or more, when it is generally accurate to »30 °C. For lower fired wares, precision cannot be achieved and it is possible only to suggest that the firing temperature was either less than 500 °C or in the 500–700 °C range. Theoretically it might be feasible and worthwhile to apply this method to samples of well-fired clay kiln structure, but as yet no such work has been carried out. Further information on the firing conditions and colour-formation of products might be possible by Mössbauer spectroscopy (Tite 1972, 291–5, 327–8) or X-ray diffraction (CBA 1970; Tite 1972, 285–7). So far as is known, however, it has not been applied to Roman pottery. Attempts to obtain information on firing conditions by colour analysis have not yet proved very successful (Tite 1972, 300–301). The great complexity of the factors affecting the colour of pottery make any data extremely difficult to interpret. Over the past few years, however, research under Professor M. Magetti at the University of Fribourg, Switzerland, has included a study of the chemical changes which take place with particular elements found in pottery fired at specific temperatures. The results of work there on Roman pottery from known kiln sites in Switzerland and elsewhere on the Continent (Magetti and Rossmanith 1981; Jornet 1980) suggest that a similar programme of analysis on Romano-British kiln products would be very worthwhile.

In the dating of pottery in general, thermoluminescence is the most widely known method. At present, however, it is too inaccurate to be of value in the study of Romano-British pottery and can only be useful in determining whether a sherd is Roman or not (Young 1980, 28). The same limitations apply to the application of geomagnetic methods for dating Romano-British pottery (inf. A. J. Clark).

On kiln sites in production over a long period, the localized sources of raw materials or the techniques of processing and firing clays may sometimes have changed in the course of time. Laboratory analysis to determine the variability of the fabric constituents of vessels from an individual site may be particularly apposite for such assemblages. The relevant methods are discussed below.

Ideally no assemblage should be studied *in vacuo*. An assessment of the affinities of a factory and its wares in relation to the surrounding region and beyond is also important. This aids the recognition of enterprises of exotic origin from purely indigenous industries, and the peripatetic from the static workshops. There is great need for kiln excavations to be followed up by the study of industries and products over wider areas, particularly by systematic field-walking and by the examination of other kiln assemblages in local museums. An assessment of kilns with related products in the Thames Estuary (Upchurch ware/black-burnished wares) indicates complete changes of emphasis in their siting (Map 17). The earliest concentrations in the 1st and early 2nd centuries lay in the Upchurch area, but by the mid 2nd to early 3rd century there was a shift immediately to the W. From the mid 3rd century onwards the greatest known density of kilns occurred in South Essex. Since the siting of kilns reflects demand, the changes must be connected, at least in part, with fluctuations in the economy of that region, the expansion and recession of its pottery trade with the Northern Frontier garrisons and, probably, with a rise in sea level and flooding in the Medway Estuary area. Other parts of Britain, such as the North Somerset Marshes and the Trent and Severn Valleys, would no doubt respond to such detailed attention.

No understanding of a kiln site would be complete without an attempt to define the marketing and distribution of the products. From such work, major factories may be distinguished from minor. Patterns of supply on a national and local level may also be analysed and charted by spacial and other geographical techniques (Hodder and Orton 1976). This is particularly difficult where factories produced undistinguished grey kitchen-wares. For these, and for many other wares, petrological and other scientific analytical methods may be required. Because of the complexity and expense of such work and the general scarcity of facilities, the problems to be tackled should be isolated carefully in advance to avoid squandering resources on fields of enquiry which can be approached macroscopically.

The establishment of a bank of scientific data on the constituents of the products of all known Romano-British kiln sites and of samples from their adjacent clay beds is, however, a matter of priority. A comprehensive corpus of such analytical data would be invaluable in identifying sources of manufacture of pottery found on non-kiln sites. It would provide an independent basis for comparison, particularly when visual differences are minimal. As yet, systematic laboratory analysis, whether petrological or chemical, has been conducted on wares from only relatively few Romano-British kiln sites, mostly by the ceramic petrology unit sponsored by the DoE at the Department of Archaeology, University of Southampton.

Analytical determinations of ceramic material fall into two main categories. One is petrological, the least expensive overall, often the quickest, and suitable for all but the finest wares. The other, chemical analysis usually by physical methods, is the most popular but normally requires expensive equipment. It is best reserved for analysing fine well-levigated wares where other methods are inappropriate.

Ceramic petrology enables non-plastic inclusions in the clay, such as distinctive minerals and rock fragments, to be identified under a polarizing microscope (Peacock 1970, 379 ff.; 1977b, 25 ff.; Young 1980, 28). From this the geographical source of such raw materials and hence the region or place of manufacture can sometimes be established if its geology is known. Thin sectioning, the main method, involves the microscopic examination of a 10 by 10 mm slice of pottery ground to transparency (Tite 1972, 215, 224–30). This technique is particularly valuable for the characterization of fabrics by observing the size, shape, colour and frequency of the grains of different minerals and of pore distribution. Such textural studies can highlight distinctive techniques of clay-preparation, vessel-forming and firing. This enables vessels from the same factory or with the same localized ceramic traditions to be isolated from similarly tempered wares made in different localities.

Heavy mineral analysis is generally used for very sandy fabrics for which thin sectioning is less informative (Peacock 1967b; Williams 1979). It is a more laborious and relatively destructive technique but has produced some very impressive results, for example when applied to black-burnished ware and Dales ware (Williams 1977; Loughlin 1977). It requires 17–27 grammes of pottery for crushing and floating in a liquid with a specific gravity of 2.9. The heavy minerals which separate and sink can then be identified microscopically and compared with geological suites of heavy minerals of known distribution. One advantage of both this and thin sectioning is that samples taken can be kept indefinitely as a record for future reference and comparison.

Because petrological techniques are inappropriate to finely levigated wares lacking diagnostic inclusions, physicochemical methods of analysis are employed to investigate the mineral composition. Even so, supplementary detailed visual or microscopic examination is always desirable. As Peacock (1977b, 25) has pointed out, this may reveal characteristics which help to explain chemical phenomena. Although a number of chemical techniques are now available or currently in process of developing archaeological applications (Young 1980, 28–31), in practice, two or three proven ones are most frequently applied to Romano-British pottery. These are neutron activation analysis (CBA 1970; Tite 1972, 273–8), X-ray fluorescence spectrography (CBA 1970; Tite 1972, 267–72; Pollard *et al.* 1981) and atomic absorption spectrophotometry (Tite 1972, 264–6; Tubbs *et al.* 1980). The last, although most accurate for elemental chemical analysis, unfortunately involves an unpleasant and very time-consuming processing procedure (Symonds 1981, 361). Optical emission spectrography (Hartley and Richards 1965; Tite 1972, 260–64), one of the earliest physicochemical techniques, is now little used. All the above methods require very small samples, none more than 5 grammes, and except for optical emission spectrography, are non-destructive. Raw data generated by such analysis is frequently fed into a computer and subjected to a series of analyses, such as discriminant and cluster analysis (Pollard *et al.* 1981; Mommsen 1981). The excavator must then interpret the results in meaningful archaeological terms (Wilson 1978, 226 ff.). Since the ability of individual physicochemical techniques to detect different elements varies (Peacock 1970, 377–8; Tite 1972, 315–23), more than one method may be preferable. It is, however, advisable to seek guidance from a professional analyst on that most appropriate to the pottery in question. Often the method will be conditioned by the equipment available at the time. For example, recent work on Rhenish wares employed X-ray fluorescence and atomic absorption spectrometry, because these were immediately accessible at the Oxford University Research Laboratory for Archaeology, and the nature of the project was likely to advance the practice of analysis (Symonds 1981). A number of University Departments of Chemistry probably have the relevant equipment. British centres conducting programmes of chemical compositional analysis on Romano-British pottery include the Department of Archaeological Sciences, University of Bradford, and the Departments of Chemistry at the University of Bristol and Queen Mary College, London. The last is currently pioneering a new method called plasma emission spectrometry (PE). This technique has the same disadvantages in sample preparation as atomic absorption spectrophotometry, but its greater accuracy for a much wider range of elements, including rare earths, may well minimize the need for much of the complicated data analysis normally applied to less precise results (inf. R. Symonds; Walsh and Howie 1980; Hart and Adams, *forthcoming*).

Most of the methods mentioned are used to analyse the core or whole fabric of a vessel. It is, however, often desirable to know the composition of the colour-coat, slip or paint applied to the surface. Such information could help to explain the significance of features or deposits on kiln sites, by providing an indication of the technical processes to which these might relate (Magetti *et al.* 1981). Auger spectroscopy, electron spectroscopy for chemical analysis (ESCA), and X-ray fluorescence spectrography are all particularly suitable for this purpose. In addition, data resulting from mass spectrometry can aid the location of the original lead source for lead glazes (Young 1980, 29–31).

It is seldom practical for substantial supplementary studies of this nature to be undertaken solely by excavators of kilns. They rarely have the time or the means to publish more than their own site and its finds. Such objectives require communal, perhaps university-based research projects, or may constitute suitable studies for D. Phil. candidates. Whether a kiln-excavation has been fully published or just completed, the importance of additional wider research on the lines indicated should not be overlooked or dismissed.

Another valuable adjunct to post-excavation work on a kiln site is the undertaking of experimental firings. In the past, many kiln experiments have been much too non-specific in their aims and achievements and, in consequence, have produced relatively little information of value. There is a need for a series of closely-controlled experimental firings of all the various kiln types, constructed in precise detail, and involving vessels of authentic form and finish manufactured in local clays and using different types of fuel. Such experiments should not be confined to the few firings that time and resources have normally permitted. Only continual firings over a period of ten or more years will provide information on the life-span of a particular type of structure. Long-term pottery-manufacturing research projects, to test theories and ideas suggested by structural and other finds, would undoubtedly be as informative on kiln technology as the Butser Ancient Farm Research Project is proving to be.

Finally, full advantage should be taken of current and past results of research relating to kilns on the Continent, where the structures of Roman kilns now appear to be of greater relevance to Roman Britain than has often been appreciated. A small European kiln-study group was recently set up. Under its aegis, and that of the Institute of Archaeology, University of Venice, annual summaries of kiln excavations in many European countries and larger papers on kilns and ceramic technology are now being published in *Revista di Archeologia*. This, it is hoped, may lead to a better understanding of pottery and tile kilns from their earliest appearance until the Medieval period.

APPENDIX A

SUMMARY LIST OF KILN SITES

For further details of each site see gazetteer in fiche at back of volume. Many of the sites listed involve entries for several kilns.

The sites are arranged according to the traditional counties pre 1974. Counties post 1974, where different, are given in square brackets.

Fiche: Diazo and Frame No.

ENGLAND

BEDFORDSHIRE

Ampthill Dolittle Mill	. . . . .	1.202
Bedford Mile Road, Elstow	. . . .	1.202–4
Bromham Clapham Gravel Pits	. . .	1.204
Cardington		
(1) Hillfoot Farm	. . . . .	1.204–5
(2) N of village	. . . . .	1.205
Eastcotts		
(1) Cotton End	. . . . .	1.205
(2) W of Harrowden	. . . .	1.206
(3) Cambridge Road	. . . .	1.206
Everton Sandy Road	. . . .	1.206
Great Barford NE of Great Barford House	. .	1.207
Harrold Harrold Lodge Farm	. . . .	1.207–10
Knotting and Souldrop NW of Souldrop village	.	1.210
Luton S of Welud's Bank, Leagrave	. . .	1.210
Sandy Sandy Cemetery	. . . .	1.211
Tempsford Tempsford Road	. . .	1.211
Toddington Fox Burrow	. . . .	1.211
Turvey E of Grindstone Hill	. . .	1.212
Wilshamstead New Farm	. . . .	1.212

BERKSHIRE

Bradfield Dark Lane	. . . .	1.214
Compton Woodrows Farm	. . . .	1.214
Hamstead Marshall		
(1) Hamstead Park Gravel Pits (East)	. .	1.215
(2) Hamstead Park Gravel Pits (West)	. .	1.215–16
[OXON] **Kennington** Cold Store	. . .	1.216
Kintbury Kintbury Holt Farm	. . .	1.217
Pangbourne Maidenhatch Farm	. . .	1.217
Shaw cum Donnington Love Lane, Shaw	. .	1.217–18

BERKSHIRE *(contd.)*

ESSEX *(contd.)*

KENT *(contd.)*

KENT *(contd.)*

LINCOLNSHIRE *(contd.)*

LINCOLSHIRE *(contd.)*

	Nettleton South Moor	3.460
	North Hykeham	
	(1) Russel Avenue	3.461
	(2) Hykeham Moor Gravel Pits	3.461
	North Willingham	
	(1) SE of Tealby Lane	3.461
	(2) E of Tealby Lane	3.462
	Norton Disney Abbey Field villa	3.462
	Owersby Owersby Moor	3.462
	Ropsley and Humby S of Hurn Wood	3.463
[HUMBERSIDE]	**Roxby cum Risby**	
	(1) E of Dragonby village	3.463
	(2) N of Westfield Holt, Roxby	3.464
	(3) Sheffields Hill, Roxby	3.464
[HUMBERSIDE]	**Scunthorpe**	
	(1) Midland Iron Mine, Conesby	3.464
	(2) S of Dragonby village	3.465–6
	South Carlton W of Middle Street	3.466–7
[HUMBERSIDE]	**South Ferriby** Ferriby Sluice Brickworks	3.467
	Tattershall Thorpe W of Tattershall Thorpe Carr	3.467
	Tealby	
	(1) W of Warren Wood, Willingham Forest	3.468
	(2) SW of Tealby village	3.468
	Walesby	
	(1) Risby Moor	3.468
	(2) Walesby Moor	3.469
	(3) W of Otby Beck	3.469–70
	(4) Otby Moor	3.470–71
	Wildsworth Whoofer Lane	3.471
[HUMBERSIDE]	**Winterton** Newport village	3.471
	Woolsthorpe/Denton Sewstern Lane iron workings	3.472

MIDDLESEX

[GREATER LONDON]	**Harrow**	
	(1) S of Wood Lane, Brockley Hill	3.475
	(2) RNO Hospital Gate Lodge, Brockley Hill	3.475
	(3) S of Brockley Hill House	3.475–6
	(4) Brockley Hill House tennis courts	3.476
	(5) S of Green Cottage, Brockley Hill	3.476–8
[GREATER LONDON]	**Hendon**	
	(1) Hilltop Café, Brockley Hill	3.478–9
	(2) Brockley Hill, Field 410, S of pond	3.479–80
[GREATER LONDON]	**Hornsey**	
	(1) Southwood Lawn Road, Highgate Village	3.481
	(2) Highgate Wood (South)	3.481
	(3) Highgate Wood (North)	3.481–5
	London	
	(1) St Paul's Cathedral	3.485
	(2) Paternoster Row/Newgate Street	3.486
	(3) London GPO site	3.486
	(4) Copthall Close/Moorgate Street	3.486
[SURREY]	**Staines** 56 High Street	3.487

NORFOLK

NORTHAMPTONSHIRE

NORTHAMPTONSHIRE *(contd.)*

Hardingstone
Houghton, Great
Houghton, Little
Irchester
Kettering
Kings Cliffe
Long Buckby
Mears Ashby
Milton Malsor
Northampton
Oundle
Quinton
Ringstead
Rothersthorpe
Rushton
Scaldwell
Southwick
Syresham
Towcester
Wakerley
Wappenham

NORTHAMPTONSHIRE *(contd.)*

Warmington W of Papley Lodge	. . . .	4.545
Weekley Weekley Quarry .	. . . .	4.545–9
Wellingborough		
(1) Hardwick Park .	. . . .	4.550
(2) 'Wellingborough' (not precisely located)	. .	4.550
Whilton Whilton Lock .	. . . .	4.551
Wollaston Lodge Farm .	. . . .	4.551
Yardley Hastings Golf Course sand pit	. . .	4.551
Yarwell Stonehill Quarries, Sulehay .	. . .	4.552

NOTTINGHAMSHIRE

East Bridgeford Castle Hill (*Margidunum*)	. .	4.554
Meering Besthorpe gravel pits .	. . .	4.555
Newark-on-Trent Farrar's Works	. . .	4.556
Nottingham W edge of Wollaton Park	. . .	4.557

OXFORDSHIRE

Asthall SE of Asthall village	. . . .	4.560
Beckley and Stowood/Elsfield Headington Wick	.	4.560
Cassington E of Cassington Mill	. . .	4.560
Dorchester		
(1) Watling Lane .	. . . .	4.561
(2) Dorchester Abbey well	. . . .	4.561
(3) Allen's Pit .	. . . .	4.561–2
Garsington Watling Road/Roman Road	. .	4.562
Hanborough Tuckwell's Gravel Pit	. . .	4.562–3
Holton Forest Hill, Red Hills	. . .	4.563
Horspath Open Brasenose	. . .	4.563
Littlemore		
(1) Ashurst Clinic, Littlemore Hospital	. . .	4.564
(2) Mount Pleasant Old Quarry	. . .	4.564
(3) Eastern Bypass .	. . . .	4.565
Marsh Baldon Golden Balls Cross-road	. .	4.565
Marston Cherwell Drive .	. . . .	4.565
Oxford		
(1) Blackbird Leys .	. . . .	4.566
(2) Rose Hill, Cowley	. . . .	4.566
(3) St Luke's Road, Cowley	. . . .	4.567
(4) Oxford School, Barracks Lane	. . .	4.568
(5) The Churchill Hospital, Headington	. .	4.568–70
(6) Harry Bear's Pit, Headington Quarry	. .	4.571
(7) Nuffield Orthopaedic Hospital	. . .	4.571
(8) Old Headington .	. . . .	4.571
Risinghurst and Sandhills Horspath Common, Shotover		4.572
Sandford-on-Thames Minchery Farm	. .	4.572
Stanton St John Poor's Land, Headington .	. .	4.572
Woodeaton		
(1) Drun's Hill .	. . . .	4.573
(2) Great Forest Grounds	. . . .	4.573

RUTLAND

[LEICS]	**Burley** Chapel Farm Quarries	. . . .	4.575
[LEICS]	**Great Casterton** Ryhall Road	. . . .	4.576

RUTLAND *(contd.)*

[LEICS]	**Greetham** W of Sewstern Lane		4.576
[LEICS]	**Market Overton** N of Market Overton village . .		4.577

SHROPSHIRE

Wroxeter
- (1) Near Bell Brook 4.579
- (2) Ismore Coppice 4.579

SOMERSET

Burnham-on-Sea
- (1) A38 bridge, Highbridge . . . 4.582
- (2) Sandway Housing Estate, Highbridge . 4.582

Chilton Polden
- (1) Outer Furlong Rhyne 4.582–3
- (2) Halter Path Drove 4.583

[AVON]   **Combe Hay**   Laporte fuller's earth mine . . . 4.583

Congresbury
- (1) Yewtree Farm 4.584
- (2) NE of Pine Apple Farm 4.584
- (3) 'Woodlands', NE of Congresbury . . . 4.585

Cossington
- (1) Decoy Pool 4.585
- (2) W of Wall Ditch 4.585
- (3) S of Gold Bridge Corner 4.586
- (4) Huntspill River, Gold Bridge Corner . . . 4.586

Edington   Burtle Moor 4.587

Huntspill, East
- (1) Gold Bridge Corner/Shaking Drove . . . 4.587–9
- (2) Cripps River/Black Ditch Rhyne 4.589
- (3) Huntspill River, N of Quaking Bridge . . . 4.590–91
- (4) River Brue, Basonbridge Farm 4.591
- (5) River Brue, Newbridge 4.592

Ilchester   NW of Roman town 4.592

Mark
- (1) Halter Path Drove 4.592
- (2) Liberty Moor 5.593

Norton Fitzwarren   Norton Bridge 5.593
Norton St Philip   Not precisely located . . . 5.593
Shepton Mallet   The Old Anglo-Bavarian Brewery . 5.594
Wedmore   Tealham Moor Drove 5.594
Woolavington   Huntspill River, E of Quaking Bridge . 5.594–5

STAFFORDSHIRE

Stoke-on-Trent   Trent Vale 5.597

SUFFOLK

Blaxhall   W of Grove Farm 5.599
Botesdale   Bridewell Lane/Chapel Lane . . . 5.599
Coddenham   Baylham House Farm . . . 5.599–600
Elmswell   E of Church Cottages 5.600
Great Welnetham   Sudbury–Bury Road, Sicklemere . 5.600

Hacheston
- (1) Lower Hacheston, 'Field III' . . . 5.601
- (2) Lower Hacheston, S of 'Field IV' . . . 5.601

YORKSHIRE: EAST RIDING and YORK

[HUMBERSIDE]	**Broomfleet** W of Weighton Lock, Faxfleet Site A .	5.678
[HUMBERSIDE]	**Holme upon Spalding Moor**	
	(1) S of Hasholme Hall	5.678
	(2) The Carrs, S of East Bursea Farm .	5.679
	(3) Bursea House complex	5.679–80
	(4) N of Bursea House	5.680
	(5) SW of Bursea Grange	5.681
	(6) Welhambridge Farm	5.681
	(7) Common Farm, Arglam	5.681
	(8) Marl Pit Farm, Major Bridge . . .	5.682
	(9) Pothill, N of Throlam Plantation . . .	5.682–3
	(10) Tollingham Airfield	5.683
	(11) S of Skiff Farm, Tollingham . . .	5.684
	(12) N of Skiff Farm, Tollingham . . .	5.684
[HUMBERSIDE]	**Lockington** Woodhouse Farm . . .	5.684
[N YORKS]	**Norton**	
	(1) Grove Bungalow/Vicarage Garden . . .	5.685
	(2) Model Farm Estate	5.685–8
	(3) The Cemetery	5.688
	(4) Wold Street	5.688
	(5) Commercial Street Primitive Chapel . . .	5.689
[N YORKS]	**Scampston** East Knapton	5.689
[N YORKS]	**York** Borthwick Institute/Ebor Brewery . . .	5.689–90

YORKSHIRE: NORTH RIDING

[N YORKS]	**Heworth Without** Tang Hall Beck, Apple Tree Farm .	6.692
[N YORKS]	**Malton** NE of Malton fort	6.692
[N YORKS]	**Oldstead** Cockerdale Wood, Cold Cam . . .	6.693
[N YORKS]	**Welburn**	
	(1) Mount Pleasant Farm, E of Whitwell-on-the-Hill .	6.693
	(2) Greets Farm, Welburn	6.694
	(3) Jamie's Crags/Castle Howard School, Crambeck .	6.694–7
	(4) NE of Welburn village	6.697
[N YORKS]	**Whitwell-on-the-hill** Cliffe House Farm, Crambe .	6.698

YORKSHIRE: WEST RIDING

[S YORKS]	**Auckley**	
	(1) Auckley sand pit	6.700
	(2) SE of Mosham Farm	6.700
	(3) Blaxton Quarry	6.700–701
[S YORKS]	**Blaxton** Mosham Wood nursery gardens . . .	6.701
[N YORKS]	**Boroughbridge**	
	(1) E of Aldborough Roman town . . .	6.701–2
	(2) Hall Arm Lane, Aldborough	6.702
[S YORKS]	**Cantley**	
	(1) Rossington Bridge Pumping Station . . .	6.703–4
	(2) Brockhole, Branton	6.704
	(3) Cantley Hall	6.705
	(4) Kilham Farm, Branton	6.705
[S YORKS]	**Doncaster**	
	(1) Carr Lane, Bessacar	6.706–7
	(2) Cantley Estate, South Kiln Group . . .	6.707–11

YORKSHIRE: WEST RIDING *(contd.)*

SCOTLAND

DUNBARTONSHIRE

WALES AND MONMOUTHSHIRE

DENBIGHSHIRE

GLAMORGANSHIRE

MONMOUTHSHIRE

APPENDIX B

RECOMMENDATIONS FOR PRESERVATION

In compiling the lists below, the criteria have been the archaeological or historical importance and rarity of kiln sites, of types of kiln structure and of kiln products, both nationally and locally. The list is based on academic considerations and does not take into account the problems of preservation.

Very few kiln sites remain unploughed. Even fewer have extant earthworks, such as waster-heaps, and many factories must have been cleared up and levelled immediately they ceased operation. Most uneroded or undisturbed kiln sites survive in old woodland or marginal scrub land. It is, therefore, particularly desirable that those remaining should be protected from damage such as afforestation, ploughing or non-archaeological digging. Areas designated for conservation, moreover, should comprise not merely the actual kilns but also their immediate surroundings, where auxiliary features may occur. There is indeed a need to locate precisely some of the kiln structures listed, and to define the exact limits of many of the factories by geophysical methods.

The following sites, which survive either as earthworks, or apparently unploughed and substantially undisturbed, seem worthy of preservation:

DERBYSHIRE

HAZELWOOD. (2) Jenny Tang Plantation

ESSEX

COLCHESTER. (7) Warren Fields

HAMPSHIRE

BINSTED
  (2) Alice Holt Forest, AH 17–18, 20–21, 41–2, 64–5
  (3) Alice Holt Forest, AH 19
  (4) Alice Holt Forest, AH 48–63
  (5) Alice Holt Forest, AH 31–7, 39–40, 43, 47
  (6) Alice Holt Forest, AH 66
  (7) Alice Holt Forest, AH 68, 73, 74
  (9) Alice Holt Forest, AH 67
  (10) Alice Holt Forest, AH 25–7
  (11) Alice Holt Forest, AH 45, 79–81
  (12) Alice Holt Forest, AH 69–72
  (13) Straits Enclosure, Alice Holt Forest, AH 75–7

FORDINGBRIDGE
  (4) SE of Boundary Bank of Sloden Enclosure (South)
  (6) Sloden Hole
  (8) Lower Sloden Enclosure I
  (9) Lower Sloden Enclosure II/Row Hill
  (10) Sloden Driftway
  (13) Amberwood Site II
  (19) Pitts Wood Enclosure (South-east), Site I
  (20) Ashley Bottom, E of Pitts Wood
  (23) Pitts Wood Enclosure (North-east)
  (24) Ashley Rails
  (25) Crock Hill (Main Group)
  (29) Islands Thorns Enclosure (Main Group)
  (30) Islands Thorns II

SHEDFIELD. (2) Hallcourt Wood (North-east)

KENT

CLIFFE AT HOO
  (3) Wharf Farm
  (4) Priory Marshes
  (5) Havenwick

GILLINGHAM. (3) Saltings E of Nor Marsh

UPCHURCH
  (4) Twinney Creek
  (7) Milfordhope East
  (11) Slayhills Salting
  (12) SW side of Sharfleet Creek
  (16) Greenborough Marshes

LINCOLNSHIRE

LINWOOD. (2) Linwode Warren

SOMERSET

CHILTON POLDEN
  (1) Outer Furling Rhyne
  (2) Halter Path Drove (*see also under* MARK)

CONGRESBURY. (2) E of Pine Apple Farm

COSSINGTON
  (1) Decoy Pool
  (2) W of Wall Ditch
  (3) S of Gold Bridge Corner
  (4) Huntspill River, Gold Bridge Corner

EDINGTON. Burtle Moor

HUNTSPILL, EAST
  (1) Gold Bridge Corner/Shaking Drove
  (2) Cripps River/Black Ditch Rhyne

MARK
   (1) Halter Path Drove (*see also under* CHILTON POLDEN)
   (2) Liberty Moor

WEDMORE. Tealham Moor Drove

WOOLAVINGTON. N of Combe Plantation

SUFFOLK

HINDERCLAY. (1) Hinderclay Wood

WILTSHIRE

SAVERNAKE
   (1) S of Column Ride
   (2) S of Bitham Pond

WILCOT. Withy Copse, Oare

YORKSHIRE, WEST RIDING

HUDDERSFIELD. Grimscar Wood

Of the many kiln concentrations under cultivation or otherwise damaged, the following have been selected as also worthy of protection from further erosion. The group includes a number of kiln complexes within urban housing areas which would nevertheless merit rescue excavation should building or redevelopment be projected.

ENGLAND

BERKSHIRE

SUNNINGWELL
   (1) Foxcombe Hill (substantial regional industry little disturbed by ploughing)
   (2) Overdale, Boar's Hill (as previous; site includes undisturbed ground to S between this and previous site)

BUCKINGHAMSHIRE

GERRARDS CROSS. (1) 'Spring Wood', Hedgerley Lane (a well-preserved kiln structure within a major rural industry)

CAMBRIDGESHIRE

HORNINGSEA. (2) S of Eye Hall (major regional kiln complex threatened by ploughing)

CHESHIRE

WARRINGTON. Kimberley Drive, Stockton Heath, Wilderspool (specialist exporting industry)

CUMBERLAND

ST CUTHBERT WITHOUT. Low Scalesceugh (an important military tilery and pottery threatened by ploughing)

DERBYSHIRE

MILFORD. (1) Chevin Golf Course (unexplored outlier of Derbyshire-ware industry)

DORSET

ARNE
   (2) Nutcrack Lane, Stoborough (a little-ploughed black-burnished ware (BB1) factory)
   (4) Redcliff Farm, Ridge (a large but little-ploughed black-burnished ware (BB1) factory)

HAMPSHIRE

ROWLANDS CASTLE. (2) W of Woodbury Lane (probable nucleus of major regional factory)

HEREFORDSHIRE

LEDBURY, RURAL. Marley Hall (Severn Valley-ware factory in area lacking known kiln sites)

HERTFORDSHIRE

ALDENHAM. (2) Loom Lane, Radlett (part of a major exporting specialist industry)

HADHAM, LITTLE. (2) Barley Hill, Bromley Hall Farm (part of a major 4th-century industry)

HADHAM, MUCH. (1) Wickham Spring Field, Bromley Hall Farm (as previous)

ST STEPHENS. Little Munden Farm, Bricket Wood (an important early exporting specialist producer)

HUNTINGDONSHIRE and PETERBOROUGH

AILSWORTH. (2) SW of Ailsworth village (unexplored Nene Valley factory)

CASTOR. (6) SW of the Moats (unexplored Nene Valley factory)

SIBSON CUM STIBBINGTON
   (3) NW of Wansford Station (major Nene Valley kiln concentration with adjacent buildings)
   (9) S of Stibbington Gravel Pits (unexcavated Nene Valley workshop)
   (10) Stibbington Gravel Pits (unexcavated Nene Valley workshop threatened by ploughing)

STANGROUND SOUTH. (2) S of Stanground Sluice (unexplored Nene Valley factory)

SUTTON. Sutton Heath (outlying Nene Valley factory with no recorded excavations)

KENT

OTFORD. SE of the Station (an early, relatively unknown specialist producer, possibly engaged in military supply)

LEICESTERSHIRE

GROBY. E of Groby quarries (kiln and adjacent building in area lacking excavated potteries)

LINCOLNSHIRE

BOURNE. Bourne Grammar School (little-excavated kiln complex in region with few known potteries)

KNAITH. N of Knaith Hall (large little-explored regional centre threatened by ploughing)

LEA. Lea Grange Farm (large and totally unexplored regional complex)

LINCOLN. (15) N of Catchwater Drain, Swanpool (unknown extension of major late specialist complex)

SOUTH CARLTON. W of Middle Street (important specialist exporter)

TATTERSHALL THORPE. W of Tattershall Thorpe Carr (isolated site in region lacking known kilns)

MIDDLESEX

HENDON
(1) Hilltop Café, Brockley Hill (earliest known site in major specialist industry)
(2) Brockley Hill, Field 410, S of pond (one of few undeveloped sites in· major kiln complex)

NORFOLK

BRAMPTON. NE of Red House Farm School (large major semi-specialist complex threatened by ploughing)

CAISTOR ST EDMUND. (1) S of S ditch of Caistor Roman town (specialist kiln totally unexplored)

ELLINGHAM. Dairy Farm (specialist centre with only limited excavation)

SHOULDHAM. Abbey Farm (large, late regional complex, little-excavated and threatened by ploughing)

NORTHAMPTONSHIRE

ECTON. North Lodge Farm (large regional complex, little-excavated and threatened by ploughing)

OXFORDSHIRE

BECKLEY AND STOWOOD/ELSFIELD. Headington Wick (a specialist workshop with a potentially-close relationship to a villa)

HORSPATH. Open Brasenose (a large specialist kiln site, ploughed but little-excavated)

MARSH BALDON. Golden Ball Cross Road (totally unexcavated specialist kilns threatened by ploughing)

RISINGHURST AND STANDHILLS. Horspath Common, Shotover (a ploughed but little-excavated specialist factory)

SUFFOLK

LAKENHEATH. (2) White Fen (an important late regional producer)

NAYLAND WITH WISSINGTON. Grove Farm, Wissington (an unexplored, early specialist centre)

STANNINGFIELD. Old Hall Farm (an unexplored, possible specialist centre)

WATTISFIELD. (1) Pear Tree Farm, Kings Lane (possibly the earliest centre in a major regional industry)

SUSSEX

COLDWALTHAM. (2) Hardham Camp (a little-known factory in an area with relatively few kiln sites)

WARWICKSHIRE

HARTSHILL. (2) Hartshill Quarry, Grange Road (large, nationally important complex near active quarry)

MANCETTER. Broad Close Field and adjoining fields to E, SW and S (large, nationally important complex, threatened by ploughing)

WILTSHIRE

MINETY. Oaksey Nursery (early specialist pottery and tilery with no excavated pottery kilns)

WORCESTERSHIRE

MALVERN LINK
(5) Grit Farm East (Severn Valley complex, in region with few known kilns)
(6) Great Buckmans Farm (as previous)

YORKSHIRE, EAST RIDING

HOLME UPON SPALDING MOOR. (6) Pothill, N of Throlam Plantation (major regional complex threatened by ploughing)

YORKSHIRE, NORTH RIDING

WELBURN. (3) Jamie's Crags/Castle Howard School, Crambeck (major, late specialist factory threatened by ploughing)

YORKSHIRE, WEST RIDING

BOROUGHBRIDGE. (2) Hall Arm Lane, Aldborough (specialist production centre supplying military markets)

WALES

DENBIGHSHIRE

HOLT. Castle Lyons Roman works depot (a major military tilery/pottery partially threatened by ploughing)

GLOSSARY

Aceramic. A term applied to a region in which pottery was not made, used, or traded on a regular basis.

Amphora. A very large two-handled pottery container for storing and transporting liquid commodities such as wine (e.g. Swan 1980, pl. 16).

Appliqué. A decorative figure or *motif* made separately, usually in a mould, and applied or fixed to the surface of a pot before slip-coating and firing (e.g. Swan 1980, fig. 1 no. 2).

Baffle. An obstacle, such as a low wall, bollard or screen, usually positioned in the stokehole or flue of a kiln to prevent a rapid rush of cold air directly into the kiln-chamber (Fig. X).

Barbotine. Relief decoration executed by trailing semi-liquid clay through the end of an implement on to a finished pottery vessel before firing, a process identical to icing a cake (e.g. Swan 1980, pls. 1, 18, 19).

Black-burnished Ware. A standard range of culinary vessel-forms manufactured in two different fabrics and widely imitated. *BB1* (black-burnished ware Category 1), was black, gritty, handmade, mainly in Dorset, and widely distributed from *c.* 120 to the late 4th century. *BB2* (black-burnished ware Category 2) was greyish, finer, wheel-thrown in the Thames Estuary area, and widely exported from *c.* 140 to the mid 3rd century (Williams 1977; Farrar 1973a).

Burgus. In this volume, a small fortified post usually controlling a main route.

Burnished. A smooth, often shiny surface, produced by rubbing a leatherhard pot with a hard object.

Calcite-gritted Ware. Pottery embodying crushed calcite (either shell or mineral grit), usually kitchen-wares such as storage-jars and cooking-pots and bowls (e.g. Swan 1980, fig. V no. 32, fig. XIII no. 80).

Campanulate Vessel. A cup or bowl with a profile shaped like an inverted bell (e.g. Gillam 211–13).

Carinated Bowl. A bowl with a sharp inward change of angle in its body (e.g. Gillam 214–17).

Castor Ware. See **Nene Valley Ware.**

Channel-rimmed Jar. A cooking-pot having a simple out-turned rim with one or more distinct grooves on it; particularly common in Northamptonshire and North Bedfordshire in the mid to late 1st century (e.g. Woods 1972, figs. 25–6 nos. 182–91).

Cheese Press. A small, flat-bottomed dish with holes and concentric ridges in the bottom and sometimes with a flat matching lid. It was presumably used for making a moist cottage-type cheese (e.g. Swan 1980, fig. XI no. 69).

Colonia (pl. *ae*). Originally a chartered land settlement of Roman citizens (especially legionary veterans) usually associated with a newly-founded town. The title signified the highest grade of civic status and was sometimes granted to existing communities considered worthy of it (e.g. the settlement adjacent to the legionary fortress at York).

Colour-coat. See **Slip.**

Comb-stamping or **stabbing.** On a pot, a repetitive series of decorative stabbing marks made with a toothed implement (e.g. Hayes and Whitley 1950, fig. 13 no. 15).

Corbels. In this volume, a series of short, horizontal projections from the kiln-wall, immediately below the raised oven-floor to support it (e.g. Fig. III.vi).

Cordon. A raised, continuous horizontal band on the exterior of a pot (e.g. Swan 1980, fig. IV no. 26).

Cornice-rim. On rough-cast and other beakers, a projecting rim, decoratively moulded as in an architectural cornice (e.g. Gillam 84–90).

Countersunk Handle. A rounded handle partly sunk into the side of a vessel (e.g. Gillam 40 and 41).

Crambeck Wares. Pottery made at Crambeck, S of Malton, Yorks. N.R., and widely distributed in the North of England and North Wales in the second half of the 4th century, including cream mortaria and parchment wares, imitation samian forms, and a range of lead-grey kitchen-wares (Corder 1928; Corder and Birley 1937).

Cross-walls. In this volume, a series of permanent, long, narrow, parallel walls, often of tile, built at regular intervals across the bottom of the combustion-chamber of a kiln at right angles to the flue-axis. A central gap in each formed a narrow corridor, an extension of the flue-axis (Fig. III.iv).

Dales Ware. Coarse shell-gritted handmade cooking-pots probably made near the Trent/Humber confluence from the mid 2nd century onwards. Sandy wheel-thrown imitations, *Dales-type* cooking-pots, were made in Lincolnshire, the Humber basin and probably the York area (Gillam 1951; Loughlin 1977).

Derbyshire Ware. Pimply high-fired lid-seated jars produced W of Derby from shortly before the mid 2nd century (Gillam

1939). Production of their lower-fired everted-rimmed predecessors (*pre-Derbyshire ware*) began in the late 1st century in the *vicus* of Little Chester fort (*see* pp. 124–5).

Everted Rim. A rim turning sharply outwards and upwards from the wall of a pot (e.g. Gillam 97–8).

Flagon. A vessel with a narrow neck, globular body, one or more handles and often a foot-ring, used for holding liquids. Its production was usually confined to specialist manufacturers (e.g. Gillam 1–20).

Flange. A prominent continuous projection from the body, neck or rim of a vessel, intended to facilitate handling (e.g. Gillam 228–32, 237–58).

Flask. A narrow-mouthed jar without handles (e.g. Gillam 36–9).

Gallo-Belgic. The latest Iron-Age culture of Gaul, particularly N and E of the Seine and Marne, before the Roman conquest. In this volume, the term is applied to imported and Romano-British pottery of a style influenced by this culture both before and after AD 43.

Hammer-head Mortarium. A mortarium with a rim and flange which form a single unit, shaped like the head of a hammer, its centre meeting the body of the vessel at right angles (e.g. Gillam 281–5).

Hemispherical Bowl. A bowl of a form comprising at least half a sphere (e.g. Gillam 195–7).

Hofheim-type Flagon. A single or double-handled flagon with a cylindrical neck and outcurved rim, triangular in section; named after types published from the mid 1st-century military site at Hofheim, Germany (Hofheim Forms 50, 51, 58, 62; *see* Swan 1980, fig. 1 no. I).

Honey Jar. A double-handled, often bulbous jar with a wide mouth (e.g. Swan 1980, fig. IV no. 24). There is no firm evidence that such jars held honey.

Huntcliffe-type Cooking-pots. Calcite-gritted cooking-pots of distinctive form with a grooved hooked rim, common in Yorks. E.R. in the 4th century and throughout the North from the mid 4th century onwards (e.g. Gillam 162, 163).

Hunt Cup. A beaker (drinking vessel) with a decorative scene depicting dog(s) hunting stag(s) or hare(s) executed *en barbotine* (e.g. Gillam 84, 85, 89).

Imitation Samian. Vessels whose form, and sometimes finish and decoration, imitated samian ware (e.g. Swan 1980, fig. X).

Lamp-filler. A globular, narrow-mouthed jar with a projecting spout of very narrow bore. It was perhaps used for filling lamps or as an infant/invalid feeding cup (e.g. Swan 1980, fig. XIV no. 85).

Lamp-holder. A shallow, flat-bottomed, asymmetric dish, shaped like the mouth of a jug, usually with a handle; thought to have been used as a container for an oil lamp (e.g. Darling 1977, fig. 6.5 no. 27, fig. 6.7 no. 39).

La Tène. A Continental Iron-Age culture named after a Swiss lake site, elements of which first appeared in parts of Britain in the Late Iron Age.

Leatherhard. The stage reached during the drying of a pot when the clay is stiff enough for the vessel to be picked up without distortion, yet soft enough to respond to pressure for burnishing, attaching handles and other finishing processes.

Lid-seated Vessel. A pot in which the rim is ledged, dished or grooved internally to keep a lid in place (e.g. Gillam 151–3).

London Ware. Late 1st-century vessels in a relatively fine burnished grey fabric. They imitated samian bowls (usually Dr. 29, 30, 31) and were often decorated with inscribed lines, impressed stamps, rouletting and compass-scribed circles. Made in the Thames Estuary area, Suffolk, Herts. and the Nene Valley in the late 1st and 2nd centuries (e.g. Swan 1980, pl. 10).

Lug Handle. A small solid-clay protuberance integral with the wall of a pot to aid handling; contrasts with the more usual Romano-British strap-handle formed of a projecting loop.

Lyon Ware. Fine colour-coated cups and beakers with rough-cast, *appliqué* or rusticated decoration. Made at Lyon (France) and imported to Britain (mainly for military markets) from *c*. AD 43–*c*. 70 (e.g. Swan 1980, fig. 1 nos. 2, 3, 5).

Malvernian Ware. A range of very coarse, simple jars, handmade on a commercial basis at several centres in the Malverns from the mid/late Iron Age onwards. They were distributed over considerable distances, particularly in the Marches, South Wales and Gloucestershire (Peacock 1967a).

Mica-dusted Wares. Pottery coated with a slip containing mica particles to give a golden or bronze-like sheen; usually of 1st or 2nd-century date.

Mortarium (pl. *a*). A stout mixing bowl with a strong lip and a pouring spout, usually dusted on the inside with hard grit (*trituration* grits) to strengthen it against wear during the pounding of foodstuffs. Its production was mainly in the hands of specialist producers (e.g. Swan 1981, figs. VI, VII).

Municipium (pl. *a*). A chartered settlement of Roman citizens or of people enjoying 'Latin rights'; *municipia* ranked next in dignity to *colonia*. The status was normally conferred on an already existing community.

'Necked' Bowl or ***Jar.*** A bowl or jar with a rim curving outwards from its shoulder to form a neck of concave quarter-round profile (e.g. Swan 1980, fig. IV no. 26); sometimes referred to as a *cavetto*-rim or neck.

Nene Valley Ware. Pottery manufactured at various sites immediately W of Peterborough, in the Lower Nene Valley (incl. Castor), and widely distributed in Roman Britain from the mid/late 2nd to late 4th century; in particular, brown or black colour-coated table-wares including hunt cups with trailed decoration *en barbotine* (e.g. Swan 1980, fig. VIII).

Non-specialist Producer. A pottery workshop making mainly kitchen-wares and not usually including table-wares (e.g. colour-coated vessels), mortaria, flagons, or unusual vessels of exotic affinities among its output.

Oxidized Ware. A fabric in which the iron oxide in the clay has absorbed as much oxygen as possible during firing. It is produced when vessels are fired with an ample and continuous supply of oxygen, usually resulting in a white, buff, orange or red colour. Pottery can be partly oxidized (indicated by colour differences between the surface and core of the fabric), or unevenly oxidized (indicated by colour differences on the surface of a vessel).

Paint. See **Slip.**

Parchment Ware. A range of table-ware, mostly bowls, in pale fabrics with simple red-brown painted decoration; popular in the mid/late 3rd and 4th centuries (e.g. Swan 1980, pls. 26, 27).

Parisian Ware. Thin, grey, burnished, stamp-decorated bowls and jars circulating mainly in Lincolnshire from the late 1st to early 3rd century (Elsdon 1982).

Pedestal. In this volume, a free-standing, raised plinth or bollard placed on the bottom of a kiln-chamber, either to support a raised oven-floor or (in single-chambered kilns) to aid the stacking of the pottery load and circulation of hot air around it (e.g. Fig. III.ii).

Pilasters. In this volume, integral short piers, buttresses or column-like projections of varying shape, protruding from the kiln-wall on the inside of the combustion-chamber, and usually intended to support the raised oven-floor of the kiln (Pls. 26, 27, and 43b).

Pipe Clay. Relatively pure clays (such as those used for tobacco pipes), containing little or no iron, and usually white or pale cream in colour.

Quern. A handmill for grinding corn, consisting of two circular stones, the lower socketed or perforated for a pivot, the upper perforated as a hopper.

Raetian Mortaria. Orange mortaria usually with lug handles, an angular cut-out spout and a glossy red-brown slip applied only on the top of the flange, rim and on the internal concave moulding. The tradition stemmed ultimately from the Continent, with factories known in Raetia, but most examples in Britain were locally made in kilns such as those at Holt, Wilderspool and near Carlisle or SW Scotland (e.g. Gillam types 268—70).

Reduced Ware. A fabric in which the iron oxide in the clay is in a low state of oxidation. It is produced when the final stages of heating and cooling are carried out without oxygen, which is removed from the solid compounds, resulting in a grey or black colour. Pottery can be partly reduced (indicated by colour differences between the surface and core of the fabric) or unevenly reduced (indicated by colour differences on the surface of a vessel).

Reeding. Horizontal grooving on the flange or rim of some types of mortaria and bowls (e.g. Swan 1980, fig. II nos. 9 and 11).

Rilling. Fine, close-set horizontal lines formed by scribing (e.g. with a comb) on the body of the vessel (e.g. Swan 1980, fig. V no. 32).

Ring-necked Flagon. A flagon with mouldings on the neck forming a series of superimposed horizontal rings (e.g. Swan 1980, fig. III no. 21).

Roller-stamping. Impressed decoration applied by a roller in a repetitive sequence. It usually comprised three or more small panels of design, with different patterns, which had been cut into the roller (e.g. Swan 1980, fig. XI no. 70).

Rough-cast. Pottery decoration consisting of small particles of dried clay or gritty material dusted over the surface, generally under a slip coating (e.g. Gillam 72–6).

Rouletting. Incised decoration made by a toothed wheel or roller (*roulette*) and applied while the vessel was turning on the potter's wheel (e.g. Gillam 42–6).

Rustic or **Rusticated Jar.** A cooking-vessel, usually in a grey fabric; during manufacture, very plastic clay was applied to the exterior of the vessel after throwing, and worked up with the fingers into rough knobs, parallel ridges or spidery encrustations (e.g. Swan 1980, pl. 14).

Samian Ware (Terra Sigillata). Glossy, red, slipped table-ware of the 1st to mid 3rd century, mostly of Gaulish origin, but widely imitated from the 1st to 4th century. The standardized plain and decorated forms are usually identified by the numbers in Dragendorff's classification (e.g. Dr. 37; cf. Swan 1980, pls. 7–9).

Saucepan-pot. A coarse, cylindrical flat-bottomed cooking-vessel shaped like a saucepan without a handle, current in central Southern England in the mid–late Iron Age (e.g. Cunliffe 1974, A15, nos. 1–3 and 5–7).

Savernake (Ware) Industry. A number of sites in North-east Wilts. (incl. kilns in Savernake Forest) making light grey flint-gritted vessels, mostly jars, from about the mid 1st to 2nd century (Annable 1962; Swan 1975).

Segmental Bowl. A bowl of which the body forms part of the segment of a sphere (e.g. Gillam 291–5, 299).

Slip; Colour-coat; Paint. In this volume, *slip* refers both to a solution of clay and water (with or without added colorants) into which a vessel is dipped, and to the resultant finish after firing. When such a slip is made darker than the paste of the vessel which it covers (by the addition of minerals), it is called a *colour-coat*. *Paint* is used for a thick slip (white or coloured) applied decoratively (by brush or other implement) to the finished surface of a pot prior to firing.

Specialist Producer. A pottery workshop whose output primarily comprised table-wares (e.g. colour-coated vessels), mortaria, flagons or vessels with special functions (often of exotic affinities). In the 1st and 2nd centuries (sometimes later), specialist producers were almost always involved in military supply.

Stoneware. Pottery fired to a high temperature, usually over 1200 °C, at which the body vitrifies.

Tazza (pl. e). A cup-like vessel with a stem and foot, usually in a pale fabric and often decorated with bands of frilling (e.g. Swan 1980, fig. XIV no. 86).

Temper. An additive to clay (e.g. sand, shell, crushed pot or charcoal) to improve workability and assist uniform drying by preventing excessive shrinking.

Tripod Vessel. A pot with three legs or feet; normally of 1st or early 2nd-century date (e.g. Cam. 45 and 63).

Upchurch Ware. Dark grey, highly burnished cooking and table-wares, including BB2, London ware and poppy-head beakers, produced at various sites on the North Kent Marshes (including Upchurch) from the middle of the 1st century onwards and widely exported from the late 1st to early 3rd century (*see* Map 17).

Vicus (pl. *i*). In this volume, a civilian settlement, urban area or village which developed near a military establishment, often to provide services for it. It had the lowest legal status accorded to a built-up area in the Roman world and would therefore have been subordinate to a higher (military) authority.

Vitrification. The formation of glassy material in a ceramic body resulting from firing at a high temperature (800 °C or more, depending on the clay constituents).

Wall-sided. Used of a bowl or mortarium whose side rises more or less vertically above a carination and terminates in a plain or relatively plain rim (e.g. Swan 1980, fig. VI no. 33).

Ware. (a) Vessels from the same production centres, e.g. Crambeck ware. (b) Vessels having the same basic characteristics of technique, e.g. colour-coated wares.

Waster. A vessel spoilt or flawed in manufacture (e.g. cracked, blistered, sintered or distorted).

CHRONOLOGY

Periods to which common reference is made

BC 25–AD 14	Augustus	Augustan
AD 14–37	Tiberius	Tiberian
AD 37–41	Gaius (Caligula)	} pre-Flavian
AD 41–54	Claudius	Claudian
AD 54–68	Nero	Neronian
AD 69–79	Vespasian	
AD 79–81	Titus	Flavian
AD 81–96	Domitian	
AD 98–117	Trajan	Trajanic
AD 117–138	Hadrian	Hadrianic
AD 138–161	Antoninus Pius	
AD 161–180	Aurelius	Antonine
AD 180–192	Commodus	
AD 193–211	Severus	
AD 211–217	Caracalla	Severan
AD 218–222	Elagabalus	
AD 222–235	Severus Alexander	

Combinations of these terms are also used, e.g. Hadrianic-Antonine, and normally in the sense of late Hadrianic to early Antonine.

BIBLIOGRAPHY AND ABBREVIATIONS

Aitken and Weaver 1962. Aitken, M. J. and Weaver, G. H. Magnetic dating: some archaeomagnetic measurements in Britain. *Archaeometry* v (1962), 4–22.

Aitken et al. 1958. Aitken, M. J., Webster, G. and Rees, A. Magnetic prospecting. *Antiquity* xxxii (1958), 270–71.

Alcock, L. 1968. Excavations at South Cadbury Castle, 1967. *Antiq. J.* xlviii (1968), 6–17.

Anderson, A. C. 1980. *A Guide to Roman Fine Wares*. Vorda Research Series 1 (1980). Highworth, Swindon.

Anderson, A. S. 1978. Wiltshire moulded imitation samian. *In* Arthur and Marsh 1978, 357–71.

Anderson, A. S. 1979. *The Roman Pottery Industry in North Wiltshire*. Swindon Archaeol. Soc. Rept. No. 2.

Anderson, A. S. 1980. Romano-British Pottery Kilns at Purton. *Wiltshire Archaeol. Natur. Hist. Mag.* lxxiii (1980), 51–8.

Anderson and Anderson 1981. Anderson, A. C. and Anderson, A. S. *Roman Pottery Research in Britain and North-West Europe*. Papers presented to Dr G. Webster. BAR Int. Series 123 (1981). Oxford.

Annable, F. K. 1954. The Roman Pottery Kilns at Cantley Housing Estate, Doncaster: Kilns 1–8 and 9–15. *Yorkshire Archaeol. J.* xxxviii (1954), 403–6.

Annable, F. K. 1960. *The Romano-British Pottery at Cantley Housing Estate, Doncaster: Kilns 1–8*. Doncaster Museum and Art Gallery Publication no. 24 (1960).

Annable, F. K. 1962. A Romano-British Pottery in Savernake Forest: Kilns 1–2. *Wiltshire Archaeol. Natur. Hist. Mag.* lviii (1962), 142–55.

Anon. 1972. The Horniman Museum Kiln Experiment at Highgate Wood. Part 1. *London Archaeol.* ii part 1 (1972), 12–17.

Anon. 1973. The Horniman Museum Kiln Experiment at Highgate Wood. Part 2. *London Archaeol.* ii part 3 (1973), 53–9.

Anthony, I. E. 1968. Excavation at Verulam Hills Field, St. Albans, 1963–4. *Hertfordshire Archaeol.* i (1968), 9–50.

Archaeol. Excav. 1971: *Archaeological Excavations for 1971* (1972). Dept. of the Environment Annual Report.

Arthur and Marsh 1978. Arthur, P. and Marsh, G. (eds.). *Early Fine Wares in Roman Britain*. BAR British Series 57 (1978). Oxford.

Artis, E. T. 1828. *The Durobrivae of Antoninus identified and illustrated in a Series of Plates exhibiting the excavated remains of that Roman Station in the vicinity of Castor, Northamptonshire.* London.

Artis, E. T. 1847. Report on recent excavations made at Sibson, near Wandsford, Northamptonshire, on the estate of the Duke of Bedford. *J. Brit. Archaeol. Assoc.* ii (1847), 164–9.

Atkinson, D. 1932. Three Caistor pottery kilns. *J. Roman Stud.* xxii (1932), 33–46.

Baker, F. T. 1937. Roman Pottery Kiln at Lincoln. *The Lincolnshire Magazine* 3.7 (1937), 1–4.

BB1: Black-burnished ware, Category 1 (*see* Glossary).

BB2: Black-burnished ware, Category 2 (*see* Glossary).

Bellhouse, R. L. 1960. Excavation in Eskdale: The Muncaster Roman Kilns. *Trans. Cumberland Westmorland Antiq. Archaeol. Soc.* lxi (1960), 1–12.

Bellhouse, R. L. 1961. Excavation in Eskdale: The Muncaster Roman Kilns (Part II). *Trans. Cumberland Westmorland Antiq. Archaeol. Soc.* lxi (1961), 47–56.

Bellhouse, R. L. 1971. The Roman tileries at Scalesceugh and Brampton. *Trans. Cumberland Westmorland Antiq. Archaeol. Soc.* lxxi (1971), 35–44.

Bennett, P. 1978. Excavations at 16–21 North Lane, Canterbury. *Archaeol. Cantiana* xciv (1978), 165–91.

Bersu, G. 1940. Excavations at Little Woodbury, Wiltshire. Part 1. The Settlement revealed by excavation. *Proc. Prehist. Soc.* vi (1940), 30–111.

Bersu et al. 1911. Bersu, G., Goessler, P. and Paret, O. Römische Töpferöfen bei Weil i Schönbuch, Walheim, und Welzheim. *Fundberichte aus Schwaben* xix (1911), 119–35.

Bird and Young 1981. Bird, J. and Young, C. J. Migrant potters – the Oxford connection. *In* Anderson and Anderson 1981, 295–312.

Birley, A. R. 1980. *The People of Roman Britain*. London.

BJ: *Bonner Jahrbüch.*

Blumstein, M. 1956. Roman Pottery from Hoo. *Archaeol. Cantiana* lxx (1956), 273–7.

BNFAS: *Bulletin of the Northamptonshire Federation of Archaeological Societies.*

Bónis, E. B. 1980. Pottery. *In* Lengyel and Radan (eds.) 1980, 357–79.

Brassington, M. 1971. A Trajanic kiln complex near Little Chester, Derby, 1968. *Antiq. J.* li (1971), 36–69.

Brassington, M. 1980. Derby Racecourse kiln excavations, 1972–3. *Antiq. J.* lx (1980), 8–47.

Brixworth 00: Pottery-forms in Woods 1972.

Brown and Sheldon 1969. Brown, A. E. and Sheldon, H. L. Early Roman Pottery Factory in North London. *London Archaeol.* i part 2 (1969), 38–44.

Brown and Sheldon 1970. Brown, A. E. and Sheldon, H. L. Highgate 1969. *London Archaeol.* i part 7 (1970), 150–54.

Brown and Sheldon 1974. Brown, A. E. and Sheldon, H. L. Highgate Wood: the Pottery and its Production. *London Archaeol.* ii part 9 (1974), 222–31.

Bruns, C. G. (ed.) 1909. *Fontes Iuris Romani Antiqui.* 7th ed. Tübingen.

Bryant, G. F. 1970. Two experimental Romano-British kiln firings at Barton-on-Humber, Lincolnshire. *J. Scunthorpe Mus. Soc.* iii part 1 (1970), 1–16.

Bryant, G. F. 1971. *Experimental Romano-British Kiln Firings at Barton-on-Humber, Lincolnshire.* Workers' Educational Assoc., Barton-on-Humber Branch, Occas. Paper I (1971).

Bryant, G. F. 1973. Experimental Romano-British Kiln Firings. *In* Detsicas 1973, 149–60.

Bryant, G. F. 1977a. A Romano-British Pottery Kiln at Claxby, Lincolnshire: Excavation, Discussion and Experimental Firings. *Lincolnshire Hist. Archaeol.* xii (1977), 5–16.

Bryant, G. F. 1977b. Experimental Kiln Firings at Barton-on-Humber, South Humberside 1971. *Medieval Archaeol.* xxi (1977), 106–23.

Bryant, G. F. 1978. Romano-British experimental kiln firings at Barton-on-Humber, England, 1968–1975. *Acta Praehistorica et Archaeologica* ix/x (1977/8), 13–22.

Bryant, G. F. 1980. Experimental firing of a replica Romano-British turf built kiln at Barton-on-Humber, 1972. *In* Buckland and Dolby 1980.

Buckland, P. C. 1976. A Romano-British Pottery Kiln Site at Branton near Doncaster. *Yorkshire Archaeol. J.* xlviii (1976), 69–82.

Buckland and Dolby 1980. Buckland, P. C. and Dolby, M. J. *A Roman Pottery Kiln Site at Blaxton Quarry, near Doncaster.* The Archaeology of Doncaster 4/1. The Roman Pottery Industry. Doncaster.

Buckland et al. 1980. Buckland, P. C., Magilton, J. R. and Dolby, M. J. The Roman pottery industries of South Yorkshire: a review. *Britannia* xi (1980), 145–64.

Bunch and Corder 1954. Bunch, B. and Corder, P. A Romano-British Pottery Kiln at Weston Favell, near Northampton. *Antiq. J.* xxxiv (1954), 218–24.

Cam. 00: Vessel-form numbers in Hawkes and Hull 1947.

Castle, S. A. 1972a. Excavations at Brockley Hill, Middlesex, *Sulloniacae* (N.G.R, TQ 174441), 1970. *Trans. London Middlesex Archaeol. Soc.* xxiii (1972), 148–59.

Castle, S. A. 1972b. A kiln of the potter Doinus. *Archaeol. J.* cxxix (1972), 69–88.

Castle, S. A. 1973a. Trial Excavations in Field 410 Brockley Hill (part 1). *London Archaeol.* ii part 2 (1973), 36–9.

Castle, S. A. 1973b. Trial Excavations at Brockley Hill, part 2. *London Archaeol.* ii part 4 (Autumn 1973), 78–83.

Castle, S. A. 1974. Excavations at Brockley Hill, Middlesex, March–May 1972. *Trans. London Middlesex Archaeol. Soc.* xxv (1974), 251–63.

Castle, S. A. 1976a. Roman Pottery from Brockley Hill, Middlesex, 1966 and 1972–4. *Trans. London Middlesex Archaeol. Soc.* xxvii (1976), 206–27.

Castle, S. A. 1976b. Roman Pottery from Radlett, 1959. *Hertfordshire Archaeol.* iv (1974–6), 149–52.

Castle and Warbis 1973. Castle, S. A. and Warbis, J. H. Excavations on Field No. 157, Brockley Hill (*Sulloniacae?*), Middlesex, February–August 1968. *Trans. London Middlesex Archaeol. Soc.* xxiv (1973), 85–110.

Catherall, P. D. 1983. A Romano-British Pottery Manufacturing Site at Oakleigh Farm, Higham, Kent. *Britannia* xiv (1983) *forthcoming*.

CBA 1970: *Handbook of Scientific Aids and Evidence for Archaeologists.* Council for British Archaeol. London.

Chaplin and Brooks 1966. Chaplin, R. E. and Brooks, R. T. Excavation of a Romano-British site at South Ockendon. *Trans. Essex Archaeol. Soc.* 3rd series, ii (1966), 83–95.

Chenet, G. 1941. *La Céramique Gallo-Romaine D'Argonne du IVe Siècle et la Terre Sigillée décorée à la Molette.* Mâcon.

Chenet and Gaudron 1955. Chenet, G. and Gaudron, G. *La Céramique Sigillée D'Argonne des IIe and IIIe Siècles.* Supplement à Gallia VI. Paris.

Childe, V. G. 1940. *Prehistoric Communities of the British Isles.* Edinburgh.

Clark, A. J. 1949. The Fourth-century Romano-British Pottery Kilns at Overwey, Tilford. *Surrey Archaeol. Collect.* li (1949), 29–56.

Clark, A. J. 1975. Archaeological Prospecting: a progress report. *J. Archaeol. Sci.* ii (1975), 297–314.

Clark, A. J. 1980. Magnetic Dating. *Sussex Archaeol. Collect.* cxviii (1980), 7–12.

Clarke, D. T.-D. 1950. A Roman Pottery Kiln at Earl Shilton. *Leicestershire and Rutland Mag.* ii part 3 (1950).

Cockle, H. 1981. Pottery Manufacture in Roman Egypt. A new papyrus. *J. Roman Stud.* lxxi (1981), 87–97.

Coleman-Smith, R. J. C. 1972. Bonfire Fired Pottery. An Introduction for Teachers, Potters and Archaeologists. Privately produced and distributed notes.

Connah, D. B. 1964. The Excavation of Romano-British kiln sites at Hamstead Marshall, Berkshire. *Archaeol. Newsletter* vii (1964), 235–7.

Corder, P. 1928. *The Roman Pottery at Crambeck, Castle Howard.* Roman Malton and District Report 1 (1928). Leeds.

Corder, P. 1932. *The Roman Pottery at Throlam, Holme-on-Spalding Moor, East Yorkshire.* Roman Malton and District Report 3 (1932). Hull.

Corder, P. 1941. A Roman pottery of the Hadrian–Antonine period at Verulamium. *Antiq. J.* xxi (1941), 271–98.

Corder, P. 1950a. *A Romano-British pottery kiln on Lincoln Racecourse.* Dept. of Adult Education, Univ. Nottingham.

Corder, P. 1950b. Kiln furniture. *In* Hayes and Whitley 1950, 20–25.

Corder, P. 1957. The Structure of Romano-British pottery kilns. *Archaeol. J.* cxiv (1957), 10–27.

Corder, P. (ed.) 1961. *The Roman Town and Villa at Great Casterton, Rutland.* Third Report for the Years 1954–8, Univ. Nottingham.

Corder and Birley 1937. Corder, P. and Birley, M. A pair of fourth-century Romano-British pottery kilns near Crambeck; with a note on the distribution of Crambeck ware. *Antiq. J.* xvii (1937), 392–413.

Corder and Kirk 1932. Corder, P. and Kirk, J. L. *A Roman Villa at Langton, near Malton, East Yorkshire.* Roman Malton and District Report 4 (1932). Leeds.

Cregeen, S. M. 1956. The Roman Excavations at Cantley Housing Estate, Doncaster. Part III. Kilns 22–25 and Iron-smelting Furnace I. *Yorkshire Archaeol. J.* xxxix (1956), 32–47.

Cregeen, S. M. 1957. The Romano-British excavations at Cantley Estate, Doncaster; the pottery from Kilns 9–25. *Yorkshire Archaeol. J.* xxxix (1957), 364–88.

Cunliffe, B. 1974. *Iron Age Communities in Britain.* London.

Cuomo di Caprio, N. 1972. Proposta di classificazione delle fornaci per ceramicae laterizi in area italiana. *Sibrium* xi (1971–2), 371–464.

Cuomo di Caprio, N. 1979a. Pottery and Tile-kilns in South Italy and Sicily. *In* McWhirr 1979a.

Cuomo di Caprio, N. 1979b. Updraught pottery kilns and tile kilns in Italy in pre-Roman and Roman times. *Acta Praehistorica et Archaeologica* ix/x (1978/9), 23–31.

Curzon and Hanson 1971. Curzon, J. B. and Hanson, W. S. The Pottery Kiln. *In* Jones, G. D. B. Excavations at Northwich (*Condate*). *Archaeol. J.* cxxviii (1971), 31–77.

Dannell, G. B. 1973. The Potter Indixivixus. *In* Detsicas 1973, 139–42.

Dannell, G. B. 1975. Longthorpe, 1974. *Dubrobrivae. A review of Nene Valley archaeology* iii (1975), 18–20.

Darling, M. 1977. Pottery from early military sites in Western Britain. *In* Dore and Greene 1977, 57–100.

Daugas et Malacher 1976. Daugas, J-P. et Malacher, F. Les Civilisations de l'Age de Fer dans le Massif Central. *La Préhistoire Française* ii (1976).

Davidson, B. K. 1967. The Late Saxon Town of Thetford: An Interim Report on the 1964–6 Excavations. *Medieval Archaeol.* xi (1967), 189–208.

Dent, J. S. 1966. A probable third ditch section from the Crambeck Quarry. *Yorkshire Archaeol. J.* xli (1966), 572–4.

Detsicas, A. P. (ed.) 1973. *Current Research in Romano-British Coarse Pottery.* C.B.A. Res. Rept. 10 (1973). London.

Detsicas, A. P. 1974. Finds from the pottery kiln(s) at Eccles, Kent. *Antiq. J.* liv (1974), 305–6.

Detsicas, A. P. 1977. First century pottery manufacture at Eccles, Kent. *In* Dore and Greene 1977, 19–36.

DoE: Department of the Environment.

Doran and Hodson 1975. Doran, J. E. and Hodson, F. R. *Mathematics and Computers in Archaeology.* Edinburgh.

Dore and Greene 1977. Dore, J. and Greene, K. (eds.). *Roman Pottery Studies in Britain and Beyond.* Papers presented to John Gillam, July 1977. BAR Suppl. Series 30 (1977). Oxford.

Down, A. 1978. *Chichester Excavations III.* Chichester.

Drury and Rodwell 1973. Drury, P. and Rodwell, W. Excavations at Gun Hill, West Tilbury. *Essex Archaeol. Hist.* v (1973), 48–112.

Dryden, H. E. L. 1885. Hunsbury or Danes Camp and the Discoveries there. *Assoc. Archit. Soc. Rept. Papers* xviii (1885), 53–61.

Dudley, H. 1949. *Early Days in North-West Lincolnshire.* Scunthorpe.

Duhamel, P. 1973a. Les fours céramiques en Gaule romaine – Etude morphologique avec répertoire des fours et ateliers. Thèse de L'Ecole pratique des Hautes Etudes, IVe section (1973).

Duhamel, P. 1973b. Les Fours Gallo-Romains. *In* Duval, P.-M. *Recherches d'Archéologie Celtic et Gallo-Romaine.* Hautes Etudes du Monde Gréco-Romain No. 5. Paris 1973.

Duhamel, P. 1974. Les Fours de Potiers. *Les Dossiers de l'Archéologie* No. 6 (1974), 54–66.

Duhamel, P. 1975. Les Ateliers Céramiques de la Gaule Romaine. *Les Dossiers de l'Archéologie* No. 8 (1975), 12–19.

Duhamel, P. 1979. Morphologie et évolution de fours céramiques en Europe Occidentale – protohistoire, monde celtique et Gaul romaine. *Acta Praehistorica et Archaeologica* ix/x (1978/9), 49–76.

Dunnett, R. 1975. *The Trinovantes.* Peoples of Roman Britain Series. London.

Elsdon, S. M. 1979. Baked Clay Objects: Iron Age. *In* Wheeler 1979, 197–210.

Elsdon, S. M. 1982. *Parisian Ware: a study of the stamped wares of the Roman period in Lincolnshire, Humberside and South Yorkshire.* Vorda Research Series 4 (1982). Highworth, Swindon.

Evans, K. J. 1974. Excavations on a Romano-British site, Wiggonholt, 1964. *Sussex Archaeol. Collect.* cxii (1974), 97–151.

Fanthorpe, C. R. 1977. *The Building and Firing of a Replica of a Romano-British, Above-Ground, Turf Built Pottery Kiln.* Doncaster Met. Bor. Council. Doncaster.

Farrar, R. A. H. 1973a. The Techniques and Sources of Romano-British Black-burnished Ware. *In* Detsicas 1973, 67–103.

Farrar, R. A. H. 1973b. The Lost Roman Pottery Site at Bagber, Milton Abbas. *Proc. Dorset Natur. Hist. Archaeol. Soc.* xcv (1973), 93–6.

Farrar, R. A. H. 1975. Interim Report on Excavations at the Romano-British Potteries at Redcliff near Wareham. *Proc. Dorset Natur. Hist. Archaeol. Soc.* xcvii (1975), 49–51.

Ferdière, A. 1975. Les Ateliers de Potiers Gallo-Romains de la

Région Centre. *Revue Archéologique de Centre* liii–liv (1975), 85–111.

Filtzinger, P. 1972. Novaesium V: Die Römische Keramik aus dem Militärbereich von Novaesium (etwa 25 bis 50 n Chr). *Limesforschungen* Bd. xi (1972). Berlin.

Fitz, J. 1980. Economic Life. *In* Lengyel and Radan (eds.) 1980, 323–35.

Fletcher, Valls, D. 1965. Tipologia des los hõrnos ceramicos romanos de España. *Archivo Español de Arquelogia* xxxviii (1965), 170–4.

Forrer, R. 1911. *Die römischen Terrasigillata – Töpfereien von Heiligenberg – Dinsheim und Ittenweiler im Elsass.* Stuttgart.

Foster, P. J. 1976. Romano-British Finds at Kettering. *Northamptonshire Archaeol.* xi (1976), 170–7.

Foster et al. 1977. Foster, P. J., Harper, R. and Watkins, S. An Iron Age and Romano-British settlement at Hardwick Park, Wellingborough, Northamptonshire. *Northamptonshire Archaeol.* xii (1977), 55–96.

Freke and Craddock 1980. Freke, D. J. and Craddock, J. Towards a Strategy for excavating Pottery Kilns and analysing Kiln Assemblages. *Sussex Archaeol. Collect.* cxviii (1980), 13–17.

Fremersdorf, F. 1922. *Römische Bildlampen.* Forschungen zur Kunstgeschichte Westeuropas. Bonn.

Frere, S. S. 1961. Excavations at Verulamium, 1960. Sixth Interim Report. *Antiq. J.* xli (1961), 72–85.

Frere, S. S. 1972. *Verulamium Excavations I.* Rept. Res. Comm. Soc. Antiq. London xxviii (1972).

Frere, S. S. 1974. *Britannia: A History of Roman Britain.* (2nd ed. 1974). London.

Frere, S. S. 1983. *Verulamium Excavations II.* Rept. Res. Comm. Soc. Antiq. London xli (1983).

Frere and Clarke 1945. Frere, S. S. and Clarke, R. R. The Romano-British Village at Needham, Norfolk. *Norfolk Archaeol.* xxviii (1945), 187–216.

Frere and St Joseph 1974. Frere, S. S. and St Joseph, J. K. The Roman Fortress at Longthorpe. *Britannia* v (1974), 129.

Friendship-Taylor, R. M. 1979. The Excavation of the Belgic and Romano-British Settlement at Quinton, Northamptonshire: Site 'B' (1973–7). *J. Northampton Mus. Art Gallery* xiii (1979), 2–176.

Fulford, M. G. 1974. The Excavation of Three Romano-British Pottery Kilns in Amberwood Inclosure, near Fritham, New Forest. *Proc. Hampshire Fld. Club Archaeol. Soc.* xxviii (1971), 5–28.

Fulford, M. G. 1975. *New Forest Roman Pottery.* BAR British Series 17 (1975). Oxford.

Gillam 00: Vessel-type numbers in Gillam, J. P. 1970. *Types of Roman Coarse Pottery Vessels in Northern Britain.* 3rd ed. Newcastle upon Tyne.

Gillam, J. P. 1939. Romano-British Derbyshire Ware. *Antiq. J.* xix (1939), 429–37.

Gillam, J. P. 1951. Dales Ware, a distinctive Romano-British Cooking-pot. *Antiq. J.* xxxi (1951), 154–64.

Gillam, J. P. 1973. Sources of Pottery found on Northern Military Sites. *In* Detsicas 1973, 53–62.

Gillam, J. P. 1976. Coarse Fumed Ware in North Britain and Beyond. *Glasgow Archaeol. J.* iv (1976), 57–80.

Gillam and Greene 1981. Gillam, J. P. and Greene, K. T. Roman Pottery and the Economy. *In* Anderson and Anderson 1981, 1–24.

Gilmour, E. F. 1955. The Roman Excavations at Cantley Housing Estate, Doncaster. *Yorkshire Archaeol. J.* xxxviii (1955), 536–45.

Goodchild, R. 1943. 'T'-shaped corn-drying ovens in Roman Britain. *Antiq. J.* xxiii (1943), 148–53.

Gose, E. 1950. *Gefässtypen der Römischen Keramik im Rheinland.* Bonner Jahrbüch, Beiheft 1, Kevelaer (1950).

G.R.II: *Germania Romana: Ein Bilder-Atlas II:* Die Burgerlichen Siedelungen. 1924. Bamberg.

Green, C. 1977. Excavations in the Roman Kiln Field at Brampton, 1973–4. *East Anglian Archaeology* 5, 31–95. Norfolk Archaeol. Unit, Gressenhall (1977).

Greene, K. T. 1979. *The Pre-Flavian Fine Wares* (Report on the Excavations at Usk, 1965–76, Vol. I, ed. W. H. Manning). Cardiff.

Gregory, A. 1979. Early Romano-British Pottery Production at Thorpe St. Andrew, Norwich. *Norfolk Archaeol.* xxxvii (1979), 202–7.

Grimes, W. F. 1930. *Holt, Denbighshire: The Works-Depôt of the Twentieth Legion at Castle Lyons.* Y Cymmrodor 41. London 1930.

Gunn, J. 1971. Firing a Roman Kiln at Chichester. *Ceramic Review* viii (1971), 10–12.

Haalebos and Koster 1981. Haalebos, J. K. and Koster, A. Marbled ware from the Netherlands. *In* Anderson and Anderson 1981, 69–92.

Hadman and Upex 1975. Hadman, J. and Upex, S. A Roman Pottery Kiln at Sulehay, near Yarwell. *Durobrivae. A review of Nene Valley Archaeology* iii (1975), 16–18.

Hagen, J. 1912. Augusteische Töpferei auf dem Fürstenberg. *Bonner Jahrbüch* cxxii (1912), 343–62.

Hagen, J. 1917. Römische Sigillata Töpferei und Ziegelei bei Sinzig. *Bonner Jahrbüch* cxxiv (1917), 170–91.

Hampe and Winter 1962. Hampe, R. and Winter, A. *Bei Töpfern und Töpferinnen in Kreta, Messenien und Zypern.* Mainz.

Hampe and Winter 1965. Hampe, R. and Winter, A. *Bei Töpfern und Zieglern in Süditalien, Sizilien und Griechenland.* Mainz.

Hannah, I. C. 1932. Roman Blast Furnace in Lincolnshire. *Antiq. J.* xii (1932), 263–8.

Harden, D. B. 1936. Two Romano-British potters'-fields near Oxford. *Oxoniensia* i (1936), 81–102.

Harding, D. W. 1972. *The Iron Age in the Upper Thames Basin.* Oxford.

Harding, D. W. 1974. *The Iron Age in Lowland Britain.* London.

Harding, W. K. 1937. Romano-British Pottery Kilns between Compton and Aldworth, Berkshire. *Trans. Newbury Dist. Fld. Club* vii (1937), 211–16.

Harris, W. E. 1935. The late Romano-British kiln in Compton, Berkshire. *Berkshire Archaeol. J.* xxxix (1935), 93–5.

Harris and Young 1974. Harris, E. and Young, C. J. The 'Overdale' kiln site at Boars Hill, near Oxford. *Oxoniensia* xxxix (1974), 12–25.

Hart and Adams, *forthcoming.* Hart, F. A. and Adams, S. J. The Chemical Analysis of Romano-British Pottery from the Alice Holt Forest, Hampshire, by means of Inductively-coupled Plasma Emission Spectrometry. *Archaeometry, forthcoming.*

Hartley, B. R. 1960. *Notes on the Roman pottery industry in the Nene Valley.* Peterborough Museum Society Occas. Papers No. 2 (1960, reprinted 1972).

Hartley, B. R. 1977. Some Wandering Potters. *In* Dore and Greene 1977, 251–61.

Hartley, K. F. 1972. The Mortarium Stamps. *In* Frere 1972, 370–81.

Hartley, K. F. 1973a. The kilns at Mancetter and Hartshill, Warwickshire. *In* Detsicas 1973, 143–7.

Hartley, K. F. 1973b. The Marketing and Distribution of Mortaria. *In* Detsicas 1973, 39–51.

Hartley, K. F. 1973c. Stamped Mortaria. *In* Hebditch, M. and Mellor, J. The Forum and Basilica of Roman Leicester. *Britannia* iv (1973), 58–9.

Hartley, K. F. 1973d. La Diffusion des Mortiers, Tuiles et d'autres Produits en Provenance des Fabriques Italiennes. *Cahiers d'Archéologie Subaquatique* ii (1973), 49–60.

Hartley, K. F. 1976a. Were mortaria made in Scotland? *Glasgow Archaeol. J.* iv (1976), 81–9.

Hartley, K. F. 1976b. The Mortarium Stamps. *In* Castle 1976a.

Hartley, K. F. 1977. Two Major Potteries producing Mortaria in the First Century AD. *In* Dore and Greene 1977, 5–17.

Hartley, K. F. 1981. Painted Fine Wares made in the Raetian Workshops near Wilderspool, Cheshire. *In* Anderson and Anderson 1981, 471–9.

Hartley and Richards 1965. Hartley, K. F. and Richards, E. E. Spectrographic Analysis of some Romano-British Mortaria. *Univ. London Inst. Archaeol. Bull.* v (1965), 25–43.

Hartley and Webster 1973. Hartley, K. F. and Webster, P. V. Romano-British Pottery Kilns near Wilderspool. *Archaeol. J.* cxxx (1973), 77–103.

Hassall, M. W. C. 1953. A Pottery Mould from Horsepath, Oxon. *Oxoniensia* xvii/xviii (1952/3), 231–4.

Hawkes, C. F. C. 1938. An unusual find in the New Forest Potteries at Linwood, Hants. *Antiq. J.* xviii (1938), 113–36.

Hawkes and Hull 1947. Hawkes, C. F. C. and Hull, M. R. *Camulodunum.* Rept. Res. Comm. Soc. Antiq. London xiv (1947).

Hayes, R. H. 1966. A Ditch at Crambeck Quarry. *Yorkshire Archaeol. J.* xli (1966), 567–71.

Hayes and Whitley 1950. Hayes, R. H. and Whitley, E. *The Roman Pottery at Norton, East Yorkshire.* Roman Malton and District Report 7 (1950). Leeds.

Heinberg and Rüger 1972. Heinberg, U. and Rüger, C. *In* Beiträge Zur Archäologie Des Römischen Rheinlands III. *Rheinisches Ausgrabungen* xii (1972). Bonn.

Helen, T. 1975. *Organisation of Roman Brick Production in the First and Second Centuries.* Annales Academiae Scientiarum Fennicae: Dissertationes Humanarum Litterarum v. Helsinki.

Hemsley, R. 1959. A Romano-British Pottery Kiln at Manduessedum. *Trans. Birmingham Warwickshire Archaeol. Soc.* lxxvii (1959), 5–17.

Hicks and Wilson 1975. Hicks, J. D. and Wilson, J. A. Romano-British Kilns at Hasholme. *E. Riding Archaeol.* ii (1975), 49–70.

Hodder and Orton 1976. Hodder, I. and Orton, C. *Spacial Analysis in Archaeology.* Cambridge.

Hodges, H. 1965. *Artefacts: an Introduction to early Materials and Technology.* 2nd ed. 1965. London.

Hodges, H. 1970. *Technology in the Ancient World.* London.

Hofheim 00: Pottery type-numbers in Ritterling, E. *Das Frührömische Lager bei Hofheim im Taunus.* Weisbaden 1913.

Hogg, R. 1965. Excavations of the Roman auxiliary Tilery, Brampton. *Trans. Cumberland Westmorland Antiq. Archaeol. Soc.* lxv (1965), 133–68.

Holden and Holmes 1980. Holden, E. W. and Holmes, J. A Romano-British Pottery Kiln at Polhill's Farm, Arlington. *Sussex Archaeol. Collect.* cxviii (1980), 57–62.

Holwerda and Braat 1946. Holwerda, J. H. and Braat, W. C. *De Holdeurn Bij Berg en Dal. Centrum van Pannenbakkerij en Aardewerkindustrie in dem Romeinschen Tijd.* Oudheidkundige Mededeelingen Nieuwe Recks Suppl. XXVI (1946).

Holzhausen Type 00: Vessel-type form numbers in Pferdehirt, B. 1976. *Die Keramik des Kastells Holzhausen.* Limesforschungen Bd. xvi (1976). Berlin.

Howe et al. 1980. Howe, M. D., Perrin, J. R. and Mackreth, D. F. *Roman Pottery from the Nene Valley: A Guide.* Peterborough City Museum Occas. Paper No. 2.

Howlett, D. R. 1960. A Romano-British Pottery Kiln at Upper Sheringham, Norfolk. *Norfolk Archaeol.* xxxii (1960), 211–19.

Hughes, H. V. 1959. A Romano-British Kiln Site at Perry Barr, Birmingham. *Trans. Birmingham Warwickshire Archaeol. Soc.* lxxvii (1959), 33–9.

Hughes, T. Mck. 1903. The War Ditches near Cherry Hinton, Cambridge. *Proc. Cambridge Antiq. Soc.* x (1898–1903), 234–7, 452–81.

Hull, M. R. 1963. *The Roman Potters' Kilns of Colchester.* Rept. Res. Comm. Soc. Antiq. London xxi (1963).

Hume, I. N. 1954. Romano-British potteries on the Upchurch Marshes. *Archaeol. Cantiana* lxviii (1954), 72–90.

Hurst, H. 1972. Excavations at Gloucester 1968–71. 1st Interim Report. *Antiq. J.* lii (1972), 24–69.

Jackson, I. A. 1962. Upchurch: Two Roman Pottery Kilns. *Archaeol. Cantiana* lxxvii (1962), 190–95.

Jackson, I. A. 1972. Romano-British pottery kiln on the Upchurch Marshes. *Kent Archaeol. Rev.* xxx (Winter 1972/3), 288–90.

Jackson, I. A. 1975a. A Preliminary Note on Briquetage from the Upchurch Marshes. *Kent Archaeol. Rev.* xl (Summer 1975), 295–8.

Jackson, I. A. 1975b. Upchurch. *Kent Archaeol. Rev.* xlii (Winter 1975), 36.

Jackson and Ambrose 1978. Jackson, D. A. and Ambrose, T. M. Excavations at Wakerley, Northants., 1972–5. *Britannia* ix (1978), 115–242.

Jacob and Lerede 1975. Jacob, J.-P. and Leredde, H. Jaulges-Villiers-Vineux. *Les Dossiers de l'Archéologie* viii (1975), 71–8.

Jenkins, F. 1956. A Roman tilery and two pottery kilns at *Durovernum* (Canterbury). *Antiq. J.* xxxvi (1956), 40–56.

Jenkins, F. 1960. Two pottery kilns and a tilery of the Roman Period at Canterbury. *Archaeol. Cantiana* lxxiv (1960), 151–61.

Johnson et al. 1961. Johnson, A. C., Coleman-Norton, P. R. and Bourne, F. C. *Ancient Roman Statutes*. University of Texas Press. Austin, U.S.A.

Johnston, D. E. 1969. Romano-British Pottery Kilns near Northampton. *Antiq. J.* xlix (1969), 75–97.

Jones, M. U. 1971. Aldborough, West Riding, 1964: Excavations at the South Gate and Bastion and at Extra-Mural Sites. *Yorkshire Archaeol. J.* xliii (1971), 39–78.

Jones and Rodwell 1973. Jones, M. U. and Rodwell, W. Romano-British Pottery Kilns from Mucking, Essex. *Trans. Essex Archaeol. Soc.* v (1973), 13–47.

Jones and Webster 1969. Jones, G. D. B. and Webster, P. V. Derbyshire Ware – A Reappraisal. *Derbyshire Archaeol. J.* lxxxix (1969), 18–24.

Jope, E. M. 1957. Ceramics. Part II: Medieval. *In* Singer *et al.* 1957, 284–310.

Jornet, A. 1981. Composition de la céramique romaine d'*Augusta Raurica* (Augst). *Schweiz mineral petrogr. Mitt.* lx (1980), 271–85.

JRS: Journal of Roman Studies.

Kay, S. O. 1962. The Romano-British Pottery Kilns at Hazelwood and Holbrook, Derbyshire. *Derbyshire Archaeol. J.* lxxxii (1962), 21–42.

King, E. 1974. Roman Kiln Material from the Borthwick Institute, Peasholme Green: a report from York Excavation Group. *In* Addyman, P. V. Excavations at York, 1972–3. First Interim Report. *Antiq. J.* liv (1974), 213–17.

King and Moore 1975. King, E. M. and Moore, M. The Romano-British Settlement at Crambe, North Yorkshire. *Annu. Rep. Yorkshire Phil. Soc. for 1974*, 64–8.

Knorr and Sprater 1927. Knorr, R. and Sprater, Fr. *Die westpfälzischen Sigillata – Töpfereien von Blickweiler und Eschweiler Hof*. Speier am Rhein.

Knowles, A. K. 1967. A Roman Pottery Kiln at Brampton, Norfolk. *Norfolk Research Committee Bulletin* xvii (1967), 12–15.

Knowles, A. K. 1977. The Roman Settlement at Brampton: Interim Report. *Britannia* viii (1977), 209–21.

Layton, C. 1829. A Roman Kiln or Furnace for making Pottery discovered at Caistor. *Archaeologia* xxii (1829), 412–4, pl. XXXVI.

Leach, B. 1976. *A Potter's Book*. 1976 ed. London.

Leather, G. M. 1973. *Roman Lancaster: Some excavation reports and some observations.* Privately produced and distributed. Garstang, Lancs.

Lengyel and Radan 1980. Lengyel, A. and Radan, G. T. B. (eds.). *The Archaeology of Roman Pannonia*. Kentucky/Budapest.

Lethbridge, T. 1948. Further Excavations at the War Ditches. *Proc. Cambridge Antiq. Soc.* xlii (1948), 117–27.

Lloyd, G. D. 1968. A Roman Pottery Kiln in the Parish of Lockington. *E. Riding Archaeol.* i (1968), 28–38.

Loeschcke, P. S. 1922. *Ton industrie von Speicher und Umgebung.* Sonderdruck aus Trierische Heimanblätter. Trier.

Loeschcke, P. S. 1928. Römische Garfässe aus Bronze, Glas und Ton im Provinzial museum Trier. *Trierer Zeitschift* iii (1928), 68–81.

Loughlin, N. 1977. Dales Ware: A Contribution to the Study of Roman Coarse Pottery. *In* Peacock 1977a, 85–146.

Ludowici, W. 1905. *Stempel-Bilder Römischer Töpfer aus meinen Ausgrabungen in Rheinzabern.* Nebst dem II. Teil der Stempel-Namen 1901–1905. Munich.

Lyne and Jefferies 1979. Lyne, M. A. B. and Jefferies, R. S. *The Alice Holt/Farnham Roman Pottery Industry.* C.B.A. Res. Rept. 30 (1979). London.

Lyne and Jefferies (unpubl.). Lyne, M. A. B. and Jefferies, R. S. Experimental Kiln Firings in Alice Holt Forest. MS records.

McWhirr, A. (ed.) 1979a. *Roman Brick and Tile. Studies in Manufacture, Distribution and Use in the Western Empire.* BAR Int. Series 68 (1979), 73–95. Oxford.

McWhirr, A. 1979b. Tile-kilns in Roman Britain. *In* McWhirr 1979a.

McWhirr and Viner 1978. McWhirr, A. and Viner, D. The Production and Distribution of Tiles in Roman Britain with particular reference to the Cirencester region. *Britannia* ix (1978), 359–77.

Magetti and Rossmanith 1981. Magetti, M. and Rossmanith, M. Archaeothermometry of Kaolinitic Clays. *Révue d'Archéometrie* Supplement 1981, 185–94.

Magetti et al. 1981. Magetti, M., Galetti, G., Schwander, H., Picon, M. and Wessicken, R. Campanian Pottery: The Nature of the Black Coating. *Archaeometry* xxiii part 2 (1981), 199–207.

Mahaney, C. 1975. Excavations at *Manduessedum*, 1964. *Trans. Birmingham Warwickshire Archaeol. Soc.* lxxxvii (1975), 18–44.

Marsden, P. R. V. 1969. The Roman Pottery Industry of London. *Trans. London Middlesex Archaeol. Soc.* xxii part 2 (1969), 39–44.

Marsh, G. 1978. Early second century fine wares in the London area. *In* Arthur and Marsh 1978, 119–223.

May, J. 1970. Dragonby: An Interim Report on Excavations on an Iron Age and Romano-British Site near Scunthorpe, Lincolnshire, 1964–9. *Antiq. J.* 1 (1970), 222–45.

May, J. 1976. *Prehistoric Lincolnshire.* History of Lincolnshire Vol. I (1976). Lincoln.

May, T. 1904. *Warrington's Roman Remains.* Warrington.

Mayes, P. 1961. The firing of a pottery kiln of Romano-British type at Boston, Lincolnshire. *Archaeometry* iv (1961), 4–30.

Mayes, P. 1962. The firing of a second pottery kiln of Romano-British type at Boston, Lincolnshire. *Archaeometry* v (1962), 80–86.

Maynard et al. 1936. Maynard, G., Brown, B., Spencer, H. E. P., Grimes, W. F. and Moore, I. E. Reports on a Roman pottery-making site at Foxledge Common, Wattisfield, Suffolk. *Proc. Suffolk Inst. Archaeol.* xxii (1936), 178–97.

Metzler and Weiller 1977. Metzler, J. and Weiller, R. Der Mittel- und Spätkaiserzeitliche Vicus. *Beiträge zur Archäologie und Numismatik des Titelbergs.* Publication de la Section Historique xci (1977), 41–4.

Miles, A. 1975. Salt-panning in Romano-British Kent. *In* de Brisay, K. W. (ed.). *Salt, the Study of an Ancient Industry.* Colchester Archaeol. Group.

Mitchelson, N. 1964. Roman Malton: The Civilian Settlement. Excavations in Orchard Field 1949–52. *Yorkshire Archaeol. J.* clxii (1964), 209–61.

Mommsen, H. 1981. Filters to sort out pottery samples of the same provenience from a data bank of Neutron activation analysis. *Archaeometry* xxiii part 2 (1981), 209–15.

Mountford et al. 1968. Mountford, A. R., Gee, J. and Simpson, G. The excavation of an early Neronian Pottery Kiln and Workshop at Trent Vale, Stoke on Trent. *N. Staffordshire J. Fld. Stud.* viii (1968), 19–38.

Musty, J. W. G. 1974. Medieval pottery kilns. *In* Evison, V. I., Hodges, H. and Hurst, J. G. (eds.). *Medieval Pottery from Excavations: studies presented to Gerald Clough Dunning, with a bibliography of his works,* 41–65. London.

Nicklin, K. 1979. The Location of Pottery Manufacture. *Man* xiv (1979), 436–58.

Noble, J. V. 1965. *The Techniques of Painted Attic Pottery.* London.

Norman and Reader 1912. Norman, P. and Reader, F. W. Further Discoveries relating to Roman London. *Archaeologia* lxiii, 257–344.

Oakley et al. 1937. Oakley, K. P., Vulliamy, C. E., Rouse, E. C. and Cottrill, F. The excavation of a Romano-British pottery kiln site near Hedgerley. *Rec. Buckinghamshire* xiii (1937), 252–80.

O'Brien, C. 1980. An experiment in pottery firing. *Antiquity* liv (1980), 57–9.

O'Brien, C. undat. *Experiments in Primitive Pottery Making Techniques.* Trent Valley Archaeological Research Committee. Dept. of Adult Education, University of Nottingham.

Oelmann, F. 1931. Ausgrabung in Vetera, 1930. *Germania* xv (1931), 221–9.

O'Neil, B. H. St J. 1928. Excavation at Mancetter 1927. *Trans. Birmingham Warwickshire Archaeol. Soc.* liii (1928), 173–95.

Orton, C. R. 1970. Production of pottery from a Romano-British kiln site: a statistical investigation. *World Archaeol.* i (1969–70), 343–58.

Orton, C. R. 1973. An experiment in the reconstruction of the pottery from a Romano-British kiln site at Highgate Wood, London. *Univ. London Inst. Archaeol. Bull.* xi (1973), 41–73.

Orton, C. R. 1975. Quantitative pottery studies: some progress, problems and prospects. *Sci. and Archaeol.* xvi (1975), 30–35.

Orton, C. R. 1978. Is pottery a Sample? *In* Cherry, J. F., Gamble, C. and Shennan, S. (eds.). *Sampling in Contemporary British Archaeology.* BAR British Series 50 (1978), 399–402.

Orton, C. R. 1980. *Mathematics in Archaeology.* London.

OS: Ordnance Survey.

Oswald and Gathercole 1956. Oswald, A. and Gathercole, P. W. Excavation at *Manduessedum* 1954–6. *Trans. Birmingham Warwickshire Archaeol. Soc.* lxxiv (1956), 30–52.

Page, W. 1898. A Romano-British pottery lately found at Radlett, Herts. *Proc. Soc. Antiq.* 2nd series, xvii (1898), 261–70.

Paret, O. 1932. *Die Römer in Württemberg.* Teil III Die Siedlungen des römischen Württemberg. Stuttgart.

Partridge, C. 1981. *Skeleton Green. A late Iron Age and Romano-British Site.* Britannia Monograph Series No. 2. London.

Pasmore, A. 1967. *New Forest Pottery Kilns and Earthworks.* Cadnam, Southampton (privately printed).

Peacock, D. P. S. 1967a. Romano-British Pottery Production in the Malvern District of Worcestershire. *Trans. Worcestershire Archaeol. Soc.* i (1967), 15–28.

Peacock, D. P. S. 1967b. The heavy mineral analysis of pottery: a preliminary report. *Archaeometry* x (1967), 97–100.

Peacock, D. P. S. 1970. The scientific analysis of ancient ceramics: a review. *World Archaeol.* i part 3 (1970), 376–89.

Peacock, D. P. S. (ed.) 1977a. *Pottery and Early Commerce: Characterisation and Trade in Roman and Later Ceramics.* London.

Peacock, D. P. S. 1977b. Ceramics in Roman and Medieval Archaeology. *In* Peacock 1977a, 21–33.

Pearce, B. W. 1930. The Roman site at Otford. *Archaeol. Cantiana* xlii (1930), 157–71.

Perrin, J. R. 1980. Pottery of 'London Ware' type from the Nene Valley. *Durobrivae. A review of Nene Valley archaeology* viii (1980), 9–10.

Philpot, F. V. 1973. An improved fluxgate gradiometer for archaeological surveys. *Prospez Archeol.* vii–viii (1972–3), 99–105.

Pitt-Rivers, A. 1892. *Excavations in Bokerley and Wansdyke, Dorset and Wilts. 1888-91 III.* London.

Pollard et al. 1981. Pollard, A.M., Hatcher, H. and Symonds, R.P. Provenance studies of 'Rhenish' pottery by comparison with *terra sigillata. Revue d'Archéometrie* v (1981), 177–85.

Prigg, H. 1881. Roman Pottery Kilns, West Stow Heath. *J. Brit. Archaeol. Ass.* xxxvii (1881), 152–5.

PSAL: *Proceedings of the Society of Antiquaries London.*

Purdy and Manby 1973. Purdy, J.G. and Manby, T.G. Excavations at the Roman Tilery at Grimescar, Huddersfield, 1964. *Yorkshire Archaeol. J.* xlv (1973), 96–107.

Rackham, O. 1976. *Trees and Woodland in the British Landscape.* London.

Rackham and Van de Put 1934. Rackham, B. and Van de Put, A. (eds.). *The Three Books of the Potter's Art, by C. Cipriano Piccolpasso.* London.

Rădulescu, A. 1969. Ateliere Meşteş găreşti Pentu ars Materiale de Constructie din Lut. *Pontice* ii (1969), 333–53.

Rawes, B. 1972. Roman Pottery Kilns at Gloucester. *Trans. Bristol Gloucestershire Archaeol. Soc.* xci (1972), 18–59.

R.E.: *Pauly's Realencyclopaedie der classischen Altertumswichenschaft. Herausgeben von Wissowa.*

Reynolds, P.J. 1976. *The Neolithic Kiln.* Butser Ancient Farm Demonstration Area Information Sheet 4. Petersfield, Hants.

Reynolds, P.J. 1977. Experimental Archaeology and the Butser Ancient Farm Project. *In* Collis, J. (ed.). *The Iron Age in Britain: a Review,* 32–40. Sheffield.

Reynolds, P.J. 1979. *Iron-Age Farm. The Butser Experiment.* London.

Reynolds, P.J. undat. *Pottery Clamp.* Butser Ancient Farm Demonstration Area Information Sheet 22. Petersfield, Hants.

Reynolds and Langley 1979. Reynolds, P.J. and Langley, J.K. Romano-British corn drying oven: an experiment. *Archaeol. J.* cxxxvi (1979), 27–42.

Rhodes, D. 1969. *Kilns: Design, Construction and Operation.* London.

Richardson, G.G.S. 1973. The Roman Tilery, Scalesceugh, 1970-1971. *Trans. Cumberland Westmorland Antiq. Archaeol. Soc.* 2nd series, lxxiii (1973), 79–89.

Richter, G.M.A. 1923. *The Craft of Athenian Pottery.* Newhaven.

Richter, G.M.A. 1957. Ceramics. Part I: From *c.* 700 B.C. to the Fall of the Roman Empire. *In* Singer *et al.* 1957, 259–83.

Rieth, A. 1960. *5000 Jahre Töpferscheibe.* Konstanz.

Rigby and Stead 1976. Rigby, V. and Stead, I.M. The Coarse Pottery. *In* Stead 1976, 136–90.

Robinson, J.F. 1978. *The Archaeology of Malton and Norton.* Yorkshire Archaeological Society. Leeds.

Rodwell, W. 1974. The Orsett 'Cock' Cropmark Site. *Essex Archaeol. Hist.* vi (1974), 13–39.

Rook, A.G. 1965. Investigation of a Belgic Occupation Site at Crookhams, Welwyn Garden City. *Hertfordshire Archaeol.* i (1965), 51–65.

Rook, A.G. 1970. Investigation of a Belgic Site at Grubs Barn, Welwyn Garden City. *Hertfordshire Archaeol.* ii (1970), 31–6.

Rottländer, R.C.A. 1966. Is Provincial-Roman pottery standardised? *Archaeometry* ix (1966), 76–91.

Rottländer, R.C.A. 1967. Standardisation of Roman provincial pottery: II, function of the decorative collar on Form Drag. 38. *Archaeometry* x (1967), 35–45.

Rottländer, R.C.A. 1977. Zur Standardisierung der Formschüsseln der Bildsigillata (Standardisierung 8). *Acta Praehistorica et Archaeologica* vii/viii (1976/7), 53–63.

Samuels, J. 1979. The Excavation of two Romano-British Pottery Kilns at Barnetby Top, South Humberside. *Lincolnshire Hist. Archaeol.* xiv (1979), 11–18.

Saunders and Havercroft 1977. Saunders, C. and Havercroft, A.B. A Kiln of the Potter Oastrius and related Excavations at Little Munden Farm, Bricket Wood. *Hertfordshire Archaeol.* v (1977), 109–56.

Scott, K. 1975. Romano-British Tile-kilns: The Arbury Tilery. *Trans. Birmingham Warwickshire Archaeol. Soc.* lxxxvii (1975), 57–67.

Shaw, M. 1979. Romano-British Pottery Kilns on Camp Hill, Northampton. *Northamptonshire Archaeol.* xiv (1979), 17–30.

Shepard, A.O. 1954. *Ceramics for the Archaeologist.* Washington, D.C.

Singer et al. 1954. Singer, C., Holmyard, E.J. and Hall, A.R. *A History of Technology Vol. I.* From Earliest Times to the Fall of Ancient Empires. Oxford.

Singer et al. 1957. Singer, C., Holmyard, E.J., Hall, A.R. and Williams, T.I. *A History of Technology Vol. II.* The Mediterranean Civilisations and the Middle Ages *c.* 700 B.C. to *c.* A.D. 1500. Reprinted 1957. Oxford.

Smedley and Owles 1961a. Smedley, N. and Owles, E. Some Suffolk Kilns: I. A Romano-British Pottery Kiln at Homersfield. *Proc. Suffolk Inst. Archaeol.* xxviii (1961), 168–83.

Smedley and Owles 1961b. Smedley, N. and Owles, E. Some Suffolk Kilns: II. Two kilns making colour-coated ware at Grimstone End, Pakenham. *Proc. Suffolk Inst. Archaeol.* xxviii (1961), 203–25.

Smedley and Owles 1964. Smedley, N. and Owles, E. Some Suffolk Kilns: III. A small kiln at Grimstone End, Pakenham. *Proc. Suffolk Inst. Archaeol.* xxix (1964), 67–72.

Smedley and Owles 1965. Smedley, N. and Owles, E. A face mould from the Romano-British Kiln Site at Homersfield. *Proc. Suffolk Inst. Archaeol.* xxx (1965), 210–12.

Smith, C.R. 1846. On Roman potters' kilns and pottery, discovered by E.T. Artis in the county of Northampton. *J. Brit. Archaeol. Ass.* i (1846), 1–9.

Smith and Todd 1974. Smith, D.J. and Todd, M. A First Century Pottery Kiln at Blackmore Thick Farm, Southwick. *J. Northampton Mus. Art Gallery* x (1974), 6–12.

Stanley and Stanley 1964. Stanley, M. and Stanley, B. The Romano-British Potters' Field at Wappenbury, Warwickshire. *Trans. Birmingham Warwickshire Archaeol. Soc.* lxxix (1964), 93–108.

Stead, I. M. 1976. *Excavations at Winterton Roman Villa and other Roman Sites in North Lincolnshire 1958-67.* Dept. of the Environment Archaeol. Report No. 9. London.

Sturdy and Young 1976. Sturdy, D. and Young, C. J. Two early Roman kilns at Tuckwell's Pit, Hanborough, Oxon. *Oxoniensia* xli (1976), 56–64.

Suggett, P. G. 1953. Report on the Excavations at Brockley Hill, Middlesex, August and September 1951. *Trans. London Middlesex Archaeol. Soc.* xi (1953), 173–88.

Suggett, P. G. 1954. Excavations at Brockley Hill, Middlesex, March 1952 to May 1953. *Trans. London Middlesex Archaeol. Soc.* xi (1954), 259–76.

Suggett, P. G. 1955. The Moxom Collection. A Romano-British Pottery Group from Brockley Hill, Middlesex. *Trans. London Middlesex Archaeol. Soc.* xviii part 1 (1955), 60–64.

Suggett, P. G. 1956. Excavations at Brockley Hill, Middlesex, August 1953 and 1954. *Trans. London Middlesex Archaeol. Soc.* xix (1956), 65–7.

Sumner, H. 1917. *The Ancient Earthworks of the New Forest.* London.

Sumner, H. 1927. *Excavations on New Forest Roman pottery sites,* with plans and illustrations of the construction of the pottery kilns, of the different wares made, and of a potter's hut. London.

Swan, V. G. 1971. The structure of Romano-British New Forest pottery kilns. *Antiquity* xlv (1971), 45–8.

Swan, V. G. 1973. Aspects of the New Forest Late-Roman Pottery Industry. *In* Detsicas 1973, 117–37.

Swan, V. G. 1975. Oare reconsidered and the origins of Savernake Ware in Wiltshire. *Britannia* vi (1975), 37–61.

Swan, V. G. 1980. *Pottery in Roman Britain.* 3rd ed. Princes Risborough.

Swan, V. G. 1981. Caistor by Norwich reconsidered and the Dating of Pottery in East Anglia. *In* Anderson and Anderson 1981, 123–55.

Swan, V. G. 1983. Inveresk Ware? *Roman Northern Frontier Seminar xv (1982), forthcoming.*

Swan, V. G., *forthcoming*. The origins of the New Forest Romano-British pottery industry, *forthcoming*.

Symonds, R. P. 1981. The application of Chemical Analysis to the study of 'Rhenish' wares. *In* Anderson and Anderson 1981, 359–68.

Tarrant and Sandford 1972. Tarrant, N. and Sandford, A. A Romano-British Kiln at Fulmer. *Rec. Buckinghamshire* xix (1972), 174–88.

Thompson, B. 1902. The Discovery of a Romano-British Pottery Kiln at Corby. *J. Northamptonshire Natur. Hist. Soc. Fld. Club* xi (1902), 261–4.

Thompson, F. H. 1958. A Romano-British pottery kiln at North Hykeham, Lincolnshire; with an appendix on the typology, dating and distribution of 'rustic' ware in Great Britain. *Antiq. J.* xxxviii (1958), 15–51.

Thompson, F. H. 1965. *Roman Cheshire,* A History of Cheshire Vol. 2. Chester.

Tildesley, J. M. 1971. Roman Pottery Kilns at Rettendon. *Essex J.* vi part 2 (1971), 30–50.

Tilson, P. 1973. A Belgic and Romano-British Site at Bromham. *Bedfordshire Archaeol. J.* viii (1973), 23–66.

Tite, M. S. 1969. Determination of the firing temperature of ancient ceramics by measurement of thermal expansion: a reassessment. *Archaeometry* xi (1969), 131–43.

Tite, M. S. 1972. *Methods of Physical Examination in Archaeology.* London.

Todd, M. 1968. 'Trent Valley Ware', a Roman coarse ware of the Middle and Lower Trent Valley. *Trans. Thoroton Soc. Nottinghamshire* lxxii (1968), 38–41.

Tubb *et al.* 1980. Tubb, A., Parker, A. J. and Nickless, G. The Analysis of Romano-British pottery by atomic absorption spectrophotometry. *Archaeometry* xxii (1980), 153–72.

Tubbs, C. R. 1969. *The New Forest: An Ecological History.* Newton Abbot.

VCH: *The Victoria History of the Counties of England.*

Vertet, H. 1979. Les fours de potiers gallo-romains du Centre de la Gaule. *Acta Praehistorica et Archaeologica* ix/x (1978/9), 145–57.

Wacher, J. S. 1973. Review of Detsicas 1973. *Archaeol. J.* cxxx (1973), 326–8.

Wacher, J. S. 1978. *Roman Britain.* London.

Wainwright, G. J. 1979. *Gussage All Saints: An Iron Age Settlement in Dorset.* Dept. of the Environment Archaeol. Report No. 10. London.

Walke, N. 1965. *Das Römische Donau Kastell Straubing-Sorviodurum.* Limesforschungen Bd. iii (1965). Berlin.

Walker, F. G. 1912. Roman pottery kilns at Horningsea, Cambridgeshire. *Proc. Cambridge Antiq. Soc.* xvii (1912), 14–69.

Walsh and Howie 1980. Walsh, J. N. and Howie, R. A. An Evaluation of the Performance of an Inductively-Coupled Plasma Source Spectrometer for the Determination of the Major and Trace Constituents of Silicate Rocks and Minerals. *Mineralogical Magazine* xliii (1980), 967–74.

WAM: *Wiltshire Archaeol. Natur. Hist. Mag.*

Watson, F. J. 1958. Romano-British kiln: building and firing a replica. *Pottery Quarterly* v (1958), 72–5.

Webster, G. 1943. A Roman Pottery at South Carlton, Lincolnshire. *Antiq. J.* xxiv (1944), 129–43.

Webster, G. 1960. A Romano-British Pottery Kiln at Rookery Lane, Lincoln. *Antiq. J.* xl (1960), 214–20.

Webster, G. 1961. An Excavation on the Roman Site at Little Chester, Derby, 1960. *Derbyshire Archaeol. J.* lxxxi (1961), 85–110.

Webster, G. 1974. *Practical Archaelogy.* 2nd ed. 1974. London.

Webster, G. (ed.) 1976. *Romano-British Coarse Pottery: a Student's Guide.* CBA Res. Rep. 6 (3rd ed. 1976). London.

Webster, G. 1977. Reflections on Romano-British studies, past, present and future. *In* Dore and Greene 1977, 317–33.

Webster, G. 1978. *Boudica, the British Revolt against Rome AD 60.* London.

Webster, G. 1980. *The Roman Invasion of Britain.* London.

Webster, G. 1981. *Rome against Caratacus.* The Roman Campaigns in Britain AD 48–58. London.

Webster *et al.* 1940. Webster, G., Jessup, R. F. and Kirkman, J. S. A Roman Pottery Kiln at Canterbury. *Archaeol. Cantiana* liii (1940), 109–36.

Webster, P. V. 1975. More British Samian Ware by the Aldgate-Pulborough Potter. *Britannia* vi (1975), 163–70.

Webster, P. V. 1976. Severn Valley Ware: A Preliminary Study. *Trans. Bristol Gloucestershire Archaeol. Soc.* xciv (1976), 18–46.

Webster and Booth 1947. Webster, G. and Booth, N. A Romano-British pottery kiln at Swanpool, near Lincoln. *Antiq. J.* xxvii (1947), 61–79.

West, S. E. 1955. Romano-British pottery kilns on West Stow Heath. *Proc. Suffolk Inst. Archaeol.* xxvi (1955), 35–53.

Wheeler, H. 1979. Excavation at Willington, Derbyshire. *Derbyshire Archaeol. J.* xcix (1979), 58–220.

Wheeler and Wheeler 1936. Wheeler, R. E. M. and Wheeler, T. V. *Verulamium, a Belgic and two Roman Cities.* Rept. Res. Comm. Soc. Antiq. London xi (1936).

Whitwell, J. B. 1982. *The Coritani: Some Aspects of the Iron Age Tribe and the Roman Civitas.* BAR British Series 99 (1982). Oxford.

Wild, J. P. 1973. A fourth-century Potter's Workshop and Kilns at Stibbington, Peterborough. *In* Detsicas 1973, 135–8.

Wild, J. P. 1974. Roman Settlement in the Lower Nene Valley. *Archaeol. J.* cxxxi (1974), 140–70.

Wild, J. P. 1977. Eine Militarische Töpferei beim Legionslager in Longthorpe, Peterborough. *Studien zu den Militargrenzen. Roms II: Vorträge des 10 Internationalen Limeskongresses in der Germania Inferior,* 75–80. Köln.

Willett, F. 1948. A Romano-British pottery kiln, Foxcombe Hill, Berkshire. *Oxoniensia* xiii (1948), 32–8.

Williams, D. F. 1977. The Romano-British Black-Burnished Industry: An Essay on Characterization by Heavy Mineral Analysis. *In* Peacock 1977a, 163–220.

Williams, D. F. 1979. The Heavy Mineral Separation of Ancient Ceramics by Centrifugation: a preliminary report. *Archaeometry* xxi part 2 (1979), 177–82.

Wilson, A. L. 1978. Elemental Analysis of Pottery in the Study of its Provenance: A Review. *J. Archaeol. Science* v (1978), 219–36.

Winbolt, S. E. 1935. Loomweights from a Kiln. *Antiq. J.* xv (1935), 474–5.

Wise, J. R. 1863. *The New Forest: Its History and Scenery.* London.

Wood, F. K. 1972 (unpubl.). Swanpool Kiln Experiment. MS account.

Woods, P. J. 1969. *Excavations at Hardingstone, Northants., 1967–8.* Northamptonshire County Council.

Woods, P. J. 1972. Brixworth Excavations. Vol. I. The Romano-British Villa, 1965–70. Part I. The Romano-British Coarse Pottery and Decorated Samian Ware. Reprinted from *J. Northampton Mus. Art Gallery* viii (1970), 3–102. Northampton 1972.

Woods, P. J. 1974. Types of Late Belgic and Early Romano-British Pottery Kilns in the Nene Valley. *Britannia* v (1974), 262–81.

Woods *et al.* 1981. Woods, P. J., Turland, R. and Hastings, P. Romano-British Kilns at Biddlesden, Buckinghamshire. *In* Anderson and Anderson 1981, 369–95.

Young, C. J. 1971. A Pottery Mould Fragment from Littlemore, Oxon. *Britannia* ii (1971), 238–41.

Young, C. J. 1972. Excavations at The Churchill Hospital, 1971: Interim Report. *Oxoniensia* xxxvii (1972), 10–31.

Young, C. J. 1977. *The Roman Pottery Industry of the Oxford Region.* BAR British Series 43 (1977). Oxford.

Young, C. J. (ed.) 1980. *Guidelines for the Processing and Publication of Roman Pottery from Excavations.* DoE Directorate of Ancient Monuments and Historic Buildings Occasional Paper No. 4. London.

INDEX

THE GAZETTEER: EDITORIAL NOTES

In the interests of economy, the gazetteer of kilns and kiln sites has been printed in the form of microfiche (at the back of the volume) and its subject-matter tabulated to facilitate rapid scanning: 'as previous' refers to the entry in the adjacent column to the left and not to that above.

Locational Information

Sites are arranged according to the traditional counties and civil parishes (pre 1974), with concordances shown, in square brackets, in Appendix A. Within each parish, the site numbers relate to kilns, kiln sites or kiln groups which appear to form single entities; for excavated sites, however, any feature, kiln or phase numbering or lettering assigned by the excavator has also been used. Where available, National Grid references to eight figures are given for most sites. For several which appear to be at risk from undesirable looting or treasure-hunting, some of the figures have been replaced by asterisks *, at the request of the relevant excavator or field-worker. The full references, however, are held in the archive of RCHM's National Monuments Record.

The Kiln Structures (columns 4–6)

In the interests of compression, the dimensions of kilns have been omitted. Kilns over 1.5 m in diameter externally have been termed 'large' and those under 1 m 'small'. Flues measuring over two-thirds of the long axis of their corresponding kiln-chambers have been described as 'long'; 'short' flues comprise a mere roofed constriction between kiln-chamber and stokehole. To facilitate a rapid assessment of the main structural details, a simple letter and number classification has been adopted for columns 4 and 5. Letters or numbers are used only when the excavation or exposure of a kiln and/or its surrounds has been sufficient to establish the presence or absence of an element as significant. 'Probable' or a '?' used in conjunction with such details may imply that evidence is slight, or that judgement is based on comparison with kilns which are adjacent or in the same region: '??' indicates even less certainty. Where interpretation differs from that of the excavator, this has been indicated in **Comments** (column 12).

The General Classification of Kiln Structures (column 4)

A = Evidence for a clamp or bonfire-firing, characterized by the absence of any temporary or permanent walling, flue, stokehole or raised oven-flooring, but where the fuel constituted the covering material of the vessels being fired: A(a): surface clamp (Fig. I.i); A(b): sunken or pit-clamp.

B = Evidence for a surface-built kiln (or a kiln sited in a very shallow depression) with single flue and a temporary lining (e.g. of turf), indicated by a clearly defined area of burning. Temporary stacking furniture and/or a temporary raised oven-floor may have been used (Fig. I.iii). For internal variations *see under* F.

C = Evidence for a surface-built kiln, as B, but with two opposing flues. For internal variations *see under* F.

D = A surface-built or very shallowly-set kiln with a single flue and a substantial permanent lining to the kiln-chamber. For internal variations *see under* F.

E = A permanent, surface-built kiln, as D, but with two opposing flues (Pl. 42). For internal variations *see under* F.

F = A circular or oval, sunken or semi-sunken kiln (*see* Fig. II), with a single flue and (usually) a permanent clay lining to the kiln-chamber. Where the subsoil is clay, such kilns may occasionally be unlined below ground level. Internal variations comprise:

(1) No evidence for the use of kiln-furniture, integral stacking aids, or a raised oven-floor: i.e. a single-chambered kiln (Fig. II.ii).

(2) Evidence for the use of temporary (portable) kiln-furniture at the bottom of the kiln-chamber to aid stacking and heat circulation, but none for a raised oven-floor: i.e. a single-chambered kiln (e.g. Pl. 39).

(3) An integral permanent structural component or feature in the kiln-chamber to aid stacking and heat circulation, but no evidence for a raised oven-floor: i.e. a single-chambered kiln (e.g. Fig. XVII).

(4) Temporary support(s) or furniture and a temporary (i.e. portable) raised oven-floor spanning all or most of the furnace-chamber (e.g. Fig. II.iii).

(5) Permanent integral support(s) and a temporary raised oven-floor spanning all or most of the furnace-chamber.

(6) Permanent integral support(s) and a permanent raised oven-floor spanning all or most of the furnace-chamber (e.g. Fig. II.v).

(7) A permanent, self-supporting raised oven-floor, i.e. one lacking any special supportive structure.

G = A circular or oval, sunken or semi-sunken kiln, as F, but with two opposing flues (e.g. Fig. XVIII). For internal variations *see under* F.

H = A square or rectangular sunken or semi-sunken kiln with a single flue (e.g. Fig. XXII). For internal variations *see under* F.

Detailed Arrangements within Kiln-chambers (column 5)

(a) Temporary, usually free-standing, prefabricated, portable pedestal(s), block(s), bollard(s) or other furniture which may or may not have supported a raised oven-floor.

(b) Pottery vessel(s), often inverted, used to support a raised oven-floor (Fig. III.i).

(c) Permanent integral free-standing pedestal(s) or bollard(s) which may or may not have supported a raised oven-floor (e.g. Fig. III.ii).

(d) A single permanent tongue or long pier, projecting from the centre back of the furnace-chamber and integral with the kiln structure, used to support a raised oven-floor (Fig. III.iii).

(e) Cross-walls – a series of permanent, narrow, parallel walls, often of tile, built at regular intervals across the bottom of the furnace-chamber at right angles to the flue-axis. A central gap in each formed a narrow corridor in the combustion-chamber – an extension of the flue-axis (Fig. III.iv).

(f) Integral pilasters, short piers, buttress or column-like projections from the kiln-wall, usually intended to support a raised oven-floor (Fig. III.v).

(g) Integral corbels projecting from the kiln-wall, immediately below the raised oven-floor to support it (Fig. III.vi).

(h) A permanent continuous ledge or kerb running along all or most of the internal circumference of the kiln-chamber, and attached to, moulded out of, or built into the kiln-wall. It either supported the raised oven-floor or aided the stacking and stability of the pottery load by keying it into the kiln-wall (Fig. III.vii).

(j) Niches or short cup or ledge-like recesses, moulded into the kiln-wall at intervals and on the same level, often used for supporting the individual bars of a raised oven-floor.

(k) Small sockets or holes poked into the kiln-wall while still plastic in order to insert the ends of the bars of a raised oven-floor (Fig. III.viii).

(m) The lip or top of the kiln-wall, flattened into a ledge and used as seating for portable flooring material such as bars (e.g. in semi-sunken kilns (Fig. III.ix).

(n) A single barrel-vault consisting of ribs of curved bars, blocks or voussoir-shaped tiles, usually acting as an underflooring to give added strength to a superimposed, flat, raised oven-floor. Occasionally the arched vault itself formed a curved raised oven-floor (e.g. Fig. XI).

(p) Two parallel barrel-vaults as (n), usually separated by a central support (e.g. a tongue), positioned on the line of the flue axis.

(q) A solid-clay platform across the back of the furnace-chamber.

Site Features and Finds (column 7)

Only those which might relate to pottery production or the status of the site in its contemporary environment are included. Additional details may also be found as **Comments** (column 12).

Pottery (column 8)

Care has been taken to exclude pottery apparently not made on the site under consideration. Where a kiln-structure alone has been excavated, without adjacent features, it is difficult to be sure whether the vessels found in association represent the products of that particular kiln, or waste material dumped from adjacent kilns. This reservation applies to most of the kiln assemblages derived from very small excavations. Where known, vessels have been listed in the approximate order of frequency.

An adequate definition of vessel-profiles is difficult without illustration. Many vessel-types were of purely local significance. Where possible, reference has been made to the type-numbers of common published forms. Comparisons have been made on the basis of form alone and generally do not take into account the fabric, details of which have been kept to a minimum except for certain unusual or specialist wares. They are in any case intended only as a pointer, since there is no substitute for personal examination of pottery. For many industries, no work has been carried out on the distributional aspects of the kiln products; the markets may therefore be assumed to have been relatively local unless otherwise stated.

Technical terms which also occur in the main text are explained in the Glossary (Appendix p. 153). For the meaning and usage of additional specialist terms found in the gazetteer, readers are referred to Webster 1976, Swan 1980 and Young 1980.

Dating (column 9)

The dating of most published kiln groups and many unpublished assemblages has been checked in the light of the revised dating of the Antonine Wall (cf. Gillam 1973) and other recent advances in Romano-British pottery studies. Inverted commas indicate the excavator's own opinion or term.

A very few of the sites listed in the gazetteer have not been plotted on the distribution maps. This is because the relevant information was received too late for it to be included there.

Printed in the UK for HMSO
Dd 717085   C25   11/83